P9-CAO-302

STUDYING BRITISH CINEMA
THE 1990s

STUDYING BRITISH CINEMA
THE 1990s
BY
EDDIE DYJA

auteur

First published in 2010 by
Auteur
The Old Surgery, 9 Pulford Road, Leighton Buzzard LU7 1AB
www.auteur.co.uk

Copyright © Auteur Publishing 2010

Designed and set by Nikki Hamlett at AMP Ltd, Dunstable, Bedfordshire

Printed and bound in India
by Imprint Digital

Cover: *The Full Monty* © BFI Stills, Posters and Designs

All rights reserved. No part of this publication may be reproduced in any material form (including photocopying or storing in any medium by electronic means and whether or not transiently or incidentally to some other use of this publication) without the permission of the copyright owner.

British Library Cataloguing-in-Publication Data
A catalogue record for this book is available from the British Library

ISBN 978-1-906733-02-5 (paperback)
ISBN 978-1-906733-03-2 (hardback)

CONTENTS

Acknowledgements...4

Introduction 5

1. The Hangover from the 1980s...7
   The Crying Game 15
   Much Ado About Nothing 27

2. Change is Going to Come..39
   Trainspotting...44
   Lock, Stock and Two Smoking Barrels 53

3. Think Global, Act Local..63
   High Fidelity...70
   Fever Pitch...80

4. From Flea-Pit to Multiplex...93
   The Full Monty 99
   Brassed Off...109

5. The Film Production Boom in Britain...121
   Four Weddings and a Funeral...129
   The World is Not Enough 137

6. It's a Lottery...151
   Billy Elliot..156
   Ratcatcher...165

7. Getting Distributed or Not..177
   Secrets and Lies..181
   Land and Freedom...190

8. Culturally Diverse...203
   East is East...207
   Babymother...216

9. Typically British..227
   Shakespeare in Love...233
   Sense and Sensibility 244

10. End of the Decade – Boom or Bust?..257
   Notting Hill..263
   Chicken Run 271

ACKNOWLEDGEMENTS

This book would not have been possible without John Atkinson, whose patience, encouragement and support I deeply appreciate. I am also deeply indebted to the professionalism, depths of knowledge and cheerfulness of the BFI National Library staff who pointed me in several right directions along the way, and none more so than the estimable Sean Delaney, who not only seemed to know the contents of every book and article I ever referred to, but also happily gave me lists to other references beyond my ken. Much of the statistical material was gleaned with help from the BFI's Information Department where Ian O'Sullivan pointed me in the direction of the best numbers to crunch, while Matt Ker helped me piece together bits from the exhibition jigsaw. I am also indebted to Tom Cabot and Sophie Contento for helping out with some key books from BFI Publishing's back catalogue.

Many thanks also go to Sharon Greaves and Nikki Hamlett who took the book to the finish line.

Finally, last but not least my thanks and love go to Linda who, without fail, encouraged me on every step of my journey through British Cinema in the 1990s.

INTRODUCTION

British cinema in the 1990s enjoyed something of a renaissance after the bleak nadir of the 1980s. Hit films such as *Four Weddings and a Funeral* (1993) and *The Full Monty* (1997) punched above their weight at the box office; *Trainspotting* (1996) and *Lock, Stock and Two Smoking Barrels* (1998) tapped the vein of youth culture not seen since the 1960s; British auteurs such as Ken Loach and Mike Leigh enjoyed a degree of success on the art house circuit; typically British themes such as brass bands in *Brassed Off* (1996), with a nod to the Social Realist tradition, made it to the big screen, as did themes of cultural diversity as in *East is East* (1999).

A new group of directors such as Michael Winterbottom, Shane Meadows and Lynne Ramsay all suggested that better and brighter things lay ahead. If that wasn't enough to convince the sceptics about the renaissance of British film, then there was also Aardman Animations, which brought family entertainment back to British cinemas.

Hand in hand with an increase in film production came a year-on-year rise in cinema attendances and a growing number of multiplexes around the country. British films increased their share of the domestic market place.

British film production also enjoyed a huge cash injection via the National Lottery whose balls first started rolling out millionaires in 1995. For some, the issue of Lottery funding for film production was seen as controversial and the appointment of the Arts Council of England to distribute funds seems, with the benefit of hindsight, to have been a bad idea. Nevertheless, Lottery-funded films gave many aspiring film-makers a fairground type attempt to test their strength in the real world of commercial film. Sadly, most failed to hit the jackpot and few went on to make other films. As a result, the 1990s are littered with curious half-baked ideas, some that had value, others that quite frankly should never have seen the light of day.

The decade also reveals a desire for the Government to promote the industry. The long process began in June 1990 with a meeting at Downing Street featuring such British film heavyweights as Richard Attenborough, David Puttnam and John Boorman. Margaret Thatcher's legacy of a free market economy conjured in the 1980s stalked and defined the film industry during the remainder of the Tory government's term. Despite New Labour's promises of a new start, the name of the game was getting 'bums on seats'. Films were primarily defined by their box-office performance and, in particular, their opening weekend performance, in the same way that television became defined by its ratings.

By the end of the decade with New Labour still culturally enjoying its honeymoon period and basking in its self-styled image of 'Cool Britannia', a new body called the Film Council was formed with the aim to build a sustainable film industry in Britain.

But despite all the reasons to be cheerful, familiar cracks were appearing within the industry. One of the largest and most traumatic events was when Dutch-owned

PolyGram sold the company, including its film division, to Seagram in 1999. In doing so it cruelly cut down what at one time had seemed a genuine attempt at creating a European-based studio system in Britain with ambitions to take on Hollywood.

In an interview in 2001 Oscar-winning British actress Emma Thompson made a scathing assessment of the British film industry. 'The very phrase depresses me. I don't think we've got a film industry, and never have had. We've been making bloody awful films.'

Her comments reopened an inevitable can of worms about the success of British film in the 1990s. Notwithstanding the awards, the critical plaudits and the talent of its actors, directors and technicians, most of the British film industry was sustained by American investment through the key areas of production, exhibition and distribution and any profits from British films generally saw their way back across to the pond to Hollywood.

There was also another strand of film financing which came from Europe and this proved important for British art house film-makers such as Loach, Leigh and Peter Greenaway who might otherwise have found funding for their projects to be impossible.

The apparent boom in film-making left some familiar doors curiously hard to open. There were still pitifully few British films made by Black and Asian film-makers and women film-makers still operated around the fringes of an industry dominated by men.

The development of mass communications via the internet during the 1990s meant that the film world was never going to be the same again. Consumerism was fuelled by the cult of celebrity, of not only the rich and famous, but the not so rich and infamous. Where once we went to the cinema, by the end of the decade we were consuming films. They were a product that we could pay for several times over in the cinema, on pay-per view television, on video and then on DVD. The 1990s made film-making a global enterprise and for a while some British films joined the party and didn't look too out of place.

Yet the overall feeling about British film in the 1990s was one of hope. The all-time low in the 1980s had been replaced by a reinvigorated industry and the promise of even better things to come. The fact that those hopes, by and large, were not realised in the 21st century can be traced back to the plans made during the 1990s to create something that many have deemed unachievable – a sustainable British film industry.

I. THE HANGOVER FROM THE 1980S

When screenwriter Colin Welland triumphantly waved his Oscar aloft and declared that: 'The British are coming,' at the 1982 Academy Awards, having just bagged the Best Original Screenplay for *Chariots of Fire* (UK, 1981) which also won Best Picture, the film world waited for the new dawn of British cinema.

The following year Richard Attenborough's *Gandhi* (UK/USA/India, 1982) also won the coveted Best Picture award, but Welland's optimistic prediction proved to be the beckoning of a false dawn. In the 1980s not only did the British not come, but the British film industry was nearly nowhere to be seen as it went on to suffer its worst decade on record in terms of film production and film attendance.

The traumas suffered by the industry in the 1980s were to inform and reshape the interest in British films in the next decade, which saw film production and film attendance rise. It is therefore inadvisable·to define the 1990s British film industry in isolation. It is important to take a step back and see how British cinema was able to stage a recovery from its lowest point and march positively forwards.

CINEMA EXHIBITION IN THE 1980S

In 1984 cinema attendance hit its lowest point in Britain when only 54 million admissions were recorded. There were just 660 cinema sites and 1,271 screens. Many cinemas had closed down while others, in need of refurbishment, gained the tag of 'fleapit'. Not surprisingly, the British public preferred the comfort of home for its entertainment and television obliged with well-made dramas and comedies, not to mention a wide range of films – albeit dated.

However, British cinema going was to undergo an entertainment revolution with the introduction of the multiplex from America. The first of these opened in Milton Keynes in 1985. The 10-screen multiplex cinema was owned by American multiplex pioneer AMC and part of a leisure complex.

The emphasis on leisure and comfort was an important ingredient of the multiplex and it lured more than one million admissions in its first year. This successful model featuring large screens, state-of-the-art sound systems, large auditoria, ample leg-room and all the popcorn and fizzy drinks you could consume, paved the way for further multiplexes to be built, so by the end of the 1980s there were 29 multiplexes in Britain with 285 screens. From 1985 until 1994 admissions to cinemas more than doubled. The multiplex revolution continued throughout the 1990s and gave an undoubted boost to cinema going in the UK. However, this would prove to be a doubled-edged sword. American companies mainly built multiplexes and quite frankly their purpose was not to show cutting-edge British movies. Profits came via bums on seats and blockbusters filled those seats.

VIDEO KILLED THE RADIO STAR

Initially, the terrible decline in cinema admissions in the UK coincided with the steady rise in videocassette recorders (VCR). In 1980 the VCR was still seen as a consumer novelty and only two per cent of homes in the UK had one. This was to change dramatically throughout the decade as the trend caught on and people built up their only personal film and television libraries. By the end of the decade 70 per cent of homes had video recorders as more film companies cottoned on to the advantages of rental and sell-through video.

In Britain the video trend was complemented by strong TV programmes. People felt comfortable going to their local video shop and renting a film for the evening. Indeed, video rental was far more popular than video ownership. Throughout the 1990s rental transactions slowly diminished while retail transactions managed a year-on-year increase. By the end of the 1990s the DVD (Digital Versatile Disc) format came along offering better picture quality and leading to a cycle of repacking, replacing and re-consuming.

FILM PRODUCTION IN THE 1980S

Number of Films Produced in the UK 1980-90

Year	Number of Films	Year	Number of Films
1980	58	1986	56
1981	40	1987	72
1982	67	1988	60
1983	37	1989	45
1984	70	1990	51
1985	58		

Source: BFI Information Services/Screen Digest/Screen Finance

THE EADY LEVY AND THE FILM ACT 1985

In 1983 a mere 37 British films were produced making it the worst year on record for British film production and directly the opposite of what many had hoped would happen after the Oscar successes of *Chariots of Fire* and *Gandhi*. The 1985 Film Act was introduced to encourage film production in Britain. It played a part in the abolition of the Eady Levy, which paradoxically had been set up to bolster film production in Britain.

The Levy was a tax on box office receipts for films that qualified as British, which meant that a proportion of the price of a cinema ticket for a film went back to the film producers. Eady money was paid to the British Film Fund Agency, which in turn was responsible for making payments to British film-makers, the Children's Film Foundation, the National Film Finance Corporation, the British Film Institute and towards training film-makers.

Initially, the Eady Levy seemed to bear fruit in the 1960s, fuelled also in part by the 'Swinging Sixties', The Beatles and the British Invasion, and directors of the calibre of Stanley Kubrick, Sidney Lumet, Roman Polanski, François Truffaut and Michaelangelo Antonioni who all found Britain an attractive place to work.

As the fortunes of the British film industry declined in the 1970s and the 1980s so too did the effectiveness of the Eady Levy. In the end the sums collected by the Levy seemed small and it appeared to be a burden on both producers and exhibitors alike.

The 1985 Act also abolished the Cinematograph Film Council and dissolved the National Film Finance Corporation, transferring its assets to British Screen Finance Limited. However, what the Film Act of 1985 failed to achieve was to present any viable solid funding alternatives to the Eady Levy, and this would cause ramifications throughout the 1990s.

TELEVISION AND FILM IN THE 1980S

While British film was to experience its worst decade in the 1980s the opposite was true for British television. It is worth remembering, in light of today's multi-channel environment, that at the start of the 1980s British viewers could only choose three channels: BBC1, BBC2, and ITV. Nevertheless, television was a different beast than it is today and it was enjoying a golden era of high-quality dramas and memorable comedies.

The TV decade brimmed with innovations such as the launch of Channel 4 in November 1982, breakfast TV complete with cosy sofas, and the establishment of cable and satellite networks with Sky broadcasting in 1989.

Money that might have gone into film was ploughed into big TV productions such as *The Borgias* (BBC2, 1981), *Brideshead Revisited* (ITV, 1981), *The Jewel in the Crown* (ITV, 1984,) *Edge of Darkness* (BBC2, 1985), and *Fortunes of War* (BBC1, 1987). This was also the decade of acclaimed social conscience dramas such as Alan Bleasdale's *Boys from the Black Stuff* (BBC2, 1982), and Dennis Potter's inventive musical thriller *The Singing Detective* (BBC1, 1986).

Memorable series also included *Auf Wiedersehen, Pet* (ITV, 1983) about the unlikely adventures of bricklayers on a construction site in Germany. Even family-orientated entertainment, such as *The Chronicles of Narnia* (BBC1, 1988), received major funding.

CHANNEL FOUR

Channel 4's entry onto the broadcasting scene had the unexpected effect of bringing television and film closer together. Up to that point rigid union agreements effectively separated film and TV production work and transmission rules didn't allow films to be transmitted until three years after their release.

New agreements between the unions and the Cinema Exhibitors' Association loosened those restrictions and Channel 4 Chief Executive Jeremy Isaacs became the first to allow allowed the fledgling channel to invest in feature films in order to recoup monies via screenings abroad.

Channel 4 invested in 134 feature films during the decade, starting a trend that would be picked up by other TV companies, notably Granada whose film division opened in 1987 and scored a notable hit with the award-winning *My Left Foot* (UK/Ireland, 1989). Channel 4's investment in films came as a real fillip for film-makers who had been struggling to find extra sources of capital.

In fact, Channel 4 was shrewd with its funding, often offering small percentages of eight, 16 or 20 per cent for films, but dangling the carrot of transmission rights to co-producers.

Suddenly, modest investment in film production seemed like it could be a viable proposition since the guarantee of TV transmission acted like something of a safety net for those film-makers fretting about getting their audiences into cinemas.

Channel 4, working with other film production companies, was keen to nurture new talent. Indeed, the remit of the fourth channel was to look for diverse and innovative tastes that differed from the traditional popular output by BBC and ITV. One such innovation was its Film on Four slot, which showcased its own films. Its budget of £6m per year was spent in co-productions as well as standalone productions in which the top amount invested was around £300,000.

As it developed Channel 4 made a deal with the Cinema Exhibitors Association that allowed films with budgets under £1.25m to be shown on TV after the film had finished its theatrical run.

Perhaps the epitome of Channel 4's film remit of the 1980s was Stephen Frears' *My Beautiful Launderette* (UK, 1985). Written by Hanif Kureshi, the quirky story of a launderette run by Johnny, a working-class white boy, and Omar, a middle-class Pakistani, who become lovers managed to tick several boxes with its take on homosexuality, class and ethnic issues. The film was successful at the box office and thus became a major feature presentation event when it was screened on TV in 1987. It is worth noting that Channel 4's co-producer was a fledgling production company called Working Title, which would dominate the British film scene in the 1990s and beyond.

Channel 4's input into film production continued to secure hits throughout the 1990s, the biggest of which were *Four Weddings and a Funeral* (UK, 1994), and *Trainspotting* (UK, 1995). Towards the end of the 1990s, Channel 4 made FilmFour a separate entity, both acting as a distributor and a production company with ambition. While Channel 4 kept to its small budget policy the film arm was secure and occasionally thrived. The moment

FilmFour overstretched itself, as it did with the £12m *Charlotte Gray* (UK/Australia/ Germany, 2001), the production arm collapsed, bringing its distribution arm down with it. Yet another British production company had succumbed to the sin of ambition without a safety net. Tellingly, FilmFour has managed to successfully regroup itself in the mid-2000s by going back to the prudent budgetary principles first established in 1982 by its parent.

HIGH HOPES FOR FILM PRODUCTION

The curious paradox about the British film industry in the 1980s is the small number of success stories, albeit short-lived, within the production sector. These included Goldcrest, HandMade Films and Palace Pictures. Others such as Channel 4, Working Title and Merchant Ivory fared much better by surviving and even thriving throughout the 1990s. All the successes can be measured on the quality of British films that were produced. Alas, the failures merely highlight the fragile nature of the film business and just how hard it is to achieve sustainable growth. In each case the key to maintaining some kind of momentum was to woo the Americans. On the one hand was the desire to make Britain an attractive and viable production base for big films, on the other Americans had to be convinced that British films would capture American audiences. In other words, when the Americans came British films seemed stable and secure but when the Americans went home the industry started to wobble, if not collapse.

Merchant Ivory Productions Ltd

Mention Merchant Ivory and it is easy to picture a stately home in a sun-drenched, pre-war location, with upper-class types embroiled in all manner of typically British stiff upper lip emotional turmoils. This clichéd view of the company, which attracted older audiences and helped boost the art house scene in Britain in the 1980s, is worthy of an examination in terms of its Britishness.

Its founders are not British – producer Ismail Merchant was born in India, while director James Ivory hailed from America. The company, which still produces films today (despite Merchant's death in 2005) has an office in New York as well as London and yet during the 1980s Merchant Ivory established itself as a purveyor of what academics labeled 'heritage films'.

Its big 1980s hit was *Room With a View* (UK, 1985), an adaptation of E.M. Forster's novel about a doomed romance set in Florence with an impressive cast list that included Maggie Smith, Helena Bonham Carter, Denholm Elliott, Daniel Day-Lewis, Simon Callow, Judi Dench, Rupert Graves and Julian Sands. This was followed by another E.M. Forster adaptation *Maurice* (UK, 1987), about the homosexual affair of two students in Cambridge in 1911.

Earlier on in the decade Merchant Ivory had offered audiences a sign of its creative intentions with two other well-received films *Heat and Dust* (UK, 1982), and *The Bostonians* (UK/USA, 1984).

Several factors were important to Merchant Ivory's success. Firstly, the founders made the type of films that interested them - generally literary adaptations that would appeal to an audience over the age of 35. Secondly, they received funding from Channel 4, and thirdly, their films were well-received in North America and they would not be compromised to make bigger pictures.

Merchant Ivory managed the trick of survival and continued to make films despite often 'sniffy' critical opinions. Indeed, in the 1990s Merchant Ivory produced a steady output of films such as *Howards End* (UK/Japan, 1991), *The Remains of the Day* (UK, 1993), *Jefferson in Paris* (UK/USA, 1995), and *A Soldier's Daughter Never Cries* (UK, 1998). None broke the standards first established in the 1980s, and the partnership was brought to a premature end when Ismail Merchant died suddenly in 2005.

HandMade Films

When ex-Beatle George Harrison stepped in to fund *Monty Python's Life of Brian* (UK 1979), after EMI withdrew support from the project, he didn't appear to have a long-term plan to create a successful film production company. However, when the film became a big hit Harrison, along with his American business manager Dennis O'Brien decided to invest in other projects under the title of HandMade Films.

They agreed to pick up the rights from Black Lion Films for the tough gangster thriller *The Long Good Friday* (UK, 1979), starring Bob Hoskins, when the production company wavered about some of its content. Their instinct again proved correct as the film went on to become an acclaimed hit.

The Python connection followed when HandMade invested in Terry Gilliam's charming fantasy feature *Time Bandits* (UK, 1981) and *The Missionary* (UK, 1981), scripted by Michael Palin. What followed was an impressive range of critically acclaimed films such as *A Private Function* (UK, 1986), *Mona Lisa* (UK, 1986), and *Withnail and I* (UK, 1986).

However, HandMade famously came unstuck due to its policy of selling distribution rights to productions around the world while films were still being made. A film starring Madonna and her then husband Sean Penn looked on paper as though it was destined for international success. Unfortunately, on celluloid *Shanghai Surprise* (UK, 1986), was a critical and box-office flop.

Lauded as the saviour of the British film industry HandMade celebrated its tenth anniversary in 1988 but the partnership between Harrison and O'Brien became strained and ultimately litigatious when it emerged that O'Brien had been guaranteeing films with Harrison's money without his knowledge. Financially, HandMade could not sustain its losses despite a hit with the comedy romp *Nuns of the Run* (UK, 1990), when the company became embroiled in a dispute with Palace Pictures which acted as distributor.

In 1994, HandMade was wound up and sold on to Paragon Entertainment. The fruits of this acquisition produced the black comedy *Intimate Relations* (UK/Canada, 1995), starring Julie Waters and Rupert Graves. However, HandMade was sold on again to Equator in 1999. In 2006, HandMade plc was relaunched to exploit the back catalogue and again dip its toe in the film industry.

Goldcrest Films

The rise of Goldcrest in the early 1980s is as spectacular as its fall in the later half of the decade. With heavyweight triumphs like *Chariots of Fire*, *Gandhi*, *The Killing Fields* (UK, 1984), not to mention the gentle Ealingesque comedy *Local Hero* (UK, 1983), Goldcrest was in danger of becoming a real force to be reckoned with on the international stage.

At first Goldcrest aimed to make films with a certain kind of Britishness that could be sold to the American market. But, as with Merchant Ivory, the British connection was in its output rather than its running since it was headed up by Canadian Jake Ebert.

When Ebert left Goldcrest in 1984 his successor James Lee embarked on an ambitious slate of films, which didn't necessary follow the Britishness formula that had delivered such success. Instead, Goldcrest embarked on three big productions *Revolution* (UK/Norway, 1985), *Absolute Beginners* (UK, 1986), and *The Mission* (UK, 1986). Of the three, only *The Mission* managed to make the type of impact of earlier productions. By then the damage had been done – both *Absolute Beginners*, which received a critical mauling and *Revolution*, which flopped at the box-office, overspent their considerable budgets.

The end soon followed for Goldcrest, which had incurred £15m losses. In 1987 it was sold to Brent Walker as a sales and distribution company rather than a production company.

Palace Pictures

Palace Pictures began life by creatively running the Scala, an art house cinema in North London, which offered its customers an eclectic choice of cult films and all-nighter screenings. Its founders Nik Powell and Stephen Woolley quickly saw the logical progression from screening cult movies to selling them via video, which they rightly guessed would become a burgeoning industry. Palace Videos output in the early 1980s featured the outrageous *Pink Flamingos* (USA, 1972), and the students' favourite cult hit *Eraserhead* (USA, 1976).

Powell and Woolley's passion for cinema meant that they were regulars on the film festival circuit and their instincts told them that there was an intelligent audience interested in edgier stuff than the diet of space-age Hollywood blockbusters and worthy stately home melodramas. They forged friendships with up-and-coming film-makers such as the Coen Brothers, Neil Jordan and Sam Raimi. The lattter's first feature *The Evil Dead* (USA, 1982) took Palace into film distribution when it released the film theatrically as well as on video. This policy led to massive video sales of the film and encouraged Palace to continue to distribute films such as *Paris Texas* (Germany/France/UK, 1984), and *Merry Christmas Mr. Lawrence* (UK/Japan, 1984). Palace's shift into film production came as other distributors started moving in on its new-found territory. It made sense to secure distribution rights by producing the film as well. Palace Pictures' first feature was the eerie re-telling of Little Red Riding Hood – Neil Jordan's *The Company of Wolves* (UK, 1984). The film met with critical acclaim and reasonable box-office success in the UK. At this point Palace Pictures had risen to the status of a mini-British film studio with fingers in the exhibition, distribution, production and video pies.

The obvious next move was to consolidate its position by achieving an international hit in Britain and North America. It invested in the musical flop *Absolute Beginners* but didn't lose money (unlike co-producer Goldcrest). It fared much better when teaming up with HandMade on the well-received *Mona Lisa* and perhaps reached its full potential with the portrayal of the Profumo affair in *Scandal* (UK/USA, 1988), which did well on both sides of the Atlantic.

However, Palace could not guarantee success and films such as *Siesta* (UK/USA, 1987), *High Spirits* (USA, 1988), and *The Big Man* (UK, 1990), failed to live up to their potential. This uneven progression could not sustain too many box-office failures. The industry appeared to lose confidence in Powell and Woolley's abilities and their last big hit film *The Crying Game* (UK/Japan, 1992) could not save the company from going under.

Powell and Woolley continued to work as producers throughout the 1990s but Palace Picture's bold attempt to become a major international force in the film industry was sadly consigned to the history books.

BFI Production Board

It would be fair to say that the 1980s saw British films achieving some spectacular commercial successes as well as disastrous flops. The British Film Institute's (BFI) Production Board was established to produce 'difficult' works – works that weren't catered for by mainstream producers. The timing was perfect since the new Channel 4 saw part of its remit to invest in experimental kinds of work and so the decade saw the brief emergence of an alternative art house cinema where the creative talents of Peter Greenaway, (*The Draughtsman's Contract*, UK, 1982), Sally Potter (*The Gold Digger's*, UK, 1983), Derek Jarman (*Caravaggio*, UK, 1986), and Terence Davis (*Distant Voices Still Lives*, UK, 1988) were given a platform. Also important was the fact that Black and Gay cinema made it onto the film radar in Britain. The public funding of the BFI was able to extend to a small distribution and exhibition service and of course the public service provider, Channel 4, would be able to screen the films on television to a far bigger audience then the independent cinema circuit.

BFI Production Board was to be replaced by the BFI Production division during the 1990s with varying degrees of low-budget art house success including *Young Soul Rebels* (UK/France/Germany/Spain, 1991); *Wittgenstein* (UK/Japan, 1993); *Under the Skin* (UK, 1997) and *Love is the Devil* (UK/France/Japan, 1998). The films occupied a peculiar position within the British film canon. They were rarely mainstream or commercial but they picked up international recognition particularly through major film festivals. At the end of the 1990s BFI Production was transferred to the Film Council where future commissions would be assigned via the New Cinema Fund.

1990 AND THE SEEDS OF RECOVERY

It is clear that the triumphs and traumas of the 1980s had led to a greater awareness of there being something wrong with the British film industry. The main lesson from the 1980s was that the industry did not have the ability to cope with films that failed. Some of the seeds of recovery had been sewn in the 1980s with the rise of the multiplex, the arrival of Channel 4 with its injection of ideas and cash, and the excitement of video. But film production still continued to stutter.

It is worth examining a couple of successful films from the early part of the 1990s; Palace Pictures' final hurrah *The Crying Game* and Kenneth Branagh's continued exploration of Shakespeare in the sun-drenched *Much Ado About Nothing* (UK/USA, 1993) to see just how the hangover from the 1980s affected film-makers in the 1990s.

The Crying Game (1992) (UK/Japan) UK Cert 18

Director: Neil Jordan

Screenplay: Neil Jordan

Producer: Stephen Woolley

Production companies: Channel Four; Palace (Soldier's Wife) Ltd; Nippon Film Development & Finance; Palace Productions in association with Eurotrustees with the participation of British Screen

Production start date: 03/11/1991 **Budget:** £2.3m (estimated)

Distributor: Mayfair **UK Release date:** 30 October 1992

UK Box Office: £2,024,849 **USA Box Office:** $62.5m

Worldwide Box Office: n/a

It is impossible to talk about Neil Jordan's taut emotional thriller without referring to the film's 'twist.' Those who have seen the film will understand why protecting this key moment is important.

Notwithstanding the 'twist', *The Crying Game* is a remarkable British film of the early 1990s in that it touches on subjects that are not conducive to box-office returns – the troubles in Northern Ireland, racial issues and sexual identity. It then adds yet another layer of issues for an audience to absorb – complex examinations of human nature and the enduring power of love, or as Col (Jim Broadbent), the barman sums up philosophically: 'Who knows the secrets of the human heart?'

This is precisely the daring type of film that Channel 4 was set up to champion. Ironic then that its controversial nature would lead many potential backers to have cold feet and ultimately bring Palace Pictures to its knees. For producers Stephen Woolley and Nik Powell this was to be a bittersweet film. After an unpromising release in Britain it proved its backers wrong by eventually doing exceptional box-office business in America and winning plaudits and awards, including six Oscar nominations, (winning one Oscar for Neil Jordan for his screenplay).

SYNOPSIS

Opening at a fairground in Armagh, Northern Ireland during the troubles, a black British soldier, Jody, is seduced and captured by Jude, a member of an IRA unit.

Jody is told that he will die if their demands to free an IRA prisoner are not met. He strikes up a rapport with one of his captors, Fergus, and asks him to visit his partner Dil in the event of his death. Fergus volunteers to shoot Jody but the soldier makes a break for freedom, only to be killed accidentally by an army convoy heading to rescue him.

Fergus escapes to London and carries out Jody's wish to contact Dil and develops a relationship with her. During foreplay, he is shocked to discover that Dil is in fact a man, but Jody's haunting memory compels Fergus to see Dil again.

When Jude turns up in London and forces Fergus to carry out an execution of a judge, Fergus feels obliged to protect Dil from any recriminations his IRA colleagues might carry out and he persuades Dil to have her hair cut and dress up as a man.

Fergus finally confesses his part in Jody's death but Dil turns the tables on Fergus by tying him up, which means he cannot carry out his assassination of the judge. Instead his former IRA colleague Maguire carries out the job but is killed, leaving Jude to find and kill Fergus. However, Jude is shot by Dil shoots Jude. Fergus prevents Dil from shooting herself and urges her to leave so he can take the blame for Jude's murder.

Fergus is thus reconciled with Dil and atones for Jody's death. The final scene shows Dil, in 'her' glamorous splendour, visiting Fergus in prison.

HOW THE FILM WAS MADE

Jordan had first come up with the idea for the film in a script he had started called 'The Soldier's Wife' in 1982. The plotline is broadly similar to that of *The Crying Game* except for the fact that the soldier's wife is a woman. However, Jordan shelved the project because of the similarities between his story and Bernard MacLaverty's novel *Cal*, published in 1983 and released as a film in 1984, in which an IRA man falls in love with the widow of an RUC policeman who was murdered on the orders of the IRA.

Jordan's film-making career, which had started so brightly with *Angel* (UK, 1982) and Palace Pictures' productions of *The Company of Wolves* and *Mona Lisa*, had taken a turn for the worse with the failure of his Hollywood films *High Spirits* and *We're No Angels* (USA, 1989). He returned to Britain to team up again with Palace Pictures and make *The Miracle* (UK/Ireland, 1990), which garnered warm reviews but poor box-office business. Nevertheless, while promoting *The Miracle* with Stephen Woolley, Jordan uniquely resolved his quandary with 'The Soldier's Wife' by making the soldier's wife a transvestite.

Woolley was thrilled when he received Jordan's script and, along with Nik Powell, set out on the long journey to find funding for the film. By now Palace Pictures was in financial trouble, partly by its own doing, partly due to bad luck, and had lost some of its financiers' trust. Woolley kept absolute faith in Jordan's ability as a writer and film-maker and launched something of a personal crusade to gain funding. However, Woolley and Powell were dealt an enormous blow when American executives found the subject matters of Northern Ireland politics, race and sexual identity far too taboo to invest in. Miramax, with whom Palace had had a good relationship, did agree to buy the American distribution rights but wouldn't put money into production.

Channel 4 also expressed its own doubts over aspects of the film and asked Jordan to come up with an alternative upbeat ending. Woolley kept up incessant pressure on Channel 4 to fund the project, even threatening to set himself alight. Taken by his commitment and passion for the project, Channel 4 then agreed to come onboard.

In the meantime, Powell had secured funding after meeting Michyo Yoshizaki of the Japanese distribution company Nippon Development & Finance. Powell and Woolley also persuaded Eurotrustees, essentially a consortium of distributors from France, Germany, Spain and Italy, which also included Palace in the UK, to fund the project. Simon Perry, the chief executive of British Screen, liked the script and agreed to invest despite the fact that earlier loss-making collaborations with Palace had created an uneasy relationship.

The budget was tight but Woolley knew that he had to press on if the project was to be realised. On Jordan's recommendation Forest Whitaker was cast as the black British soldier. This caused consternation among some black members of the UK actors' union Equity. Woolley was unrepentant knowing that the casting of an American actor, who had caught his eye in the biopic of *Bird* (USA, 1988), would enhance the film's international sales potential. In the end some still griped about Whitaker's hard-to-place London accent, the fact that he seemed too physically bulky to pass for a British soldier (and this presumably also included his cricketing credentials) but these criticisms seem harsh in the context of Whitaker's subtle performance as the not-so-vulnerable Jody, who manages to unlock the key to Fergus' troubled mind in order to make his doomed break for freedom.

There was criticism too of the casting of British actress Miranda Richardson as Jude, the failed femme fatale, but she went on to be nominated for Best Supporting Actress in the 1993 BAFTAs.

The biggest casting headache proved to be the film's greatest triumph – that of Dil. Jordan was adamant that Dil had to be credible as a woman in order for the plot twist to work – this point was unsuccessfully disputed by Channel 4 who would have preferred that Dil was revealed as a transvestite straightaway. After numerous casting sessions it soon became clear that the person who was to play Dil would have to be an unknown actor (so that audiences would be none the wiser), or failing that a transvestite with no formal acting ability. In the end newcomer Jaye Davidson fitted the part to perfection. Even on repeat viewings with full knowledge of 'the twist' Davidson's 'performance' as a glamorous, slightly vulnerable woman is convincing. Indeed, the delicious irony in the film is that Davidson seems decidedly less at ease as a man in cricket whites.

The film, which necessitated the tightest of schedules, commenced shooting in Northern Ireland on 3 November 1991, but even then Woolley had to raid the tills of the Scala Cinema, which he owned and from which Palace began, in order to pay cast and crew.

KEY ISSUES

It is interesting that potential (and some actual) financiers thought that Jordan's script contained so many sensitive or taboo subjects that the film would become a box-office turn off. Jordan's fate as a hit film-maker was also called to question, as was confidence in the ability of Powell and Woolley's Palace Pictures to pay its way. And yet it is to their credit that Jordan, Powell and Woolley held their nerve and continued to have an unflinching belief in their controversial project.

The Troubles

The Crying Game is set during the troubles in Northern Ireland when the Provisional IRA is waging its terrorist campaign against those seen to be supporting the unionist cause, including the British government and the British troops originally sent over in 1969 to keep the peace. The IRA's aim was to bring an end to British rule and return to a united Ireland.

Seen from the perspective of the Peace Process and the power-sharing Northern Ireland Assembly, which took office in May 2007, the film perhaps contains pathways towards peace and reconciliation. In order to survive Fergus embraces change, no matter how difficult it may be to accept. Stephen Rea as Fergus, a regular in Jordan films, earned an Oscar nomination for his performance of a man in crisis negotiating a tricky emotional minefield to inner peace.

Generally, the politics of the film tend to be personalised. It is clear that Fergus is going through some soul searching, maybe not to do with the cause that he has been fighting for, but with the numbing effect the violence has had on him personally. Jody makes indirect references to the IRA and their struggles, but he does say at one point that Fergus is 'a good soldier', perhaps as an acknowledgement that both men are reluctantly carrying out orders.

Fergus is warned several times not to get too close to the prisoner because it becomes increasingly likely that Jody will be shot. In the final event, Fergus volunteers to carry out the execution. As Fergus leads Jody out into the woods Maguire begins to issue Jody with an official statement from the IRA justifying the action. However, Fergus reacts angrily to Maguire and cuts him short before leading Jody on. At this point Fergus appears to abandon his old cause and adopts a new deeply personal cause. Our sympathies, which at this point have been with Jody, shift to the moral dilemma facing Fergus.

The critics were split in their opinions of how the IRA characters were portrayed. When the film opened in October 1992, the IRA had renewed a bombing campaign on mainland Britain leading the British press to be a little wary about its content. Some critics in Britain were not happy with having Fergus, an active member of the IRA, as the hero in the film, particularly one with a conscience. Others felt that the characters of Jude, who seems to lack any kind of compassion, and Maguire, who seems unswervingly loyal and committed to the point of carrying out the suicide attack on the judge in a British street, were too harshly drawn. At one point Jude pistol-whips Jody when he gives her some backchat and in London Maguire stubs out his cigarette on Fergus's hand when he does the same.

Yet if Maguire and Jude lack humanity then the British soldiers are presented in a worse light with their extreme and brutal recrimination in the aftermath of Jody's accidental death. They strafe the glasshouse where Jody had been kept captive, mow down two of his kidnappers and riddle the cottage with bullets. The attack is completely impersonal and the scene ends with the glasshouse in which Jody had been held in flames.

Fergus' escape from the British army in Northern Ireland and from the IRA carries with it a neutral aspect. To regain his humanity he needs to abandon his past. By the time Jude turns up and tells him that his desertion led to a court martial and that he was spared his own execution because he was to carry out the assassination of a target in London, Fergus' life has moved on.

When he tries to tell Jude: 'I'm out', he does not do so as a political statement. His desire to leave the IRA is part of his wider personal quest to reconnect with his human side. However, disillusioned though Fergus may be, he still looks capable of carrying out the hit on the judge. Indeed, Fergus demonstrates that violence can be used to good effect, principally when he rescues Dil from her abusive boyfriend Dave (Ralph Brown) by beating him up. He also uses menace when he defends Dil's honour from the sexist jibes of property developer Deveroux (Tony Slattery) issuing the curt inquiry: 'Do you ever pick your teeth up with broken fingers?'

Jordan uses the troubles as a backdrop to constructing the story. But one gets the feeling that his principle concern was to make a film about the personal dilemmas of Jody, Fergus and Dil to form the basis of a complex love triangle. Nevertheless, without the brooding presence of the IRA the film would not be able to work as a film-noir thriller, particularly in its final act when Jude and Maguire show up in London.

Race

Jordan was keen to write a scenario whereby he brought two protagonists together who were essentially part of a minority – a black British soldier on a tour of duty and a Catholic IRA man in Northern Ireland. It is clear that part of Fergus' sympathy towards Jody comes, albeit unstated, from the fact that he is black. At one point an exasperated Fergus cries: 'What the fuck were you doing here?' This is a double-edged, or possibly triple-edged, exclamation aimed at the British army's presence in Northern Ireland, why a black man should join the army, and possibly why a black soldier should be picked up by a white woman.

The interesting part of The Crying Game is that amid all the tension and suspense there is very little in the way of racial tension. The Metro bar in London is seen as a cosmopolitan bar where a person's identity is almost seen as irrelevant. In fact the film opens with the beginnings of an interracial relationship with Jude seducing a slightly drunk Jody. In this case Jude has no desires for Jody but is acting to lure him away so that he can be kidnapped. Jude later despises Jody but her disgust seems little to do with the colour of his skin. She also teases Fergus by calling Dil a 'black chick' (while apparently holding some Robinson's Jam, infamous for its golliwogs on its jam jar labels) but this is rather more out of jealousy.

In London Fergus meets up with Dil but the issue of her racial origin is not mentioned. On their first meeting in the hairdressers when Dil is washing Fergus' hair she makes an attempt to place his accent, finally, incorrectly and possibly ironically, labelling Fergus as Scottish, something that Fergus makes no effort to correct.

The biggest reference to racism comes when Jody declares to Fergus: 'So, I get sent to the one place they call you nigger to your face.' While Fergus glibly tells Jody not to take the jibes personally, he is prickly when Jody refers to him as 'Paddy'. Ironically, Fergus is subject to more racism himself when he comes to London and Devoroux insists on calling him 'Pat'. Yet the issue of race is an important part of the melting pot as *The Crying Game* reaches its boiling point, since it forms part of a larger issue surrounding identity.

The Twist/Sexuality

Rather than call the film The Soldier's Wife, Jordan's original title, the film was named after Dave Barry's maudlin ballad, *The Crying Game*, from 1964. The song, which appears in three different versions in the film (including the end credits), deals with love and loss in a persuasive, simplistic way:

> First there are kisses, then there are sighs
> And then before you know where you are
> You're sayin' goodbye

Love and loss are certainly at the heart of the film's core. However, in order to reach this point the audience is teased into undertaking a bewildering sexual orienteering course.

The first obstacle thrown in the audience's way is in the characters of Jude and Jody who seem to be embarking on a passionate fling. Their names are sexually ambiguous since Jude can be a male name and Jody can certainly be female.

Fergus is presented as a rather masculine, heterosexual man and he kisses Jude tenderly, leaving the audience to guess the extent of their relationship. When Fergus shows concern about her seduction of Jody she replies: 'I thought of you.' Indeed, he gently jibes Jude about how much she seemed to be enjoying her sexual encounter with Jody. Any doubts about the pleasure involved are dashed when Jody lunges at Jude at the first opportunity they have after he is captured. This rebuttal is returned with interest when later Jude strikes Jody with the butt of her pistol, confirming that their liaison had been nothing but a sham. Later on in London when Jude, sporting a new harder look, has tracked Fergus down, she rather aggressively suggests having sex with him, which he definitively rejects.

Jody on the other hand first flatters Fergus by saying that he is handsome. He tells Fergus that: 'I didn't even fancy her' referring to Jude as not his type, and this leads Jody to show Fergus a photograph of Dil. Fergus is duly impressed and says: 'She'd be anybody's type.' Fergus asks if that is his wife, which Jody does not refute. Another clue as to what is to come after Jude hits Jody: 'Women are trouble,' he sobs and then adds: 'Dil, she's no trouble.' Jody's love for Dil is genuine and the strength of this is confirmed when Fergus talks to Dil about Jody.

An interesting shift of power comes when Jody, who has his hands tied behind his back, requests Fergus to hold his penis while he urinates, (earlier a more vulnerable Jody had urinated in a toilet tent at the fair with one hand while still holding Jude's hand as she waited outside for him). Fergus reacts awkwardly as if his masculinity is threatened. However, the two men are bonded by this incident when Fergus casually quips: 'The pleasure was all mine'. We don't know that Jody's hearty laughter reveals a secondary reason since our reasoning tells us later on in the film that Jody was gay or bisexual.

The Metro, the bar where Dil hangs out in London and where Fergus nervously follows her to buy her a drink, does not seem like a transvestite bar until after Dil has revealed herself to be a man. The barman Col initially acts as an interpreter between the confident Dil and the sheepish Fergus, even though they can hear each other. Col even feels obliged to tip Fergus off that Dil isn't what she seems but fails as she comes on stage to give an impressively sultry mime to her theme tune – the Crying Game.

Fergus, like the audience, is intrigued by Dil – the soldier's wife. He cements his relationship with Dil when he witnesses and then steps in to beat up Dave, Dil's abusive, apparently heterosexual, boyfriend. During Fergus' first major sexual encounter Fergus attempts to put his hand up Dil's skirt but is rebuffed (which mirrors Jody's own exploration of Jude). Instead, Dil gives him a blow job during which Fergus is haunted by the image of Jody. It is as if he is guilt-ridden and needs assurances that it is morally acceptable to continue with his relationship with Dil.

The shock/horror revelation comes when Dil and Fergus prepare to have penetrative sex together and Fergus gently pulls off her robe to find a flat chest and a penis. It is as though Fergus has found the missing piece of a jigsaw puzzle – and what a revelation! His reaction is one of bemusement and mild rage. He strikes Dil as she attempts to comfort him and proceeds to throw up in the sink, making his apologies and leaving. The film could have ended here when Fergus sees an image of a smiling Jody dressed up in his cricket whites and exacting some sort of revenge.

Indeed, the guilt that Fergus feels for Jody's death is the reason that he agrees to see Dil again, if only to clarify in his mind the details of what has happened. In the meantime, Fergus is able to issue some mixed gender quips. Maguire asks: 'What's she like between the sheets?' Fergus retorts: 'definitely unusual.' Deveroux taunts Fergus, having been rebuffed for referring to Dil as 'Pat's tart'. He continues sarcastically: 'Of course, she's not a lady,' to which Fergus replies: 'She's not that either.' Dil dismisses the blurring of her sexual identity as merely 'details', a sentiment that is echoed by Col in the Metro.

In a film of many twists, the next comes as no less of a surprise. Despite his disappointment of learning that Dil is a man – 'I kinda liked you as a girl.' – Fergus continues a friendship, bordering on romance, with Dil and makes sure that Dil is protected from Jude, with whom he witnesses a catty scene where the two love interests in Fergus's life eye each other up. Knowing that Dil is in danger, having identified Jude but not knowing that she is a terrorist – 'is she Scottish too?' she asks – Fergus persuades Dil to cut her hair and pose as a man. She does this in a rather contrived, unconvincing, clumsy fashion by wearing Jody's cricket whites. Dil as a man suddenly seems less convincing than Dil as a woman.

Redemption

Fergus's bizarre journey is one of righting a wrong and being able to live with himself. In this respect Jody gives him a head start with his recital of the ancient fable of the Scorpion and the Frog, which definitely unsettles Fergus. A scorpion asks a frog to carry him across the river. The frog is afraid of being stung, but the scorpion reasons that if he stung the frog they would both die. Reassured by the logic the frog agrees, but in mid-stream the scorpion stings the frog leading both to their death. When the frog asks why, the scorpion explains, 'it's in my nature.' Fergus doesn't see the point of the story until Jody explains that it is against Fergus' nature to act violently.

It is because of Fergus's nature to do the right thing that he tracks Dil down in the first place and carries out Jody's request to look after her. But for Fergus to truly become free he knows that at some point he will have to confess to Dil that he had a hand in Jody's death. For a while it seems as though Fergus will not be able to explain since his personal relationship with Dil has become too close. Ironically, when Fergus is facing a deadly situation with his mission to assassinate the judge he finally finds the courage to tell Dil what happens. Unfortunately, Dil is drunk and hazy due to prescribed drugs at the time and it is only in the morning that Fergus' confession becomes clear.

In another twist to the story Dil ties Fergus to the bed, effectively imprisoning him and so condemning him to death by his IRA colleagues when he fails to carry out the assassination of the judge.

The tables are turned yet again when coolly Dil shoots Jude, who has turned up to kill Fergus. Dil exacts revenge from Jude's initial seduction of Jody. He then prevents Dil from turning the gun on herself.

Fergus sees that taking responsibility for Jude's murder is the only option of truly avenging Jody's death. In the final awkward scene of the film the heavy burden of guilt is lifted from Fergus' shoulders as Dil visits him in prison. Fergus is free at last and has realised not only that love conquers all but that redemption is possible if you are prepared to accept change within yourself.

SCENE ANALYSIS – FERGUS AND JODY IN THE GLASSHOUSE

Although two thirds of The Crying Game occurs in London, Fergus' intense relationship with Jody establishes something about Fergus' character and his motivation for seeking out and befriending Dil. It also plants an uneasy image of Jody in our minds and although Jody is killed off his presence continues to influence and inform both Fergus and Dil throughout the remainder of the film. Importantly, Jody's short-lived scenes in the dilapidated glasshouse, rather like his partially visible face, only serve to reveal part of the truth and allows Jody to exact a calculated ambush of his own. Although Jody wears a hood, it is Fergus who is left in the dark about the true nature of Jody's relationship with Dil.

Jordan and his cameraman Ian Wilson benefited from the autumnal hues of the exterior shots and used the effect of sunlight pouring through the panes in the glasshouse, which assumed the symbolism of a jail with the window frames suggesting prison bars and the overgrown twines adding to the feeling of barbed entrapment. The lighting also serves to distinguish captor from captive with Fergus generally being placed in the light while Jody is normally situated in the shade, thereby suggesting his own shadowy nature. The scenes in the glasshouse are also played with hardly any musical backdrop at all, creating an intimate atmosphere.

There is a subtle difference in tone in Fergus' voice from when he directs Jody into the glasshouse to his faltering guidance when he emerges later with the man with whom he has struck up a relationship. As well as being separated by lighting, the camera movements establish a distance between the two men. As they settle in the glasshouse the camera first follows Fergus and then slowly steers past him to settle on a physical space between Fergus and Jody when they are framed together as Fergus (on the left of the screen) feeds Jody, on the right, with a bar of chocolate. Gradually the physical distance between the two men is broken down.

When Fergus removes Jody's hood for the first time Jody is framed in the centre of screen whereas Fergus occupies either the left side of the screen or the right hand – maintaining a distance from Jody. When Jody beckons Fergus over to see his photos of Dil, Fergus is not facing Jody and speaks to him over his shoulder. At the point that Fergus wanders over to Jody, gun in hand, to take out his wallet the camera tilts slightly, a move which emphasises not only Jody's uncomfortable position but also Fergus' compliance to his prisoner's request. The men are now closer in the frame than the preceding mid-shots.

It is also interesting that Fergus first shows a picture of Dil and Jody to Jody before it is revealed to the audience in a large close-up. The photo is peculiar since neither Dil or

Jody are looking at each other (Jody's eyes are closed). Dil is captured more in the light than Jody with a dark dividing line seemingly separating them. When Fergus asks Jody: 'Is she your wife?' we are shown a closer image of Dil; the light in the photo draws attention to how she looks. Later on this picture, along with other pictures of Jody in his cricket whites, will be seen in Dil's flat.

In the following short scene Jody's growing confidence is confirmed when he gets Fergus to help him urinate. Physically Jody and Fergus are close but when the two appear in shot Jody's physical presence seems a lot bigger on screen than Fergus, whose stature is diminished. Jody now has the upper hand as he issues instructions to Fergus to help him pee.

The next time the two are alone in the glasshouse doubts have entered Fergus' mind as Jody plays his mind games by telling the story of the scorpion and the frog. As he recounts the story Fergus slowly walks away, again with his back to Jody, and the camera follows him as he walks behind some garden boxes where he faces Jody. As Jody delivers the concluding line – 'it's in my nature' – the camera takes Fergus' view, which puts Jody, hood uncovering his mouth, in the centre of the frame. The shot cuts to a thoughtful Fergus who is also in the centre of the frame asking Jody what the story means. The camera follows Fergus back to Jody as he removes the hood. By this time the bond between the men has been forged even though Fergus is unsettled.

The next shot features a slow forward pan, which sees the two men chatting on equal footing about where they would like to be if it wasn't for their current circumstances. The camera veers towards a close shot of Fergus who is again chatting with his back to Jody. Now, Fergus occupies the centre of the screen with Jody framed to his right. Their intimate moments are interrupted with a cut to a wider shot allowing Jude to enter the room and the camera moves around as she breaks up the space occupied by Fergus and Jody.

Jude leaves the glasshouse having pistol-whipped Jody and the camera returns to Fergus as he goes to Jody's aid. As he lifts the hood there is a cut to a powerful close-up, which reveals Jody's bloodied lip. This is followed by a similar close-up of Fergus' face as he asks Jody if he is all right. Jody continues to speak with only his lips and chin visible along with the textures of the hood. The physical distance and indeed the emotional distance between Fergus and Jody are drawn together with tight head and shoulder shots putting the two close in the frame as Jody compels Fergus to find Dil and make sure that she is all right.

Fergus and Jody's final scene in the glasshouse has Jody with his hood again up to his lips but this time his tears and emotions are inescapable. The camera draws to Fergus who knows he has to execute Jody as he admits: 'No, I'm not good for much.'

The delicately played scenes between Fergus and Jody set in the quiet confines of an isolated glasshouse are literally shattered with Jody's unexpected death and the army's ruthless reprisal. The careful way the scenes are constructed makes Fergus' journey to find Dil not only plausible but, from a dramatic point of view, necessary.

REACTION

By the time *The Crying Game* was released in Britain in 1992, the game was up for Palace Pictures which had been declared bankrupt in April of that year. Initially, it looked as though the film would prove to be a disappointing endnote to what had been an adventurous company. Due to financial problems Palace didn't distribute the film in Britain itself, leaving it to Mayfair to negotiate the delicate matter of promoting the film as a thriller with a twist. Mayfair struggled and despite quite good reviews particularly in the broadsheets – and the well-kept embargo on 'the twist' – the film did eventually do reasonable business in Britain with final box office receipts of £2,024,849.

In America the situation was completely different. Miramax's promotion was inspired. It indulged in some mild exploitation marketing, labelling *The Crying Game* as 'the film that everyone is talking about'; it created a film-noir poster featuring a sultry looking Miranda Richardson as Jude with the tagline: 'Sex. Murder. Betrayal. In Neil Jordan's new thriller, nothing is what it seems – *The Crying Game* … play it at your own risk.'

The campaign hit a nerve with American audiences. The reviews, not too bothered about the political aspects of the film, were enthusiastic, revelling in the sexual politics and violence and comparisons were made with the two Hitchcock classics *Vertigo* (1958) and *Psycho* (1960). They also shared a childlike delight in not revealing the secret within the film to the point that one of the earliest reviews in the *Los Angeles Times* had a headline which said: 'Don't Read Any Further If You Haven't Seen This Film.'

Ironically, with the film doing exceptional box-office business, the cat was truly let out of the bag when Davison was nominated as Best Actor in a Supporting Role at the Oscars. Jordan picked up an Academy Award for the screenplay and this led on to a renewed interest of the film in Britain. *The Crying Game* grossed around $62.5m in the USA, the majority going to Miramax rather than the beleaguered Palace team.

In the end Woolley and Powell could issue a collective 'We told you so!' and went on to produce films in the 1990s often under the guise of Scala Productions: *Twentyfourseven* (UK, 1997), and *Little Voice* (UK/USA, 1998). Woolley continued to support the work of Jordan as they combined on *Michael Collins* (USA, 1996), *The Butcher Boy* (Ireland/USA, 1997) and *The End of the Affair* (USA/Germany, 1999).

Much Ado About Nothing (1993) (UK/USA) UK Cert PG

Director: Kenneth Branagh

Screenplay: Kenneth Branagh (from William Shakespeare)

Producers: Stephen Evans; David Parfitt; Kenneth Branagh

Production companies: Samuel Goldwyn Company; Renaissance Films; BBC Films; First City Features

Production start date: 03/08/1992 **Budget:** £5.60m (estimated)

Distributor: Entertainment **UK Release date:** 27 August 1993

UK Box Office: £5,505,603 **USA Box Office:** $22.5m

Worldwide Box Office: n/a

While Palace Pictures prepared to go under in the early 1990s, the same cannot be said of Kenneth Branagh, who burst on to the film scene with his bold and self-assured version of Shakespeare's *Henry V* (UK, 1989), which he directed, acted in and adapted. The working class protestant Belfast boy, who had moved with his family to Reading in 1969 as a consequence of the troubles in Northern Ireland, now embarked on yet another phase of his life, that of Britain's latest auteur, drawing comparisons to no less luminaries as Olivier and the young Orson Welles.

His passionate mission was to make Shakespeare accessible on the screen to a wide audience. Having established himself as a theatre actor and director via RADA and the formation of his Renaissance Theatre Company, Branagh had dipped his toe in a few film roles, the most notable as a World War 1 veteran excavating in a country church in *A Month in the Country* (UK, 1987). He also came to prominence on television in the BBC's seven-part serial *The Fortunes of War* (1987), a role that would see Branagh meeting his co-star and future wife, Emma Thompson.

The ambitious Branagh set up Renaissance Films with his friend David Parfitt to fund the production of *Henry V*. The international success and acclaim of *Henry V* gave him the chance to woo Hollywood with eyes on future bigger prizes. He directed and starred in Paramount Picture's thriller *Dead Again* (USA, 1991) co-starring alongside Emma Thompson. The film did good box-office business and Branagh returned to Britain to make the slightly self-conscious ensemble piece *Peter's Friends* (UK/USA, 1992) also featuring Thompson, and a host of British friends such as Stephen Fry, Hugh Lawrie, Imelda Staunton, Richard Briers and Phyllida Law (Emma Thompson's mother).

Branagh even had time to write the first part of his memoirs *Beginning* (1989) which lifted eyebrows even further. Branagh and Thompson were at the height of their celebrity status as a couple when he announced his next step to decamp to the hills of Tuscany and produce a version of Shakespeare's romantic comedy *Much Ado About Nothing*.

SYNOPSIS

Set in the sun-drenched hills of the Italian town of Messina, Leonato, a respected nobleman lives with his young daughter Hero, his spirited niece, Beatrice, and his older brother, Antonio. Their idyllic lifestyle is pleasantly disturbed when friends of Leonato return from a war, led by the prince Don Pedro and the young noblemen Claudio and the wise-cracking Benedick, Don John, Don Pedro's illegitimate brother, and Borachio and Conrade both loyal to Don John.

Claudio is smitten with Hero and the two announce their plans to marry. Meanwhile, Don Pedro, Claudio and Lenoato along with Hero and Ursula trick Benedick and Beatrice into believing that one loves the other, thereby speeding up their true feelings for each other. However, Don John is intent on destroying everyone's happiness. He arranges for Borachio to make love to Margaret and convinces Don Pedro and Claudio that they are witnessing Hero being unfaithful. Distraught and enraged, Claudio humiliates a bemused and heartbroken Hero at the altar by accusing her of lechery.

Leonato, urged by the friar, sets out to discover the truth and Antonio and the Friar decide to pretend that Hero has died in the wake of the calamitous revelation. The upheaval forces Benedick and Beatrice confess their love to one another but Beatrice sets Benedict a challenge to protect Hero's honour by challenging Claudio to a duel, which Benedick reluctantly agrees on.

Don John's deceit is revealed when some night watchman overhear Borachio bragging to Conrade about his crime. The two men are arrested by the dim-witted constable Dogberry and his gormless companion Verges.

Before Benedick can take on Claudio everyone learns about Borachio's set-up with Margaret. Leonato seizes the opportunity to clear his daughter's name and unite the two lovers once more by telling Claudio that in order to atone for Hero's death he must pin up a notice on Hero's tomb proclaiming her true virtue and then marry Antonio's daughter.

Back in the chapel Claudio unveils his new bride and is shocked to see that she is Hero. Both are happily reconciled. In the meantime, Benedick and Beatrice engage in one final verbal battle of wits before also agreeing to marry.

HOW THE FILM WAS MADE

With the success of *Henry V* acting as a benchmark and some box-office success in America behind him with *Dead Again* Branagh felt confident to look to America for funding of his next project. In 1988 his Renaissance Theatre Company had undertaken a four-play British Isles tour where he had played Benedick, the misguided confirmed bachelor, in *Much Ado About Nothing*. Images of sun-drenched Tuscan hillsides, gallant soldiers on horseback, beautiful women, flowing flagons of wine, lots of laughter and a host of tomfoolery persuaded him that this would be a project as bold in its own way as *Henry V*.

The Samuel Goldwyn Company, which had produced *Peter's Friends*, was ready to hear Branagh's pitch. He reiterated his mission to make Shakespeare accessible to the public by making a bold choice with *Much Ado About Nothing*, a play that had not been filmed in English before. Branagh assured his main backers that this version would be sexy with a sumptuous location and the added draw of top Hollywood stars such as Denzel Washington, Keanu Reeves and Michael Keaton, plus his wife Emma Thompson, who had just turned in an Oscar-winning performance in the Merchant Ivory film *Howards End*.

British support came from Branagh's own Renaissance Films and BBC Films. In August 1992 filming commenced at the beautiful Villa Vignamaggio, Greve, near Sienna in Italy over a period of eight weeks. Branagh brought the film in on budget and on time.

KEY ISSUES

Within the opening five minutes of the film the audience has been transported to an idyllic sun-drenched Tuscan Villa; heard Beatrice carefully recite the words of song 'Sigh no more ladies, sigh no more' – (following the words slowly on the screen); seen the arrival of Don Pedro and his virile men riding into the scene as if they were the Magnificent Seven; and finally witnessed bronzed naked bodies as both men and women separately throw themselves into various baths for a quick freshen-up. Branagh, having grabbed our attention with sun, sex and suggestiveness, moves on to presenting Shakespeare's *Much Ado About Nothing*.

The trouble with Shakespeare

To some modern audiences, and particularly cinema audiences not used to much taxing dialogue, Shakespeare's language is difficult to grasp with its clever puns, classical references and peculiar delivery. The key to enjoyment is perseverance and allowing the plots to unravel.

Branagh uses a few devices to guide an audience unfamiliar with Shakespeare's quick-fire word play. Keen to make the exchanges tighter, his adaptation trims some lines so that the dialogue between the actors flows at the pace modern audiences expect.

For instance, when Don Pedro concludes the scheme to bring Benedick and Beatrice together, he does so with a couple of sharp lines (in bold) while Shakespeare gives far more detail:

> 'And Benedick is not the unhopefullest husband that I know. Thus far can I praise him: he is of a noble strain, of approved valour, and confirmed honesty. I will teach you how to humour your cousin that she shall fall in love with Benedick; and I, [to Leonato and Claudio] with your two helps, will so practice on Benedick that, in despite of his quick wit and his queasy stomach, he shall fall in love with Beatrice. **If we can do this, Cupid is no longer an archer; his glory is ours, for we are the only love-gods. Go in with me, and I will tell you my drift.'**

Branagh also cuts out a few short scenes superfluous to our understanding and he switches scenes from the play, presumably for cinematic effect. For example, with Claudio and Hero betrothed and the scheme to bring Benedick and Beatrice together revealed, the camera gets a shot of the intense Don John and his men leaving the party. In the play the next scene shows Borachio hatching his plot to discredit Hero by using Margaret at Hero's window, whereas Branagh decides to delay this scene, preferring to insert the lighter one involving Benedick and Beatrice.

In other cases such as the high-speed banter between Beatrice and Benedick, Branagh is happy for Shakespeare's language to go relatively untouched.

> Benedick: God keep your ladyship still in mind, so some gentleman or other shall scape a predestinate scratched face.
>
> Beatrice: Scratching could not make it worse, and 'twere such a face as yours were.
>
> Benedick: Well, you are a rare parrot-teacher.
>
> Beatrice: A bird of the tongue is better than a beast of yours.
>
> Benedick: I would my horse had the speed of your tongue, and so good a continuer. But keep your way, a God's name, I have done.

The early quick-fire exchanges between Beatrice and Benedick are met with plenty of laughter and knowing smiles to signal merriment. The background laughter (rather liked canned laughter) nudges us along so although we may not always get all the references, we get the gist.

Background music is also used throughout the film as an indicator of how we should be feeling at the time – happy, sad, concerned. An example how music is used to alter the moods comes in the scene after the first spat at the altar when Benedick and Beatrice are left alone and for the first time declare their love for each other. The background music, while not being too intrusive, is suitably romantic. However, as soon as Beatrice tells Benedick to 'kill Claudio,' the sentimental strings come to a halt and are followed by a more menacing, darker stab of music.

The lushness of the scenery and the colours producing varying qualities of natural light were also important factors in establishing the almost magical mood. This works perfectly in the flamboyant masked party scene where the colours are particularly vibrant. For Branagh it was a perfect backdrop in which to film (having been largely confined to a studio when filming *Henry V*).

Finally, Branagh tries to have the actors act as naturally as possible while reciting the lines to give the impression that they are engaging in real conversations. The themes of love, betrayal, misunderstanding, loss and reconciliation, not to mention the quick-fire wit, call for a range of believable emotions.

In this respect he deliberately chose to break up any preconceived notion of how the actors would speak by adding a mix of American actors to lend new texture, nuances and dynamics to the action.

Casting of US actors

Branagh was keen to shatter the myth that American actors don't get Shakespeare and so can't do the Bard justice. This notion is discussed in Al Pacino's own unusual semi-documentary take on Shakespeare's Richard III, *Looking for Richard* (USA, 1996), in which Branagh appears as a British interviewee explaining how to decipher Shakespeare's iambic pentameter.

Of the four US actors Denzel Washington has perhaps the most difficult role to play, since Don Pedro is an authority figure who acts as a conduit to the love interest between Claudio and Hero, and also between Beatrice and Benedick. As a result Washington is partly called upon to use his natural dignity and poise and act amiably rather than display any tortured emotions of rage, envy or spite.

Those emotions are given to the brooding figure of Keanu Reeves as Don John – not quite a pantomime villain but close. In the play Don John is Don Pedro's bastard brother, so there is a slight uneasiness in Branagh's version of casting a white man to play a black man's half-brother. As the villain of the piece Don John maintains a look of distain throughout the action, but emotionally the audience is not given much indication as to why he bears a grudge to Don Pedro, or Claudio for that matter.

The principle love interest in the film comes from Robert Sean Leonard as the love-smitten Claudio. Claudio is a youthful, impulsive character, which Leonard is able to capture. Indeed, his role calls for him to be smitten, conniving (when helping Don Pedro and Leonato to bring Benedick and Beatrice together), angry (when rebuffing Hero at the altar) and remorseful.

Of the four American actors Michael Keaton's performance as Dogberry, with his cod-pirate, Pythonesque actions are the most noteworthy. Clearly drawing influence from characters in *Monty Python and the Holy Grail* (UK, 1974), (both Dogberry and his side-kick Verges ride imaginary horses), Keaton's comic performance is deliberately over the top. Indeed, the slapstick anarchic elements (in which Ben Elton provides a good foil) seem out of place with the rest of the film. It is also ironic that the character of Dogsberry seems to take time to grasp what is being said to him, possibly to highlight the whole 'doing Shakespeare' debate.

In the final analysis the critics were undecided about the effectiveness of their performances, particularly in light of the rather more self-assured performance served up by Richard Briers as the benevolent Leonato. However, Branagh had another card up his sleeve and that was the chemistry between himself and his wife.

Ken and Em

Branagh and Thompson were at their height of their powers professionally as Britain's most talented, ambitious celebrity couple. They were the toast of Hollywood, who respected their Oscar nominations and triumphs. In Britain, the media tended to be rather dour, reaching for that unpleasant trait of trying to knock successful people, particular ambitious ones, off their perch. The satirical TV show *Spitting Image* (ITV) was an example of how they were lambasted and the 'luvvie' tag stuck with them leading to jokes such as Thompson coming home and Branagh shouting: 'I'm in the kitchen,' to which Thompson replies: 'Can I be in that as well?'

Benedick and Beatrice seemed ideal casting for them. Both characters are fiercely independent, quick-witted and somewhat obstinate. Branagh thought that both he and Thompson shared some of those traits, which would lead to exchanges reminiscent of the classic movies of Spencer Tracy and Katharine Hepburn. Whether the snap, crackle and pop performances work is ultimately down to personal judgment, there is always a knowing sense when the couple are on screen.

Thompson's Beatrice comes across a tad too sensible and intelligent. In the meantime, Branagh's Benedick manages the egotistical buffoon bit well but is less assured when he is in love. As a result it is easy to see how he can be conned into believing that Beatrice loves him but less convincing to see how Beatrice gets taken in by the same premise.

Much Ado About Nothing would be their last film together and the bickering lovers in the film would play out similar scenes in real life. Branagh would have a relationship with Helena Bonham Carter, his next co-star in *Mary Shelley's Frankenstein* (UK/USA/Japan, 1994). Thompson met her second husband, actor Greg Wise, on the set of *Sense and Sensibility* (USA, 1995).

SCENE ANALYSIS — SCREENING BENEDICK'S SOLILOQUYS

Branagh's backdrops were the hills and countryside and the sun-drenched splendour of Villa Vignamaggio with the majority of action taking place outdoors. Naturally, the cinematic cards dealt to Branagh – the ability of the camera to move around the actors; the framing of dialogue between characters; close-up shots of reactions and having visible physical spaces from which the actors can arrive and depart – helped offset the problems of staging Shakespeare on the screen. But perhaps the biggest challenge was how to film soliloquies. In the theatre the actor is not alone when they speak their soliloquy, since the theatre audience is present to absorb their words. On the screen a soliloquy merely gives the impression of someone talking to themselves.

The sequence in Much Ado Nothing that begins with Benedick's soliloquy on why he won't marry and ends with both Benedick and Beatrice in love, is a useful way to see how Branagh uses the cinematic elements to keep the action flowing and the way he employs camera movement, props and non-diegetic music (background music that appears within the action on the screen) to make the soliloquy seem less absurd.

Having faded to black from the previous night time masked ball sequence, an establishing shot takes us into daylight and the gardens with the camera panning down between two lines of thick green hedges. In the next shot Benedick appears in full shot from the left screen from a pathway between the hedges, carrying a deckchair. The deckchair acts as a comic prop but also as an initial distraction from Benedick's opening soliloquy, which is filmed in one shot with the camera moving with Benedick, who stays in the centre of the screen, down a path before he sits by the fountain where the camera slowly zooms closer in on his face. On the one hand Benedick is shown sharing his thoughts, emotions and motives with the audience. But this is not a theatre audience. Branagh chooses not to have Benedick look into the camera. Indeed, his gaze studiously avoids making any contact in the direction of the audience. To do so would set an awkward precedent – with the audience expecting intimate revelations to camera throughout the remainder of the action.

In effect Benedick is seen merely talking to himself and the audience is left to trust, within the context of the action, that this is normal behaviour. The gradual zoom to Benedick suggests that he is merely thinking out aloud – even though his facial reactions and hand movements are quite expressive when he lists some attributes that he could fall for in a woman: 'Rich she shall be and that's certain, wise and I'll have none.' His train of thought is interrupted by Don Pedro's laughter as he arrives with Claudio and Leonato to set their trap. A long shot featuring the fountain and its surroundings allows Benedick to beat a comic retreat with his deckchair prop.

The physical space of the fountain and surrounding area is then explored as Don Pedro asks for the 'Cry no more Ladies', song to be played. The camera moves around the fountain catching those at the villa going about their work (with washing bundles, wicker baskets and weeding) while the song gathers momentum from its solo guitar instrumentation as a three-male choir joins in and additional non-diegetic music is added in the form of an orchestral accompaniment.

Don Pedro and Claudio and Leonato settle by the fountain, a space they occupy throughout the scene, and speak in raised voices. The deckchair is used for a slapstick moment when Benedick falls through it just when he overhears that Beatrice loves him. The jolly nature of the scene is enhanced by the jovial background music, which then accompanies the three plotters' conversation. Benedick is seen comically flitting in between the hedges as the three men sit together by the fountain and is occasionally seen in a close-up taking in his reactions to what they have said. There are a couple of shots from Benedick's perspective where he sees the men from a distance sitting by the fountain but can't see their faces. Another comic moment comes where Benedick lets out a short cry of indignation when he is accused of having 'a contemptable spirit'. Fearing that he might have been discovered he mimics a bird. At this point the light music stops to allow the bird sound to become amplified and allow the three men to respond before the music resumes again to Benedick's relief.

As the men leave the fountain area Benedick occupies their space and begins a new soliloquy, this time with light romantic music locked into his train of thought rising and falling with his own words, particularly at the point where he exclaims in astonished delight: 'For I will be horribly in love with her.' Again the camera follows Benedick around the fountain in a single shot keeping him in the centre of the frame and is locked in to his movements. It stops when Benedick stops and starts moving when he moves again. He is filmed in a mid-shot from the waist up until again the camera subtly moves closer in to his face. In this way Branagh adds cinematic sound and movement to embellish the awkward nature of Benedick's second soliloquy.

The physical comedy continues as Benedick self-consciously sprawls himself on the ledge of the fountain as Beatrice approaches. Benedick's facial reactions to Beatrice's fairly straightforward invitation – 'Against my will I am sent to bid you to come in to dinner' – confirm that he believes Beatrice loves him and ends by his misguided interpretation of her entreaty by concluding: 'There's a double meaning in that'.

With Benedick hooked, Hero and Ursula are left to trick Beatrice as she makes her way down the path back to the main house. Once again the light comic music is employed as Beatrice is stopped in her tracks when she overhears that Benedick loves her. Comically, she also flits behind a hedge to hear better what is being said. This time her prop is a statue that barely conceals her. Indeed, in this sequence Beatrice is generally caught in the centre background between Hero and Ursula or, like Benedick, caught in close-up as she reacts to what is said.

As Hero and Ursula run giggling away from the scene we are offered Beatrice's brief soliloquy, which is accompanied by a tracking camera movement and uplifting music. Beatrice reaches her prop, a swing, and is framed holding on to the two ropes before joyously taking to the swing.

The conclusion to this whole sequence has a rather daft Benedick skipping in the fountain superimposed with a blissfully happy Beatrice on the swing. Both are captured together in this sequence which uses the gardens effectively as a backdrop as Beatrice appears to swing through mid-air while Benedick sloshes about in the water accompanied by a rousing orchestra celebrating their newly discovered love before the screen fades to black.

REACTION

The attempts at deriding Branagh in Britain were enough for him to agree to release the film in America first. Ironically, the launch of the film offered Branagh some respite from the sniping with an impressive array of mates turning up at the British charity premiere including Sir Richard Attenborough, Sir John Mills, Anthony Andrews, Amanda Donohoe, Geraldine McEwan, Helena Bonham Carter, Hugh Laurie and Stephen Fry. Branagh even reported hearing crowds outside the cinema cheering 'Up the British film industry', which pleased him.

The film received fairly good reviews but not all the critics were convinced by the performance of the American actors. Nevertheless, box-office receipts were generally good and many anticipated Branagh's next venture.

His next project, *Mary Shelley's Frankenstein*, had a comparatively large budget of £19 million, starred himself and Robert De Niro and was filmed, at the director's request, in Britain. It proved to be a disappointment both critically and at the box-office. The rest of the decade saw him back in Shakespeare territory directing and scripting a film about staging Hamlet *In the Bleak Midwinter* (UK, 1995), followed by the real deal – an ambitious and well-received version of *Hamlet* (UK/USA, 1996) and an inventive 1930s musical take on *Love's Labor's Lost* (UK/USA/France, 1999). He also played Iago in a film version of *Othello* (USA, 1995).

CONCLUSION

The Crying Game and *Much Ado About Nothing* are two examples of British films that were affected by what had gone on in the 1980s. There is a paradox that the downside of the

1980s where production companies ended up overstretching themselves should result in a film like *The Crying Game* – although an international hit it saw the end of the dynamic Palace Pictures. For Powell, Woolley and Jordan the 1980s had been heady formative years, whereas the remainder of the 1990s was one of regrouping.

Branagh had also tasted success in the 1980s and his star continued to rise in the early part of the 1990s. However, he too succumbed to an ambitious project too far in *Mary Shelley's Frankenstein*. Nevertheless, as an actor and director Branagh proved to be resilient and worked on interesting projects throughout the decade, perhaps with not such acclaim but certainly with less derision.

FURTHER READING

Back to the Future: The Fall and Rise of the British Film Industry in the 1980s
Wickham, Phil and Mettler, Erinna (BFI National Library, Information Services, 2005)

Producing the Goods: UK Film Production 1991-2001
Wickham, Phil (BFI National Library, Information Services, 2003)

Always Look on the Bright Side of Life: The Inside Story of HandMade Films
Sellars, Robert (Metro Books, 2003)

The Egos Have Landed: The Rise and Fall of Palace Pictures
Finney, Angus (Heinemann, 1996)

My Indecision Is Final: The Spectacular Rise and Fall of Goldcrest Films.
Eberts, Jake and Illot, Terry (Atlantic Monthly Press, 1990)

British Television, An Illustrated Guide, 2nd Edition
Vahimagi, Tise (Oxford University Press, 1996)

BFI Film and Television Handbook (BFI, editions from 1983–2005)

Selected reviews/articles/references

The Crying Game

Sight & Sound V2. N.7 (1 Nov 1992) P.40 by Romney, Jonathan

Empire N.41 (1 Nov 1992) P.40 by Salisbury, Mark

The Crying Game
Giles, Jane (BFI Publishing, 1997)

Contemporary British Cinema 16+ Source Guide Guides
Mettler, Erinna; Ormsby, Andrew; Reeve, David; Dupin, Christophe (BFI National Library, 2003) www.bfi.org.uk/filmtvinfo/publications/16+/

DVD: *The Crying Game*: Special Edition (Optimum Releasing, 2006)

Much Ado About Nothing

Sight & Sound V3. N.9 (1 Sept 1993) P.50-51 by Felperin, Leslie

Empire N.51 (1 Sept 1993) P.78-84 by Dawson, Jeff

Much Ado About Nothing, Shakespeare, William. The Arden Shakespeare edited by A.R.Humphreys (Routledge, 1991)

Shakespeare 16+ Source Guide Guides
Kerameos, Anastasia; Ormsby Andrew; Evers Bronia; Gardoqui Iratxe (BFI National Library, 2007)

www.bfi.org.uk/filmtvinfo/publications/16+/

The Kenneth Branagh Compendium – www.branaghcompendium.com

2. CHANGE IS GOING TO COME

At the beginning of 1990 the British film industry was in crisis. Film production had reached its nadir when in the previous year only 30 films had been made - the lowest total recorded since 1914. Paradoxically, interest in film in Britain was showing signs of recovery. American companies had continued to build multiplexes and the comfortable surroundings increased cinema-going. Naturally enough, with so little British product around, people were flocking to see Hollywood films. The video market in Britain had taken off both in rental and retail terms and the British public was a close second only to the USA in its consumption of feature films in the home. Cable and satellite TV had also been thrown into the mix with the launch of Sky and BSB, which would shortly merge as BSkyB and their film channels. Furthermore, British film-making and technical talent was universally recognised. In the 1990 Academy Awards, British and Irish individuals won eight Oscars:

Best Actor: Daniel Day Lewis for *My Left Foot*

Best Actress: Jessica Tandy for *Driving Miss Daisy*

Best Supporting Actress: Brenda Fricker for *My Left Foot*

Best Cinematography: Freddie Francis for *Glory*

Best Costume: Phyllis Dalton for *Henry V*

Best Live Action Short: James Hendrie for *Work Experience*

Best Sound Effects Editing: Richard Hymns for *Indiana Jones and the Lost Crusade*

Best Art Direction: Anton Furst for *Batman*

Indiana Jones and the Lost Crusade, the top box-office film in the UK in 1989, had been made at the Elstree Studios, while *Batman*, which was third, had utilised Pinewood's facilities and locations around Hertfordshire and Bedfordshire. But these were all Hollywood productions utilising British expertise and none of the vast profits directly benefited the British industry. Quite clearly something had to change if the indigenous British film industry, particularly the production sector, was to be regarded as anything more than a cottage industry. The answer lay in the hands of the government.

It was widely agreed within film circles that the Conservative government had showed little interest in the arts, let alone film, during Margaret Thatcher's long term in office. The government had abolished the Eady Levy, a tax on box-office receipts for films that qualified as British, and introduced the Film Act 1985 (See Chapter 1). Crucially, beyond the formation of British Screen Finance, little else was done to encourage investors to make films in Britain, leaving film-makers isolated and with empty pockets.

DOWNING STREET SEMINAR

On 15 June 1990, Margaret Thatcher hosted a seminar led by Sir Richard Attenborough and leading British film-makers and producers including David Puttnam, John Boorman, Lynda Myles and Simon Relph, the chief executive of British Screen. Also at the meeting were representatives from the big studios in the USA.

The British delegation patiently explained how the film industry worked in Britain with the wide separation between UK production, distribution and exhibition meaning that producers had to work hard to get any money back at all and there was little chance of extra funds to make further British films and build on successes. There seemed no incentives for overseas film-makers to come over and make films to create inward investment and, lamentably, the public had a greater appetite for Hollywood movies over homespun fare. Also of interest was Britain's lack of co-production opportunities with the rest of Europe, where schemes existed to help producers and governments generally offered subsidies to their indigenous film industries.

And yet the film industry in Britain offered much in terms of its expertise both in creative and technical areas. Although countries from Eastern Europe were offering film locations abroad at generous rates, the Americans still saw Britain as a halfway house to break into the European market. At the meeting, Lew Wasserman, head of Universal, declared that: 'Britain has the opportunity to be the Hollywood of Europe.' The Americans seemed keen to support film in Britain if they felt they were involved in a growing market. The talent that Britain had to offer was not a problem, rather it was whether there was a desire to rebuild what had become a stagnant industry.

At the end of the meeting an agenda for change was agreed. Working groups were set up to look at marketing opportunities and fiscal incentives and £5m was offered for European co-productions. There was, however, a wariness about actual government subsidies for films since countries with subsidy programmes such as Germany, France and Australia had poor returns in terms of money that was invested and in some cases many films never made it to the screens.

The Downing Street meeting didn't in itself change the fortunes of the film industry overnight and the cautious approach suggested evolution rather than revolution. Nevertheless, Richard Attenborough and his delegation had put British film on the political agenda and the fortunes of film production in the UK in terms of output and investment significantly rose across the decade. A change had come. Some five months after the Downing Street seminar Thatcher had resigned as Prime Minister and had been replaced by John Major. His term in office merely signalled the end of one political era and the beginning of a new cultural and media-friendly era led by Tony Blair's New Labour.

DEPARTMENT OF CULTURE MEDIA AND SPORT

Prior to the 1990s politicians had showed an awkward ambivalence towards the arts. This changed during the 1990s, first in 1992 following John Major's surprise victory in the election with the creation of the Department for National Heritage. The large department took over responsibilities held before by trade and sports and covered the arts, media, heritage and sport. Reflecting its wide ranging, leisure-orientated remit, its first minister, David Mellor, was quickly nicknamed 'Minister for Fun' by the press. The department was also responsible for overseeing the setting up of the National Lottery regulator Camelot and selecting the Arts Council to distribute Lottery funding for arts projects.

The 1997 election heralded the end of 15 years of Tory rule. Blair swept to power in a moment symbolised by the catchy tune, 'Things Can Only Get Better' by D:Ream. By then ministers not only knew a bit more about the arts but actively courted them. The first New Labour Culture Secretary, Chris Smith, was no exception. Reflecting that the word 'heritage' had connotations with the past, he changed the department's name to the Department for Culture, Media and Sport (DCMS), the subtle difference being an emphasis on the cultural life of the country as well as concentrating on film, broadcasting, sport and the arts as before. The Department even spawned the first ever Minister For Film, Tom Clarke.

TAX BREAKS

Much of the decade was taken up with film industry people appealing to the Treasury to create tax incentives for overseas investors, particularly write-offs on production costs. An early breakthrough came when tax relief was offered under Section 42 of the Finance (No. 2) Act 1992 for British qualifying films. Section 42 usually allows benefits for films with budgets greater than £15 million. Tax relief allows a 100 per cent write-off of production and acquisition expenditure over a period of three years.

In 1997 the government, in an effort to help small independent film-makers, added to the relief for British qualifying films costing £15 million or less by increasing the amount that could be written off under Section 48 of the Finance (No 2) Act 1997. Section 48 allowed 100 per cent write-off for production or acquisition costs when the film was completed. Unlike Section 42, however, Section 48 was subject to review dates, which continued to be extended up to 2006.

'Sale and leaseback' became the mechanism through which the UK's tax breaks for British qualifying feature films were channelled. A producer or production company can reduce its borrowing (approximately 10-15 per cent of the budget) by selling the rights to the film to a UK purchaser, who can claim tax relief on the purchase price while leasing the rights back to the seller.

Rules on what constituted a British qualifying film were also loosened when in 1999 the DCMS added a new definition. The Department cited *Little Voice* (UK/USA, 1998), as an example of a film which could not be defined as British under the old Films Act 1985 (although filmed in the UK with a UK cast, too much of its soundtrack had been recorded outside the UK). Under the government's new rules the main qualification for classification as a 'British film' would be that 70 per cent of a film's budget should be spent in the UK – still effectively allowing for a third of the film's budget on location abroad. The system also required film-makers to spend 70 per cent of their labour costs (for personnel involved in the film) on European and Commonwealth citizens, but it also allowed for the occasional 'star' import to take part in a film, such as Julia Roberts in *Notting Hill* (UK/USA, 1999).

EUROPE

Despite Britain's political obstinacy in Europe in relation to the Maastricht Treaty, the creation of the European Union in 1993 encouraged some British film-makers to forge co-production links with countries in Europe. The European Co-production Fund (ECF) was set up to stimulate joint productions with other European countries. In 1993, Britain finally joined Eurimages, the film fund of the Council of Europe, which aimed to stimulate film production by offering funds for European co-production, exhibition and distribution. By 1995, the government had withdrawn from Eurimages for economic reasons, much to the chagrin of the British film community, but Britain joined in the European Commission's MEDIA programme, which provided funding and other support for European partners.

Certainly, the top British art house directors embraced European co-productions for their work during the decade, among them:

Peter Greenaway – *Prospero's Books*, (UK/Netherlands/France/Italy/Japan, 1991); *The Baby of Macon*, (UK/Netherlands/France/Germany, 1993); *The Pillow Book*, (UK/Netherlands/France/Luxembourg, 1995)

Sally Potter – *Orlando*, (UK/Russia/Italy/France/Netherlands, 1992); *The Tango Lesson* (UK/France/Argentina/Japan/Germany, 1997)

Ken Loach – *Land and Freedom*, (UK/Spain/Germany, 1995); *Carla's Song*, (UK/Germany/Spain, 1996); *My Name is Joe*, (UK/Germany/France/Italy/Spain, 1998)

The cross-border co-operation between European countries and the greater freedom of movement meant that the British film industry could no longer act in splendid isolation if it wished to survive – not just by making films, but by having them shown on an international stage. In any case, countries such as Germany were also successfully vying for the attentions of the American's for film backing.

BRITISH SCREEN FINANCE

Set up in 1986, British Screen received a small government grant which went towards supporting British talent in commercially viable productions for the cinema, which might otherwise had found difficulty in attracting mainstream commercial backing. Between 1986 and 1999 it invested in some 150 productions. They included *The Crying Game*; *Orlando*; *Naked* (UK, 1993); *Land and Freedom*; *Sliding Doors* (UK/USA 1997); and *Hilary and Jackie* (UK, 1998).

BRITISH FILM COMMISSION AND THE FORMATION OF THE FILM COUNCIL

One tangible consequence of the Downing Street seminar was the creation of the British Film Commission in 1991, whose aim was to promote the UK as an international production centre and to encourage the use of British locations, services, facilities and personnel. Regional film commissions and offices sprung up around Britain, offering potential film-makers the opportunity to use their areas for filming locations.

This open-arms policy also saw the formation of the London Film Commission in 1995 to assist film and television people wanting to use London as a location and partly funded by the government and the private sector. The government also set up a British Film Office in Los Angeles in 1998 to facilitate the needs of American film-makers wishing to film in the UK.

The navel gazing into the industry continued when the government's cinema working group published an all-embracing, optimistic document on the industry called *A Bigger Picture* in March 1998 with calls for better training facilities via the training body Skillset. The DCMS had noted an improvement in British film production over the course of the decade and was taken by the idea of creating sustainable film industry structures.

As the decade progressed and debates about British film continued it was decided to create a separate strategic agency to develop the film industry and the film culture in the UK. It resulted in the launch of the Film Council in October 1999 in an effort to achieve the seemingly impossible and build up cohesive sustainable structures in the British film industry. It officially came into being on 1 April 2000 but before then had taken over the responsibility and subsumed the functions of a number of government-supported organisations, including the British Film Commission; the Arts Council of England's Lottery Film Department; and the British Film Institute's Production Department and British Screen Finance.

The thorny issue of a government film subsidy was largely handed over to the distribution of Lottery funds for film projects (see Chapter 6). However, the initial poor returns from Lottery-funded films seemed to reflect government fears about film subsidies and in a bid to consolidate film production the decade ended with the announcement that three film franchises would be created to benefit from Lottery funds.

These were DNA, the Film Consortium and Pathé.

Though met with scepticism from certain quarters, there was no doubt that New Labour had taken film and film culture seriously. While the political landscape of the country had changed so too had the impression, largely brought about by skilled-media manipulators known as spin doctors, that there was a cultural renaissance. 'Cool Britannia' had arrived and, surely, for the creative industries things could only get better.

To emphasise the mood of change came several films by new film-makers that seemed to breathe new life and energy into British cinema and provide the world with something beyond costume dramas and rom-coms. In this section I'll consider two films from the 1990s which illustrate this cultural mood swing and renewed confidence: *Trainspotting* and *Lock, Stock and Two Smoking Barrels*.

Trainspotting (1995) (UK) UK Cert 18

Director: Danny Boyle

Screenplay: John Hodge (based on the novel by Irvine Welsh)

Producer: Andrew MacDonald

Production companies: Figment Films;, Noel Gay Motion Picture Company; Channel Four; Channel 4 Films; Film Finances Ltd (completion bond)

Production start date: 22/05/1995 **Budget:** £1.76m (estimated)

Distributor: Universal Pictures **UK Release date:** 23 February 1996

UK Box Office: £12,433,450 **USA Box Office**: $16.5m

Worldwide Box Office: $72m

Quentin Tarantino's *Reservoir Dogs* (USA, 1992) and *Pulp Fiction* (USA, 1994) set an unprecedented blueprint for independent film-makers in Britain. Aspiring film-makers were enchanted by Tarantino's quirky, humorous dialogue, stylised violence, glamorous anti-heroes, uncompromising shots of drug abuse, and clever use of music (such as 'Stuck in the Middle with You' in *Reservoir Dogs* and 'You Never Can Tell' in *Pulp Fiction*). Tarantino was talking to a young audience but this was not easily defined as the 15-30 demographic – this was an indie audience prepared to give the mainstream a miss from time to time – an audience that seemed to know where Tarantino was coming from.

In Britain the notion of having the finger on the pulse of popular youth culture had been sadly lacking in the early part of the 1990s. But all that was to change when two Scots and an Englishman created a film that almost defined the change in the political and social cultural arena in Britain. That film was *Trainspotting*.

The team that created *Trainspotting* consisted of Andrew MacDonald, the grandson of Emeric Pressburger and brother of Oscar-winning director Kevin; fellow Scot John Hodge, a trainee doctor who he met at the Edinburgh Festival; and director Danny Boyle, born in Bury, Lancashire. When he met MacDonald and Hodge he had been working on *Mr Wroe's Virgins* (BBC, 1993). Their production company was called Figment Films.

They burst onto the British film scene with their first feature, the surprisingly dark and stylish thriller *Shallow Grave* (UK, 1994) set in Edinburgh, which starred Ewan McGregor, Christopher Eccleston and Kerry Fox. The film, which was almost wholly funded by Channel Four with additional funding from the Glasgow Film Fund, became the highest grossing wholly UK release of the year. The triumvirate next turned their attentions to *Trainspotting*, the cult novel written by Irvine Welsh.

SYNOPSIS

In late 1980s Edinburgh, Renton a young man in his twenties, declares in voice-over that he has opted out of normal lifestyle choices in favour of heroin. He describes the detailed preparations needed to come off heroin but concedes that he needs one last hit to ease him in. He describes the downside of coming off heroin is that he has to mix with his friends.

He is seen in a park with Sick Boy aiming his air-rifle at passers-by. He then meets Spud as both go for job interviews. Next we meet the psychotic Begbie.

Renton flirts self-consciously but successfully with a young girl, Diane (Kelly Macdonald), and the two have sex. To his horror he sees Diane in her school uniform the next morning and has an awkward breakfast with her parents.

After a depressing visit to the Highlands with Sick Boy, Spud and another friend, Tommy, Renton decides to go back onto heroin. Tommy is dumped by his girlfriend, Lizzy, and urges Renton to give him heroin as a solace, after which he becomes addicted and contracts HIV. In the meantime, another junkie Allison loses her baby daughter Dawn, who dies in her cot. The group discovers that Sick Boy was the father. Renton and Spud are apprehended after stealing from a department store. Spud goes to jail while Renton voluntarily enlists in a drug treatment programme.

Renton cannot last very long without going back to his dealer but suffers an overdose, which leads him to hospital where his life is saved. Renton's parents take control and help him beat his addiction by locking him in his room, although not before he suffers disturbing hallucinations.

Seeking a new life in London as a property-letting agent his happiness is interrupted by the death of Tommy. Sick Boy, Begbie and Spud join Renton in London where they sell some heroin for £16,000. Disgusted by Begbie's violence Renton decides to steal the money.

Spud wakes to see Renton leaving with the bag of money but keeps quiet. Begbie trashes the hotel when he awakes, Sick Boy goes home empty-handed and Spud finds a wad of money left by Renton in a locker. Meanwhile Renton tries to start a new life.

HOW IT WAS MADE

The success of *Shallow Grave* prompted Channel Four to invest in another Edinburgh-based tale. Author Irvine Welsh gave his blessing to the project and even agreed to appear in the film as Renton's less reliable drug dealer, Mikey Forrester. His novel is written in the form of episodic first person narrations from the various characters who live in, or around Leith, Edinburgh, who either use or form part of a group of friends who use heroin. The writing uses Scottish vernacular phrases which are spelt out phonetically such as 'Tommy sais tae us: – Hi Franco, is that boy gittin lippy?' and the novel does not follow a linear narrative. The film-makers felt that the multi-narrative approach might prove too much for a audience to absorb and so Hodge's solution was to make Renton the central character and have him act as the main narrator (although not exclusively). This device works well in bringing various characters in and out of what becomes a more coherent story with Renton's philosophical voiced-over observations analysing character traits.

Despite its Edinburgh setting most of the Scottish filming took place in Glasgow apart from the memorable opening chase sequence, which was filmed on Princes Street, Edinburgh. The Figment Films team again cast McGregor in the main role but also found a superb supporting cast of Ewen Bremner, Robert Carlyle, Jonny Lee Miller and Kelly Macdonald that would become synonymous with the marketing and success of the film.

KEY ISSUES

Heroin addiction and the knock-on effects it has on a group of friends is the obvious key issue surrounding *Trainspotting*. In this respect the film places us in the unreliable hands of Renton to guide us through his own self-redemption and journey to kick the habit but in so doing the film casts its net far wider and examines the values of late twentieth century British society. In the end the film is all about the pursuit and longing for true happiness as an antidote to a modern world seemingly strewn with misery.

Drugs

In the novel, Tommy, who has just broken up with Lizzy, asks Renton to explain to him the feeling that heroin gives him. In the book Renton is against Tommy trying heroin but nevertheless he gives a considered reply: 'Smack's an honest drug… It doesnae alter yir consciousness. It just gies ye a hit and a sense ay well-being. Eftir that, ye see the misery ay the world as it is, and ye cannae anaesthetise yirself against it.'

In the film Renton's desire to take heroin is more ambiguous: 'I chose not to choose life: I chose something else. And the reasons? There are no reasons. Who need reasons when you've got heroin?' But as for its effect he leaves us with little doubt: 'Take the best orgasm you've ever had, multiply by 1,000, and you're still nowhere near it.'

In both instances it is clear that heroin has a destructive effect on the individuals who take it. The book is able to go into more detail about the complex issue that results in a moth-to-a-flame type of dependency. The film does not have the same amount of time but ensures that the drug-taking is not glamorised. Nevertheless, there is a stylishness and speed about the film that takes the audience on a trip even though we do not witness any real lasting highs but rather share in assorted episodes of lows.

By the mid-1990s the rave culture in Britain was in full flow and ecstasy was the new happy drug of young people's choice. The schoolgirl Dianne comments knowingly to Renton at one point: 'The world is changing, music is changing, even drugs are changing.' An audience of potential thrill-seekers could easily relate to Renton and his mates and the film acknowledges the acid-house scene when Renton and Begbie go to a London club to celebrate Begbie's win on the horses.

Trainspotting taps into the youthful vein of hedonism, drugs-for-fun and the endless pursuit of the next high — but it does so quite objectively. The arguments about whether the film acts 'responsibly' centre on its graphic depiction of drug abuse rather than the scenes of withdrawal and dependency. Throughout the film writer Hodge, who previously studied medicine at the University of Edinburgh, displays his knowledge of the subject of addiction. At one point Renton issues a list of drugs that were available via the National Health Service: 'We took morphine, diamorphine, cyclozine, codeine, temazepam, nitrezepam, phenobarbitone, sodium amytal dextropropoxyphene, methadone, nalbuphine, pethidine, pentazocine, buprenorphine, dextromoramide chlormethiazole. The streets are awash with drugs that you can have for unhappiness and pain, and we took them all.'

The film has some nice comic set-pieces and, because of this, the film-makers were seen by some to be trivialising drugs by turning the film into something entertaining. Indeed, this accusation might be true of how the film trivialises crime by showing a fast sequence of petty thefts to the languid soundtrack of Iggy Pop's 'Nightclubbing'.

However, the film-makers clearly didn't pull any punches when showing how unglamorous heroin addiction becomes. Tommy's decline from fit non-drug taking person to wasted junkie through to HIV AIDS-infected corpse is shocking, only to be dwarfed by the scene comes when Allison's baby dies in her cot while the gang has been shooting up. Suddenly, the droll witticisms that have made the drug users quite likeable dry up as reality kicks in. Sick Boy's reaction is to cry but the screaming Allison is only placated when Renton, himself unable to quite comprehend the horror, decides that he would 'cook up'. Even this rather pathetic gesture comes with a price as Renton concedes: 'So I cooked up and she got a hit, but only after me. That went without saying.'

HIV and AIDS is an issue that lurks in the background of the film, and again the film-makers make an interesting departure from the book during Renton's sexual encounter with Dianne. In the book he has unprotected sex, and while knowing that he is clean he is wracked with fear that he might have become infected by this encounter, reasoning incorrectly that if Dianne slept with him then she has probably had many partners. In the film Renton is seen pulling off a condom after being banished to the couch by Dianne. This is a strong message sent out to the audience – even a character like Renton acts responsibly over safe sex.

Ironically, Sick Boy's big drug deal which bags Begbie, Spud and Renton the sum of £16,000 offers Renton his chance for salvation and to cut away from his mates and start a new life – clean. However, when Tommy persuades Renton, Spud and Sick Boy to go for a walk in 'the great outdoors' and breathe fresh air, the friends reject the notion as boring and a waste of time. In the end heroin is seen as an escape for those unable to attain the goals that society has mapped out for them. In this respect *Trainspotting* also serves up a critique of a different cocktail - that of Thatcherism in the 1980s.

Choose life/Thatcherism

In *Trainspotting*'s opening sequence Renton and Spud are being chased by security guards and Renton's voice-over proclaims: 'Choose life. Choose a job. Choose a career. Choose a family, choose a fucking big television, choose washing machines, cars, compact disc players, and electrical tin openers'. Later on Renton's aspirations begin to be realised in London when he works in a lettings office. Tellingly, with his life seemingly sorted out, he declares: 'There was no such thing as society and even if there was, I most certainly had nothing to do with it. For the first time in my adult life I was almost content.' In this statement Renton echoes Thatcher's own philosophy about the individual: 'There are individual men and women and there are families and no government can do anything except through people and people look to themselves first… There is no such thing as society'.

Renton's attempts at belonging seems in some ways an extreme reaction to his youthful, nihilistic rebellion where boredom, the dole and few opportunities for fulfillment lead him and his mates down the path to drug addiction. Not only does Renton want to conform to society's rules, he metaphorically gets on his bike and finds a job in London, willing to embrace a positive change in his life.

As he enthusiastically maps out his future based on society's expectations, his final voice-over, which comes over as part confession, part manifesto speech, leaves a somewhat shallow, joyless ring since it generally embraces a new soulless addiction to materialism: 'I'm going to be just like you: the job, the family, the fucking big television, the washing machine, the car, the compact disc and electrical tin opener, good health, low cholesterol, dental insurance, mortgage, starter home, leisurewear, luggage, three-piece suite, DIY, game shows, junk food, children, walks in the park, nine to five, good at golf, washing the car, choice of sweaters, family Christmas, indexed pension, tax exemption, clearing the gutters, getting by, looking ahead, to the day you die.' It is fitting that Renton's face blurs as the voice-over proclaims his intentions to become an anonymous, unremarkable consumer.

Choose music

As Diane succinctly points out to Renton, 'music is changing'. By 1996, Britpop had arrived on the scene and the film features these influences by melding tracks from some of the top bands of the day such as Blur, Pulp, Elastica, Brian Eno, New Order, Primal Scream and Sleeper to marry with the action. Three key film-defining musical sequences stand out. The first, Iggy Pop's 'Lust for Life' perfectly accompanies the adrenaline-fuelled opening sequence, the chase through Edinburgh's streets. The second is Lou Reed's hymn to a heroin hit, 'Perfect Day', which ironically underpins Renton's near-fatal overdose as he is bundled in an undignified manner in and out of a taxi on his way to the hospital. But perhaps the track that defines the film as a contemporary piece of work is Underworld's thumping hit 'Born Slippy' near the end of the film as Renton executes his plan to steal the bag of money. The soundtrack album of *Trainspotting* perfectly suited not only the mood of the film but the mood of the times and it was no surprise when it picked up the Brit Award for Best Soundtrack in 1997.

Choose fantasy

Since drug taking is part of the theme of the film it is interesting how matters relating to drug taking in terms of perception and perspective are portrayed. Swanney's dingy flat where Renton and his mates shoot up is sparse but filmed using vivid bright reds and green to give the subtle impression of an enhanced awareness. There are also three quite pointed surreal scenes, which add to a hallucinogenic effect.

The first is when Renton enters 'the worst toilet in Scotland' and dives in to the faeces-struned, stinking toilet bowl to recover his lost suppositories. The ghastly scene is transformed as Renton is seen swimming underwater, as if searching for pearls at the bottom of the ocean. His momentary euphoria of finding his drugs is counterbalanced by the reality of just how low he has had to sink.

Renton's overdose sequence in Swanney's flat shows the carpet upon which he lays giving way and sinking into a grave-like hole which casually awaits his death. Renton seems to be at peace but quite clearly there is a frantic rush to revive him.

However, the key fantasy moment comes in Renton's withdrawal sequence when his parents lock him in a bedroom to go through his cold turkey ordeal.

SCENE ANALYSIS – CHOOSE COLD TURKEY

Part of the appeal of *Trainspotting* is its cinematic style which includes sharp cuts, retrospective shots, scenes often drenched in red and delicately offset with green via a door, a shirt or a pillow, the use of false perspectives and the occasional blurring of reality and fantasy – not to mention heart-thumping background music. On top of this we have Renton's voice-over recounting his fraught journey from addiction to some semblance of mainstream normality. All these elements combine to give the film a dynamic edge, which still seems fresh today. The harrowing cold turkey sequence where we witness Renton's recent life haunting him via his delirious state is not only one of the most visually arresting in the film but also contains many of the film's stylistic motifs.

Renton's parents put their son to bed in his bedroom of prison cell proportions and lock the door. The close-up shot of the lock gives way to the thumping, relentless beat of Underworld's 'Dark and Long', which plays in the background. A dark dull brown colour (almost like congealed blood) permeates the scene, adding a deadening element to events.

The room darkens, with any light appearing over the top of the bed and the camera zooms over from the door to see an uncomfortable Renton trying to adjust his position with his sheets. Renton's voice-over states that 'I don't feel the sickness yet, but it's in the post, that's for sure'.

The next shot gives us a false perspective from behind Renton's bed facing the door to the room. Unexpectedly there appears movement, as if Renton's bed is a trolley and he is being pulled away from the door. We see the weird shot of the room moving into a space we know that it cannot occupy, signalling the start of Renton's delirious withdrawal. The shot cuts to a head shot of Renton preparing to encounter his demons.

His attention is drawn to the sound of a girl singing a love song to him. The next cut reveals Diane in her school uniform, sitting cross-legged at the end of Renton's bed, her face smiling almost wistfully, framed in the centre of the picture and caught in some light against the dark, brooding background.

As Diane's voice fades a new clunking sound makes Renton stir but this time it is the real image of his parents coming into his room with food. Renton responds by begging to return to the clinic. When they leave the room Renton pulls the sheets over his head. The camera joins him for an intimate shot, drenched with a delicate orange hue, as Renton turns and a new false perspective is revealed as Begbie, fag in mouth, appears under the sheets with Renton (the bed is only a single). Begbie threatens Renton with violence if he doesn't come off drugs. The fantasy shot switches back to reality via a seamless special effect as a shocked Renton turns back from under the bed clothes.

His relief lasts only seconds as now the sound of a baby can be heard and Renton fixes his gaze on the far end of the room where he sees Allison's dead baby crawling upside down on the ceiling towards him in an unusual, sinister special effect shot. As Renton plunges his head in the pillow, caught between the worlds of hallucination and reality, we get a long shot of the scene from the perspective of the door and we see the baby continue to makes its progress along the ceiling.

Next Renton's perceptions are interrupted by the sound of an organ from what turns out to be a TV quiz show. Renton's head turns and the shot cuts to a full screen of a television set and a quiz show, the type that his parents might be watching. As the presenter quizzes the panelist about the AIDS virus we see the contestants actually are Renton's parents. He pops his head out of the sheets again to witnesses Sick Boy sitting on a chair at the end of his bed with his mother standing by the door declaiming 'just say no'.

Now the hallucinations come thick and fast. As the baby's cries can be heard the camera angle appears from the top of the wardrobe looking down at Renton as the baby's progress towards him continues. Childlike himself, Renton clutches his pillow for comfort, turning his head into it, but more aural sounds force him to turn around. This time he sees Spud (in long shot) sitting on top of his wardrobe in a prison costume with his chains banging and staring directly at Renton and exacerbating his feelings of guilt.

Momentarily Renton seems calm as a close-up shot of the TV quiz show host cuts to Renton almost contemplating the answer and then unexpectedly to the bedroom wall where a shadow encroaches from the right hand side revealing a ghost-like Tommy who answers the question correctly before berating Renton about the supposed benefits of heroin. The next cut has a long shot from above looking down on Renton in bed as he attempts to reason with Tommy before his gaze turns upwards towards a cry from the baby.

There follows a sequence of rapid cuts culminating in a reference to the famous scene in *The Exorcist* (William Friedkin, 1973) as the baby turns her head 180 degrees towards Renton. The rapidity intensifies as Renton screams for all to stop. Each shot is intercut with Tommy sidling along the wall, Spud clunking his chains and the baby falling off the ceiling towards Renton (seen first from his and then the baby's perspective). His screams continue as he is seen from above in a hysterical, half-foetal position. The next intercut brings Renton's mother and father looking concerned. Renton's father calls out, 'Mark, Mark'. As Renton appears to wake and become reorientated his father ends the cold turkey sequence by saying 'There's something we need to do'.

Although the fantasy sequence ends when they urge Renton to take an HIV test the background music continues as Renton has his test and then is seen in a state of depression while around him his parents and his friends (captured in fast motion to his stillness) celebrate their bingo success. Even when the scene shifts to the estate where Tommy lives the music from Renton's nightmare can be heard until it finally ends with Renton at Tommy's door.

REACTION

The film-makers had one last trick up their sleeve – the film's release was supported by a carefully thought-out marketing campaign. Distributor PolyGram Filmed Entertainment invested a massive £850,000 for publicity. This represented almost 50 per cent again of the film's modest £1.75m budget but it proved to be money well spent. Design consultants Stylorouge, who had experience on pop artwork presentations, were brought in to design the poster.

The line-up of the orange poster for *Trainspotting* featuring Renton, Begbie, Sick Boy, Spud and Dianne (but not Tommy, as actor Kevin McKidd was not available for the photo shoot) hit just the right note. The characters are staring out in intriguing poses – Begbie gives a v sign, Dianne appears to be growling, Sick Boy apes Sean Connery as James Bond using his fingers like a gun, Spud looks friendly and benign, while Renton is feverishly clutching himself. With the exception of Renton the characters all exude a spirit of exuberance.

The film garnered good reviews with general praise for its bold pace and visual presentation and fine performances from McGregor and Carlyle. The critics were quick to pick up Boyle's non-judgemental stance on the depiction of drugs. There was even an over-exuberant line of tubthumping from *Empire* magazine: 'Hollywood come in please, your time is up, not only can we compete, we can knock you into the ground.' The film brought in more than £12m at the UK box-office, following on from where *Shallow Grave* had left off by making it the top wholly UK production of 1996 and the ninth biggest at the UK box-office overall. The film did well in America too, distributed by Miramax, although some of the broad Scottish accents were deemed incomprehensible for American audiences and the first 20 minutes had to be overdubbed. Perhaps anticipating this is a subtitled scene in a club when Tommy speaks to Spud.

Figment's next film, set in America, had McGregor playing alongside Cameron Diaz and Holly Hunter in *A Life Less Ordinary* (UK, 1997). Figment's collective finger taken off the British cultural pulse, Boyle and co served up an entertaining, but mainstream, American caper movie.

Lock, Stock and Two Smoking Barrels (1998) (UK) UK Cert 18

Director: Guy Ritchie

Screenplay: Guy Ritchie

Producer: Matthew Vaughn

Production companies: SKA Films; Summit Entertainment; the Steve Tisch Group

Production start date: 04/1997 **Budget:** £2.6m (estimated)

Distributor: PolyGram Filmed Entertainment/Universal **UK Release date:** 28 August 1998

UK Box Office: £11,784,141 **USA Box Office:** $3.6m

Worldwide Box Office: $ 25.2m

When Guy Ritchie's self-assured, debut feature, which he wrote and directed, was released in 1998, Tarantino comparisons abounded with critics citing both *Pulp Fiction* and *Reservoir Dogs* as major influences. Tarantino had merely blasted a door wide open to inspire young film-makers to emulate his style, wit and knowledge of popular culture.

Two years after *Pulp Fiction*, *Trainspotting* had taken up the mantle with a fast, stylish film, preparing the way for *Lock, Stock and Two Smoking Barrels* to win over a similar audience.

However, there was more to *Lock, Stock...* than an intricate homage to the king of American indie, since Ritchie tapped into a richer vein of British film and television culture. The director admitted that *The Long Good Friday*, had been a principle influence and that connection is seen through the casting of P.H.Moriarty, Alan Ford and Dexter Fletcher who appear in both films. Additionally, several hit British TV shows – the unremittingly bleak soap *EastEnders* (BBC), the eternally optimistic sitcom *Only Fools and Horses* (BBC), the cheekily roguish serial *Minder* (ITV) and the gritty police drama *The Sweeney* (ITV) – provide better signposts for appreciating the backdrop and the comedy of the film. There's even a nod to comedian Harry Enfield's creation 'The Scousers' in the form of Dean (Jake Abraham) and Gary (Victor McGuire), the two inept crooks from Liverpool.

The mid-1990s had witnessed the rise and rise of 'lad culture', where drinking lager, going to football and eyeing up 'totty' were seen as natural lifestyle options for young men. *Loaded* magazine, launched in 1994, was a typical example of how the British media encouraged this trend and Ritchie's film came along at just the right time for blokey blokes to identify with the sitcom style heroes Eddie (Nick Moran), Tom (Jason Flemyng), Soap (Dexter Fletcher) and Bacon (Jason Statham).

Throw in a smattering of classic cars, the surprise 'acting' debut of former footballer Vinnie Jones, the presence of a bona fide ex-East End criminal in Lenny McLean, a director who previously worked on commercials and music videos, an edgy soundtrack and a cameo appearance from Sting and you have a promising cocktail for a hit film.

However, being both a British film and a debut feature, Ritchie struggled to get funding. It is arguably his greatest achievement that he succeeded for a film that has a plethora of characters and complicated plotline.

SYNOPSIS

Set amongst the criminal world in London's East End, four mates Eddie, Bacon, Tom and Soap need to find £50,000 or face having their fingers cut off after gangster 'Hatchet' Harry Londsdale beats Eddie in a rigged game of poker.

In the meantime 'Hatchet' Harry gets his chief henchman Barry the Baptist to organise the theft of a pair of valuable antique shotguns, which are about to go on auction. Barry hires two incompetent burglars, Gary and Dean, who sell on the antique shotguns to Nick the Greek much to Barry's fury and they are told to recover them.

Meanwhile, Eddie and his mates ambush his criminal neighbour Dog and his gang as they raid some ex-public school-boy dope marijuana-growing dealers. Quirky, tough gang leader Rory Breaker sets out with his henchmen to sort out Eddie and his mates when

Nick the Greek tries to sell him back the stolen marijuana which Rory owns.

In the bloodbath that ensues Rory stumbles upon Dog and his gang also waiting for Eddie. Dog escapes with the two antique shotguns and scrambles out of the bloodbath but runs into Big Chris who, with his young son Little Chris, works for 'Hatchet 'Harry as debt collectors. Chris takes the guns and the bag containing Eddie's money and heads to 'Hatchet' Harrys.

More mayhem follows when Gary and Dean appear trying to get hold of the shotguns. 'Hatchet' Harry kills Dean, leading Gary to kill 'Hatchet' Harry, which in turn leads to Barry killing Gary – but not before Gary has time to kill Barry.

Eddie and Tom turn up yet again to survey another death scene. Eddie takes the money and leaves while Tom lingers behind to take the antique shotguns only to encounter Big Chris who has just killed Dog. Big Chris takes the money from Eddie.

Eddie and his mates are arrested but released. With the shotguns implicating them they demand that Tom disposes of the shotguns by throwing them off a bridge.

In a final twist, Big Chris leaves Eddie and his mates with the bag, which contains an antiques catalogue where they learn the true value of the shotguns. They desperately try to phone Tom who is left dangling on the edge of the bridge trying to retrieve the shotguns.

HOW IT WAS MADE

Guy Ritchie came to make *Lock, Stock…* after a career in pop promos and commercials, which funded his film-making ambitions. His calling card was a short film called *The Hard Case* (UK, 1995), which like *Lock, Stock…*, dealt with the theme of card sharks. After this he met producer Mathew Vaughn and set up SKA Films.

The film's final budget is around £2.6m, although some estimates place it as less. Yet as first time film-makers in their 20s, Ritchie and Vaughn seemed too much of a risk to most potential investors, even at this relatively modest price. However, financing came from some influential sources, notably executive producer Trudie Styler, who had seen *The Hard Case*. Her involvement led to the cameo appearance of her husband Sting (and subsequently would lead to Ritchie meeting his future wife, Madonna). Further backing came from American producer Steve Tisch and the promise of distribution outside the UK from American distributor Summit Entertainment.

The six-week shoot began in November 1997 in London locations around Bethnal Green, Shoreditch and Borough Market, Southwark. In the end PolyGram picked up the UK distribution for the film. The buzz created by the film was helped by the presence of ex-footballer Vinnie Jones, trading on his hard man image acquired through his footballing career. Equally intriguing was the casting of former bare-knuckle fighter turned actor,

Lenny McClean, who had genuine East End gang associations. The film was set for its UK release in late autumn 1998.

KEY ISSUES

Ritchie claimed in an interview, with no apparent sense of irony, that the British gangster genre was an area that had not been fully exploited. Unfortunately, many other British film-makers were contemporaneously thinking exactly the same thing and British films became awash with gangland themes although few managed to combine humour, violence and style as successfully as Ritchie.

British Gangster Movies

Prior to *Lock, Stock...* British films in the 1990s about the gangster underworld included *The Krays* (UK, 1990), and *Face* (UK/South Africa, 1997). But within two years of the release of *Lock, Stock...*, the genre seemed to pick up a vicious life of its own with a quick succession of gangster movies vying for cinema screen space. They included *Essex Boys* (UK, 2000); *Gangster No 1* (UK, 2000); *Love, Honour, and Obey* (UK, 1999); and *Sexy Beast* (UK/USA/Spain, 2000.

In Ritchie's film nearly every character seems to be involved in some sort of criminal activity. Eddie and his mates are the amoral heroes of the story; 'Hatchet' Harry is the villainous porn king; Dog has a vicious gang, Rory Breaker is the black drug baron; Greg and Dean are hapless Liverpudlian thieves; and finally there are the posh marijuana growers. There are only three women - one is a topless dancer and the other two are minor characters.

Ritchie conjures up an almost cartoon-like world befitting its crime caper status, one in which violence occurs in order to resolve his complicated plot rather than to give us any real insights into the working of violent criminal minds. He seems more concerned with being a storyteller rather than a social commentator and *Lock, Stock...* is less about gangsters but more about the gang of friends who get involved in a deadly, dangerous underworld. In this respect, the bond of trust and genuine warm friendship that exists between Eddie, Tom, Bacon and Soap saves the film from becoming an amoral blood bath.

Violence

Towards the end of the film a musical homage to Ennio Morricone from Sergio Leone's spaghetti Western *For a Few Dollars More* (Italy/Germany/Spain, 1965) is played out while the body count reaches its peak. Death arrives frequently and violently with a total of 17 brutal killings. Of these, Big Chris exacts the nastiest revenge by slamming the despicable

Dog's head repeatedly with a car door. Yet Big Chris feels morally justified since Dog had threatened to kill Little Chris. Elsewhere there seems little compulsion to enter into any consideration about what is right or wrong and the killings are generally carried out with little emotion.

However, Ritchie is careful in his depiction of violence. On the one hand he does not shy away from showing it while portraying his villains as lovable; on the other he draws a fine line between depicting it for dramatic effect or gratuitous sensationalism. Most of the worst scenes are played out of camera shot; we see Dog throw a knife at his hapless victim rather than actually stabbing him; the bloody shoot-out in Eddie's flat is witnessed from outside rather than amid the carnage; Plank and Rory Breaker point guns closely at each other but we only hear the shots being fired. However, we do see plenty of bodies and we do see plenty of shooting.

Despite the grisly events, the film doesn't feel particularly violent, thanks to the tone, which is that of a comic gangster romp. Some acts of violence are even played for (very) dark laughs such as 'Hatchet' Harry clubbing someone to death with a dildo, or Gary's frizzy hair being parted by a shotgun blast.

Humour

The British tradition for comedy crime capers can be traced back to films like *The Italian Job* (UK/USA, 1969), *The Wrong Arm of the Law* (UK, 1963), and *The Lavender Hill Mob* (UK, 1957). *Lock, Stock...* feels like a self-conscious contemporary update of that theme. Ritchie's witty 'cockney' script ensures that most of the characters are armed with a constant arsenal of one-liners, witty reposts or bemused exclamations:

Rory Breaker: If you hold back anything, I'll kill ya. If you bend the truth, or I think you're bending the truth, I'll kill ya. If you forget anything, I'll kill ya. In fact, you're gonna have to work very hard to stay alive Nick. Now, do you understand everything I've just said? Cause' if you don't, I'll kill ya!

There are amusing asides such as the scene when a man comes staggering out of the door of a pub, which Tom, Bacon and Soap continue to enter regardless; the gunfight at Eddie's flat develops to the tune of *Zorba the Greek*; and a luckless traffic warden gets a comedic biffing from Eddie and his mates for no other reason than he is a traffic warden.

But Ritchie is careful not to overplay the comic touches for fear they might get in the way of his intricate plotline, itself the source of some of the humour. The film ends with one last ironic twist with Tom dangling (in another likely nod to *The Italian Job*) from a bridge with the priceless guns almost within his grasp.

Style

When the film was released some critics thought that Ritchie had over used stylistic tricks gleaned from his time making pop promos and commercials. Yet part of the appeal of the film is precisely this fresh approach with a careful use of slow motion, quick cuts, freeze frames, speed-up shots and comic subtitles — camera work and editing that a generation, weaned on MTV would appreciate. The camera work and the film's autumnal lighting featuring delicate yellow, brown and orange hues also make it a visually distinctive piece of work.

The pace of the film is generally at getaway car speed, helped along with an eclectic soundtrack featuring a smattering of old and new tunes from Dusty Springfield to The Stone Roses and onto the theme from *Zorba the Greek* (1964).

Without the exuberant style and flair, the witty script and a great team effort from the cast, Ritchie's film might easily have become another embarrassing low-budget British flop but he succeeded in conjuring up something that felt fresh, lively and original.

SCENE ANALYSIS — PLAY YOUR CARDS RIGHT

The high-stakes card game is perhaps the most showy, stylised sequence. With close-up shots of men playing poker and combinations of slo-mo action and speeded-up footage, it has the feeling of an upmarket commercial.

The game takes place in a boxing ring which affords Ritchie and his cinematographer, Tim Maurice-Jones, the luxury of some visual sparring, close quarters action and finally Eddie being caught by Harry Hatchet's sucker punch, which leaves him reeling as he eventual steps out of the ring. The blurry Eddie walks stunned from the card game accompanied by double-exposed images of his bewildered self. It is fast-paced and played against the appropriate backing track of The Castaways one hit *Liar, Liar*.

Initially, the camera takes in the action from a ring-side perspective, moving slowly on the outside of the ring before concluding in a speeded-up motion to establish the positions of the people at the table. We are then dealt a series of shots from roughly the centre of the table looking at those involved in the game, the first being Eddie who spins his chip into the centre of the screen. This establishes Eddie's confidence and precedes a series of quick close-up cuts showing different angles of the game in progress and clues to how Eddie will be duped: an overhead shot of cards being dealt; a coin being rolled along the knuckles of a hand; a close shot of Barry drinking coffee; a black and white TV monitor shot of Eddie's card as Harry looks up; a close-up, back in colour, of cards being viewed discreetly; chips being flicked and then tossed into a pile.

Shots from the centre of the table of the other players follow, giving the impression of someone in the corner of a ring responding to an action. Eddie flicks a card in slow motion to the centre of the table; a player blows his cigar smoke at the screen; Eddie places his hand carefully in the centre (his image goes out of focus when he does so); more chips are thrown in; cards are discarded in slow motion before returning to the correct speed or thrown into the centre and caught in freeze frame. At one point Eddie's knuckles are captured in close-up as he cuts the pack and we sense that the action is going Eddie's way. A scream on the record signifies a breakthrough for Eddie and we see a shot of two of the players; one throws his card while the other sits eyes down looking punch-drunk at his worthless cards. In the next shot a confident Eddie sweeps up his winnings.

There follows a sequence of close-up shots of the players smiling – except Harry, whose point of view up to this moment has not been captured in the series of fast cuts. When we do see him his face is framed in close-up showing an intense concentration. He's not laughing – yet.

The card game action is interrupted as a player is ejected – Tanya mouths the word 'out' perfectly in synch with the vocal track. This break allows the vocal track of the ejected man shouting: 'give me back my money' to play along with the music track which fades.

The previously rapid action, which conveyed Eddie's winning streak, is now contrasted with slower action shots against the sultry duotone lighting prevalent elsewhere in the film. Slower camera movements around the table and Barry's spying on the game is revealed in full. The soundtrack music has gone. Instead the camera's attentions turn to the two main heavyweights in the scene, Eddie and Harry, with an intense close-up of their pupils dilating.

Eddie is framed on the left hand side of the screen with a close-up shot of his head as he confidently raises the stakes. However, when the camera cuts to a close-up of Harry on the right of the screen his close-up is tighter in on his face, far more intense and dominant. During their exchanges Harry's extreme close-up is dropped momentarily when he says: 'Is there anything else you want to say?' Eddie gets an extreme close-up when he declares 'No, I think I'd rather just turn them over', perhaps implying that Eddie has resumed his upper hand. But Harry's extreme close-up returns when he says 'No, you need five hundred grand to see me'.

As Harry moves in for his knock-out punch the camera circles him in his mid-shot and cuts to a similar movement showing Eddie now looking vulnerable. As Harry shows his hand the camera shows his knuckles in close-up moving towards the centre of the screen. Each time a card is turned over there follows a quick cut to Eddie as the camera makes a slow forward motion towards Eddie's expressionless face until the third card is revealed and Eddie reels from the shock, reinforced with a superimposed image of himself. As he gets up from the table a new piece of music kicks in as his wobbly movements and shell-shocked impression are caught in a subtle set of superimpositions, the camera seemingly swaying with Eddie's unsteady movements as he makes his way out of the ring as a beaten man.

Eddie leaves the boxing gym and the CCTV-like angle of the camera captures him lurching into the street and bending over, coughing up the bitter taste of his defeat and the realisation that he has to explain to his mates about the debt they will have to pay.

REACTION

Prior to its release Lenny Mclean, who had become ill during filming, died from brain and lung cancer. The film was dedicated to him using his nickname 'The Guv'nor', while billboard posters were altered to show his image.

The film picked up good reviews with many praising Ritchie's fresh, stylish approach. Comparisons with Tarantino were inevitable but nevertheless *Lock, Stock…* was widely perceived as a modern British classic.

Vinnie Jones was singled out for praise but the rest of the cast, including newcomer Jason Statham, soon aquired celebrity status with the laddish side of the media, which lapped up a British equivalent of the classic American Rat Pack. But the British press couldn't resist a swipe at someone so young and apparently successful as Ritchie and columnists were quick to label the director, born to an upper middle-class family in Hertfordshire, as a 'mockney', a derisive term for those who adopt cockney accents to gain 'street cred'.

Despite minor carping, the film passed the £11m mark in box-office takings in the UK, making it the second highest box-office taker of 1998 behind Gwyneth Paltrow's hit *Sliding Doors*. British awards followed with Ritchie picking up Most Promising Newcomer at the Evening Standard British Film Awards 1999 and Screenwriter of the Year at the influential London Critics Circle Awards 1999. The film also won the Audience Award at the 1999 BAFTAs.

It was less of a success in America, the plot complexities and the array of 'cockney' characters apparently proving slightly harder to digest, but it continued to make great box-office returns worldwide, finally accruing some £50m. For Ritchie and his cast the future looked bright.

CONCLUSION

According to the Britmovie website (www britmovie co uk) *Lock, Stock…* was 'Hailed as *The Long Good Friday* for the *Trainspotting* generation'. There *are* some similarities between *Trainspotting* and Ritchie's movie. Both feature an opening chase sequence when characters are introduced by voice-over, while the pursuit of drugs provides the backdrop to the action leading to sports bags loaded with cash. Both films also contain a strong sense of cultural and regional identity – *Trainspotting* is set among drug users in Leith, Edinburgh, while *Lock, Stock…* depicts cockney petty crooks chancing their arm against hard criminals in London's East End.

Both films also succeed by reflecting the energy and enthusiasm of the teams behind them. The two straddle a moment of political change in Britain with *Trainspotting* released in 1996 bidding farewell to the increasingly discredited Tory Government which would fall in the 1997 election; while *Lock, Stock...* takes place in the early optimistic triumph of the New Labour Government. These films, complete with carefully selected soundtracks, appealed to an audience of twenty-somethings who understood their cultural and social nuances and found that perhaps there could be cool alternatives to Hollywood mainstream movies.

FURTHER READING

The View From Downing Street
Headland, Jane and Relph, Simon (BFI, 1991)

A Bigger Picture: The Report of the Film Policy Review Group
(Department of Culture, Media and Sport, 1998)

Towards a Sustainable UK Film Industry
(Film Council, 2000)

British Cinema of the 90s
Murphy, Robert (ed.) (BFI, 2001) Chapter Four – The Film Industry and the Government: 'Endless Mr Beans and Mr Bonds?' by Miller, Toby

Choose life: Ewan McGregor and the British film revival
Brooks, Xan. (London: Chameleon, 1998).

BFI Film and Television Handbook (BFI, editions from 1983–2005)

Selected reviews/articles/references

Department Media for Culture and Sport – www.culture.gov.uk

UK Film Council – www.ukfilmcouncil.org.uk

British Council Films and Television Department – www.britfilms.com

Trainspotting

Sight & Sound V.6 N.3 (1 March 1996) P.52-53 by Kemp, Philip

Empire N.81 (1 March 1996) P.28-29 by Nathan, Ian

Smith, Murray *Trainspotting* (BFI Publishing, 2002)

A British Success: Making and Selling Trainspotting
Sight & Sound Supplement, Money (1 Sept 1996)

Language Barrier
Premiere (UK) V.4 N.6 (Jul 1996) P.27

Contemporary British Cinema 16+ Source Guide Guides
Mettler, Erinna; Ormsby, Andrew; Reeve, David; Dupin, Christophe (BFI National Library, 2003) www.bfi.org.uk/filmtvinfo/publications/16+/

Marketing 16+ Source Guide Guides
Forbes, Tessa; Ker Matt; Delaney Sean (BFI National Library, 2000)
www.bfi.org.uk/filmtvinfo/publications/16+/

Trainspotting
Welsh, Irving (Vintage, New Edition 1994)

DVD: *Trainspotting the Definitive Edition* (Universal Pictures UK, 2003)

Lock, Stock and Two Smoking Barrels

Sight & Sound V.8 N.9 (1 Sept 1998) P.46-47 by Leigh, Danny

Empire N.111 (1 Sept 1998) P. 35 by Newman, Kim

DVD: *Lock, Stock and Two Smoking Barrels* (2 Disc Special Edition) (Universal Pictures UK, 2005)

3. THINK GLOBAL, ACT LOCAL

While the decade saw the government and representatives from the British film industry working out ways of improving film production in Britain, the world media marketplace went global. Technological advances in digital telecommunications dramatically transformed the way people received information and communicated with each other. They were persuaded to consume more, were given more choice of viewing programmes and films and were presented with new viewing and listening formats.

The dominant players in control of the news and television networks, the systems of film distribution and exhibition and information technologies were in a strong position to influence the way we thought about the world. Subtly or unsubtly the notion of globalisation, a uniformed view of the world driven by consumerism, seeped into our lives, whether this came from Coca-Cola, MacDonalds, Nike or our subscriptions to satellite TV channels, our mobile phones, our upgraded personal computers or merely from our desire to see the latest blockbuster at our new multiplex. Evidence of this benign invasion was increasingly represented by the term 'branding' and by the endless march of the marketing machine. By the end of the decade the term convergence, the option to combine various media formats for presentation, became the buzzword in executive offices and among media experts in the broadsheets.

It is ironic that during this time efforts were made to bolster British cinema. While it is clear that America would always hold the keys, opportunities presented themselves for the USA to cooperate with other nations. Britain, sharing a common language, was its obvious ally.

Pressure became greater for British film producers to make films that would not just appeal to local but global audiences. Art-house cinema, which included foreign language films, noticed a dramatic dip as fewer and fewer cinemas in the UK bothered to show subtitled films unless they had won an Oscar.

But as the decade progressed so too did the proliferation of sequels. Catering for the tastes of mass audiences meant that something had to give, and that inevitably meant quality. By the end of the decade British television had joined in and embraced the notion of reality TV shows with like Big Brother, which premiered in the Netherlands in 1999 and has since become a global phenomena. Reality TV had arrived, as anticipated in *The Truman Show* (USA, 1998). These shows pulled in big audiences and cash but, sadly, also dumbed down television.

All this left British film-makers with a dilemma. Would they hold onto their principles and make the films that they wanted to make, particularly the art-house directors who not only had to find funding but saw their audience slowly dwindle.

Breakdown of percentage of films released in the UK by country

	1990	1991	1992	1993	1994	1995	1996	1997	1998	1999	2000
USA	65.25	55.14	56.40	58.26	54.36	59.50	58.33	53.88	48.33	37.75	36.65
USA/UK		1.00	1.70	2.90	1.74	2.82	7.20	7.39	4.26	4.60	4.97
UK	11.00	14.61	10.80	6.61	11.85	8.81	8.34	9.51	9.12	10.71	8.63
UK/Co-production			7.50	3.72	3.50	6.34	7.58	11.97	9.42	9.95	10.20
Other Co-production				4.95	2.43	5.28	4.55	4.92	2.74	00.51	8.90
Europe	16.50	24.25	16.60	15.30	17.07	10.91	10.60	8.80	15.19	19.14	16.49
Other	7.25	5.00	7.00	8.26	9.05	6.34	3.40	3.53	10.94	17.34	14.13
Releases in UK	262	267	241	242	287	284	264	284	329	392	382

Sources: AC Nielsen EDI/Screen Finance/BFI

The US domination of the British market was not a new phenomenon. Historically, the pioneers of American cinema tended to be film exhibitors as well as film-makers. They understood the concept of keeping cinemas full and audiences happy. In this respect the policy of telling good stories and giving the public what they wanted paid dividends.

The table above shows how US releases dominated the decade in the UK. However, the figure does show that by the end of the 1990s that dominance had tapered off. Part of the explanation for this is that US producers had joined forces in Europe for more co-productions. However, what the table really shows is that despite the growth in UK film production, the amount of home-grown films was relatively low; even adding up the co-productions 1997 was the only year when British films accounted for more than a quarter of the films released in the UK. The British film industry remained fragmented with only occasional tie-ins between production, distribution and exhibition, unlike the major companies in the US who had years to perfect the smooth integration of their industry.

What was also galling from a British point of view is that American audiences got to see films (even many British films) before the British. The barometer of success lay in the opening weekend phenomena and more often than not it was an American audience that got to judge whether a film would be a hit in Britain or not.

THE WORLD WIDE WEB

An indication of just how alert the major Hollywood Studios were to change can be demonstrated with the discovery and development of the World Wide Web at the beginning of the 1990s.

The World Wide Web was created in 1989 by Sir Tim Berners-Lee, a British computer developer with a physics degree from Oxford and working in Geneva. He had a desire to create a universal free electronic encyclopaedia of information that the world could share. In August 1991 he posted his first short summary about his invention on the internet. What is remarkable was the uptake of the technology. Whereas radio and television took decades to build up audiences of more than 50 million listeners or viewers, that same figure was achieved in just four years, from universities to companies, and eventually into people's homes.

The Internet Movie Database (IMDb) started as a result of film enthusiasts posting information from a Usenet newsgroup about actresses with beautiful eyes. From this point onwards more information was posted so that in 1990 a viable list of actor information could be published and was launched in October 1990. By 1998, with dot. coms springing up all over the world, IMDb was acquired by Amazon.com, one of the first companies to sell goods over the internet. This was an example of the dot.com bubble, when the stock market went mad for the dot.coms, and saw dot.coms grow at an astonishing rate between the mid-1990s until the turn of the century when the bubble burst. Computer geeks came into their own, as the language of html looked set to dominate the world. However, after the 'visions' of aspiring venture capitalists had become less rose-tinted, the internet became more of the egalitarian universal font of knowledge that Berners-Lee had first envisaged.

The film world was quick to see the possibilities of the internet as an additional marketing tool. Previously, studios had to rely on trailers in cinemas for their forthcoming releases. Now they could create them on specially-designed pages. *The Blair Witch Project* (USA, 1999) Dir Daniel Myrick, Eduardo Sánchez, even created a whole back history of the Blair Witch and put up on a web page. Not only did this generate interest in the forthcoming film, it created an aura behind the content of the horror film, implying that it might have been true. All this succeeded in hyping up the film for its release – and naturally audiences lapped it up, whether they believed in it or not.

The table overleaf demonstrates the changing of people's video consumerism habits. By the beginning of the decade video rentals dominated the video market with 277 transactions amassing a value of £418m. The 1990's boom in consumerism, which encouraged ownership of films, saw a dramatic change with 114 million retail transactions in the year 2000 bring in the massive sum of £1,104m.

The UK Video/DVD Market 1990–2000

Year	Retail Video millions	Retail DVD millions	Value Video (£m)	Value DVD (£m)	Rental Video millions	Value Video (£m)
1990	40		374		277	418
1991	45		440		253	407
1992	48		506		222	389
1993	60		643		184	350
1994	66		698		167	339
1995	73		789		167	351
1996	79		803		175	382
1997	87		858		161	369
1998	100		940		186	437
1999	96	4	882	68	174	408
2000	114	16.6	1104	264	186	444

Source: BFI The Stats An overview of the film, television, video and DVD industries 1990-2003

Meanwhile, the rental market started to show signs of decline as the new kid on the block - the DVD – made its entrance in 1999. This signalled the beginning of a new era where the digital format allowed for more information to be placed on the disc. Bonus features were added to films which could involve as little as the original trailer or as much as the director's commentary, deleted scenes, behind-the-scenes look at how the film was made and interviews with the stars.

In the space of some 20 years the VHS videotape format was to become as much of a secondary format as vinyl records had at the end of the 1980s when they were replaced by CDs. The film *High Fidelity* (UK/USA 2000) shows a period of time of time when vinyl was still the best format for records, where people used cassette tapes to make compilations, when CDs were still frowned upon by purists and digital downloads did not dominate the marketplace. In a twist, the film was promoted in the UK on a CD Rom given free with the *Independent* newspaper, which featured some clips and music from the film – an example of how convergence was used to promote a theatrical film.

Total revenues from films no longer depended on the takings at the box-office. With the right marketing push and carefully placed tie-ins, TV, DVD satellite and cable deals could potentially greatly increase their profits and even in some cases boost films that had not performed as well as expected at the box-office.

TELEVISION

The free market fervour of the Conservative government made an impact on the terrestrial television industry around 1990 with the Broadcasting Act of 1991. The Act gave 15 regional franchises to ITV companies that passed the 'quality' threshold. Thames Television, surprisingly, lost out to Carlton. Both ITV and BBC were required to commission 25 per cent of programmes from independent producers. Many now see this as a period when ITV was destabilised and competition for TV ratings overshadowed the desire to produce quality programmes. This in turn would have a consequence for the film industry, which up to this point had lived in the shadow of television. Now the two came closer together with Channel 4, BBC Films, and Granada all funding film productions, with the obvious advantages of having exclusive rights to film premieres on their channels.

However, by the end of the decade terrestrial television, even with the Spice Girl's assisted launch of Channel Five in 1997, was beginning to look decidedly old hat with the threat posed by satellite and cable channels and the promises of digital broadcasting systems.

Satellite and cable TV had a slow introduction to the UK during the 1990s. Rupert Murdoch's Sky Television launched in February 1989 to be followed by British Satellite Broadcasting in March 1990. The two fledging companies very soon merged to form British Sky Broadcasting in November 1990. They offered up a menu of news, sports and movies. The movies tended to be blockbusters and viewers could subscribe to them if they wanted to see them early and then pay more, on top of their annual subscriptions, for films and sporting events.

In 1992, the Football League joined forces with BSkyB to create the Premier League, which would be bolstered by TV money. The English game would never be the same again as The Premier League quickly established itself to be a top TV draw and in time top foreign players were lured to Britain by the promise of greater exposure and money. In this respect, Nick Hornby's film *Fever Pitch* (UK, 1996), seems as dated in its own way with regard to football and football habits as *High Fidelity* is to music and music formats.

The proliferation of channels offering more choice had media commentators initially drooling at the prospect of an end to media monopolies and the prospect of niche TV channels where viewers could choose what to watch based on their interests. However, quirky channels such as the Landscape Channel, offering stress free viewing, were bumped off ever-changing cable TV menus, while shopping channels like QVC went from strength to strength. It gradually dawned on the commentators that more meant more or less the same. As TV programmes became increasingly formulaic, viewers voted with their feet and, interestingly, cinema attendances rose during the 1990s while TV executives found themselves facing new challenges to keep their audiences.

COMPUTER GAMES

Alongside video and DVD spin-offs, the 1990s saw the steady rise in popularity of computer games with the breakthrough *Wolfenstein* making its appearance in 1992, to be followed rapidly by *Doom* in 1993 and, of course, British-made *Lara Croft's Tomb Raider* (released in 1996). PCs speeded up to take into account the need for fast responses and the steady development of Microsoft Windows by the mid-1990s allowed games and their graphics to become more sophisticated. Companies like Nintendo and Playstation developed their own personalised consoles, which became 'must-have' presents for a whole generation of mainly male children.

Action movies, including the Bond films such as *The World is Not Enough*, (UK/USA, 1999), were accompanied by action-packed shoot 'em-ups with parallel settings to the films. Hollywood was not impervious to the popularity of computer games and quickly turned its attentions to transforming them into films such as *Super Mario Bros.* (USA, 1993); *Street Fighter* (USA, 1994); *Mortal Kombat* (USA, 1995); and *Wing Commander* (USA, 1999). The success of these films eventually led to co-UK productions such as *Lara Croft Tomb Raider* (USA/UK/Germany/France/Japan, 2001) and *Resident Evil* (UK/Germany/France, 2002). Even the art house circuit was not impervious to the phenomena when *Run Lola Run* (Germany, 1998), and its three episodic repeated runs alluded to repeat plays in arcade or video game.

The film industry also responded to the developing digital technology by employing it notably in action films. A breakthrough in computer generated imagery (CGI) resulted in the first feature film by Pixar Animation Studios called *Toy Story* (USA, 1995), which had a similar impact on the animation film world as Disney's first full-length feature *Snow White and the Seven Dwarfs* (USA, 1937), some 60 years earlier.

MAGAZINES

Another by-product of the proliferation of channels and entertainment portals was the growth of the cult of the celebrity. *Hello!* magazine, first published in 1988, spawned a whole host of glossy celebrity lifestyle magazines such as *OK* Magazine launched in 1990, *Now* launched in 1997 and *Heat* in 1999. By the end of the decade, the magazines didn't just focus on royalty, top actors or top pop stars; almost anyone who had had 15 minutes of fame on television, or was merely rich, became a celebrity.

Again, this was skillfully anticipated in the film *To Die For* (USA, 1995), with its prophetic line espousing the shallowness of our global society: 'You aren't really anybody in America if you're not on TV.' Aspirational lifestyles became the focus of TV programmes as the world seemed to embrace consumerism – what better way to sell your products than have a top celebrity telling you 'because you're worth it.?'

This global presence in the UK was even felt in the world of film magazines. At the start of the decade *Sight & Sound*, the serious film quarterly, and its partner the *Monthly Film Bulletin*, both published by the British Film Institute, received a rude jolt with the publication of Emap's *Empire*. Not only was *Empire* monthly, it had colour photos, and lots of them and aimed at a mainstream audience. It unashamedly championed box-office films and pandered to a growing cinema audience. Among the features of forthcoming attractions the magazine printed endless lists of favourite scenes from films, anticipating or possibly contributing to, the trend for top 100 lists that now fill up TV schedules.

Not surprisingly, it also drew handy advertising revenue from the major studios and still had room for the odd paragraph here and there about art house films. *Sight & Sound*, whose serious look at cinema had been edited by Penelope Huston since the 1950s, responded by going monthly, installing a new editor in Philip Dodd and merging the *Monthly Film Bulletin*. However, the editorial policy remained geared at a high-brow audience and was noted for championing Iranian cinema throughout the 1990s while *Empire* and its main rival *Total Film*, from Future Publishing, launched in 1997, continued along their populist paths.

Ironically, the emergence of British cinema was squeezed out, caught somewhere between the two extremes of popular and worthy. Both *Empire* and *Sight and Sound* reviewed *The Full Monty* but neither anticipated that it would become the biggest British success of the decade. It was only when the box-office till registers were ringing that both magazines considered the phenomena in their own ways.

GLOBAL AUDIENCE

All these changes were to have a subtle influence on film-making. Local stories had to have some sort of global appeal if producers were to have any chance of getting their money back. Similarly, in the UK the perceived upturn in the British film industries fortunes, particularly in the production sector, meant that producers could look beyond Britain and North America for their box-office returns if they found the right subject to attract a global audience. Cracking that nut would surely bring more money in with promises of making bigger and better pictures.

Certainly, globalisation was having a peculiar 'back to the future' effect on films designed to win over global audiences. Films like *Speed* (USA, 1994) needed little translation. In effect, they were a sophisticated form of silent film — full of thrills and spills and very little dialogue. However, blockbuster films in the 1990s were far from silent. A soundtrack of some sort was *de rigueur* to guide the audience through a range of emotions — calm, tense, agitated, enraged, aroused.

If this was the case at the top end of the market then film-makers were inevitably having to work harder to persuade studios, producers or financiers that their projects were worth a gamble. In the UK, the growth of the exhibition market came at a price - exhibitors wanted bums on seats and the multiplexes wanted punters to spend money on popcorn and soft drinks. They were not going to achieve this by screening unknown low-budget British films with first-time directors and unfamiliar casts. Their priorities were to bring in the big movies. However, even regular cinemagoers can get tired of too much popcorn. The policy of packing out cinema screens with the *Jurassic Parks*, the latest *Star Wars* prequel or whatever Disney wanted to release was fine when they were worth watching, but big budget, highly-hyped films can flop badly, whereas films with a slow burn, word of mouth uptake can surprise – witness *The Full Monty*.

Nevertheless, by the end of the 1990s the global marketplace was resounding to the sound of cash till registers where people were encouraged to pay for a film, not once but several times over – in the cinema, through a pay-per-view satellite subscription, on video or DVD, and via associated materials such as the obligatory soundtrack of the movie or the book of the film.

This section focuses on two local stories by the same British author, Nick Hornby, and sees how these films were handled in relation to the British film industry. In *Fever Pitch* the film stayed local, whereas in *High Fidelity* the ambitions of the film-makers took the film from somewhere off the Holloway Road in Islington, North London and transported it to Chicago.

High Fidelity (2000) (UK/US) UK Cert 15

Director: Stephen Frears

Screenplay: D.V. De Vincentis; Steve Pink;, John Cusack;, Scott Rosenberg (based on the novel by Nick Hornby)

Producers: Tim Bevan; Rudd Simmons

Production companies: Touchstone Pictures; Working Title Films; Dogstar Films; New Crime Productions; Top Five Productions

Production start date: 29/04/1999 **Budget:** £12.5m (estimated)

Distributor: Buena Vista International **UK Release date:** 21 June 2000

UK Box Office: £5,078,025 **USA Box Office:** $27.3m

Worldwide Box Office: $35.8m

By the end of the 1990s there was a genuine feeling that British cinema had come out of the doldrums and the notion of 'Cool Britannia' helped to reinforce Britain's cultural impact on the world, which included books, film and music. Brit pop had gone some way to re-establish British cultural identity, as had a handful of hit British films. When *Notting Hill* was released the area of Notting Hill was deemed a 'cool' place to set a film and London was a 'cool' place to visit anyway.

It therefore came as somewhat of of shock to learn that writer Nick Hornby's perfectly observed, international best-selling book about the peculiar male psyche in relation to lists, music, women and compilation tapes set in 'ultra cool' North London called *High Fidelity* was going to be made into a film – set not in Islington but Chicago!

Unlike the film *Fever Pitch*, for which Hornby had written the screenplay based on his cult first autobiographical novel about his obsession with Arsenal football, he was happy to let American actor John Cusack and his friends take his 'global' themes onto a much bigger stage. This was not to be a low-budget hit British film funded by Channel 4; this was going to be a film made by the Walt Disney Corporation through the aegis of Touchstone Pictures and with a big budget (in British terms). The treatment of *High Fidelity* was in essence what globalisation is all about.

SYNOPSIS

Set in Chicago, Championship Vinyl record shop owner and former DJ Rob Gordon is devastated when his girlfriend Laura leaves him. Rob reveals, in the form of flashbacks, his five most memorable break-ups in chronological order.

Rob's relationship with Barry and Dick, who help out in his shop and share his musical obsessions, is strained due to Laura's break-up but he still goes with Barry and Dick to a bar to see singer Marie DeSalle perform.

Laura's friend Liz, who has been sympathetic to Rob, storms into the record shop and berates Rob for the way he has treated Laura, which Rob reveals in flashbacks. Rob re-examines the nature of his failed relationship in a bid to win Laura back. He decides to revisit all of his past all-time, top five break-up girl friends in order to make sense of his own failures and achieve some sort of self-knowledge that will allow him to move on. One by one Rob reaches closure in a series of meetings with his ex-girlfriends.

During this process Rob learns that Laura is seeing Ian. An obsessed Rob meets up with Laura in a vain attempt to win her back. She delights him by saying that she and Ian have not had sex yet. Rob is euphoric and then inexplicitly goes on to sleep with Marie DeSalle.

The turning point in Laura and Rob's relationship is when Laura's father dies and Rob attends the funeral and the two reconcile by getting back together in her car. Laura arranges a gig where Rob can DJ again. Rob confides in Laura that he has at last lost the need to meet his perfect fantasy woman and he asks Laura to marry him. Laura is both amused and moved.

At the successful launch party, Barry's band makes a surprisingly good debut performance much to Rob's relief and delight.

HOW IT WAS MADE

Hornby's hit follow-up to his debut book was published in 1995 and soon became an international best seller and shortly afterwards gained a film industry buzz since Touchstone Pictures (Disney's film outlet for PG-rated films) had purchased the film rights. It was muted that Mike Newell, who had scored such a transatlantic hit with *Four Weddings and a Funeral*, would direct, thereby giving the film some British credibility. However, rumours came out that American actor John Cusack was to star as the main character of Rob.

In fact, John Cusack not only came on board as the lead role, he also took ownership of the film by co-writing the screenplay, co-producing the film (New Crime Productions was the film arm of his theatre company called The New Criminals) as well as acting as co-music supervisor. Hornby's book had struck a chord with Cusack and his co-writers D.V. De Vincentis, Steve Pink and Scott Rosenberg. They recognised the male character of Rob – aimless, anally-retentive, self-opinionated, self-obsessed, self-deluding, self-deprecating, man/child – as a universal character and controversially figured that it didn't matter where you placed Rob (in the Western world); his faults, failings, traits and nuances would have a universal resonance. The writing team immediately visualised Chicago settings and Cusack went as far to state that the backdrop of Chicago was to function like an additional character. Apart from that strong association, the writers and the producers felt that location didn't alter the essence of the book. Hornby could also see the bigger picture – the extra exposure the film would give him as the author would be good for future projects.

However, the film does have British involvement via Working Title Films, which had established offices in America but had begun to add a string of 'British' hits to its collection including *Four Weddings and a Funeral* and *Notting Hill*. In the end, Mike Newell stepped down from the director's chair to become executive producer alongside co-founder of short-lived production company Dogstar Films. The producers felt that some sort of British sensibility was still needed to steer the project and Stephen Frears, who had first established himself as a director with his quirky Channel 4 film *My Beautiful Launderette* and had directed John Cusack in *The Grifters* (USA, 1990), was brought on board.

Frears initially shared a British sense of disappointment that the film was to be set in Chicago but quickly came to the same conclusion as Cusack and his colleagues that the actual setting didn't matter since the themes were universal. In the end Frears felt that the film worked well away from its London location. The film also lent itself to Rob confiding to the audience, an intimate straight to camera style reminiscent of Michael Caine in *Alfie* (1965), and to a lesser extent Woody Allen in *Annie Hall* (USA, 1977). There is also an influence in Wayne Wang's intimate and down-to-earth film *Smoke* (USA, 1995) about a group of regular customers of a tobacconist store, starring Harvey Keitel and William Hurt.

Frears realised that the film would stand or fall by establishing a similar tight-knit community through his main characters. Cusack had already bagged the main role of Rob and was entirely convincing and comfortable as a 'man with a problem'. Equally effective was the contrast to the energetic, brash, performance that Jack Black gives to Barry, which is perfectly countered-balanced by Todd Louiso's timid and softly spoken interpretation of Dick. These three male roles remain true to the essence of the characters Hornby created (but without their British accents).

Slightly more intriguing, Frears picked Danish actress Iben Hjejle to provide the female match to Rob's long journey to achieve stability in his relationship. As if to emphasise a point her accent is American (in the film Laura is subtly assigned Danish roots via her mother who has an accent and the evidence of small Danish flags on the mantelpiece in Laura's parents home). Her performance is universal – and without doubt Iben Hjejle could have played Laura (with an English accent) had the film been set in London.

The film had been in development since 1997 and finally commenced production in April 1999. It was released in America in March 2000 before its British release in June 2000.

KEY ISSUES

Essentially both the film and the book deal with the agonising analysis of relationships and holding on to them. The meaning of love, betrayal and reconciliation all follow suit but are always accompanied by musical references. In this way the book and the film deal with the anally-retentive world inhabited by men who love music, record shops and making compilation tapes for friends and lovers.

Everyday I write the book

On the whole the film of *High Fidelity* remains faithful to Hornby's book and retains its best lines and witty observations.

At the beginning of the film, an intense Rob asks the audience 'What came first, the music or the misery? Did I listen to music because I was miserable? Or was I miserable because I listened to music?' Hornby chooses to begin with a list and then a description of Rob's 'five memorable split-ups, in chronological order' before introducing the dangers of listening to too much music.

The book takes its time to recall and revisit the top-five most memorable break-ups including one (number three Jackie Allen) whose scenes of break-up and revisiting are not included in the film. In fact, the film mucks up the chronological order by have Rob recall his break-ups via Alison Ashmore, Penny Hardwick, Charlie Nicholson and Sarah Kendrew (relegating Jackie Allen to five and dismissing her in a line which enables Laura to break into Rob's all-time top five break-ups – with a bullet). However, the film milieu does not have the luxury to linger and expand on scenes and characters and minor adjustments are necessary.

Hornby's book articulates a particular male trait of being obsessive about music and facts – more as a source of comfort than a true source of joy. The overriding sentiment is expressed in the line 'What really matters is what you like, not what you are like.' Anyone who has ever entered a second-hand record shop and flipped endlessly through record and CD racks will know exactly where Hornby's characters are coming from – when they take a break from making definitive pronouncements about the music they rate they turn their attention in a similarly uncompromising way to other areas of popular culture. The same applies to the art of making compilation tapes.

The book also has endless top five lists, predicting a future when TV shows would contain top 100 lists and magazines follow suit by sacrificing proper journalism for any quick-fit list-making exercise.

Geographically, Hornby takes us to North London locations via references to Crouch End, Holloway, Seven Sisters Road and Camden. In the book, he takes the long hike to South London when he, Barry and Dick see Marie DeSalle for a second time (a scene not included in the film). Frears' film trusts Cusack's reinterpretation of locations in Chicago settings (Lincoln Park, Lane Technical High School, Wicker Park, and on the Red Line Wilson Platform).

Emotionally, in the book Rob is leaning more to the 'new man' than to the lad, with references to art house cinema, an appreciation of books and the fact that he cleans the toilet from time to time. In many ways he is in touch with his feminine side and often appreciates Laura's point of view. He is self-deprecating and self-chastising and he acts unfaithfully, which make him flawed. Both the book and the film reveal the contradiction in Rob's character that while he is self-assured about musical tastes he struggles to articulate his real feelings for Laura. This tension is ultimately resolved when having just got back with Laura, Rob finds himself making a tape for Caroline, a journalist and cries out to himself: 'When's it all going to fucking stop?' He finally pledges himself to Laura and the book ends with his triumphant DJ'ing gig accompanied by Barry's band's excellent debut. In the book his band changes its name from Sonic Death Monkey to Backbeat and knocks out a set of 1960's beat music classics – Route 66, Long Tall Sally, Money, Do You Love Me? In the Midnight Hour and La Bamba. Rob starts to compile a tape for Laura in his head and the book ends with the line 'Tonight, for the first time ever, I can sort of see how it's done.'

American without tears

A hypothetical debate, worthy of the book itself, about setting the film in London would throw up some interesting British casting issues. Could Colin Firth, Ewan McGregor, Robert Carlyle, or even Tim Roth have fitted the character of Rob? The debate is academic – John Cusack was Rob. He owned the part. Nevertheless, in his first flashback scene when Rob takes us back in time in his early youth and recalls break-up number 1 (Alison Ashmore), we see young boys practicing swings with their baseball bats. This is possibly the only time in the film where the film places us firmly in America, whereas the rest of the film stays truer to a universal environment and attitudes.

The film only strays into the realms of Hollywood with the inclusion of a lovely cameo by Tim Robbins as Ian, and the slightly more self-indulgent inclusion of Bruce Springsteen (although in fairness this is also in keeping with the book where Rob decides to revisit his failed girlfriends before it's too late, an idea he compares to Springsteen's song Bobby Jean. In the book Rob states: 'I'd like my life to be like a Bruce Springsteen song.')

One of the funniest moments in the film (which is freely interpreted from the book) is when Ian walks into the record store and gently confronts Rob about his stalking and endless phone calls. Rob's response is played out in a couple of fantasy attacks, one in which the mild-mannered Dick slams a phone into Ian's face – the reality is a meek backdown from Rob.

Another device not included in the book is the storyline of the thieving skate-boarding punks that Rob chooses to promote by issuing a CD. This is possibly included in the film to emphasise Laura's point that Rob need no longer be a professional critic all his life and that he could instead become 'part of it.'

In the book a character called Johnny carries out the shoplifting rather than the skateboarders. The inclusion of the skateboarders takes the film out of Hornby territory and it feels more American than universal even though skateboards are not exclusively American.

In the book Marie DeSalle is a white American singer songwriter. In the film she keeps her American identity but she is black. Hypothetically, would it be likely that Rob would have fallen for an English singer songwriter? Somehow it seems unlikely.

Ironically, music became the issue that threw the film unexpectedly back to Britain. Apparently, John Cusack, D.V. De Vincentis, Steve Pink, and Scott Rosenberg had long 'Hornbyesque' debates about what to put in. Music is used throughout the film, often subtly to accompany the story's narrative. The tracks heard in the store – *I Can't Stand the Rain* by Ann Peebles and *I'm Wrong About Everything* by John Wesley Harding – are contrasted with more obvious musical devices such as Queen's *We Are the Champions* when Rob learns that Laura hasn't slept with Ian – yet.

British musical references fared pretty well with name checks to The Jesus And Mary Chain, Echo And The Bunnymen, The Clash and The Smiths. There were also three rather big musical plugs for Belle and Sebastian, the Beta Band and Stiff Little Fingers during scenes in the record store. After the film was released the Beta Band benefited as a result of Rob/John Cusack's direct plug – he tells Dick under his breath: 'I will now sell five copies of The Three EPs by The Beta Band' and proceeds to play *Dry the Rain*. In this moment alone the film is not only being faithful to the book it is entering a meaningful marriage where the setting of the action doesn't seem so important – its heart is in the right place.

The film ends in the club when Barry's band (no longer called Sonic Death Monkey but Barry Jive and the Uptown Five) opens with Rob's 'greatest record of all time' *Let's Get it On* by Marvin Gaye. The film gives the record more credence than in the book by linking it to Rob and Laura's relationship. In a cinematic sense this makes much more sense than using *Route 66*, and of course the happy ending is transformed by Barry's magnificent metamorphosis from foul-mouthed, elitist, record-accumulating obsessive to cool soul singer with attitude. The film ends with Rob compiling a tape for Laura.

Girl's talk

The film has too many cynical edges to make it an out-and-out romantic comedy but if you remove the musical reference scenes there lurks a rom com film of a love lost and a love regained.

Rob's low points are usually indicated with rather pathetic scenes of him feeling sorry for himself in the rain, whether it be from a call-box outside Ian's apartment or sitting on the bench after Laura's father's funeral.

Because the film is seen entirely from his point of view we get very little in the way of a female insight into the events as they unfold, other than the sequences when his ex-girlfriends discuss the origins of their break-ups. However, it would be fair to say that the film appeals to both sexes. For men (possibly more than women) there is the obvious delight in sharing an interest in Rob, Barry and Dirk's musical tastes – elitist though they may be. Yet both men and women can relate to the traumatic break-ups. In confiding so directly Rob exposes some typical male traits both negative – he's selfish, lazy, unable to commit, ego-centric, and unreliable – and positive – deep down he's caring, honest and in his own way quite charismatic. Laura seems to have more power in the relationship in her ability to make the big decisions to leave, and then to return, whereas Rob is seen to be vulnerable most of the time. This vulnerability leads him to make some poor choices (such as sleeping with Marie DeSalle).

Whether or not these stereotypical views apply, it seems that *High Fidelity* works on a level that embraces the subject of sexual politics and it is refreshing to see Rob's character, and to a lesser extent Laura's, painted grey. It makes their relationship all the more believable.

Lip service

The device used to have Rob talk direct to camera (and thereby the audience) is a great feature of the film. Frears could have employed a voice-over narration, but this would not have been as effective. What we get instead is a character who trusts us, the audience, enough to confide his most personal thoughts. This allows the interior monologues from the book to come alive in the film, particularly on two occasions.

The scene where Liz storms into Rob's record shop and calls him: 'A fucking arsehole', leads Rob to confess to the audience about his four terrible misdemeanours with Laura (that he had an affair when she was pregnant, that it led indirectly to her abortion, that he owes her money, and that he said he would consider seeing someone else). At a point when the audience could very easily go off Rob and agree with Liz, Rob allows us back onto his side by explaining the contexts of his acts. He does this while travelling to work on a train and furtively looks around the train carriage before continuing his confession. We are Rob's mates and we travel on this journey with him.

Another scene sets Rob near a river where he tells us five things he misses about Laura. His list appears trite and trivial yet somehow provides us with an intimate glimpse of his true feelings to Laura and we recognise that he actually loves her. 'Three. I miss her smell and the way she tastes. It's the mystery of human chemistry and I don't understand it. Some people, as far as your senses are concerned, just feel like home.' This particular strong revelation appears to bring Rob to a swell of momentary emotional speechlessness so that when he moves to the fourth thing on his list he has to show us it via his fingers before he regains his flow and talks about the attributes which he think gives Laura grace.

Elsewhere, Rob sometimes moderates his voice when he feels other characters might still hear him such as when we see him in bed next to Marie DeSalle as she sleeps the morning after their one-night stand.

SCENE ANALYSIS – LITTLE TRIGGERS

The straight-to-camera talking device enhances our understanding of the inner workings of Rob's obsessive and sometimes tormented mind and is used to great effect. This also serves as just one of the triggers that prompt frequent flashbacks to incidents in the past, which sometimes leads to flashbacks within flashbacks before the action returns comically to the train of thought that Rob had been sharing with his audience. Underpinning this of course is the constant use and celebration of music within the film, which holds a special position in setting scenes, understanding people's characters, or simply as a performance to be enjoyed.

Straight from the beginning with its short opening title we hear the sound of a stylus being applied to a record and then see an extreme close-up of the physical splendour of a section of an LP record with light caressing the grooves as the music plays the film's first track, *You're Gonna Miss Me* by the Thirteenth Floor Elevators. The first cut then shows a close-up of the sound system that is conveying this music and in the darkened room the camera follows the coil of Rob's headphones until it stops at his back of his head. The next cut shows us a dark shot of a close-up of his face placed in the centre of the screen, framed with headphones still on as he speaks directly to the camera for the first time. We engage in what appears to be his philosophical correlation between pop music and being miserable before the camera cuts to Laura in his apartment putting on her coat to leave. She jerks the lead from out of the music system and so cuts off Rob's train of thought as he turns to her.

In this short introduction we have seen the physical nature of Rob's fascination - vinyl records which will be apparent later in the film as their physical nature is treated with reverence. At one point Rob is seen dusting some ex-jukebox singles with care. We are also subtly directed to the warped way that Rob's knowledge of music works. His girlfriend is about to leave him and yet he still has time to find and play a song called *You're Gonna Miss Me*. Laura's action of taking the lead out of the sound system takes Rob from his fantasy world into the real world. Rob's apartment, complete with his beloved, impressive record collection, is dimly lit to suit his mood but later on in the film we actually see daylight – not least when Laura teases him about his top five occupations.

Having slammed the door after Laura leaves Rob returns to talk to camera by charting his top five break-ups. The camera on a long shot in his apartment stays trained on Rob as he walks (talking all the time) up and resumes his close-up. It breaks away as Rob shouts after Laura (who couldn't possibly hear him) and then switches the record back on, turning the volume up. Having screamed out to Laura from his window (a shot seen from her perspective) Rob calms down and sits in his listening chair and switches the music off before addressing the audience again. As he is framed sitting comfortably in a mid shot he reflects on break-up number one and the film takes us into the first of many flashbacks to the tune of *I Want Candy* by Bow Wow Wow, which fades in as the camera catches Rob in reflective mode.

Next we cut to the park and we hear Rob talk in voice-over as the camera tracks a group of teenage girls dressed in mid-1970's fashion as they walk past boys preoccupied by baseball. To confirm Rob's notion about girls: 'One moment they weren't there, not in any form that interested us anyway,' the girls walk on the other side of some fencing looking towards the inside, while the boys generally keep their eyes focussed on the game until a young Rob is approached and led away by Alison Ashmore. We see the young couple kissing and the shots are interrupted by returning to Rob in his present day chair before returning to Rob being usurped by Kevin Bannister at which point the music on the record (ending on shouts of 'hey! hey!' ends abruptly) and Rob's friend closes the flash book with the amusing retort of 'slut.'

In the next moment Rob's strange sense of satisfaction in chronicling these painful break-ups is shown as the camera slowly draws away from Rob in his seat, revealing a cigarette in his hand (the film often displays Rob with a cigarette). The next cut takes us out of Rob's apartment and onto the platform of the train station as he goes to work. Again, trains make up part of the physical geography of the film, which uses real locations in Chicago as part of its urban backdrop.

On the platform Rob's piece to the camera is interesting since fellow commuters waiting for his train pay him no attention. It is though Rob is with a friend – rather than talking to himself. This time, flashback number two comes after he has listed Penny Hardwick's top five artists, the last being Elton John eliciting a cut to the tune of *Crocodile Rock* and a flashback (complete with more fashion indicators) to Rob's days at high school. Cusack convincingly plays the younger version of himself and again the flashback ends abruptly on another moment – the explosion in the chemistry class that follows the news that Penny had sex shortly after he dumped her.

In the next shot we see Rob reaching his work place where he addresses the camera, which is filming him from a high angle as he makes his way to open the store. Rob faces up while he talks and the camera drops down to his level. The physical process of opening up the shop, turning on the lights and walking into shot further establishes Rob's world. Dick's quiet entrance and selection of the gentle Belle and Sebastian's track contrasts dramatically with Barry's explosive entrance as he tosses Dick's cassette from the player and replaces it with Walking on Sunshine by Katrina and the Waves. The film manages to convey both Barry and Dick's personalities with the help of the soundtrack.

As the action progresses it seems that Rob has lost his train of thought and might not confide in us anymore. This feeling is dispersed as Rob finally addresses his audience and continues his list of break-ups, clearly establishing how the narrative will ebb and flow.

REACTION

The predictable hooh-hah accompanying the film's release in Britain was the issue of switching the setting from London to Chicago. To some this seemed unnecessary, particularly in the light of the big box-office success of *Notting Hill* featuring a bloke in his thirties running an unsuccessful bookstore instead of record shop. *High Fidelity* did quite well at the UK box-office, passing the £5m mark, but this should be tempered in terms of the money it cost to make.

By and large, the film won over the critics who concurred that it stayed true to its source material. In particular, Cusack seemed appropriate as the lead character of Rob, and Black and Louiso drew plaudits, but Catherine Zeta-Jones' cameo as Rob's sophisticated but ultimately shallow ex, was also appreciated. Some critics couldn't resist the temptation of writing their reviews in the style of the film and the book – top five reasons why to like *High Fidelity*. Apart from praise for the wry and witty script, the film was appreciated for how down to earth it felt and the fact that it was character-driven.

High Fidelity worked well as a film in its own right, although for fans of the book there still lingers a tinge of regret at not seeing the film set somewhere up the Seven Sisters Road. It also made those same people realise what they suspected all along – that 'Cool Britannia' was just a meaningless marketing tool.

Hornby's next book, *About a Boy*, was also adapted as a film with Hornby taking credit as executive producer and with Working Title again its production company. The film, which starred Hugh Grant, Toni Collette, Rachel Weisz and Nicholas Hoult, was released in 2002 and became a big budget success. This time the location was true to the book and shot in London.

Fever Pitch (1996) (UK) UK Cert 15

Director: David Evans

Screenplay: Nick Hornby (based on the book Fever Pitch by Nick Hornby)

Producer: Amanda Posey

Production companies: Channel 4 Films; Wildgaze Films

Production start date: 1996 **Budget:** £1.75m (estimated)

Distributor: Film Four Distributors **UK Release date:** 4 April 1997

UK Box Office: £766,121 **USA Box Office:** $0.13m

Worldwide Box Office: n/a

Hornby's best-selling, cathartic book on the agonies and occasional ecstasies of being a
football fan didn't appear to have enough about it to warrant a feature film but it came
along at the right time in terms of the re-invention of the British bloke – lager, football,
gigs, girls and cars. In 1996, England staged the European Football Championship and
David Baddiel and Frank Skinner, with a little help from Ian Broudie, summed up an ironic
mood of optimism with their anthem *Three Lions. Fantasy Football,* hosted by Baddiel
and Skinner, seized on the universal truths espoused in Hornby's book: that the majority
of football fans, irrespective of who they support are the same – they are hopeless
obsessives and eternal pessimists. Hornby's book, which comes from a middle-class
perspective, now serves as an historical point just before the Premiership was invented
with its cosmopolitan influx of players from around the world, its branding and its pay-per
view coverage on Sky television. Football was about to go global.

The Beautiful Game, as Pele coined it, is played and watched to the level that Hornby's
book describes in most corners of the world, bar North America. The 1994 World Cup
was a big success in the United States, but this is a place where football isn't even called
football. So, the decision to turn *Fever Pitch* – a male-specific, Arsenal-orientated, fan-
based take on a sport that Hollywood would have little interest in – was a bold one. This
was to be a British film about a British subject matter.

SYNOPSIS

Set in London during the 1988/89 football season, Paul Ashworth, an English teacher
in his mid-thirties, works at a North London comprehensive school. His single greatest
obsession is Arsenal football club. He has a laid-back, sometimes unorthodox approach
to teaching, whereas new teacher Sarah Hughes is a strict disciplinarian and is initially
antagonised by Paul's carefree approach.

Paul and Sarah become unlikely partners, but Sarah is exasperated by Paul's strict adherence to worshipping Arsenal and several times she catches him thinking only about his team.

Paul's complicated love hate relationship with Arsenal is seen via flashbacks starting in the late 1960s where his recently divorced father takes the young Paul to his first football match.

Paul coaches his school team and identifies with and encourages Robert, a young Arsenal fan in his class. The headmaster Ted offers Paul a vacant head of year position. Paul rather glibly turns it down. Tensions between Paul and Sarah grow after he reluctantly takes her to an Arsenal match in the wake of the Hillsborough stadium disaster and Paul finally works out that she is pregnant.

In a childlike manner Paul feels that he is prepared to commit to Sarah. He tries to persuade Sarah to buy a flat with him very close to the Highbury stadium. But his obsession for Arsenal seem to make the couple irreconcilable.

Issues are brought to a head on the day of Arsenal's crunch title decider, away at Liverpool on the last day of school term when Arsenal are required to win by two clear goals. Paul and his best mate Steve watch the match on TV in Paul's flat, while Sarah is invited by her fifth form class to an end of term party. The affirmation that Sarah is a good teacher somehow lifts her out of her doldrums. She leaves the party and takes a cab to join Paul.

The two are eventually reconciled after Arsenal win in the last seconds of the match and an impromptu party starts around the Highbury ground.

HOW IT WAS MADE

Channel 4 funded the film but there was also executive producer support from the former Palace Picture team of Stephen Woolley (a life-long Spurs supporter) and Nik Powell (Arsenal). Hornby wrote the screenplay himself and created the character Paul based on himself in order to add a romantic interest in Sarah. The process of adapting the book and turning it into a viable film took more than four years before it was ready to go into production.

The great casting coup was to get Colin Firth to play the lead role. Firth had recently set pulses racing in his steamy portrayal of Darcy in the BBC's adaptation of *Pride and Prejudice*. The casting was in part designed to draw in a female audience who may have otherwise given a film about football a wide berth. Other cast members generally were known for their TV work such as Neil Pearson (*Drop the Dead Donkey*) Holly Aird (*Soldier, Soldier*) Ruth Gemmell (*Band of Gold*) and Mark Strong (*Our Friends in the North*). Strong was also a bona fide Arsenal fan, whereas Firth, rather like the character of Sarah, inevitably learned to become one through Hornby's persuasive influence.

David Evans, who had also cut his teeth on television mainly with the series *Common as Muck*, had actually read the book before publication and was keen to convey the spirit of the game as seen through the eyes of a supporter. However, the intention was to create a romantic comedy and deliberately start the film from the premise of boy meets girl – the football would come later.

Hornby's geographical locations were well replicated in London and Maidenhead with much action taking in and around the roads leading to the Highbury stadium itself. However, the terrace scenes showing Arsenal's North Bank were actually shot at Fulham's Craven Cottage due to the fact that Arsenal had become an all-seater stadium.

The production team also had to pay attention to period details such as hairdos and fashions that were prevalent from the late 1960s to the early 1970s. This was reflected in the choice of soundtrack, featuring songs from the relevant era (such as Harry J Allstars and Slade from the early period and The Smiths and Van Morrison later on), which Hornby oversaw in the manner befitting the man who would next write *High Fidelity*.

The film took six weeks to shoot from May 1996, finishing around the start of Euro 1996 in England where for one month in June football was coming home.

KEY ISSUES

From the start it was clear that the producers were going to pitch the film as a romantic comedy rather than a film about football fandom and the marketing people had some fun with their tag lines – 'Life gets complicated when you love one woman and worship eleven men!' and 'A ~~football~~ *love* match made in heaven.' However, *Fever Pitch* is more than a romantic comedy, for it also looks at the subject of identity and belonging, albeit in an unusual way.

Identity

Those who had read and enjoyed Hornby's book are not disappointed with the replaying of the major scenes but in the film Hornby is able to delve deeper into Paul's motivation for supporting Arsenal and why winning the championship is so important.

Early on Paul's voice-over states: 'We all have our reasons for loving things the way we do,' and is followed by a flashback to his recently divorced father taking his young son to his first match. In the car on the way to the game the young Paul confesses that he's not really into football but the events of the day become like an epiphany for him. In the café with the cynical old men and in the stands with people shouting and swearing, Paul finds a new family.

Football becomes a compensation for Paul for losing out on his father through his divorce. The pain of that separation is channelled through Paul's devotion to Arsenal and supporting the team links Paul with his mother and father. After Arsenal score a scrambled goal in the first match Paul turns to his father and says: 'Terry Neil – he's good isn't he?' much to his father's delight. Later on, having had an adventure at Reading (where Paul's mum had unintentionally bought him a ticket at the home end) Paul is delighted when his mother engages in an informed conversation about the match with him and ends by saying: 'We're good in cups aren't we?' Even Paul's little sister seems to know a bit about football.

Supporting Arsenal gives Paul his identity and his sense of security. His need for security appears so extreme that he chooses to live in a flat as close to the Highbury Stadium as possible. Paul's empathy with his pupil Robert, a devoted Arsenal fan, is evident when during a parent's meeting he persuades Robert's newly-divorced mum to take her son to Arsenal. This is like a form of transference where Paul sees the value of belonging to something that will always be there week in week out.

His problems occur later when he encounters Sarah, who unsettles him by offering him an alternative identity. Perhaps influenced by his separation Paul reacts angrily to his friend Steve about the prospect of his relationship with Sarah by saying: 'What's the point of that anyway? It's just a waste of fucking time.' Nevertheless, Paul and Sarah do set off on an uneasy relationship where Paul is not prepared to compromise on his devotion to Arsenal, much to Sarah's increasing desperation.

Unpredictably, Paul appears delighted when he discovers that Sarah is pregnant. He even seems keen to settle down. At one point he shocks his friend by stating that maybe some things are more important than football after all. He abandons his natural inclination to pessimism by predicting, accurately, a 5-0 victory to Arsenal.

However, a bad result against Derby tests his new resolve and he converts to type and feels more upset about the defeat than missing out on the head of year post. An exasperated Sarah makes her biggest error by stating: 'It's only a game.' Paul is infuriated that Sarah cannot grasp his reluctance to loosen his grip on his ties with Arsenal and states that when friends talk about Arsenal they think of him. However, Paul reacts with anger with a sideswipe at Sarah saying: 'One day you'll learn to care about something you can't tick.'

Paul's need for a deep-rooted emotional pay-off reaches its peak during Arsenal's dramatic title decider with Liverpool at Anfield and Michael Thomas' last gasp goal both unites Paul and frees him from his past. In Paul's mind Arsenal's victory is a symbolic gesture showing him that he can also commit to Sarah and the deep-rooted anxiety associated with losing, and loss is, at that moment exorcised. Paul knows full well that life and football aren't inextricably linked and that Arsenal will not always win championships.

Symbolically, Arsenal's victory lifts years of uncertainty and self-doubt. Paul is freed up of his emotional responsibilities to Arsenal with someone real. He concludes in voice-over: 'My relationship with Arsenal changed… I have my own life again.' Victory celebrations on the streets outside the Highbury stadium convince Sarah too about the strength of feeling, of identity and belonging that Paul has felt through his support of Arsenal. In a real sense and in the party atmosphere of the street she too experiences first-hand how much belonging to this community means.

A game of two halves

While Paul is quite stubbornly clear about his identity and his allegiance to Arsenal, Sarah's own identity comes under some scrutiny during her relationship with Paul. During the course of their rather unromantic courtship Paul calls her 'uptight' and later on refers to her as 'Miss Jean Brodie' and finally, via the most unromantic, backhanded compliment in rom com history, likens her to Arsenal manager George Graham: 'mean, dour and unapproachable.' However, by this point, with Paul and Sarah linking up again, Sarah has been on her own journey of self-discovery.

Her victory comes during the fifth form party. Her invitation is unexpected but when a pupil makes a speech affirming all Sarah's qualities she experiences a modest but real sense of worth. Her dedication has paid off. In this respect Sarah mirrors Paul in her uncompromising attitude to her work ethic. The problem that remains for Sarah and Paul is whether these two opposite forces will match up.

One of the amusing things about their relationship is how consistently antagonistic they are to each other. Sarah first confides in her friend Jo that Paul is a 'Yobbo', while Paul is dismissive of her predictable stereotyping of him as a football yob despite conceding to his friend Paul in a typically understated British male way that Sarah 'is not unattractive.'

Sarah and Paul's confidants Jo and Steve make interesting foils. Jo comes across as a pre-Bridget Jones character – sometimes seen alone tucking into a tub of ice cream and warning Sarah about the missionary zeal in which men set out convert women to their hobbies. Steve and Paul could be characters out of the British sit-com *Men Behaving Badly* except that their obsession is football rather than women.

The course of love in *Fever Pitch* follows the usual trajectory of rom coms – boy meets girl, they engage in some type of foreplay, they fall in love, argue, separate, and then they get back for a happy ending. Sarah and Paul's foreplay consists of the following exchange: Paul: 'Do you mind if I smoke?' Sarah: 'Yes… But you can stay the night if you want.' Their passionate first embrace is followed by Sarah's practical entreaty: 'Not on the carpet, I can't afford it.'

It is unclear if Paul and Sarah ever declare love for one another – Paul rather flippantly says that they make a good team but he seems to save his passion for the North Bank at Highbury. The couple have plenty of arguments, mainly about football: 'We live our lives in years Paul, from January through to December,' says Sarah at one point when Paul insists on talking about seasons. But ultimately they too are drawn back together tenderly by the peculiar force of Arsenal's victory. By that time it appears that Paul has finally grown up, although the couple's happiness is achieved purely on Paul's terms and seemingly Sarah is prepared to compromise on everything.

About a boy

When Paul's pupil Robert tentatively asks if Paul will accompany him to the next Arsenal game Paul responds: 'Saturday is one day in the week when I'm not a responsible adult. A bit like you but not as sensible.' We see close-cut sequences of the young Paul screaming and shouting at a match next to the adult Paul acting in much the same way. Indeed, we see plenty of evidence of Paul holding on to his childlike manner – he jumps up and down with his school-team when they score, he plays Subbuteo football with his mate Steve and perhaps, worst of all, sets fire to a napkin in the Indian Restaurant when having a serious talk about Sarah's pregnancy. She is prompted to exclaim in mock horror: 'I've just been impregnated by a 12-year-old.'

Paradoxically, the 12-year-old Paul seems more mature than the 30-something Paul. The young boy joyfully absorbs all around him including the opinions of the old men in the café. The young Paul very quickly makes his own assessments of players and recycles them to his pleased father.

The interesting issue that Hornby's character raises is that clinging on to youthful ideas and dreams is not such a bad thing compared with the drudgery and predictability of adult life. Sarah counters the argument that she was merely a child when the extent of her ambitions where to marry David Cassidy and pass her mock O-levels, but now she has moved on and these dreams no longer apply.

Paul's ability to communicate to school children at their level makes him appear to be a suitable candidate for head of year and yet makes him so dismissive when the headmaster offers him the position. Nevertheless, the film likes to give the impression that Paul is a good teacher. His childlike state is abandoned in most of the scenes where he is with Sarah. Sarah's pregnancy acts as a late awakening of Paul's adult responsibilities (even though he seems to express them in a juvenile manner). His disastrous interview for the head of year post sees him dressed smartly in a suit and tie and his attempts to act like a responsible adult are undermined by a governor (a cameo from Stephen Rea) who keeps turning the subject back to football.

By the end of the film Paul seems prepared to loosen ties with his inner 12-year-old boy that has accompanied him on so many matches – but maybe not entirely.

It's a funny old game

The backdrop to the film is of course, football and *Fever Pitch* scores highly among other films about football by presenting the game from purely the spectator's point of view. David Evans' flashback shots of young Paul walking into Highbury Stadium past sizzling onions on hot dog stands, programme sellers, mixing with other fans, the surges in the stands, the agonies and ecstasies, are instantly familiar to those who used to go to football matches before the all-seater stadium was introduced. Evans perfectly captures the key moments that shaped young Paul's destiny – the first glimpse of the hallowed Highbury turf, the rugged atmosphere in the stadium and the spontaneous reactions of the crowd. Rather than turn to the action on the pitch, the camera is nearly always turned on the crowd.

Other footballing moments are brought via television highlights, video clips and the *Saint and Greasvie* show from the late 1980s. While the book covers the Hillsborough tragedy in greater depth – an event which changed how football supporters would be treated – the film also shows Sarah and Paul observing and reacting to footage of the tragedy.

In terms of live action the film goes to a non-league game between Royal Oak and Ongar where Paul and Steve discuss their footballing ambitions and the thrill of playing at a stadium with floodlights. The film also follows the adult Paul (complete in classic 1971 double-winning Arsenal top) as he coaches his school team to near-victory in a cup competition.

Football matches that Paul attends are presented on the screen in clicking old-style teleprinter fashion. However, the final championship decider is shown on the television (during an era when league matches were shown, free and live on terrestrial television).

Finally, there is the Highbury Stadium whose benign presence acts like an additional character in the film and a place where Paul and Sarah ultimately share a happy ending.

SCENE ANALYSIS - IT'S ALL UP FOR GRABS NOW

In order to tie up the outstanding issues, the climax of the film needs to effectively convey the drama of Arsenal's last gasp victory, contextualise what it means to Paul and Sarah, and then release the couple to meet in a double-edged celebration in the streets outside the Highbury stadium.

Arsenal's triumph over Liverpool is presented via the actual ITV television footage of the game including the authentic Brian Moore commentary and David Pleat's summaries.

The universal shared experience of witnessing an event at the same time via television is neatly emphasised by a set of cuts to those watching the match from the comfort of their homes.

Paul in his armchair and Steve on the sofa (wearing Arsenal replica tops) sit apart with their gaze on the bottom left hand corner of the screen. We then cut to Sarah (wearing a red dress with white dots – Arsenal colours) as she wanders from the garden to the room of her party and turns the TV on to check the score.

A shot of Arsenal player Michael Thomas running back after an Arsenal attack leads to a cut to Robert and his mum sitting side by side on the sofa (both wearing Arsenal shirts). Robert's mum's assertion that 'Mickey Thomas' is her favourite is met with a sharp 'shut up mum, he's useless" by Robert as the film affords the first of two sly winks to the audience who know the outcome of the game.

Our next shot comes as a surprise as we see Jo, legs curled up on the sofa, pick up her remote to turn the TV on. She sees some football action, changes channels to a film (a brief shot from *Mona Lisa*) before she flicks back to the football. This time the TV action is interrupted by the sound of a telephone.

We switch to Paul's mum sitting comfortably curled up on the sofa wearing an Arsenal scarf with her cat (wearing an Arsenal rosette). As she speaks on the phone to her daughter we see an Arsenal attack develop. We get Paul's mum's initial reaction as she sits forward as we see the footage of the ball going over the bar. This leads to a sequence of quick cuts showing other reactions – Paul and Steve groan; Robert holds his hands to his face while his mum's sighs; Jo reacts as if she wants Arsenal to win and then the sequence returns back to Paul and Steve where the camera remains.

When Paul suggests to Steve that they should go out the comfortable low angle that has held him and Steve in the frame swings from behind the TV to allow Paul to get up and put his jacket on. When half-time arrives we finally see a full shot of a television set with picture from Paul's perspective looking towards Steve.

Paul and Steve's next exchanges are caught with single close-up shots. First, Steve talks to Paul from his sofa almost over his shoulder and the shot then switches to Paul standing, sulking, coat on near the door ready to leave. This serves as the half-time interval as Paul claims he'll watch the next few minutes of the game. His constant agitation serves to bring the climax of the action towards boiling point.

The next clip from the match takes us to Arsenal's first goal. This time the cuts of celebrations go from Steve, to Paul, to Robert and mum standing, to Paul's mum (scaring the cat off the sofa).

When the TV footage and commentary conveniently tell us that there is quarter of an hour of the match remaining it serves as a cue to take us back to Sarah at the party as she has set herself up with a chair in front of the TV. Her fascination with the match is interrupted with her presentation where Sarah stands and gets her own personal moment of glory as her pupils acknowledge her worth. We then see Sarah's dash via taxi to get to Paul accompanied by the soundtrack party music, which has momentarily taken the place of the TV commentary.

While Sarah is happy and preparing to be reconciled, Paul is still agitated and he starts pacing slowly up and down as he drones on. At this point the camera slowly tracks his movements, while Steve remains on the sofa focusing on the TV in the corner.

The doorbell then cuts into the scene with one minute to go and cuts to the TV footage confirm this. As the buzzer goes off one more time Paul darts to the window and hurls abuse out of the window. The next cut reveals Sarah stranding arms folded at his doorway unimpressed by Paul's hysterical invective.

The device to get Paul out of the room (as he rushes downstairs to open the door having released that Sarah has arrived) is necessary as the climax of the match is orchestrated so that Paul, now has to make a mad rush back up the stairs to see the famous Michael Thomas goal.

Suddenly, Steve's face is caught as the camera zooms close in to catch his expression. Comically he screams Paul's name as the TV footage is slowed down (with the original commentary at normal speed) and we see a strange slow motion sequence of Paul returning to the room, shots of Steve still screaming and the ball going into the net.

Paul and Steve's ecstasy is caught in a big close-up, followed by a shot of Michael Thomas's unusual headstand goal celebration which allows for a final sequence of shots – Paul and Steve on the floor, Robert and his mum dancing in a circle, Jo shouting 'yes, yes, yes,' and Paul's mum standing on her sofa punching the air and waving her scarf. The jubilations are sharply contrasted to the next shot of a pensive Sarah walking on the streets outside the stadium.

The end of the match is shown from her point of view as we hear three peeps of the full-time whistle. At this point Sarah's gaze is on the entrance to the famous Highbury stadium where out of nowhere she conjures up a vision of a deliriously happy young Paul celebrating the victory. Sarah becomes enveloped by the celebrating fans and joins in with the celebrations eventually meeting up and embracing Paul, thereby allowing the film to execute a traditional rom com ending.

REACTION

The film opened to reasonable reviews in 1997 and performed quite well, in Britain notching up £766,121 at the box-office. British reviewers generally saw the film as a genial, low-budget movie with the feel of an extended TV drama.

In the end Fever Pitch possibly failed to completely convince its target audience. Those who had enjoyed Hornby's autobiographical account of the pains of being a football fan may have not appreciated the romantic interest in the film. Equally, football fans from around the country may not have been keen to see a film based on an Arsenal fan's delight in winning the league in 1989. Meanwhile, those wishing to see a romantic comedy starring Firth may have felt that there was too much emphasis on football and flashbacks.

For this reason the film did not fare well in the USA. Football was not rated very highly and so American audiences were unlikely to get too carried away with Paul's obsession with his team. Also, the low-key romance was not quite what American audiences were used to in their rom coms; there were too many English references and no token American acting presence to appeal on a wider global level.

Hornby (who appears in the film as a teacher of an opposing team) enjoyed greater success via his next book *High Fidelity*, but *Fever Pitch* did bring Hornby into contact with the producer Amanda Posey, who he eventually married. Hornby's book and, in part, the film also led to a mood swing in Britain about football and supporters. Supporters were no longer classed as 'yobbos' and programmes like Baddiel and Skinner's *Fantasy Football* helped endorse Hornby's more measured view of the football fan. The success of Euro 1996 in Britain built on the feel-good factor and football was heavily promoted as a family, middle-class pursuit with obligatory shots of young women in the crowd.

The British film industry too responded by hosting its own five-aside annual industry football tournament (the first one at Highbury) run by Stewart Till, then president of PolyGram Filmed Entertainment and supported by the likes of Sir Alan Parker.

CONCLUSION

At times it is possible to see traces of *High Fidelity* in *Fever Pitch*. At one point Paul questions: 'Life's shit because Arsenal are shit, or the other way round?' which echoes the opening statement in *High Fidelity*. Later on in Paul's flat Sarah is flipping through Paul's record collection and asks him if he has anything by Bread to which Paul snaps rather like Rob Gordon: 'Do I look like the sort of man who would have a Bread album?' Indeed, both films deal with issues of obsessive, self-indulgent, 30-something males with relationship problems. Both films hark back to activities that are no longer so prevalent – fewer people now go to record shops to buy vinyl records and in most top football grounds terraces have given way to seats, depriving fans of the close physical presence of other fans. Both films also rely on flashback scenes to explain the current actions of their lead characters.

Yet, these two films are worlds apart. Both aim to present local character-driven stories of love and obsession but the one set in America reached a far wider audience. Could *High Fidelity* have been made in North London, where the book was set? Hornby is on record as saying that it didn't matter where it was set but it seems significant that in 2005 his idea from *Fever Pitch* was transposed to America, into a baseball setting – the film appears on DVD under the title *Perfect Catch*.

The Farrelly Brothers version stars Drew Barrymore and Jimmy Fallon and is naturally based more on Hornby's screenplay for *Fever Pitch* than his original book, but this time it turns in an account of a baseball fan's obsession with the Boston Red Sox. The film did

OK in the States, bringing in more than $42m, but it only took £636,547 in the UK. In both cases the local outscored the global, but it is hard to imagine that this would have been the same case had football been America's number one national game and had the cast of the original *Fever Pitch* included an American actor or actress.

The setting of *High Fidelity* unintentionally exposed the frailty of the British film industry. Despite the creative impetus from Britain, the country with the most money and the greatest influence on the cinema world stage dominated. In truth, the notion that Britain could compete on its own terms without financial assistance from the US seemed like a case of wishful thinking.

FURTHER READING

Global Hollywood
Miller, Toby; Govil, Niti; McMurria, John; Maxwell, Richard (BFI, 2001)

Runaway World: How Globalisation Is Reshaping Our Lives
Giddens, Anthony (Routledge, 2002)

The Stats An overview of the film, television, video and DVD industries 1990-2003
(BFI National Library, BFI Information Services, 2006)

British Television, An Illustrated Guide, 2nd Edition
Vahimagi, Tise (Oxford University Press, 1996)

BFI Film and Television Handbook (BFI, editions from 1990–2005)

Selected reviews/articles/references

Puttnam Hails New Digital Age by Dunkley, Cathy
The Hollywood Reporter, (19 July, 1999)

British Video Association – www.bva.org.uk
Nick Hornby – www.nickhornby.co.uk

High Fidelity

Sight & Sound V.10 N.8 (1 Aug 2000) P.31-37. 47-48 by Medhurst, Andy
Empire N.134 (1 Aug) P.52 by Freer, Ian

Stylus Challenge by Anwar, Brett
Film Review N. 596 (1 Aug 2000) P.32

High Fidelity
Hornby, Nick (Penguin Books Ltd; New Ed edition, 2000)

DVD: *High Fidelity* (Buena Vista, 2001)

Fever Pitch

Sight & Sound V.7 N.4 (1 April) P.41-42 by MacNab, Geoffrey

Empire N.95 (1 May 1997) P.48 by Hamilton, Jake

Catch of the day by Jeffries, Neil
Empire N.94 (April 1997) P.68-42

Fever Pitch
Hornby, Nick (Penguin Books Ltd; New Ed edition, 2000)

4. FROM FLEA-PIT TO MULTIPLEX

Compared to the gloomy days of the 1980s when admissions sunk to an all-time low of 54 million in 1984, British cinemagoers were enticed back to see films during the 1990s and cinema admissions generally rose year-on-year, bar two minor blips in 1995 and 1998.

UK cinema admission (millions) 1990-2000

1990	97.37	1996	123.80
1991	100.29	1997	139.30
1992	103.64	1998	135.50
1993	114.36	1999	139.75
1994	123.53	2000	142.50
1995	114.56		

Source: Screen Digest/CAA/Nielsen EDI/Screen Finance
BFI Film and Television Handbook 2003

MULTIPLEX BOOM

It is a great irony that the British cinema exhibition sector was boosted by American and French companies who chose to invest in a programme of expansion via the creation of the multiplex, usually classed as cinemas with five or more screens and offering the public a bite to eat or a drink as well as a choice of film to view.

Another element that typified the multiplexes is that they had quite an even geographical spread. They tended to be situated either just out of big towns, making them accessible by car, or around shopping centres. In the relatively short period between April 1990 and March 1991 multiplexes sprung up in Edinburgh (12 screens, UCI), York (12 screens, Warner Brothers), Preston (10 screens, UCI), Basingstoke (10 screens, Warner Brothers), Gloucester (six screens, MGM Cinemas), Chester (six screens, MGM), Ipswich (five screens, Rank), and London Mezzanine (five screens, Rank).

As a result of the expansion many independent cinemas closed down, but this did not lead to a downturn in the number of sites and screens. Indeed, the influx and steady growth of multiplexes during the 1990s stimulated an interest in cinema in the UK and made smaller chains and independents fight hard to stay afloat.

Clearly, the rise in cinema-going had a direct correlation to the number of sites and screens available to people throughout the country.

Multiplex sites and screens 1990-2000

Year	Multiplex sites	Screens
1990	41	395
1991	57	523
1992	65	575
1993	70	625
1994	77	687
1995	82	723
1996	96	862
1997	115	1,074
1998	150	1,341
1999	177	1,606
2000	209	1,863

Source: Screen Finance/ X25 Partnership/ Dodona Research
The Stats, BFI Information Services

In 1990, the rapid building programme of multiplexes had added 40 sites from the first UK multiplex established at The Point, Milton Keynes in 1985. This represented 5 per cent of the 737 cinema sites in the UK. Significantly, the 41 sites accounted for 22 per cent of the 1,685 screens. Ten years later the number of multiplex sites had risen to 209, representing 30 per cent of all sites in the UK, while the number of multiplex screens now accounted for a whopping 63 per cent of all screens. The steady rise in the multiplex building programme resulted in a fall of 51 sites in the UK from 737 in 1990 to 686 in 2000. But the building programme showed little sign of abating, so much so that in June 2000 a 30-screen Warner Village Cinema opened at StarCity in Birmingham, inspiring the creation of a new term for the exhibition sector – the megaplex.

UK Sites and Screens 1990-2000

Year	Total sites	Total screens
1990	737	1,685
1991	724	1,789
1992	735	1,845
1993	723	1,890
1994	734	1,969
1995	743	2,019

1996	742	2,166
1997	747	2,383
1998	759	2,564
1999	692	2,758
2000	686	2,954

Source: Screen Finance/Dodona Research

The Stats, BFI Information Services

Beyond the number crunching, the decade saw significant blockbusters and family-orientated fare to keep the growing cinema audience coming back for more. It is no surprise that Hollywood blockbusters dominated with *Titanic* (USA, 1997) Dir James Cameron, combining a tragic love story, Leonardo Di Caprio, Kate Winslet and stunning special effects to become the top box-office attraction of the decade. But the pleasing aspect from a British point of view is the appearance of two British films in the top films list, with *The Full Monty*, proudly holding its own as the top British film of the decade.

Top Films at the UK box-office 1990-2000

	Film	Distributor	Box Office (£)
1990	*Ghost* (USA)	UIP	17.3
1991	*Robin Hood Prince of Thieves* (USA)	Warner Brothers US	20.1
1992	*Basic Instinct* (USA/France)	Guild	15.4
1993	*Jurassic Park* (USA)	UIP	46.5
1994	*Four Weddings and a Funeral* (UK/USA)	Rank	27.7
1995	*Batman Forever* (USA)	Warner Brothers	20.0
1996	*Independence Day* (USA)	Twentieth Century Fox	37.0
1997	*The Full Monty* (UK/USA)	Twentieth Century Fox	46.2
1998	*Titanic* (USA)	Twentieth Century Fox	68.9
1999	*Star Wars Episode 1: The Phantom Menace* (USA)	Twentieth Century Fox	50.9
2000	*Toy Story 2* (USA)	Buena Vista	43.4

Source: *The Stats, BFI Information Services*

The growth in cinema admissions and the type of film now available benefited the young. The key audience aged between 15 and 24 warmed to the new cinema environments. By the late 1990s only 12 per cent of the over-35 age went to the cinema once a month or more compared with 58 per cent of the 15-24 age group. This was galling for the over 35s who made up 52 per cent of the population at the time, but might have been put off the cinema after decades of attending flea-pits.

Furthermore, not content with the rise in cinema attendances in Britain, some media commentators, usually representing the over-35 brigade, began to bemoan the lack of choice that the new cinema experience was offering the viewer. There was even a strange distinction coined – popcorn and carrot cake – between those who enjoyed popular films at their local cinemas and those who preferred art house films. The carrot cake brigade had hoped that some screens might be put aside for niche cinema to show the odd foreign language film or classic.

Indeed, City Screen, which ran the Picturehouse chain of independent cinemas was formed in 1989 as an antidote to the mass-market appeal of the multiplex cinema. With an emphasis on local communities and championing independent films, its first cinema was the Phoenix in Oxford. In 1992 Clapham Picturehouse opened and City Screen continued a steady progression of new builds and acquisitions targeting cities with large student populations such as Cambridge, London, Brighton and York.

CINEMA CHAINS

Hand in hand with the growth of more sites and screens came a bewildering number of changes, mergers and takeover bids within the major cinema chains as the rise in cinema audiences made the UK an attractive market. Overseas operators such as Hoyts in Australia and Ster Century in South Africa were also looking towards the burgeoning UK market.

Odeon

The UK's dominant chain during the 1990s was the Odeon group. Oscar Deutsch, who was born in Birmingham to Hungarian Jewish parents, founded Odeon cinemas in the UK in 1928. It soon grew to become the foremost chain in the UK with publicists claiming convincingly that the name derived from the motto: 'Oscar Deutsch Entertains Our Nation.' The chain had a long association with the Rank organisation during a period of the 1930s and 1940s when Britain had something resembling an integrated film industry. By the time of Deutsch's death in 1941, 258 cinemas had been established, many noted for their spectacular interiors and art-deco look. Despite boasting the largest cinema in UK, The Odeon Leicester Square, which still hosts many of London's West End film premieres, other single Odeon cinemas around the country faced closures during the 1970s and 1980s, many converted into bingo halls. Nevertheless, Odeon Cinemas remained dominant with more than 415 screens and 79 sites by the end of 1999. Since the turn of the century the company was sold first to Cinven, a European private equity firm, in 2000, which also picked up the ABC chain. Eventually Terra Firma purchased it and merged it with United Cinemas International to establish itself as Europe's most prominent chain.

ABC

In the 1940s Associated British Cinemas (ABC) was second only to the Odeon chain in the UK. The cinema circuit was briefly revived in the 1990s. First in the early 1990s it was sold to MGM before being taken on by Cinven. In 1996, it was the largest chain in Britain in terms of sites, numbering 92. By the end of the decade a further merger with Odeon cinemas signalled its end.

Virgin Cinemas

By the mid-1980s Virgin Cinemas had landed MGM, Britain's biggest chain of cinemas, which boasted 142 sites and 411 screens in the UK in 1990. However, only a third of the cinemas were multi-screen, which was where the majority of the profits came from. Four years after acquiring MGM cinema chain for £195m, Virgin struck up a deal with UGC, which was worth £215.

UGC

French-owned company UGC entered the UK, at the end of the 1990s, specialising in multiplex cinemas. By the end of the decade the company ran 36 sites with a total of 312 screens. In 1999 the group acquired Virgin Cinemas before itself being taken over a year later to become part of the Cineworld Group.

Cine-UK

New York born Steve Wiener set up Cine-UK having worked in the early part of the 1990s for Warner Brothers. Initially, its impact on the UK market was slow with 13 sites and 146 screens. However, the enterprise would eventually lead to the acquisition of French Group UGC in 2004 and the combined group traded under the term Cineworld. The first Cineworld was opened in Stevenage in July 1996 and consisted of 12 screens.

Showcase

In the 1990s National Amusements Inc. based in Dedham, Massachusetts, was the world's leading exhibitor and established its foothold in the UK in the late 1980s with its Showcase stable of cinemas. By 1999, Showcase cinemas accounted for 16 sites with 221 screens.

UCI

UCI was a chain made up of a partnership between Paramount Pictures and Universal Studios and opened the first multiplex in the UK in 1985. Its level of expansion in the UK remained modest during the 1990s with 21 sites in 1990, rising gradually to 31 in 1990. Among those were the Empire and the Plaza in London's West End. By 2004, Terra Firma, which had also acquired the Odeon chain, took it over.

Warner Village

American-owned Warner Village's expansion into the UK's exhibition market saw its sites rise from five in 1990 to 28 in 1999, with 200 screens. In 2003, SBC International Cinemas acquired it and immediately rebranded the chain as Vue.

Small chains and independents

The remainder of the exhibition sector in the UK was made up of small chains such as Apollo Cinemas, which had 14 cinemas by the end of the decade, Caledonian Cinemas in Scotland, and Hollywood cinemas, which operated in East Anglia. The rest of the country was made up of a large sector of standalone theatres that saw their cumulative sites dwindle from 437 in 1994 to 376 in 1999, despite boasting 794 screens by the end of the decade.

BUMS ON SEATS

The bottom line, so to speak, for exhibitors was bums on seats and multiplexes were not averse to offering up more than one of their screens to a particularly popular film such as *Titanic*. That struck a cautionary note, however, when the slight dip in admissions in the UK was partly blamed on the poor crop of blockbusters coming from Hollywood. In the end audiences don't mind being dictated to provided they are entertained.

There were naturally misgivings. As early as 1993 the Monopolies and Mergers Commission looked at the sometimes cosy relationship between some distributors and the major chains, in this case the MGM circuit. However, within a couple of years the marketplace had become quite competitive with the growth of UCI, Showcase, Warner and Virgin Cinemas taking over from MGM.

There was also a growing concern that the UK cinema market was being homogenised by the pervading march of Hollywood blockbusters. There were increasing calls for multiplexes to set aside screens for a wider range of cinema, including the growing stack of British-made films that ironically were struggling to get released having struggled to be made in the first place.

Luckily, signs that some cinema operators were seizing opportunities to set aside some screens came via Asian films, or Bollywood films, which found their way onto cinema screens during the latter part of the 1990s where there were significant Asian populations.

The fate of British films, particularly those with American backers, often lay in the hands of American audiences where thumbs up meant that exhibitors might be persuaded by distributors to show the film on the few screens not showing *Titanic*. In the mid-1990s, two similar British films, both successful (one phenomenally so), both with American backing and both with quirky British themes *The Full Monty* and *Brassed Off* would take different routes to their box-office success. *The Full Monty*, released on 224 screens, premiered in America and, benefiting from its US reception, encouraged exhibitors to book it in Britain. Meanwhile, *Brassed Off*, released on 203 screens, premiered in Britain before its release in America and arguably had to work harder to earn its share of the box-office spoils.

The Full Monty (1997) (UK/USA) UK Cert 15

Director: Peter Cattaneo

Screenplay: Simon Beaufoy

Producer: Uberto Pasolini,

Production companies: Twentieth Century Fox Film Corporation; Redwave Films

Production start date: 29/04/1996 **Budget:** £2.2m (estimated)

Distributor: Twentieth Century Fox **UK Release date:** 29 August 1997

UK Box Office: £52,232,058 **USA Box Office:** $45.9m

Worldwide Box Office: $211m

Remarkably, *The Full Monty*, which was made on a modest budget of £2.2m, became the most successful British film in the 1990s at the UK box-office, finishing with receipts of £52m at home and banking $211m worldwide. Its success coincided with a steady upsurge in cinema attendances in the UK.

Over a decade on *The Full Monty* remains one of the most commercially successful British films of all time with worldwide box-office receipts of more than £160m. What is amazing about its clout is that it achieved it without massive marketing, relying instead on the slow-burn effect that comes from word of mouth. Indeed, no one in the British press, which gave the film generally good reviews on its release, could forsee it becoming such a hit. Trade magazine Empire only carried a review at first, but picked up more on the film when it became a box-office phenomena.

Its initial release in the UK did not suggest that it would be anything other than a modest low-budget British film. However, the film owed much to its American backer Fox Searchlight whose marketing seemed to strike a peculiar chord with American audiences. Over time, the build-up in interest meant that British audiences flocked to see this unlikely comedy featuring unemployed steel workers in Sheffield who become male strippers to earn some extra cash.

Yet *The Full Monty* deserves its place at the top table of British films in the 1990s since it punches above its weight in some of the themes and issues that it explores – unemployment, male emasculation, gender roles and urban decay.

On closer examination *The Full Monty* shows traces of other British film traditions – the ensemble cast is reminiscent of Ealing comedies, the slightly bawdy subject matter would not seem out of place in a Carry On film, and the gloomy social commentary and northern setting, albeit sugar sweetened, is a reminder of British social realism films of the 1960s. However, the film is set in the mid-1980s at a time when Margaret Thatcher's government was shutting down Britain's traditional industrial base and espousing the virtues of free market economies and individualism. Without ever mentioning politics, *The Full Monty* provides a portrait of the consequences of Thatcherism in industrialised communities – unemployment, alienation and a shifting of traditional working class values and roles. The film also serves as an example of a typically British film from 1990s at its very best.

SYNOPSIS

Gaz and Dave, two unemployed steelworkers in Sheffield, and Gaz's son Nathan are returning from an unsuccessful mission to pinch steel girders from the disused steelworks. They pass the local working men's club, which is holding a women's night only featuring the Chippendales, an all-male striptease troupe.

Gaz needs to earn cash when he learns that ex-wife Mandy has slapped a court order on him preventing access to his son for lack of maintenance payments amounting to £700. He considers setting up a male striptease troupe of his own.

Gradually, with Dave's reluctant support, they recruit men: the hapless suicidal Lomper; their former foreman Gerald whose job interview they attempt to sabotage; a slightly older man called Horse who has some good dance moves; and the younger Guy who cannot dance but is exceptionally well-endowed.

Dave becomes increasingly self-conscious about his body size. His anxiety is coupled with a loss of self-esteem, which his loving wife Jean notices but is unable to help him with.

Meanwhile, Gaz's desperation to find £100 deposit for a venue leads him to reluctantly take Nathan's savings when Nathan insists. Gaz proceeds to up the ante by announcing to some women on the street that the show will be better than the Chippendales because the performers will go 'the full monty'.

During an 'undress' rehearsal in front of Horse's family at the steelworkers a policeman raids the premises. The raid brings unexpected publicity to the men and ticket sales soar. Dave confesses to Jean what he has been up to but breaks down, only to find Jean reassuring him.

With Dave returning for the big night it is Gaz's turn to have last minute nerves. His final impetus to go on stage is the knowledge that Mandy is in the audience without her new partner Terry. The men perform their act to an ecstatic audience.

HOW IT WAS MADE

It is unclear where the original idea for the story came from. Co-producer Paul Bucknor lay claim to it via his male stripper script called Satisfaction but the writers of a play from 1987 called *Ladies Night* claimed in a court case that their work had had been plagiarised. What is certain is that the driving force behind *The Full Monty* was Italian-born producer Uberto Pasolini, who had cut his teeth in the film business in the 1980s by working on *The Mission*, and producing the US comedy *Palookaville* (USA, 1995), by which time he had formed his own production company in Britain called Redwave Films. Impressed by Ken Loach's film *Raining Stones* (UK, 1993), Pasolini wanted to achieve an ensemble comedy, which tapped into Loach's social commentary sensibilities.

Pasolini drafted in promising writer Simon Beaufoy, who was from West Yorkshire and had graduated from the Bournemouth Film School, to write an original script. Director Peter Cattaneo was mainly directing TV programmes such as *Teenage Health Freak* (Channel 4) when he came to Pasolini's attention in a programme from the Love Bites series on BBC2 in 1995 called *Loved Up*.

Pasolini secured only development funding from Channel 4. His big break came when he approached Fox Searchlight, the low-budget film distribution division of 20th Century Fox, with the script. The company agreed to co-produce the film and crucially allowed Pasolini and his team a great deal of creative freedom.

As with many low-budget British films, the cast was made up of actors who were relatively unknown and would be character-driven. The exception was Robert Carlyle, who was already notching up a decent CV through films like *Riff Raff*, (UK, 1991), *Trainspotting*, and *Carla's Song* (UK/Germany/Spain, 1996), plus TV appearances in *Cracker* (ITV) and the series *Hamish MacBeth* (BBC). Carlyle had also appeared in *Priest* (UK, 1994), which featured Tom Wilkinson, Paul Barber and Lesley Sharp.

It was filmed on location in and around the city of Sheffield. Most interesting was that the climax when the men revealed all wasn't going to appear in the original draft. It was shot in one take on the insistence of the actors. The tangible excitement generated in the audience, which featured 400 extras, was real enough and led to the believable, spontaneous scene.

The film required some additional footage since it appeared short and so there are some scenes, notably the men playing football, where Carlyle does not appear since he was contracted to film elsewhere. Nevertheless, the film was finally unzipped to an unsuspecting world at the influential Sundance Film Festival in American in January 1997 before its UK release in August 1997.

KEY ISSUES

At its heart *The Full Monty* is a gentle, even lightweight comedy. But brooding beneath the surface is something quite serious. Thatcherism succeeded in reviving the British economy but it also produced dire social consequences. Industrial production fell, while unemployment tripled during her three terms in office. In 1997 when *The Full Monty* was made Britain had the highest childhood-poverty rate in Europe. Working class communities were in crisis as they came to terms with the new world order.

It's a man's world

The opening scene of the film shows Gaz, Dave and Nathan trying to salvage a girder from the ruins of their closed down steelworks. Perhaps symbolically, the unemployed men in *The Full Monty* spend their time trying to salvage some sort of dignity in a world that no longer seems to require their services. Where once the steel works gave men their livelihoods and a common bond, now the job club and the dole queue unite them.

Of all the male characters Gerald, the former foreman, attempts to maintain his traditional male role as breadwinner. Indeed, we see him apply for, being interviewed and landing a job. His journey appears straightforward other than the fact that he has been unemployed for six months and cannot bring himself to tell his wife. He is crushed when it looks like he has blown the interview and crest fallen when the bailiffs come in and his wife learns the truth. Ironically, her desire for material goods and holidays is not as great as her desire for the truth.

Nevertheless, Gerald maintains his managerial role of Gaz's striptease group by teaching them to dance, drilling them and instilling discipline. His ability to manage comes naturally.

Gaz is the most agitated and driven character. He philosophically announces that: 'Men are dinosaurs' and 'A few more years, and men won't exist,' and constantly challenges the social order by refusing to take on what he regards as menial jobs. We learn later that he has served time in prison and continues to have an amoral attitude to petty crime, encouraging Dave to steal the *Flashdance* video and later a black suit for Lomper's mother's funeral. However, Gaz is also driven by his desire to maintain his relationship with his son Nathan and prove to his ex-wife Mandy that he is worth something after all. Nathan gives Gaz his reaffirmation by saying that it was he who made the show happen. Indeed, Gaz demonstrates not only drive and vision but leadership qualities. Ironically, his entrepreneurial zeal and free market economy success via the male striptease scheme shows him taking on rather than embracing the core of Thatcherism. At one point he coaxes his fellow workers by dangling the carrot in front of them by saying: 'Folks don't laugh so loud when you've a grand in your back pocket.'

Dave's journey into salvaging his pride is harder. His loss of self-confidence and self-esteem is shown in every scene with his wife Jean. His depression means that he has no sex drive and his poor self-image makes him fearful that Jean will leave him. Throughout the film he is labelled as 'a fat bastard', which in normal working circumstances he could laugh off. However, the idea of stripping merely heightens his anxieties and fears. He wants to earn money and show his worth but he cannot. He quits the strip group and takes on the job as a security guard in the store. But quite clearly this does not help his self-esteem. Dave's crisis is resolved when Jean challenges him whether he is having an affair. 'Who would want to see this?' to which Jean lovingly replies: 'I would,' which restores Dave's confidence.

Horse's character is interesting since he is an unemployed black man (with a dodgy hip) who is not stigmatised due to the colour of his skin. Indeed, black stereotypes of natural rhythm and being well-endowed are wheeled out for comic effect. Another more positive stereotype of close-knit black families is introduced where female members of Horse's family, including his grandmother and his cousin, are brought in to be the audience.

At the bottom of the pile is Lomper, who ironically has a job as a security guard and even plays in the works band. He also lives at home with his elderly mother, appears to be a social misfit, a loner and this leads him to become suicidal. Lomper is also gay but possibly not aware of this fact. When Gaz and Dave offer him friendship he gains a new sense of purpose and confidence. From this moment he gets a new lease of life and ultimately finds happiness and release in his relationship with Guy.

Subtly or otherwise, the male make up of the group takes quite a diverse cut through a cross section of British society in terms of race, colour and sexuality. But what unifies the men is a desire to get their self-respect back and earn some money in the meantime.

The most mature male character in the film appears to be Gaz's son Nathan. Not only does he stump up the money to put a deposit down on the hall where the show will take place, he also acts as Gaz's conscience. Nathan is the one who gives Gaz his self-belief and crucially gives him a final talking to when Gaz's resolve wobbles just before the show begins. He disapproves of Gaz's wreckless schemes and craves a proper relationship with his father. Economically, Gaz cannot provide his son with enough money to watch Sheffield United play Manchester United, but emotionally Gaz is driven to maintain contact with his son.

As for the other men, Gaz and Dave in particular display childish qualities, most notably when being playing with the gnomes during Gerald's interview. Perhaps one of the most charming scenes is when the men are seen in training on the outskirts of Sheffield and take part in a kick-about where not only do they bond, they become like little boys again – joyful and carefree.

A woman's place is…?

While the men in the film struggle to find their new roles in society, the same cannot be said for the women. Admittedly, they are secondary characters but all of them exude confidence and a sense of pragmatic realism sadly lacking in their male counterparts. In a film that turns the feminist notion of the 'male gaze' on its head, the female characters are not viewed as sex objects (give or take Gaz and Dave's points scoring system of women who pass them by) and any ogling comes from them.

The scene in the Working Man's club when Gaz and Nathan witness the women's reaction to the Chippendales has some Orwellian overtones from *Animal Farm*. Here is ladies only night where women appear as bawdy as the men they are replacing.

Mandy, Gaz's wife, is economically stable and appears to have a senior job in the factory where she works. We see that she has a good lifestyle and, lives in a good house with a new car and a partner who also appears to be affluent. She seems exasperated by Gaz's lack of responsibility and general immature attitude to work. We do not learn whether Gaz wins Mandy back by the end of the film, but there is an implication that she is pleased that Gaz has finally made an effort and achieved something.

Dave's wife Jean also works in the store and so is the breadwinner in their household. Her problem is to convince Dave that she loves him for who he is rather than what he does. However, what is evident is that the two have a breakdown in communications because it is only when Dave is forced to admit that he was part of Gaz's plan that their relationship is resolved. Dave immediately has his confidence restored.

A breakdown in communication leads to an ultimate breakdown in the marriage of Gerald and Linda. They represent a traditional working couple with Gerald as breadwinner and his wife as housewife. Linda reveals a materialistic and consumer-driven zeal that is perhaps ahead of its time. Sadly, their marriage does not appear to have a happy ending.

The lunchbox has landed

Inevitably, a film about amateur male strippers is bound to bring up issues surrounding the body. Gaz and Dave are seen on a couple of occasions rating a passing woman out of 10 but otherwise the attentions are turned firmly at the male body. And the men all have occasion to comment unfavourably at each other's bodies. This issue is best illustrated in the exchange when the lads are round Gerald's house to use his sun-bed and Lomper is admiring a woman in a magazine.

> Dave: I mean, what if next Friday 400 women turn 'round and say 'He's too fat, he's too old and he's a pigeon-chested little tosser.' What happens then, eh?
>
> Horse: They wouldn't say that, would they?
>
> Dave: Why not? He's just said her tits are too big.
>
> Lomper: That's different. We're... blokes.
>
> Dave: Yeah, and?

Dave is the male character who suffers most from his slightly rotund appearance. At one point Gerald exclaims: 'Fat is a feminist issue.' to which Dave replies: 'What's that supposed to mean?' For Dave, being overweight is a universal issue, which he also quite wrongly associates with a lack of sex appeal to his wife, or anyone else for that matter.

Of the strippers Guy has the most stereotypically perfect body. He is muscular but toned and his audition illicits Gaz's observation 'Gentlemen, the lunchbox has landed.' Ironically, Guy who turns out to be gay, falls for the rather pale and weedy looking Lomper.

The film challenges preconceived views of sexual attractiveness and basically rubbishes them. The ultimate irony is that far from degrading the men as they perform their perfectly choreographed routine, it actually empowers them.

You've got to laugh

The Full Monty tackles serious issues but it sets out with a gentle, good-hearted, sense of humour. The script is exceptionally tight and littered with one-liners and witty rejoinders.

The affection the characters show for each other rubs off on the audience and makes us care more for them.

Lomper's attempted suicide could, in another film, be bleak and depressing. In *The Full Monty* Dave shoves an ungrateful Lomper back into his carbon-fumed car before the scene cuts to a theoretical debate on the best way to commit suicide – drowning, jumping of a high place, having a mate smash a car into you. In this sequence Lomper reveals in deadpan the reasons why he can't achieve any of these – he can't swim, he's afraid of heights and he has no mates. The joke may not be hilarious but it enables Gaz and Dave to adopt Lomper as their new mate.

There are visually funny jokes featuring the men stripping – Gaz's first attempt to show his style is cut short to the sound of a record being hastily removed as his shirt gets caught and the scene where the men strip to their varied collection of undies is visually amusing and made more so when the bailiffs beat a hasty retreat having encountered the semi-naked men.

There are plenty of quirky moments such as the Arsenal off-side trap routine when the men are first seen trying to work out their routine, Dave's assessment of the welding abilities of the actress Jennifer Beals in *Flashdance* (1983) and the gnome provocation at Gerald's interview.

Perhaps the most famous comic scene, the *Hot Stuff* dole queue dance, is the one that is most stage managed but it works in moving the story along by telling the audience that the training is beginning to work and the men are up for the challenge. Throughout the film negative issues are rarely allowed to fester. They are replaced by positive alternatives or caught short with some humour, such as Dave sitting in his shed wrapping his stomach with cling-film while eating a chocolate bar.

By the end the audience gets served up with a Hollywood style happy ending with the exuberant performance, which in itself is a comic treat down to the choice of Tom Jones's *You can leave your hat on*.

SCENE ANALYSIS – YOU CAN LEAVE YOUR HAT ON

The first thing to note about the finale is the perfect choice of song – Randy Newman's *You Can Leave Your Hat On* – and the equally perfect choice of singer, Tom Jones, who recorded it especially for the film and delivers it with great machismo. On its own the tune is sexy, intimate and erotic with a male singer getting his female partner to take their clothes off (and of course leave their hat on). In the context of *The Full Monty* the tune retains its sexy theme but the eroticism is diminished somewhat by the gender role reversal as the men take their jackets off instead of a dress. The hat is obviously a key motif in the song. Very playfully the song instructs: 'You can leave your hat on,' when in fact the hat not only comes flying off but gives the audience its full monty moment.

The costume the men wear is similar to Dave's security guard uniform. Perhaps their striptease symbolically releases them from having to take on any job, in the reluctant way Dave worked as security guard, and quite literally liberates them by shedding the constraints of a uniform and revealing their manhood.

Another feature of the scene is the live audience in the club, whose actions and wild cheers are genuine. The camera often looks from the perspective of the stage or a particular dancer to the audience, sometimes picking out a significant group of women, sometimes just getting a reaction as another item of clothing is removed. As the dance unfolds the film subtly ties up the loose ends by including reactions shots of other characters linked to those on stage.

As the men enter the stage one by one and line up we get to see several shots from the point of view of the audience looking up at the stage – one from the centre of the stage capturing all the men in a row, and one from looking from the left of the stage slightly closer up, giving a mid-shot of the men starting their routine, and a third shot slightly to the right that moves towards the centre. A closer shot from the right hand side cuts to a shot of Mandy clapping her hands surveying the men. This enables a connection to be made to Gaz who, among the commotion, shares a significant scene with Nathan in the dressing room (with the sound of cheers and music in the background). Nathan's orders to Gaz to go on stage allows the troupe to become complete again.

As Gaz bounces on to the stage in front of his mates to additional applause the connection with Mandy is restablished with a shot of her enthusiastically cheering his arrival and someone from the audience shouting: 'Come on Gaz.' There follow two quick shots showing first Dave with his thumbs up and then Gaz acknowledging the gesture. A little later on a similar couple of shots has Nathan swaying and a cut to Gaz acknowledging him.

In terms of some of the dance steps performed there is a nod to Gerald's ballroom dancing movements as at one stage Gaz and Dave shimmy back to back towards the centre of stage. The next cut goes to a table in the club where a group of women, including Linda, are laughing at the spectacle. As the men twirl and toss their ties into the audience we get shots of the audience catching them including one of Horse's family. This is followed by an odd shot of Lomper's brass band situated at the back of the hall apparently playing in time with the music as one of the songs distinctive brass stabs is heard and the shot cuts to Lomper looking over and back to the band giving him the thumbs up.

Guy, who is clearly enjoying the dance, gets to do a leap and a slide across the stage and seductively starts to take his shirt off, commanding the centre of the stage. This is sharply contrasted with a shot of Dave's brief moment of doubt before he takes off his shirt. His personal moment of triumph is reaffirmed with the next shot back to Linda's table and their cheers. Again we hear someone shout: 'Come on Dave'.

While the shots of the enthusiastic audience are intercut with the men continuing their routine, the camera picks up a mid-shot from behind Guy's back as he is about to throw his shirt off to three figures of unsmiling policemen, who are nevertheless watching the show rather incredulously. This allows another joke within the routine at the expense of the police as the costumes the dancers have been wearing have been similar to police uniforms.

By the time the dancers are down to their red thongs and hats we are offered another shot from the audience's perspective of the whole stage, but this time there is a single silhouetted woman dancing, not quite obstructing our view of the action, but perhaps suggesting something might occur soon.

By the time the thongs come off and the hats cover the dancer's private parts the crowd is reaching a fever pitch, chanting 'Off, off, off' and the shots into the audience reflect the growing frenzy. It is noticeable throughout the whole sequence that not only is the audience smiling but the actors too are captured reacting to the commotion.

One last tease is left for the audience as the men (their buttocks bared for all to see) are seen in formation. A close-up shot of Linda shows her momentarily hiding her face with Dave's shirt, which she has caught, almost daring us to believe that the men will go the whole way. The next cut gives us a back view to the men as they wander to the centre of the stage. The 'will they, won't they' moment is clearly not an issue as a shot of two women shouting: 'Off!' is captured before the men execute one last tease as they sway momentarily together with their hats in front of their genitals. A shot of Gaz, Horse and Lomper shows them with smirks on their faces as they swing round with buttocks facing the audience in a move that brings the men into a formation. Then, just as the last notes of the tune are played, we get a long shot from behind the stage with the six men in the centre of the frame and the whole audience visible in the background.

The issue of whether to show their genitals are not is resolved as the men turn to face the audience and as the music stops they fling their hats in to the audience and are caught in freeze frame, with a flashbulb going off in between Dave's buttocks. As the men are in their moment of glory Tom Jones signs off with an extended cry of 'You can leave your hat on.'

REACTION

Nobody predicted that the success of *The Full Monty* would be down to word of mouth recommendations. This was one of those a rare occasions when an audience dictates to the distributors and producers on the amount of coverage that the film should have.

Anne Dudley picked up an Academy Award in 1998 for Best Music, Original Musical or Comedy Score and the film's profile was further boosted with nominations for Best Director, Best Picture and Best Original Screenplay. Other awards included BAFTAs for Best Film, Best Performance by an Actor in a Leading Role (Robert Carlyle) and Supporting Role (Tom Wilkinson). Many other awards came, including The London Critics Circle giving British Newcomer of the Year Awards to Peter Cattaneo, Producer award to Uberto Pasolini and British Screenwriter of the Year to Simon Beaufoy as well as another award to Carlyle.

It has to be said that the critics liked the film but generally didn't see anything beyond a well-construct low-budget feel-good, British comedy. Once it had built up some momentum in America the British press was delighted to support the success.

Perhaps the essence of the film could be summed up by the industry journal *Variety*: 'It's one of those rare pics, however, where the bigness and generosity of the characters make the smallness of the budget unimportant.'

The film even gained a royal seal of approval when in 1998 Prince Charles re-enacted the dole queue dance much to the delight of the press.

The film inspired a Broadway musical of the same name set in America and it is in America that the profits of the film nestled. For while *The Full Monty* is undoubtedly a successful British movie in its creative and artistic output, and while it is also true that British cinemas enjoyed the benefits of box-office success, financially the real winner was Fox Searchlight, handsomely rewarded for taking a chance.

Brassed Off (1996) (UK/USA) UK Cert 15

Director: Mark Herman

Screenplay: Mark Herman

Producer: Steve Abbott

Production companies: Channel Four Television Corporation; Prominent Features;, Miramax Films

Production start date: 1996 **Budget:** £2.53m (estimated)

Distributor: Film Four Distributors **UK Release date:** 01 November 1996

UK Box Office: £3,388,319 **USA Box Office:** $2.5m

Worldwide Box Office: n/a

Rather like *The Full Monty* the title of *Brassed Off* suggests that it is going to be a quirky British comedy. This time the action shifts from Sheffield to South Yorkshire, the industry under threat is coal mining, and the thing that unites the men is the local colliery brass band. It is easy to tick the boxes comparing the similar themes in both these films – Thatcherism, unemployment, a northern community under threat, disillusioned men, marital breakdown or unrest, strong women, brass bands, bailiffs, suicide attempts, unusual alternative means of earning money (stripping and children's entertainer) and a rousing finale. However, whereas *The Full Monty* steers clear of overt political comment in favour of light humour, *Brassed Off* offers a gritty, harsh commentary on the legacy of Thatcher's impact on traditional working class industries. There is humour and even a sentimental underbelly to *Brassed Off*, but it is also uncompromising in its attack on the Conservative policies of the mid-1980. The twist in this tail comes from the colliery brass band, which ultimately gives hope to the men and their community and proves that there are nobler things than financial imperatives. Though bloodied, the spirit of the unemployed miners, rather like those of their steelworker counterparts in *The Full Monty*, is not broken.

SYNOPSIS

Set in the early 1990s in the coal-mining town of Grimley, the community braces itself for possible pit closure. Danny a retired miner, proudly runs the colliery brass band. A tense rehearsal is unexpectedly interrupted with the arrival of Gloria, a young woman who not only grew up in Grimley but is the daughter of Arthur Mullins who once ran the band.

Her playing earns the respect of the all-male band members. The youngest, Andy, is unsettled since he had a fling with Gloria when they were both younger. The two re-establish their relationship.

The miners are asked to ballot on whether to accept a generous redundancy package. After a shambolic, drunken display the band agrees to keep going, which means taking part in the semi-finals of a national competition, while the pit remains open. Danny is relieved and urges his debt-ridden son Phil to buy a new trombone. He earns some money by donning his Mr Chuckles clown's uniform and puts a down payment on a new trombone, but unsuccessfully lies to his wife Sandra about it. The bailiffs arrive and Sandra leaves, taking the children with her.

Gloria's connections to the management team are discovered and she is ostracised although she still takes part in the band. The band wins its semi-final but then learns the result of the ballot – four to one in favour of redundancy. As the bands reflect on the devastating news Danny collapses in the street and is rushed to hospital.

In despair Phil, in clown's outfit, breaks down at a Harvest Festival performance and unsuccessfully attempts to hang himself at the colliery. He is reunited in hospital with his father who is horrified to learn how close his son had come to killing himself. Phil then breaks the news that the band can't afford to go to the finals.

However, money is made available when Gloria confronts the management team. She is paid off but gives a cheque to the band so that they can play in the final.

In London, Harry lead the band to victory. Surprisingly, Danny appears having discharged himself and makes an impassioned acceptance speech and shocks the audience by refusing to take the trophy. The band and their wives, including Sandra, go for a night on the town with the trophy reclaimed.

HOW IT WAS MADE

Mark Herman got the idea for Brassed Off after reading an article about a brass band about to disband due to lack of funds. He teamed up with Steve Abbot, a fellow Yorkshire man, under the aegis of Abbot's Production company Prominent Features, which had been set up with the Monty Python team. Abbot had worked with Herman on his directorial debut Blame it on the Bellboy (UK, 1992). Channel Four picked up on the script and the film's funding was secured when American independent Miramax invested in this very British picture.

The British actors were largely known to British audiences for their character actor work on television with the exception of Ewan McGregor, whose career in the mid-1990s was at its busiest. Pete Postlethwaite was also a busy actor on both sides of the Atlantic, appearing in diverse roles in films such as The Last of the Mohicans (USA, 1992), In the Name of the Father (UK/USA/Ireland, 1993) and the American hit The Usual Suspects (USA, 1995). Tara Fitzgerald had recently appeared alongside Hugh Grant in two films Sirens (UK/Australia, 1994) and The Englishman Who Went up a Hill But Came Down a Mountain (UK/USA, 1995).

The cast was asked to do a Yorkshire accent and also required to learn the rudiments of their instruments in order to look convincing, while Postlewaithe took lessons in conducting. The authentic brass band sound came from the Grimethorpe Colliery band. Herman made a tiny adjustment by ironically naming the community Grimley but the storyline follows some of the actual events faced by the Grimethorpe Colliery band when in 1992 pit closures were announced just five days before the band won in the National Brass Band Championships at the Royal Albert Hall, London. Herman filmed in Grimethorpe at the colliery near Barnsley, Yorkshire and in London with other brass bands, thereby merging the fiction with reality. Indeed, the film often places the fictional characters into real settings, which occasionally gives it a verité feel.

KEY ISSUES

The dismantling of what was once a thriving coal industry and its dire consequences hardly seems a laughing matter and the humour in *Brassed Off* tends to be more bitter than sweet. However, the never say die spirit of those involved is given a fresh approach with the deep traditional sounds of a brass band. Danny's notion that the band and its music are a symbol of a community's desire to hold itself together with pride and dignity eventually proves to be true.

Partly political broadcast

In *The Full Monty* the characters have accepted their lot and the film steers clear of directly blaming the government for their plight. *Brassed Off* is a far angrier film. It principally uses the father and son team of Danny and Phil to issue forthright swipes against the policies of the Tory party, while the remainder of the characters seem quite pragmatic and resigned to their fates.

Phil, at breaking point and dressed as Mr Chuckles, is the first to make a rant about how God created the Tory party despite being 'right out of brains, right out of hearts, and right out of vocal chords' – rather inappropriately in front of a group of bemused children.

McKenzie, who represents management, is the smiling, insincere, manipulative symbol of the government who has come in to do a job, and does so with the minimum of emotional involvement and the maximum of efficiency. Although our hearts are with the miners and their community, we share their feeling of being held to ransom. The offer put on the table is generous – but comes with strings attached – if the miner's refuse redundancy the offer is greatly reduced. Even Phil's attempt at rallying the men in order to keep the mine open seems forlorn and half-hearted. 'Say no to blackmail and yes to keeping the pit alive,' is met with enthusiastic cheers from the miners but in the end the men opt for the money, much to the smarmy satisfaction of McKenzie.

Gloria's harsh lesson in politics arrives when she confronts McKenzie. The man who oozes fake charm is adept at swatting her indignant rage away, as he is at making 1,000 men redundant. He has no moral qualms about it. He tells her that the decision to close the pit had been made two years earlier: 'Coal is dead,' he tells her.

In the end the person who makes the greatest moral and emotional statement is Danny, who up to this point has stayed politically neutral. His drive and desire seems entirely wrapped up with the brass band. However, Phil's suicide attempt shocks Danny out of his idealised world and into the real world. *Brassed Off*'s key moment is not Grimley's victory at the Albert Hall but Danny's impassioned speech, condemning the government's heartless policies and the public's general apathy in accepting them.

> 'Because over the last ten years, this bloody government has systematically destroyed an entire industry. Our industry. And not just our industry - our communities, our homes, our lives. All in the name of 'progress'. And for a few lousy bob… But when it comes to losing the will to live, to breathe, the point is - if this lot were seals or whales, you'd all be up in bloody arms. But they're not, are they, no, no they're not. They're just ordinary common-or-garden honest, decent human beings. And not one of them with an ounce of bloody hope left. Oh aye, they can knock out a bloody good tune. But what the fuck does that matter?'

Whereas Phil's audience were innocent children, the audience at the Albert Hall responds with a standing ovation. Grimley wins a moral as well as a musical victory but ultimately the government's programme of pit closures and its policy of nuclear power is unchanged. Like the fate of the men in *The Full Monty*, we are left to speculate how their lives will pan out.

It's a man's world

In the opening sequences of *Brassed Off* we get to see real miners at work, emerging blackened by the soot of the mines and showering afterwards. In these few instances we could be forgiven for thinking that we were watching a documentary about the hard and uncompromising work of a miner.

The Yorkshiremen in Harman's film conform to a stereotype of being gruff, dour and heavy on the irony: 'She's a bit careless with the crockery, your Sandra!'. They like their beer, regard that a woman's place is in the home and quietly make sexist comments whenever a young woman appears. There is no attempt to suggest otherwise, even Andy who represents the younger generation is committed to following in the colliery town's footsteps – birth, coalmine, brass band, and death. Nevertheless, Andy is both realistic and idealistic when explaining to a sceptical Gloria that the decision to close the pit has already been made. He pins his flag to the mast by declaring that he will vote to keep the pit alive even though he has: 'No hope, just principles.'

The threat of pit closure undermines the men's self-confidence and this is illustrated in Phil's character – he seems to be ahead of the others in losing his job, his wife, his children, his home and his will to live. Dressed up as Mr Chuckles Phil cuts a tragic-comic character. After his first outing as Mr Chuckles the mother paying him wryly observes that being a clown isn't his main job. Phil responds by saying that he is a miner, and then adds:

'You remember them, love? Dinosaurs, dodos, miners.' When he tries to confront the bailiffs, dressed in his clown's outfit, his manhood has been undermined and his ultimate humiliation is when he fails to kill himself. The scene with him swinging for dear life in his costume is grotesque and chilling – the joke isn't funny anymore.

Ultimately, the men retain their dignity and pride with the one last thing they have control over – the brass band.

Blowing your own euphonium

Deeply embedded within the core of *Brassed Off* is the brass band music performed by the Grimethorpe Colliery Band. It acts as the film's conscience as music is seen and heard in actual performance or serves as the soundtrack.

The musical choices include familiar tunes such as *Jerusalem*, *Colonel Bogey*, *All Things Bright and Beautiful* and the *Floral Dance* (once turned into a chart hit for the Brighouse and Rastrick Brass Band, who also get nod and wink mentions in the film).

Gloria's debut of *Concerto En Aranjuez* (known as 'Orange Juice' to the Grimley Band) is particularly effective and moving. Similarly, the band manages an emotional intensity with its rendition of *Danny Boy* as Danny lies awake in hospital and joyfully sends a dour message via a nurse: 'He says your tenor horn is too soft!' At the Albert Hall *The William Tell Overture* surprisingly thunders out with rage and power and allows us to see Harry regain his confidence and self-belief with his dynamic conducting.

The joy of the film is believing that the actors not only care for the music they are playing, but apparently seem to be playing it. Danny's passion for the band, which he sees very much as a living symbol for the survival of a community, is well realised by Postlethwaite's performance. He exudes authority both moral and musical, but the pay off for Danny is when the music is good. The men, naturally, don't scrub up to his high standards. At one point Phil tries to reason with Danny: 'I love this band – we all do – but there's other things in life, you know, that's more important,' to which Danny offers a curt reply: 'Not in mine there isn't.' However, there are also nice glimpses throughout the film such as a shot of Harry and Ernie discussing a piece and making playing motions with their fingers. Phil's desire to please his father even leads him to buy a new trombone, which he can't even afford, and Harry patiently corrects people when they refer to his instrument as a trumpet: 'It's a euphonium,' he states. Harry also comes round to believing that the band has some worth. 'At least people listen to us,' he explains to his wife.

Because the music appears to be played live we don't have to suspend our disbelief too much to appreciate its power and significance. But the music also serves as the hope that the men and the community seem to have lost and offers joy to others – this can be witnessed in the heats of the competition where real delight is captured in the faces of the audiences.

Just like a woman

The role of women in *Brassed Off* differs slightly from that of *The Full Monty*. Gloria is introduced as a love interest and sex object but she also represents a modern woman set for a successful career and already economically independent. Gloria's gesture of giving money to fund the final demonstrates her economic power despite the fact that she too has been made unemployed. Gloria knows that she will be able to find work again. She is self-assured in the male milieu of the brass band and is quite happy to trade sexual innuendos with the older men. She also makes most of the running with Andy in her attempt to rekindle the old flames of their teenage romance by first asking him out and then asking him for a euphemistic cup of coffee. Even right at the end she teases Andy to kiss by commenting on Yorkshiremen's traditional lack of showing emotion.

Yet in the male world she is not treated as an equal and is despised for being part of the management team set to destroy the community, which ironically she grew up in and left for a different kind of life. In the end Gloria has to fight hard to earn the respect of the miners, who find it equally hard to accept that she is cut from the same cloth as them. Danny is the only man to have no qualms about her value, but this is based on his admiration for her grandfather. In the end Gloria does win the miners over by funding the trip to London. 'This time we've not lost before we start,' she states, emphasising that she was merely a pawn in the management's game and has learnt her lesson the hard way. Ironically, her naïve idealism does not go down well with her boss, McKenzie, who feels obliged to patronise her.

The other women in the film have stayed put in Grimley's past. Their strength is their unity, which is demonstrated by their picket-line vigils in support of the miners. Both Vera and Ida work at the local store but generally the implications are that the woman's role is to support their men. Harry's wife appears the most active by daily appearing at the colliery gates with other women supporting the miners. Her influence becomes apparent when she finally speaks to Harry as they pass each other and berates him for his lack of drive. Harry eventually responds to this jibe by taking over Danny's baton when Danny lies ill in hospital.

The film gives us a happy resolution to Phil and Sandra's break-up but not before Sandra takes control over a hopeless situation by leaving Phil. Sandra is seen at the end of her tether, having to bring up the kids with no financial support. As in *The Full Monty* children seem mature beyond their years and one of Sandra's children philosophically states: 'I don't like seeing Dad sad, Mum, but I'd sooner see him sad than not see him at all.'

SCENE ANALYSIS - TRIUMPH AND DISASTER

By the time the band goes to Halifax to play in the semi-final heat the film has reached a crucial stage with many of the elements on a knife-edge. Not only is the focus on whether the band will rally round after its last shambolic display and win through to the final, but the results of the ballot to keep the pit open are due on the same day. Left to simmer is the on-off relationship between Andy and Gloria.

The semi-final scene mirrors an earlier sequence when Gloria first enters the male enclave and performs *Concerto En Aranjuez*. Her moving performance is intercut with scenes of the union negotiating with management. The semi-final sequence enlarges on the themes already established and moves the narrative along by showing several strands that apparently happen simultaneously – the band playing in the semi-final, Sandra reaching breaking point, the announcement of the ballot result, the reaction of the community, and finally management's apparent satisfaction of a job well done.

In a sequence that lasts five minutes the dramatic elements in the plot are not only explained but signposts are added to two additional points – Danny's collapse in the street and Phil's suicide attempt. All this information is presented with the soundtrack of the band performing *Florentiner March*, composed by Julius Fučík.

The film often mixes *verité* scenes along with the action, such as the band's performance set against the splendour of the Piece Hall in Halifax. The backdrop allows for the camera not only to move in and out of the crowd, looking up to the bandstand, but also to move around the pillars in order to get a better view of the band playing.

Starting with a point of view shot from the top of a balcony, which moves between the pillars to get a long shot view of the band playing in a bandstand in front of a crowd below (just as a flock of pigeons flies overhead), we see a real band performance from the perspective of those in the audience. Other shots showing us the real event in progress include a brief glimpse of another brass band looking on and a long shot from just above the audience's heads, which captures the band framed within the roman columns of the bandstand. Closer in, a low shot from behind two people sitting at the front moves up again to reveal the full band playing. This last moment is sandwiched between two shots of actual Grimethorpe band members playing – first a close-up of a horn player, then a close-up as the cymbols crash together.

An early set of shots shows Danny in his central role conducting the band, intercut with close-up shots of the characters playing their instruments intently – Andy and Gloria framed together, Harry looking in Danny's direction, and Phil with Ernie in the background. Danny's expression suggests his growing satisfaction with the standard of the performance.

The upbeat mood in Halifax is contrasted as the action swings to events back in Grimley as the music continues to play on the soundtrack – Sandra struggles with the kids and her washing while we then hear the results of the ballot. A series of shots catches the contrasting reactions of the men – the miner who wanted to take the money gives a small victory clench of his fist, the union officials look on wearily and a shot captures one of those against taking the money look up with distain as his colleagues shuffle pass before bowing and shaking his head.

This segment is interrupted as we return to the strand in the story affecting Sandra's relationship with Phil. From the ballot result a cut takes us to Sandra discovering Phil's trombone receipt in one of his pockets. The camera zooms into her face as she picks up the paper, followed by a close-up of the receipt seen from her point of view, back to a shot of her reaction and then cuts back to Halifax to show a close-up shot of Phil, who strokes his trombone just before he plays.

We then see management's reaction to the ballot result intercut with the consequences of Phil's trombone purchase. With miners walking out on a road behind him, the camera captures McKenzie on his mobile phone smiling and the camera moves around allowing other miners to pass through. Meanwhile, the action cuts back to the bailiffs calling in on Sandra, who stands at the door holding her baby. We go back to a shot of McKenzie departing the scene. A crane shot rises to show his car leave as he reads his paper.

There follows a set of beautifully composed, almost slow motion, dreamlike shots showing miners and other people in the community slowly walking from the pit. At one point we just see the shot of a group of miners caught in the reflection of a puddle as everyone seems to walk in quiet desolation in a direction away from the pit towards the camera. The movement of the people as they cross each others paths is particularly effective in conveying a sense of aimlessness. At one point a shot shows a miner sitting stunned on the pavement, casually passed by someone walking with their bicycle. The slow retreat from the pit site also shows Rita talking to a friend as the women leave their campsite. Their expressions are sombre, their understanding of the severity of the situation complete.

Finally, with Sandra joining her children in a huddle in the centre of a room, we see furniture being removed from the house before it is time to return to the bandstand in Halifax with the band unaware of the dire drama that they have left behind. The rousing finish of the performance is slightly punctured when Danny coughs slightly, but otherwise he is shown looking on with pride.

The euphoria experienced by the band when the result confirms their victory lasts barely seconds. The cheers and hugs are replaced with a cut to the coach leaving Grimley. As it departs down the hill from left to right from filling the screen, it reveals a delicately composed shot of the brass band members who are almost silhouetted in a scattered formation looking towards a sign with the colliery just visible on the horizon. The Grimley Colliery sign, which is read from Danny's point of view, reveals the terrible truth. Scrawled in red it reads 'We fought and lost' - a bitter irony when the brass band had just fought and won their semi-final.

REACTION

In the UK the film received warm reviews with press concentrating on the social context of the film and the brass bands rather than its slightly contrived ending, which unites all the characters. The packed devices within the story – Danny's collapse, Phil's marriage on the rocks, the inevitable feel-good victory – were generally accepted, whereas some thought the weakness of the film lay in its love story between Andy and Gloria. This is ironic since in America Miramax felt the British fascination with brass bands might not translate well and so pitched the film as a romantic comedy (it was called *Brassed Off!* in the States). Nevertheless, the strong ensemble cast performances rightly drew praise. In the end the heart of the film with its echoes of social realism was warmly received and the fact that it also reflects the Grimethorpe Colliery Band's history added positive weight to its critical appreciation.

The film performed modestly in the States but in Britain in 1996 it became the second most successful British film at the UK box-office (behind *Trainspotting*). In Europe and Japan audiences were also appreciative and the film secured awards in France, Germany and Japan to go along with its British awards, which included the Peter Sellers Award for Comedy at the 1997 Evening Standard British Film Awards.

While the film did not quite capture the public's imagination in the same way *The Full Monty* had, *Brassed Off* served as another example of low-budget British film-making at its best. One of the offshoots was a renewed interest in brass. The soundtrack album by Grimethorpe Colliery Band sold 60,000 copies and was nominated for a BAFTA.

CONCLUSION

Today, *Brassed Off* is often seen as a companion piece to *The Full Monty*. The typically British film of a brass band coupled with its social conscience and its look at communities clinging on to their self-respect made it compelling. However, its Britishness was not enough to turn it into an international hit, whereas *The Full Monty* also paraded its Britishness but had a more global appeal and feelgood factor.

Ultimately, *The Full Monty* had more sex appeal and more youth appeal with its use of music. In an age where marketing and spin-offs were increasingly vital to a film's success, the choice of music mattered. Though the brass band sound in *Brassed Off* was undeniably effective, it was not the stuff that a fast-growing MTV generation particularly wanted to get into. On the other hand, *The Full Monty*, whose original downbeat score won an Oscar, contained a soundtrack featuring disco floor-fillers such as Donna Summer's *Hot Stuff*, Hot Chocolate's *You Sexy Thing*, and of course, Tom Jones' *You Can Leave Your Hat On*.

Essentially both films were low-budget comedies, which performed better than expected. Both had American backing and both had some Channel Four involvement. Ironically,

Channel Four considered *Brassed Off* to be a better bet than *The Full Monty* and allowed it to be distributed by FilmFour, whereas *The Full Monty* had the bigger backing of Fox Searchlight. Equally important was that both films owed some of their success to *Four Weddings and a Funeral*, with American film companies sniffing around for similar Brit comedies.

Whatever the merits of the two films, it was clear that the British cinema-going public emerged as the clear winner during the 1990s. Moreover, there was not only a home audience for well-made British films, but an international audience too.

By the end of the 1990s cinema in the UK had become reinvigorated, largely with the investment of foreign money. During this expansion, the challenge for the British film-makers was to make sufficiently popular films to encourage more of the major distributors to take a chance on British products. The trouble was that despite the success of films like *The Full Monty* and *Brassed Off* there lurked plenty of British films that appeared half-baked with a lack of script development.

FURTHER READING

British Cinema of the 90s
Murphy, Robert (ed.) (BFI, 2001) Chapter 5 – Spoilt for Choice? Multiplexes in the 90s by Hanson, Stuart

The Stats An overview of the film, television, video and DVD industries 1990-2003
(BFI National Library, BFI Information Services, 2006)

BFI Film and Television Handbook (BFI, editions from 1990–2005)

Selected reviews/articles/references

The Cinema Exhibitors' Association – www.cinemauk.org.uk

The Full Monty

Sight & Sound V.7 N.9 (1 Sept) P.43 by Caplan, Nina

Empire N.99 (1 Sept 1997) P.48 by Brown, Deborah

Variety (11 August 1997) P.52 by Elley, Derek

The Full Monty
Domaille, Kate (York Press, 2000)

Contemporary British Cinema 16+ Source Guide Guides
Mettler, Erinna; Ormsby, Andrew; Reeve, David; Dupin, Christophe (BFI National Library,

2003) www.bfi.org.uk/filmtvinfo/publications/16+/

DVD: *The Full Monty* (2 Disc Special Edition) (20th Century Fox Home Entertainment, 2006

Brassed Off

Sight & Sound V.6 N.11 (1 Nov 1996) P.44 by MacNab, Geoffrey

Empire N.90 (1 Dec 1996) P.44 by Freer, Ian

Movie Connections: *Brassed Off* (BBC Scotland, 22 October 2007)

5. THE FILM PRODUCTION BOOM IN BRITAIN

There can be little doubt that film production in the UK experienced a much sought-after boom after the low point in 1989 when only 30 films were produced. The rise in the number of titles was generally uneven but led to 128 titles in the UK in 1996. This was the biggest number since the 1957 when 138 films were made.

Number and Value of UK Films 1989-1999

Year	Titles	Current prices (£m)	Year	Titles	Current prices (£m)
1989	30	104.7	1995	78	402.4
1990	60	217.4	1996	128	741.4
1991	59	243.2	1997	116	562.8
1992	47	184.9	1998	88	509.3
1993	67	224.1	1999	100	549.2
1994	84	455.2			

Source: *Screen Finance/BFI Film and Television Handbook 2003*

What also changed was the amount of money ploughed into film production with the average budget rising from £3.62m in 1990 to £5.49m in 1999. It is clear that extra money allocated for film production – money from the National Lottery, which started flowing from 19 November 1994, initiatives like the £5m set aside for the European Co-production fund and the return of Bond films in the mid-1990s – all helped to boost the budget balances. Furthermore, UK studios were keen to host Hollywood productions and a steady stream of blockbusters were made in the UK. They included *Star Wars Episode One – The Phantom Menace* (USA, 1999); *Saving Private Ryan* (USA, 1998); and *Gladiator* (USA, 2000), even if they technically did not qualify as British films. The special relationship with American films was also a business relationship and as much to do with how sterling was faring against the dollar, when paradoxically a weak pound is advantageous to Hollywood studio bosses.

A quick glance at the big budget productions filmed in the UK over the decade shows that the majority were American and lacking any real cultural connection with Britain. The only 'British' film in the top budget list was the French co-production of *Little Buddha* (UK/France, 1993), starring Keanu Reeves. It was produced by Jeremy Thomas and his Recorded Picture Company with the French company CiBy 2000 also producing. Beyond that one could pick out Stephen Woolley's involvement in Neil Jordan's *Interview With the Vampire* (1993) and point at Ridley Scott direction of *Gladiator* as evidence of guiding British involvement in these films.

Top production budget of films made in the UK 1990-1999

Year	Title	Budget £m (approx)
1990	*Robin Hood Prince of Thieves*	26m
1991	*Alien 3*	24m
1992	*Little Buddha*	18m
1993	*Interview With the Vampire*	30m
1994	*Judge Dredd*	30m
1995	*Mission Impossible*	48.3m
1996	*The Fifth Element*	50m
1997	*Saving Private Ryan*	50m
1998	*Entrapment*	51.6m
1999	*Gladiator*	92m

Source: The Stats, BFI Information Department

The majority of British films released in the 1990s had to make do with budgets averaging around £2.5m or less, as was the case with the top British box-office draws of the decade – *Four Weddings and a Funeral* (£2m), *Trainspotting* (£1.76m) and *The Full Monty* (£2.2m). This, if anything, proves that big budgets don't necessarily equate to big box-office returns. Beyond the big British hits it's worth noting some other British films during the period – demonstrating the breadth of creative talent that existed within the industry and the wide range of subject matters that often would inform audiences, local and global, of British cultural matters.

Riff Raff (UK, 1991)

Production Companies: Channel 4; Parallax Pictures

Starring Robert Carlyle, Ricky Tomlinson and Emer McCourt, Ken Loach's comedy drama is about a drifter who finds work on a building site in London and moves into a squat with aspiring singer, Susan. Having returned to feature film-making with *Hidden Agenda* (UK, 1990), Loach's follow-up made in 1990 re-established his position as Britain's leading social realist film-maker.

Truly, Madly, Deeply (UK, 1992)

Production Companies: BBC Films in association with BBC Enterprises; Lionheart TV International

Anthony Minghella's whimsical debut feature film follows a bereaved woman whose cello-playing husband returns from the dead to comfort her until it is time for both to move on. Minghella quickly established himself on the international arena and enjoyed Oscar-winning success in the 1990s with *The English Patient* (USA, 1996) and five nominations for *The Talented Mr. Ripley* (USA, 1999).

Bhaji on the Beach (UK, 1993)

Production Companies: Umbi Films; sponsor Channel 4

Gurinder Chadha's comedy drama about an Asian women's group outing to Blackpool for the day shows a side of multi-cultural Britain that had been widely neglected. It was ground-breaking not just for its topic but for the fact that its film-maker should not only be a woman but an Asian woman working in a predominantly white male industry.

Backbeat (UK/Germany 1994)

Production Companies: PolyGram Filmproduction GmbH presented by PolyGram Filmed Entertainment; Scala Productions in association with Channel 4 Films; Scala/Woolley/Powell/Dyer; Forthcoming Productions

The film examines the relationship between John Lennon and Stuart Sutcliffe while the Beatles were in Hamburg before Beatlemania beckoned. Iain Softley would go on to make the adaptation of the Henry James novel, *Wings of the Dove* (UK/USA, 1997). Meanwhile, Ian Hart took the role of Lennon, a part he had already played in *The Hours and the Times* (USA, 1992) Dir Christopher Münch. Hart would appear in many British-made films in the 1990s, including Loach's *Land and Freedom* (UK/Spain/Germany, 1995).

Priest (UK, 1994)

Production Company: BBC Films

Originally made for TV, Antonia Bird's story starring Linus Roache, Tom Wilkinson and Robert Carlyle traces the life of a young gay Catholic priest who is appointed to a working-class parish in Liverpool. Wilkinson and Carlyle would team up later in *The Full Monty*. Bird would next travel to the USA to make *Mad Love* (USA, 1995) before returning to the UK for the gangster film *Face* (UK/South Africa, 1997) again starring Carlyle.

Small Faces (UK, 1996)

Production Companies: BBC Films; BBC Scotland; Glasgow Film Fund; Billy MacKinnon Media; Skyline Film and Television Productions

The drama set in Glasgow in 1968 deals with a widowed woman and her three sons as they become involved in crime and gang warfare. Director Gillies MacKinnon would go on to tackle the relationship between First World War poets Siegfried Sassoon and Wilfred Owen in *Regeneration* (UK/Canada, 1997) and then work with Kate Winslet on the 1970s hippy trail to Morocco in *Hideous Kinky* (UK/France, 1998).

Gallivant (UK, 1996)

Production Companies: Tall Stories; Arts Council of England in association with British Film Institute; Channel 4

Film-maker Andrew Kötting's idiosyncratic documentary journey all around the coastline of Britain brings him together with Gladys, his 85-year-old grandmother, and Eden, his seven-year-old daughter, who has Joubert's syndrome. Somehow issues of age and disability become secondary and the personal relationship between the family members becomes compelling, set as it is against the landscape of the British Isles.

Twentyfourseven (UK, 1997)

Production Companies: BBC Films; Scala Productions

Set in Nottingham, Shane Meadows' first full-length feature, made in black and white, stars Bob Hoskins as a middle-aged man trying to re-establish a former boxing club as a way to bring a sense of purpose to the local teenagers. The response to the film quickly established Meadows as a bright new British talent.

Wonderland (UK, 1999)

Production Companies: PolyGram Films (UK) Limited; Kismet Film Company; Revolution Films for PolyGram Filmed Entertainment presented by BBC Films; Universal Pictures International.

By the time Michael Winterbottom had made this episodic drama set over four days he had already established his unpredictable directorial choices via his bleak Hardy adaptation *Jude* (UK, 1996), the emotionally uplifting *Welcome to Sarajevo* (UK/USA, 1997), and the romantic drama *With or Without You* (UK, 1999). In the 2000s Winterbottom would continue to surprise and delight with an eclectic range of topics from the Manchester rave scene to asylum seekers.

There's Only One Jimmy Grimble (UK/France 2000)

Production Companies: Pathé Fund Limited; Sarah Radclyffe Productions; Impact Pictures presented by Pathé Pictures in association with Arts Council of England; Studio Canal +

This tale is based around a 15-year-old Manchester City supporter whose footballing fortunes are transformed when he is given a pair of football boots that he believes helps him play better. This premise closely resembles that of the comic strip *Billy's Boots*, which first appeared in *Scorcher* in 1970.

All these films with the exception of *Backbeat* (£2.9m), *Wonderland* (£4m) and *There's Only One Jimmy Grimble* (£3m) were made with budgets of £2m or less, proving that success is not always gauged by accountants. What the titles also show is a willingness for producers to step away from the traditional British film safe bets – heritage movies and comedies – by dealing more with contemporary cultural, political and social British themes.

Success proved sweeter for the few smaller budget films that made a lasting impression than the big hitting blockbusters that grind out their box-office revenue on the back of massive marketing campaigns and saturate British cinemas.

Film-makers in Britain don't necessarily warm to marketing babble – demographic charts are not their key motives for making films and the temptation to make their films first and worry about the box-office consequences later is both a strength and a weakness. The fine balance between commerce and culture was one that many struggled to meet. In America, as British producer David Puttnam pointed out in a speech in 1999 there was no such dilemma:

> 'On this side of the Atlantic, we've allowed production, distribution and exhibition to become fatally separate. The result is a series of small cottage industries instead of a modern, fully integrated business... The Americans, by contrast, have developed not just the product but a level of marketing expertise which is capable of successfully turning its hand to financing and delivering just about any kind of entertainment.'

> 'Today's movies are really 'brand names'. Every single film put out by the Hollywood studios is, in a way, its own brand which, when successful, becomes a locomotive dragging behind it many, many other sectors of the economy, everything from fashion to fast food chains, books, and video games.'

British film-makers, including Lord Puttnam, only had to look at the 1980s to see British companies who attempted to build an integrated system go under, among them Goldcrest, Handmade and Palace Pictures. Furthermore, the 1990s saw more or less the end of the Rank Organisation, once a leading symbol of the British film industry. Rank had ceased film production in the 1980s and sold its distribution arm to Carlton Communications in 1997.

Nevertheless, during the 1990s there seemed more opportunities for companies to learn the lessons from the past and embrace the challenge of film-making in the UK and there emerged several UK-based production companies that enjoyed a fair share of success.

Working Title

The toast of the British film industry in the 1990s was Working Title Films founded by Tim Bevan and Sarah Radclyffe in the late 1980s. The company is perhaps best known for its Hugh Grant-led vehicles and Richard Curtis-scripted comedies, but the company also has a strong association with the Coen Brothers' films, demonstrating its ambition to look beyond the British Isles.

From the late 1980s Working Title had close associations with PolyGram. Radclyffe left the company in 1993 and was replaced by American producer Eric Fellner. In 1994, the company struck gold with the surprise hit *Four Weddings and a Funeral* and did not think twice about following the same formula using Hugh Grant's star talents to good effect in the follow-up, *Notting Hill*.

In between times the company continued to show its ambitions to make commercially successful British films with the releases of *Bean* (UK, 1997); *The Borrowers* (UK, 1997); *The Big Lebowski* (USA/UK, 1998); *Elizabeth* (UK, 1998) and *Plunkett & Macleane* (UK, 1999). All these films benefited from larger than usual budgets for British movies and close associations with Universal Pictures, which not only distributes Working Titles films but also owns a large stake in the company.

In 1999 the company, which had established its own offices in London and Los Angeles, set up a low-budget arm called WT2 and again reaped rewards in the form of *Billy Elliot* (UK, 2000). The close relationship with America was also demonstrated when *High Fidelity* was whisked away from Islington to Chicago.

Working Title's continued success throughout the 2000s has been built largely around its earlier hits with more comedies, some modern adaptations, the odd gamble here and there but otherwise a steady ship generally bolstered by solid American backing.

PolyGram Filmed Entertainment

For a moment in the 1990s it looked as though PolyGram might have pulled off the trick of creating an integrated film corporation specialising in British movies. Paradoxically, the company was technically not British at all but owned by Dutch electronics giant Philips. This in the end would prove to be vital as the ambitions of the British film industry revival were rudely interrupted when in 1998 Philips sold PolyGram to Seagram, a Canadian drinks conglomerate. However, for the majority of the 1990s PolyGram enjoyed a period of success. It invested shrewdly in British films such as *Four Weddings and a Funeral*, *Bean*,

Shallow Grave, Lock, Stock and Two Smoking Barrels and *Spiceworld* (UK, 1997).

PolyGram's film arm, which was based in the UK, worked closely in partnership with other production companies such as Working Title in the UK and Propaganda (*Being John Malkovich* (USA, 1999)) and Interscope (*Jumanji* (USA, 1995)) in America. However, its power base came from its distribution arm. During its rise it acquired ownership of Gramercy Pictures in America and released *The Usual Suspects*, as well as establishing an international network. Michael Kuhn was the company's president, while Stewart Till headed up PolyGram Film International in London.

Seagram already owned Universal and simply merged PolyGram's production and distribution side with Universal's operations after the sale – and then it was gone.

Channel 4/FilmFour

From the debris of film production in the 1980s Channel 4 emerged in the 1990s unscathed, largely down to its frugal policy of investing small amounts in British films. Its roots were in television and the theatrical releases that it benefited would ultimately have their TV premieres on Channel 4. During the 1990s, either as Film Four International, Channel 4 Films or the eventual FilmFour, the film arm of the TV company shared a considerable amount of success.

As British film fortunes changed for the better in 1991 with the Merchant Ivory hit *Howards End* Dir James Ivory, so too did Channel 4's ambitions. The ubiquitous *Four Weddings and Funeral*, into which Channel 4 had put a modest investment, paid handsome dividends when the film was first screened on TV in November 1995, gaining a huge audience of 11 million.

There were plenty of other reasons for Film Four to be cheerful in the 1990s. It was involved in *Trainspotting, Brassed Off, Secrets and Lies* (UK, 1995), *My Name is Joe* (UK/France/Germany/Italy/Spain, 1999) and *East is East* (UK, 1999). By 1998 FilmFour, under Paul Webster, was set up as a standalone feature film division, which would tie in with FilmFour the distribution arm. The plan was to expand its ambitions and invest more money in production. Very quickly the strategy backfired and as the company went into the 2000s its last box-office success, *East is East* in 1998, seemed increasingly further away. Poor box-office performances of films like *Lucky Break* (UK/USA/Germany, 2001) and *Charlotte Gray* spelled the end. In July 2002, managing director Mark Thompson decreed that FilmFour should cease to operate and the distribution arm was closed down, while the production division was downsized back into the TV station with a view to getting back to Channel 4's basic lower investment strategy for films.

BBC Films

While Channel 4's film division eventually crashed and burned, BBC Films managed to maintain a well-balanced, if sometimes low-key presence during the 1990s, punctuated with critically-acclaimed films such as *Jude, Wilde* (UK/USA/Japan/Germany, 1997), *Mrs Brown* (UK/USA/Ireland, 1997) and *Ratcatcher* (UK/France, 1999). Like Channel 4, the BBC could screen the premieres of its films. Unlike Channel 4, it kept its investments low.

Many of the early BBC2 films came as part of a Screen Two series such as *Enchanted April* (UK, 1991), and Anthony Minghella's debut *Truly, Madly, Deeply*. Both gained theatrical screenings.

By 1993 BBC Films began dipping its toes into the water by linking with films such as Kenneth Branagh's *Much Ado About Nothing* and Mike Newell's *An Awfully Big Adventure* (UK/USA/Ireland/France, 1994). By 1996 BBC had become more sure-footed, co-producing films such as *The Van* (UK/USA/Ireland, 1996) and *Jude*. Its steady output continued throughout the decade with modest successes at the UK box-office offset with critical acclaim of films such as *Regeneration*.

Mark Shivas was the head of BBC Films until 1997 when David Thompson replaced him. The relative stability might be attributed to its public-funded body and the BBC enjoyed a rise in fortunes during the 1990s as the public continued to pay the licence fee.

PLEASE RELEASE ME

The production boom for UK films in the 1990s also revealed a weakness within the British film industry, and that came in the area of distribution. Despite the apparent success of some British titles both commercially and critically, many of the newly-made films struggled to find slots for release. Worse still, many lay unreleased. This frailty in the system meant that sustaining a real impetus in promoting British films would always be a problem, particularly since the industry was largely beholden to the major film distributors from America.

Unfortunately, for British film-makers, (all film-makers) small budgets meant that the chances of success were slim and the chances of making money slimmer still. This section looks at two contrasting types of British film produced in the 1990s – *Four Weddings and A Funeral* and *The World is Not Enough* (1999). The former was a low-budget upstart that went on to become one of the top films of the decade and kicked down the door for other films to follow, while the latter had a big budget and was part of a reinvigorated franchise, which invested heavily in British studios, technicians and know-how.

Four Weddings and A Funeral (1994) (UK) UK Cert 15

Director: Mike Newell

Screenplay: Richard Curtis

Producer: Duncan Kenworthy

Production companies: Working Title Films; PolyGram Filmed Entertainment; Channel 4 Films

Production start date: 31/05/1993 **Budget:** £2m (estimated)

Distributor: Rank/PolyGram, Carlton Film Distributors Limited

UK Release date: 13 May 1994

UK Box Office: £27,762,648 **USA Box Office:** $52.7m

Worldwide Box Office: $244.1m

If you were to pick the single most influential British film from the 1990s then it would most likely be the light, feel-good, romantic comedy *Four Weddings and a Funeral*. It kickstarted a perceived revival in British film fortunes, created an international star in Hugh Grant and, perhaps most significantly, was a big success in America. The knock-on effect was for UK audiences to become aware that British films could punch their weight on the global stage.

The film was important in other ways since it utilised a British team featuring a production arm via Working Title and Channel 4 and a distribution arm via PolyGram. The script was also written by Richard Curtis, who had already established himself as a writer of sitcoms on TV with *Black Adder* (BBC) and *Bean* (ITV). In an industry where feature films are a risky business the team behind *Four Weddings and a Funeral* seemed to have found the closest thing to a successful formula. Crudely put, this included a combination of Hugh Grant, an American actress – in this case Andie Macdowell – a good supporting British cast, Working Title Films in combination with PolyGram, and a script by Curtis.

But as with all success stories timing is important. *Four Weddings and a Funeral* struck a chord with the public at just the right time. It also benefited from the type of musical tie-in that had made Bryan Adams' *(Everything I Do) I Do It For You* a few years earlier synonymous with *Robin Hood Prince of Thieves* (USA, 1991). It's easy to forget that superstar Elton John actually sings at the opening and closing of the film (*But Not For Me* and *Chapel of Love*), since the hit over the summer of 1994 was Wet, Wet, Wet's version of the old Trogg's song *Love is All Around*, which stayed at number one for 15 weeks – not bad for some extended publicity for the film. All these factors turned a modest British comedy film into an international hit.

SYNOPSIS

A group of eight friends gather for the wedding of Angus and Laura. Charles, the best man, notices the enigmatic American Carrie, who he falls for immediately. After the wedding Charles catches up with her and they spend the night together before she returns to America the next morning.

A few months later wedding number two arrives with Bernard and Lydia. Charles finds himself on a table with several of his ex-girlfriends and later encounters another ex-girlfriend, Henrietta, who grills him about commitment issues. His evening appears to pick up when he again encounters Carrie, but his joy turns to misery when she informs him that she is engaged to a wealthy Scottish MP called Hamish. Nevertheless, Charles and Carrie end up spending another night together.

Charles and his friends receive an invite to Carrie's wedding in Scotland. Charles goes to look for a present and bumps into Carrie. Awkwardly he declares his love for her and proposes that she might consider not marrying Hamish. She is touched by his offer but declines.

Carrie's wedding at a Scottish castle proves to be a traumatic affair. The whole proceedings are brought to a shocking end when the larger-than-life Gareth dies suddenly of a heart attack. The next time the friends are gathered together is at Gareth's funeral where Gareth's partner, Matthew, concludes his moving speech by reciting a poem by W.H. Auden.

Some months later another Charles as prepares to marry Henrietta he yet again bumps into Carrie, who tells him that she has separated from her husband. At the altar Henrietta lays Charles out with a hefty punch when he claims not to be sure about marrying her. He is left with his friends to reflect what he has done. Carrie appears at his door. Charles proposes that he and Carrie never marry, which she accepts.

HOW IT WAS MADE

The team that created *Four Weddings and a Funeral* had partly worked with each other before. PolyGram and Working Title had recently produced the Hanif Kureishi drama *London Kills Me* (UK, 1991), while Curtis had scripted the comedy *The Tall Guy* (UK, 1989), which Working Title produced. Curtis' strong script for *Four Weddings and a Funeral* convinced PolyGram's Michael Kuhn that the film would work. Channel 4 Films was brought on board with modest expectations but all parties thought the film would bring in a small profit.

Grant had first come to the public's attention in Merchant Ivory's *Maurice* (UK, 1987). His career did not take off from this point but he had just starred in Polanski's *Bitter Moon* (France/UK) alongside Kristin Scott Thomas (who also caught the eye) and completed a part in another Merchant Ivory production, *The Remains of the Day*. American actress Andie MacDowell was fast establishing her star credentials with a string of successful films including *sex, lies and videotape* (USA, 1989), *Green Card* (Australia/France 1990); and *Groundhog Day* (USA, 1993).

Charles's brother in the film is deaf-mute and appropriately David Bower, a deaf actor, was sought for the role. The remainder of the cast were noted more for their British TV work.

Director Mike Newell came to the film with a pedigree of more than 30 years' work encompassing TV drama series like *Budgie* in the 1970s and diverse film work, including *The Man in the Iron Mask* (UK/USA, 1977), *The Awakening* (UK/USA, 1980) and the acclaimed *Dance With A Stranger* (UK, 1984).

Most of the filming took part around the Home Counties or in London, with Rotherfield Park in Hampshire standing in for the Scottish location. The locations became quite a feature with an assortment of magnificent stately homes and St. Bartholomew-the-Great church in Clerkenwell. There is even a shot set outside the National Film Theatre at the Southbank, perhaps as a nod and a wink to film buffs, while Charles first declares his love for Carrie not far from where Juliet Stevenson and Michael Maloney had filmed a scene in *Truly, Madly, Deeply*.

Test screenings took place in America and received favourable reactions with the exception of a nagging desire from audiences keen to know what happened next to all the leading characters. The film-makers quickly resolved the problem by constructing a neat ending credit sequence showing how everyone lived happily ever after – including one final joke with Fiona placed next to Prince Charles. American distributor Gramercy also asked the film-makers to come up with an alternative title, arguing that any reference to death in a title spells a similar fatal outcome at the box-office. Luckily, the producers stuck to their guns and *Four Weddings and a Funeral* made its first appearance at the influential Sundance festival in 1994. The film opened in America first in March but was overshadowed by the tabloid frenzy generated at the UK premiere in May 1994 when Liz

Hurley, (Hugh Grant's girlfriend) appeared wearing a black Versace dress apparently held together by safety pins.

KEY ISSUES

In a sense the success of *Four Weddings and a Funeral* comes from the fact that this very British comedy based around traditional values and middle-class manners pandered to the American market first and foremost. Symbolically, the romance between Charles and Carrie reflects the wooing of this film to the Americans.

Atlantic crossing

Four Weddings and a Funeral gave the Americans a stereotypical, almost idyllic, vision of Britain full of slightly eccentric men and attractive if slightly uptight women, neither seeming to have real occupations and swanning in and around stately homes and castles as if they were updated characters from a Jane Austen novel. The film almost harks back to a post-war era where the ruling classes still had the upper hand and the church maintained an influence over people's lives.

On another level *Four Weddings and a Funeral* also seems to chime with John Major's government calling for 'family values'. At each wedding the desire of those unattached is to find a partner and marry. It is only at the end of the film that Charles rejects the institution of marriage in favour of co-habiting with his supposed life-long partner Carrie. The unrest in the film is not of a social nature, nor of an ethnic one, but of an emotional kind. But then again, this film had no pretentious other than to be a light romantic comedy.

There are amusing references to Princess Diana and Prince Charles, which gently remind audiences of the Royal Family. But the traffic isn't all one-way for Americans are teased for their brash stereotypical manner and Carrie herself at her wedding refers to the prospect of Brits spending time with their American guests. She even evokes lines from John Lennon ('love is the answer, and you know that for sure') as another reminder to the American audience of Britain's cultural heritage. The choice of W.H. Auden's *Funeral Blues* at Gareth's funeral is apt since the British-born poet spent most of his later life in America.

Finally, it is implied that the mere fact that Carrie is American, (and we actually learn her occupation – fashion editor) makes her even more glamorous to Charles, who up to this time has rejected a succession of British women. Quite incidentally, Scarlett also ends up falling for a man from Texas who she meets at Carrie's wedding, further cementing the transatlantic bond.

The importance of being Charles

Grant became an international star as a result of his performance as the amiable, witty, self-deprecating buffoon Charles. His character, conjured up by Curtis, comes across somewhere between the Dr. Simon Sparrow character played by British actor Dirk Bogarde in the *Doctor* films of the 1950s and 1960s and the neurotic angst displayed by Woody Allen in his films from the 1970s and early 1980s. His character, rather like Bogarde, is meant to appeal to a female audience.

However, Charles cannot be categorised as an upper-class twit. Despite his mainly posh friends, Charles is no match for Tom, the true upper-class twit in the film, played with just the right degree of good-natured naivety by James Fleet. Charles seems to have something about him and is quite clearly a success 'with the ladies', as is demonstrated by the scene where he shares a table with an assortment of his ex-girlfriends. Even his awkwardness with Carrie, which she presumably finds quaint, does not prevent him from ending up in bed with her, not once but twice during the course of their unusual courtship.

His friends seem to like him even though he is disorganised. But he does not seem wilful or malicious. Even when tackling the slightly unhinged Henrietta at the second wedding he comes across sympathetically – though the evidence suggests that in the past he may well have acted like a cad. even 'Duck face' is prepared to give him the benefit of doubt and agree to marry him again – before he lets her down. In the end, Charles is portrayed as vulnerable and slightly lost, but not without desire, which in Carrie's eyes makes him 'lovely'.

It is also worth mentioning Charles' close relationship with his deaf-mute brother David. This shows more of his caring nature, but also leads to more unexpected humour in the form of signing, which acts like a secret code between the two brothers.

Carrie on loving

What we know about the characters in the film largely comes from our experiences of them at the four weddings and the funeral and we generally have to fill in the gaps. However, the relationship we constantly see is the main one between Carrie and Charles.

Other than her good looks and American background it is hard to see what Charles sees in Carrie but he obliges us by falling in love at first sight. It is also not clear quite what she sees in Charles, other than his good looks, his English background and his best man's speech. In an amusingly frank scene she goes through a list of all the lovers she has had in her life. The total comes to 33 (Charles is number 32). Even with these stats Charles continues to pursue her as the 'one' in his life.

When Charles first enquires about Carrie, Fiona dismisses his prospects by saying that she is out of his league. From this point Charles always appears inferior to her. Although he is keen, he is also insecure by her presence. She calls the shots in their first sexual liaison, inviting Charles into her room and making the first move to kiss him. The next morning she announces that she is leaving for America but not before teasing him by suggesting that having slept with her he ought to do the honourable thing and marry her.

The next time Carrie bumps into Charles she announces that she is getting engaged, but still the couple go off to spend the night together. It comes as some surprise that when Charles finishes stuttering his undying love for her using the title of David Cassidy and the Partridge Family's big hit *I Think I Love You* as his inspiration, that Carrie should say: 'That was very romantic' and still carries out her plan to marry Hamish even though it is hard to see any chemistry between the two of them.

However, as the song says, *Love is all Around*. In the end, Carrie's arrival at Charles' wedding to Henrietta comes as little surprise. By this point it seems clear that Charles and Carrie are destined to be together. Charles finally wins Carrie over by doing something that she didn't do, rejecting her potential spouse at the altar. The denouement for the two people with commitment issues is that they agree not to marry.

Weddings

One of the key devices in *Four Weddings and a Funeral* is witnessing the wedding clichés being played out. We see the constant late arrivals, the lost wedding rings, the awful best man's speech, terrible dancing at the reception, the bemused elder relatives, the bridesmaid getting off with someone, and the bride being jilted at the altar.

Another wedding favourite, the mispronounced wedding vows, is given a wonderfully comic twist when the novice priest (Rowan Atkinson) rather than the bride and groom stumbles over the words and struggles with names. Atkinson gives a marvellous cameo performance full of perfect comic timing and adds to the many comic layers already evident in the film. Another unexpected scene features the newly-wed bride and groom bonking while Charles hides waiting to come out. Once again, the comic timing is perfect.

Four Weddings also works as a spectacle in its own right with the backdrop of each wedding ceremony being pleasing on the eye. The audience sees people dress up in their best wedding suits and dresses, including Carrie and her rather distinctive large hat, which draws attention to her sense of individuality.

Funeral for a friend

In a film that plays for laughs the funeral scene is handled with a great deal of care and skill. The wedding scenes are played out with joyful if sometimes disrespectful abandon with plenty of laughter, while the funeral is treated as a solemn occasion with not a hint of a funny cliché. Part of the success of the scene is that we have already enjoyed Gareth as a larger-than-life character. This time it is Matthew who comes to the fore with his speech and his recital of W.H. Auden's *Funeral Blues* poem. It is one of the strengths of the film that Matthew and Gareth's gay relationship is presented as quite normal – the irony is that they had found love whereas their friends are seeking it.

Yet the pursuit of love that our characters have been striving for is achieved in the chapel. Quite clearly, the strong bond between the friends is evident in the funeral scene. We know very little about their other lives but we do get a strong set of their unity and their affection for one another.

SCENE ANALYSIS – I DO

Our perceptions of how the rom-com formula is going to be resolved are thrown in disarray when we are teased by the wedding invitation to Charles' wedding with his betrothed name masked by a flower. Charles surprisingly finds himself in church about to marry Henrietta. However, Carrie's appearance at the wedding and the news that her short-lived marriage to Hamish did not work out, neatly and somewhat cruelly makes her available to Charles on his big day. Naturally, Charles is thrown into turmoil and the film teases us further into guessing how, if at all, he might dump 'Duck face' at the altar.

As the doors of the church open Henrietta enters the church to the familiar strains of Mendelssohn's Wedding March and is beautifully captured as if from the point of view of a wedding photographer, framed between two sets of flowers, her proud father at her side.

The next shot, from her point of view, gives her a view of the altar as the congregation turn to face her and Charles and Matthew step out, slightly nervously. A close-up shows Charles and Matthew turn to face the bride and cuts to a similar close-up of Henrietta wearing a look of triumph behind her veil. We then see a shot of Charles, to the left of the frame and in focus, turn back to face the altar as Henrietta and her father, who are in the background and out of focus, make their way towards him.

Henrietta and her father are then seen together as she yanks his arm and says 'Not so tight Dad.' This moment makes the audience realise that Henrietta has not changed for the better. A close-up of Charles confirms his turmoil – is he really going to make the mistake of marrying Henrietta when the woman he really loves is in the congregation?

As Henrietta approaches Charles we see her tension. She briefly closes her eyes and then gives a quick look across to Charles before facing the altar again. In contrast, a close-up of Charles reveals real uncertainty when first he looks politely, almost apologetically, towards Henrietta before smiling politely in the direction of the vicar.

As the vicar begins his address we get some quick cuts showing reactions from key members of the congregation looking on intently – Bernard and Lydia (wedding number 2) and Angus and Laura (wedding number 1 – complete with their twins), and a shot of

Charles' friends in a neat line. At this point the whole service seems entirely normal until we get a close-up of the vicar's face as he continues his opening about the sanctity of marriage and says '...and therefore is not by any to be enterprised.'

The vicar's words, so familiar in church wedding ceremonies, hit home to Charles as the camera begins a subtle, slow zoom into Charles and then cuts away to the vicar where a slightly faster zoom occurs. Now the camera shows most of the vicar's face on screen with his lips becoming prominent as his words continue to impact on Charles. The vicar concludes with: 'Therefore if any man can show any just cause why they may not lawfully be joined together, let them speak now or hereafter forever hold his peace.' At this point a short, sharp piece of non-diegetic music is introduced, featuring rising staccato strings creating additional tension, abruptly interrupted by the sound of a knocking noise from the congregation.

Not for the first time the film teases us by making us unsure – is this the moment for Carrie to speak out? Will Fiona make an unexpected entreaty? No. We are given a great moment of irony when Charles' deaf-mute brother David 'speaks', thereby adding a little twist on the cliché of someone interrupting a service at this key moment.

The fact that Charles interprets while his brother signs to him enables Charles to find the courage to say what he feels. As with all their exchanges helpful subtitles appear on screen for the benefit of the audience, except this time Charles' interpretation falters when David signs: 'You've got to marry the person you love with your whole heart.' And despite the enormity of this statement David still manages to give the audience a laugh by concluding: 'And by the way your flies are undone'.

The next sequence returns to close-ups when Charles turns to the vicar to confess: 'He says he suspects the groom loves someone else.' We get two cuts to Henrietta's distraught reaction, followed by a shot of Charles' friends, the most noticeable being Fiona as she raises her eyes to the heavens in disbelief. Interestingly, we don't get a shot of Carrie's reaction to any of these exchanges. The film will keep us guessing just a little longer.

The script then manages to contrive an aural and visual punchline. The vicar looks at Charles and determinedly asks: 'Do you love someone else? Do you Charles?'. The comic timing is increased by a series of quick reaction shots as Charles prepares his answer – Fiona mouthing 'No', Angus and Laura holding their babies, Bernard and Lydia looking concerned, Scarlet and Tom with wide eyes, Henrietta preparing for the worst and finally the action returns to Charles as he utters 'I do'. No sooner has Charles uttered these words than a screaming Henrietta lays him out with a swift, heart-felt right-hander. As Charles lays spread out on the church floor the camera looks down on him from above and pans slowly upwards to the roof of the church as Henrietta's screeches can be heard among the mayhem.

With Henrietta now out of the way the film can move on to its natural rom-com conclusion. But once again we are teased. When there is a knock on the door Charles insists on opening it, preparing to face the music. But as the door opens it reveals none other than a rain-drenched Carrie and the film's promised romance reaches its natural conclusion, but not before yet another twist is introduced with this time Charles proposing that he and Carrie don't ever get married. This time Carrie gets to answer 'I do' and as lighting strikes, thunder rumbles and the background music moves to its romantic crescendo, Charles and Carrie embrace with a tender kiss.

REACTION

The film became an unexpected success and drew some fulsome reviews with the British press quick to pick up on its appeal to the American audience. Writing her review in *The Independent*, Sheila Johnson gave some snippets from American reviews including this from *The Houston Chronicle*: 'If you've ever thought to yourself, gee I love British humour, this is as good as it gets.'

Some even went as far as to declare it a modern classic, while others such as Hugo Davenport in *The Sunday Telegraph* simply purred their approval: 'It has just the right mix of the romantic and the risqué, the witty and the wistful, glossed with a sheen of pure class.'

The cast got good reviews with special mention going to Atkinson, but the undisputed star of the film was Grant. Many recognised that his foppish charm and his floppish locks could go a long way in Hollywood. The film made brisk business at the box-office and thanks to Wet, Wet, Wet's extended run in the charts it remained in the public eye and it became Britain's highest box-office film of all time (at that time) by netting £27,762,648 in the UK and more than $244m worldwide.

The film garnered many awards, including BAFTAs for Grant, Kristin Scott Thomas, and Mike Newell and winning the Best Film. Grant went on to win a Golden Globe Award and the Peter Sellers Award for Comedy at the Evening Standard British Film Awards. Scott Thomas picked up Best Actress Award at the Evening Standard British Film Awards where Curtis was presented with the Best Screenplay Award.

The World is Not Enough (1999) (UK/USA) UK Cert 12

Director: Michael Apted

Screenplay: Neal Purvis; Robert Wade; Bruce Feirstein

Producers: Michael G. Wilson; Barbara Broccoli

Production companies: Danjaq LLC; United Artists Corporation; Eon Productions

Production start date: 11/01/1999 **Budget:** £72m (estimated)

Distributor: UIP **UK Release date:** 26 November 1999

UK Box Office: £28,576,504 **USA Box Office:** $126.9m

Worldwide Box Office: $ 352m

Despite the success of Ian Fleming's novels, the first Bond film *Dr. No* (UK, 1962), had been hard for producers Cubby Broccoli and Harry Saltzman and their company Eon Productions to sell. United Artists stumped up a modest budget for the film, which to everyone's surprise became the surprise hit of 1962. Crucially, the interior work was filmed at Pinewood, which would become the home of James Bond films and a mainstay of the British film industry. A British franchise film had been born and more Bond films followed with greater budgets, more sophisticated gadgets and bigger sets.

In terms of the British cinema the Bond films have proved a massive investment for the British film industry. This investment was not merely on the big budgets lavished on Bond films for the industry in Britain had invested in the infrastructure of future film productions. In 1977 a huge purpose-built sound stage was built at Pinewood Studios to accommodate the needs of action sequences in *The Spy Who Loved Me* (UK, 1977). The building became known as the 007 Stage, which featured a massive water tank.

The 1990s were a crucial time for the Bond franchise. First, the Cold War ended as a consequence of Soviet president Mikhail Gorbachev's programme of social and economic reforms and other revolutions within former Eastern Bloc countries followed – symbolised by protesters chipping away at the Berlin Wall in November 1989. Bond's natural enemies in Eastern Europe were coming in from the cold.

In the early part of the 1990s the Bond machine had got embroiled in a dispute between MGM/UA and Eon Productions. However, with issues settled and Irish-born Pierce Brosnan picked to play the new Bond, the franchise was given new impetus with its first film in more than six years – *GoldenEye* (UK/USA, 1995). With Pinewood Studios fully booked, a new studio was created for the film in a former Rolls-Royce aero-engine factory at Leavesden in Hertfordshire.

The box-office success of this film showed that the public still adored 007 and more films followed. However, the Bond legacy also suffered a loss with the death of its legendary producer Cubby Broccoli in 1996. This did not signal the end for the Bond dynasty since the reins of the franchise passed on to Broccoli's stepson Michael G. Wilson and daughter Barbara Broccoli.

This commitment was taken a stage further when a decision was made to build Eon Studios to accommodate the next Bond film *Tomorrow Never Dies* (UK/USA, 1997).

With all this baggage behind it *The World is Not Enough*, the 19th Bond in the series, quickly leapt into production and while keeping to the tried and trusted formula of other Bond films also captured the tail end of 'Cool Britannia' and the aspirations of New Labour in Britain.

SYNOPSIS

British oil tycoon Sir Robert King is killed in an audacious bomb attack, which takes place inside MI6 Headquarters in London. The shocked MI6 team regroups to learn that the assassin was working for the anarchist terrorist Renard, who has a bullet lodged in his brain rendering him impervious to pain and touch and which will ultimately kill him. M assigns Bond to protect King's daughter Elektra who had previously been kidnapped, tortured and held to ransom by Renard.

Proudly, Elektra takes control of her father's business affairs by overseeing the construction of a massive oil pipeline. Bond establishes a close rapport with her after the couple survive an attack during a skiing trip but is puzzled by her actions, notably when she gambles and loses a large sum of money at a casino owned by ex-Russian Mafia boss Valentin Zukovsky.

Bond learns that one of Elektra's bodyguards is working for Renard. He kills the bodyguard and goes to a weapons base in Kazakhstan where he meets American nuclear physicist Christmas Jones (who is working to dismantle plutonium at the site). At the same time Renard steals a large quantity of plutonium, which Bond is helpless to prevent.

Bond now suspects that Renard and Elektra are somehow linked. He and Jones enter a pipeline to intercept a suspected nuclear bomb planted by Renard. However, Bond allows the bomb to explode when he realises that not enough plutonium has been used for a nuclear bomb and that Renard will assume that he has been killed.

Elektra captures M. Meanwhile, Renard hijacks a Russian nuclear submarine, skippered by Zukovsky's nephew, with the aim to detonate a nuclear blast near Istanbul so that other pipelines would be destroyed leaving Elektra to rule the world with her own oil pipeline project.

With time running out Bond enlists Zukovsky's help to find Renard. One of Zukovsky's men, Bull, plants a bomb in the operations room but Bond and Jones avoid injury. However, they are captured and Elektra chooses to torture Bond for her pleasure, while she offers Jones as a parting gift to her one-time lover Renard, and she is taken aboard the submarine.

Zukovsky manages to get into Elektra's hideout and frees Bond when he learns that his nephew has been killed, but not before Elektra fatally shoots him. Bond in turn frees M and gives chase to Elektra and eventually kills her when she refuses to call Renard off.

Bond dives onboard the submarine and frees Jones. Its controls are sabotaged and in an ensuing struggle with Renard he is impaled with a plutonium rod. With the nuclear reactor unarmed Bond and Jones beat a hasty retreat as the submarine is destroyed.

HOW IT WAS MADE

There is a strong British connection in the production of *The World is Not Enough*, particularly with the surprise decision to choose British director Michael Apted to direct. Apted was apparently thrilled to take over the big budget controls of a Bond film. He had an impressive record of credits to his name stretching back to TV work in the 1960s (with the ground-breaking, seven-yearly updates to Granada's *Seven-Up* perhaps his most notable); in the 1970s with films like *Stardust* (UK, 1974); and then working in Hollywood on films such as *Coal Miner's Daughter* (USA, 1981); *Gorky Park* (USA, 1983); *Gorillas in the Mist* (USA, 1988); and *Nell* (USA, 1994).

Writers Neal Purvis and Robert Wade were not yet a tried and tested team. Their work to date had been the well-received *Let Him Have It* (UK, 1991) and the yet to be released (at the time) comedy costume drama *Plunkett & Macleane*. Bruce Fierstein, who had scripted *GoldenEye* and *Tomorrow Never Dies*, was drafted in later to bolster the screenplay.

The film also brought back British production designer and stalwart of many Bond movies, Peter Lamont, who had just picked up one of the many Oscars bestowed on *Titanic* (USA, 1997), for Best Art Direction - Set Decoration.

The 007 Stage at Pinewood was used to recreate the nuclear test facility and the gigantic water tank was used in the caviar factory scenes and the final action shots set on the Bosphorus. At one stage three crews comprising more than 500 technicians were filming sequences.

As befits a Bond film, the locations picked out were eye-catching, not least in the open pre-credits sequence which has Bond chasing his female assassin from the actual MI6 building in a speed boat along the Thames, finishing up in the great symbol of New Labour's hope for the future – the Millennium Dome in Greenwich. Other notable locations included glimpses of the stunning Guggenheim Museum in Bilbao, as well as

Spain, Istanbul, Turkey and the French Alps (posing as the Carpathian Mountains).

For the third Bond in a row the main male villain is British, this time Robert Carlyle playing a Bosnian terrorist, fresh from critical acclaim in *Trainspotting* and *The Full Monty*. Other British interest include the 1990's version of the MI6 team, featuring the talents of M (Judi Dench), Q (Desmond Llewelyn), Moneypenny (Samantha Bond) with the additional novelty of John Cleese appearing as Q's understudy. Robbie Coltrane also reprises his role as the Russian Mafia maverick Valentin Zukosky. British breakbeat artist Goldie was another surprise addition to the cast, playing the two-timing villain Bull. Added to this could be included the theme tune by Garbage, who were closely associated with the Indie Britpop scene of the mid-to late 1990s.

This just left the Bond women. French actress Sophie Marceau, probably best known to a global audience for her role as Princess Isabella in *Braveheart* (USA, 1995), was selected to pick the villainous seductress Elektra King. Meanwhile, American rising starlet Denise Richards had stormed to the public's attention in the Paul Verhoeven sci-fi romp *Starship Troopers* (USA, 1997).

Originally intended for a release in 2000, *The World is Not Enough* complete with an up-to-date reference to the millennium bug, was released to the world in November 1999 just in time for Christmas.

KEY ISSUES

As with all film franchises the key issues are to give the devoted expectant audience what they want. However, the Bond franchise was already three decades and four Bonds old. It was clear that the film still had mass popular global appeal, but the trick was to make a film that would not tamper with the winning formula and yet still offer aficionados enough new tasty items to satisfy their hunger for more.

Shaken not stirred

For Bond fans *The World is Not Enough* ticks off most expectations, including Bond's trademark response to enquiries to his name: 'Bond – James Bond'. Also, in near parody fashion he orders his usual Vodka Martini with ice at Zukovsky's Casino – 'shaken not stirred'. For fans the film can also be judged on how well or otherwise the regular elements of a Bond film are executed.

Pre-title sequence

At around 14 minutes the customary pre-title sequence in *The World is Not Enough* is the longest ever for a Bond film. It serves as an adrenaline-fuelled action short in its own right when Bond takes part in a spectacular speedboat chase along the Thames, starting with an implausible leap from the MI6 building and ending at the Millennium Dome.

The Dome, for which New Labour under Tony Blair had high hopes with its boldness and its symbolism of cultural and educational excellence, opened to the public on 1st January 2000 and stayed open for just a year. Nevertheless, at the time that Bond dangled perilously off the end of a hot air balloon only to fall onto the canvas, it was still a public curiosity.

Gadgets

Bond doesn't have too many gadgets in the film. His x-ray spectacles are used largely to see who is packing what weapons at the casino and also for some fairly restrained voyeurism. His Omega watch contains a powerfully strong grappling hook but perhaps his inflatable jacket, which seems a bit cumbersome when Q's assistant first comically demonstrates it, becomes the pick of the gadgets when the inflatable air-bag ball ingeniously prevents Bond and Elektra from being buried from the avalanche.

Car

For car enthusiasts Bond's BMW Z8 is a powerful sports car, which Bond is able to start remotely via his key-chain. The vehicle also fires missiles.

Villains

Bond has two main villains. First is the terrorist known as Renard, who we see projected in a hologramic presentation at MI6's base in Scotland. Carlyle's role is peculiar because as the plot thickens he becomes almost secondary to Bond's main rival, Elektra King, whose manipulative nature and lust for power is gradually revealed as the plot unfolds. This dual-pronged villain combination is an inventive contribution to the film.

Glamour women

Marceau succeeds in her role as the beautiful femme fatale and largely overshadows Bond's other main glamour interest, Dr. Christmas Jones. Whether intentional or not, when Bond first meets Jones she climbs out of her protective clothing to display more or less an outfit similar to that worn by the well-established games console icon Lara Croft. Dr. Christmas Jones is no less dynamic, if perhaps a little less athletic and her academic, scientific qualifications in theory match those of Bond. Denise Richards was possibly brought in to appeal more to the MTV generation and has the odd distinction of being the token American presence in the film.

Guns, explosions and counter clocks

There are plenty of explosions and shooting to keep even the most determined somnambulist from dropping off. All the shots aimed at Bond miss their target but Bond tends to reply with uncanny accuracy. The most chilling moment is when Bond carries out his threat to kill Elektra by shooting her at point blank range – we are thus reminded of 007's status as a deadly killer. Equally important to the nail-biting tension is the handy device of counter-clocks ticking down to zero and this film obliges on more than one occasion. Add to this chase scenes on water, on skis or on foot and you have a breathless itinerary of all-action hero movies.

One-liners

'If you're Q does this make him R?' Bond quips to Q, to which R played by John Cleese replies: 'Ah yes, the legendary 007 wit – or at least half of it.'

Some Bond films have been criticised for playing too much for laughs, particularly in the jocular era of Roger Moore.

Brosnan is a far more intense Bond. He obliges with a string of one-liners such as his retort to the question: 'What happened to Davidov?' to which Bond, having bumped him off, replies: 'He was buried with work.' Generally, Brosnan's delivery comes with a hardened irony, rather than that of a comedian.

The finale

There is never a doubt that Bond will triumph, save the world and win the girl at the end of an exhausting fight with his villain. The end of *The World is Not Enough* features a battle within the claustrophobic, water-drenched confines of a submarine and lacks the spectacle of the pre-sequence set piece. Nevertheless, the audience still has to discover if Renard will die and whether Bond can pull off the rescue of Dr. Christmas Jones.

Music

Finally, the choice of music and credit sequence in the film is another Bond constant. The choice of British indie band Garbage may have raised some eyebrows. The tune of *The World is Not Enough* was written by the film's composer David Arnold and Don Black but only appears during the film's belated credit sequence. Elsewhere, the timeless James Bond Theme, composed by Monty Norman for *Dr. No*, is reintroduced during action sequences. This is an interesting move to connect the past Bond films with the new, and is also reflected in the closing credits where a techno-mix of the theme is used instead of a reprise of the title tune.

Suspend your disbelief

Action films require the audience to suspend their disbelief. Fans of the genre do this readily and enjoy the spectacle of explosions, chases and general mayhem. The fantasy world where the hero has some narrow brushes with death but always comes out with his hair intact is one that an audience either subscribes to or not. Even so, an audience's credulity should not be stretched too far, otherwise the action movie is in danger of becoming some sort of manic pantomime. Indeed, Robbie Coltrane's comic role as Zukovsky is the closest the film skates to providing a pantomime villain, albeit with his heart in the right place.

The World is Not Enough tests the audience's sense of plausibility throughout its complex plotline. While the elements of terrorist assassination, kidnapping and the construction on an oil pipeline are believable, other insertions into the plot are less convincing. A prime example is Bond's injury during his buffeted fall onto the Millennium Dome. The next time we see Bond he is wearing a sling and the medical opinion shown via x-ray is that he has dislocated his shoulder. This device is used to show Bond's determination to exact revenge for his failure to spot a booby-trapped bomb that kills Sir Robert King. Bond's predictable medical clean-bill of health suggests that the special agent will experience pain if he exerts himself. However, Bond skis, jumps and generally frolics without any sign of a twinge. So when later on Renard grabs hold of Bond's supposed vulnerable joint and he responds with a cry of agony the audience surely cannot believe he is in pain on this occasion.

Similarly, Renard's perplexing injury of the soon-to-be-fatal bullet in his head, which not only makes him stronger but also impervious to pain, takes a lot of swallowing. In terms of the plot it is an interesting device to justify his actions. Renard no longer cares because he knows he is going to die and so his amoral killing spree makes sense. His dedication to Elektra is also revealed as a strange play of sexual jealousy when Renard reveals his impotence to Elektra's steamy availability.

There are plenty of other examples to taunt the casual viewer such as the effortless way Bond can refresh and take himself off to an exotic location. However, the joy of Bond films is often based around marvelling at the liberties the film-makers are prepared to take in order to bring the audience regular thrilling sequences.

The spy who shagged me

James Bond's sexual proclivity was parodied in the title of the Austin Powers spoof *The Spy Who Shagged Me* (USA, 1999), which was released in July 1999. Along with his Licence to Kill Bond seems quite free to have any woman he desires – well, almost any woman – and the film is full of double entendres – such as the cigar girl asking Bond, 'Would you like to check my figures?' to which he replies: 'I'm sure they're perfectly rounded.' In the 1990 series of Bond films Bond indulges in what seem like pointless flirtations with Moneypenny, played with just the right amount of coy aloofness by Samantha Bond.

Otherwise, Bond scores three sexual conquests during the film. His first is Dr. Molly Warmflash (Serena Scott-Thomas) who is seduced into giving Bond a clean bill of health.

Bond's conquest of Elektra is less straightforward and more in keeping with cross and double-crossing ethics of international spies. Indeed, the onscreen chemistry between Brosnan and Marceau makes the sexual power play between them one of the unexpected features of the film. The two appear to be brought physically close together after a near death experience when Bond saves Elektra's life on the ski-slope. She teases Bond most of the time. When he first declines her advances she says: 'Who's afraid now Mr Bond.' Later on Elektra quite literally turns the screw on Bond when she attempts to torture him whilst straddling him in an attempt at sadomasochistic pleasure. 'I've always had power over men,' she declares. For once Bond seems powerless to overcome her and her use of sex as a powerful weapon not only has him fooled but has thrown up an unlikely rival in Renard. Indeed, jealousy and revenge is used throughout the film as a plot device.

Elektra enjoys Renard's jealousy when he asks if Bond was a skilful lover. Elektra's swift execution is therefore quite a shock to observe, since quite clearly Bond has wiped out any feelings for her.

Much easier for Bond is his seduction of Dr. Christmas Jones who we are reliably informed has no interest in men. After surviving the pipeline explosion Jones asks about Bond's relationship with Elektra, to which he retorts: 'It was purely plutonic.' Bond saves Jones's life in the submarine and presumably her honour from Renard, after which how can she resist? And it seems her name Christmas, which also ties in neatly with the release date of the film, leads to another double entendre. 'I thought Christmas only comes once a year.'

SCENE ANALYSIS — TALES OF THE RIVERBANK

Bond films have always prided themselves by filming as many as the action shots 'for real' as possible. In constructing the chase sequence along the Thames the elements of Bond – action, location, glamour, gadgets, explosions, Bond theme music, humour, and surprise – are all thrown into the mix as the sequence, which took months to prepare and more than six weeks to shoot, begins.

Our first glimpse of the Thames comes from Bond's point of view as the explosion that kills Sir Robert King leaves a huge gap in the wall of the M16 building, the twisted debris acting as a border to a shot which, when the smoke clears, shows us a boat in the centre of the screen on the Thames with Lambeth Bridge in the background. This establishes the location of the action. As Bond's focus becomes clearer we cut to a shot of the Cigar Girl training a machine gun at him.

By now the background music replacing the sound of the alarm ringing has kicked in and will be heard throughout the chase sequence mixing familiar elements from the Bond themes of old (including the famous guitar riff) with strains from the theme tune to *The*

World is Not Enough. Other sounds punctuating the chase sequence are the regular sprays of water, the whirring sound of Bond's powerboat as it flies through the air, and the intermittent sound of gun fire, crashing sounds and one oil barrel explosion.

As Bond slips into the prototype powerboat and opens a hatch ready for launch we get our first comedy moment as Q waves his hands in the air and cries out: 'Stop, stop, it isn't finished.' We then see a fantastical shot of a section of the MI6 building open and the boat come flying through the air. Close-up shots on the choppy waters of the Thames establish that the chase is on as Bond's boat speeds along and the Cigar Girl glances over her shoulder and we get her point of view of Bond in pursuit. As the Cigar Girl turns on the throttle we cut to an aerial shot of the two boats chasing each other. A close-up shot looking at Bond allows the audience to see that he (rather than a stuntman) is really steering the boat and the scene is punctuated by the first of the boat's gadget shots as we get a close-up of the array of switches and devices that will propel his boat closer towards his target.

A picture postcard shot of the Houses of Parliament from the air is quickly contrasted with a shot taken from the side of Bond's boat, which not only frames the Houses of Parliament whizzing by in the background, but also shows his boat tantalisingly close to the Cigar Girl's boat. As the two boats go under Lambeth Bridge the camera, which has been following from above, sweeps down and follows them.

A second dose of humour follows as the Cigar Girl's turn in the water completely soaks Bond (a second soaking follows later when she fires a shot-gun at him) before her craft then plunges into and destroys a pier – caught from three different angles in a series of quick cuts. The next sequence of action is established with a close-up shot of Bond's boat's boosters firing. The pursuit continues up a narrow dock passage, which allows Bond to execute a remarkable about-turn in his boat in order to catch up with the Cigar Girl.

The next sequence of shots feature rapid cuts (including shot/reverse shot sequences) building up to the moment when Bond's boat flips into a 360-spin over the Cigar Girl's boat. The boat impacts in slow motion (seen from her perspective), and spins across the boat (seen from two angles) before plunging in the water. Cigar Girl gets up to start the boat and we move to the next segment of the chase.

A conveniently closing bridge allows Bond to find a new gadget – the dive button – and the shot captures him underwater as he comically adjusts his tie. Just as it looks as though the Cigar Girl has escaped (indicated by the music slowing down) we return to a shot of a sat-nav system within Bond's boat which allows him to take a short cut and so enter a new segment of the sequence. The music obliges by regaining its electrobeat tempo.

The visual comedy continues when this time two traffic wardens clamping a car are soaked in a shot when Bond's boat makes a sharp turn and creates a huge amount of spray. The familiar Bond theme is now in evidence as the boat smashes through an LCC boat shed and goes onto dry land, cutting across the road as an old red Routemaster bus passes by. Now two police cars chase Bond as he smashes through a fish market, a restaurant and finally an outdoor table before revealing the end of his route as he rejoins the Thames at the Millennium Dome.

To confirm our understanding of this sequence we see Bond travelling down river followed by a shot of the Cigar Girl with the Dome in the background travelling up river. Their positions relative to each other are shown by a shot of the sat-nav system in Bond's boat, which is then swapped with an aerial shot showing both boats approaching each other with the Dome prominently in the picture.

The final element of the chase reaches its conclusion as Bond's torpedoes allow the Cigar Girl to steer her boat to the banks of the area before the Dome where a hot air balloon allows her a route for escape. Bond's own departure from his boat is spectacular as it makes one final leap above the Cigar Girl's burning boat and the camera captures a shot of the boat flying in the air, two ropes dangling, and Bond leaping in mid-air and grabbing hold of a rope.

From the fast pace of the water we have the slightly more sedate action of Bond dangling from the line. One shot from the Cigar's Girl's perspective has the roof of the Dome as a backdrop as Bond looks up and tries to strike a deal with her. A genuine surprise occurs when the Cigar Girl blows herself up in the balloon rather than face 'him', thereby giving us a key plot indicator of the ruthlessness of Renard. The breathless opening sequence ends with a fabulous shot of Bond's fall being broken by the roof of the Dome. Indeed, the fall looks painful as Bond misses one set of supporting wires before hanging on to another. At this point we finally cut to the title sequence.

REACTION

The World is Not Enough premiered in the UK on 26 November 1999, a week after it had been released in the USA. It quickly became the highest grossing film in the history of Bond movies, clocking up worldwide box-office receipts of $352m. All the 1990's Bond films eased any doubts that the franchise could not survive a post-cold war climate. The public's appetite for 007 remained unabated. Bond was back.

The critics were not entirely convinced. Most enjoyed the pre-title sequence on the Thames and thought that Brosnan delivered a good performance, many citing some evidence of Bond's brooding character emerging. Marceau's performance also drew positive responses, as did the cosy scenes featuring the British MI6 team. Most also agreed that the film struck just the right balance of action with humour. However, many critics felt that Carlyle's villain gave the actor little to work with and Denise Richard's character seemed far too implausible as a nuclear physicist. Nevertheless, *The World is Not Enough* proved to a global audience that even a slightly under par Bond film still packed a powerful punch.

Bond came back, but not as quickly as he had done in the 1990s. *Die Another Day* (UK/USA, 2002), was not only the 20th in the series but also marked the 40th anniversary of the series. It surpassed *The World is Not Enough*'s box-office success with a worldwide gross box-office taking of more than $450m. However, the film marked the end of Brosnan's involvement with 007 and he was replaced by Daniel Craig.

The World is Not Enough also marked the last appearance from Desmond Llewelyn, who died on 20 December 1999. The actor had played Q 17 times, starting as early as *From Russia With Love* (UK/USA, 1964), when his character was known as Boothroyd.

CONCLUSION

The success of *Four Weddings and a Funeral* should not be underestimated. It not only led to a renewed interest in British films but renewed investment as well. Other successful romantic comedies followed, notably *Sliding Doors*, which used the *Four Weddings* 'formula' by including an American actress, Gwyneth Paltrow (who starred opposite John Hannah). This in turn encouraged women to return to the ever-growing comfort of the cinema with more films aimed at their enjoyment.

The Bond franchise looks set to continue. Not only were the Bond films box-office draws at the cinema but the series found grateful homes on video and DVD shelves. Also a testimony to their draw is that Bond films regularly bring in large audiences on terrestrial television. In 1999 no fewer than 10 Bond films made it into the top 20 list of feature films shown on terrestrial television. Top of the pile was *GoldenEye*, which brought ITV (which screened all the Bond films) an audience of 13.23 million. When *The World is Not Enough* was premiered on terrestrial television in 2001 it was the third most popular feature film with an audience of 9.80 million. Remarkably, eight other Bond films still made the top 20 list for that year.

The real legacy that the Bond franchise brought to the British film industry was the investment in film studios, which had a knock-on effect by encouraging other big budget films to be shot in Britain. The Leavesden Studios that were built to accommodate *GoldenEye* now hosted Britain's latest most successful franchise – the Harry Potter films.

As a footnote to the value of the investment ploughed into the Bond films, in 2006 a fire badly damaged the 007 Stage during the filming of *Casino Royale*. Within six months the damaged stage had been replaced.

FURTHER READING

One Hundred Films and a Funeral: The Life and Death of PolyGram Films
Kuhn, Michael (Thorogood, 2002)

Producing the Goods? UK Film Production since 1991.
Wickham, Phil (BFI National Library, BFI Information Services, 2003)

British Cinema of the 90s
Murphy, Robert (ed.) (BFI, 2001) Chapter 1 – A Path through the Moral Maze by Murphy, Robert
Chapter 6 – Pathways into the Industry by Ogborn, Kate

The Stats An overview of the film, television, video and DVD industries 1990-2003
(BFI National Library, BFI Information Services, 2006)

BFI Film and Television Handbook (BFI, editions from 1990–2005)

Selected reviews/articles/references

That Shrinking Feeling by Geoffrey MacNab
Sight & Sound, Vol.12 No.10. (October 2002) P. 18-20

Working Title Films – www.workingtitlefilms.com

BBC Films – www.bbc.co.uk/bbcfilms

Film 4 – www.channel4.com/film/ffproductions

Mercharnt Ivory – www.merchantivory.com

The British Council Film Division – www.britfilms.com

Four Weddings and a Funeral

Sight & Sound V.4 N.6 (1 June 1994) P.46 by Myers, Caren
Empire N.60 (1 June 1994) P.24-25 by Thomas, Philip

Made here, big over there by Johnson, Sheila
The Independent 27th April 1994

The anatomy of a movie by Nathan, Ian
Empire N.67 (1 Jan 95) P.98-103

Contemporary British Cinema 16+ Source Guide Guides
Mettler, Erinna; Ormsby, Andrew; Reeve, David; Dupin, Christophe (BFI National Library, 2003) www.bfi.org.uk/filmtvinfo/publications/16+/

The World is Not Enough

Sight & Sound V.10 N.1 (1 Jan 2000) P.62-63 by Arroyo, José

Empire N.127 (1 Jan 2000) P.12-13 by Newman, Kim

Cinefantastique Vol.31 No.9.(December 1999) P.32-55 by Wilson, Michael G.

Licence to Thrill: A cultural history of the James Bond films
Chapman, James (Tauris, revised edition, 2007)

The James Bond Phenomenon: A Critical Reader
Lindner, Christoph (Editor) (Manchester University Press, 2003)

The Essential Bond: The Authorized Guide to The World of 007
Pfeiffer, Lee and Worral, Dave (Boxtree, 2002)

Bond 16+ Source Guide Guides
Smart, Emma; Delaney, Sean; Khan, Ayesha; Clarke, Nicola; Williamson, Tracey (BFI National Library, 2006)

DVD: *The World is Not Enough*: Special Edition (MGM Entertainment, 2003)

6. IT'S A LOTTERY

On 19 November 1994, 22 million UK television viewers witnessed 49 bouncing balls being rotated wildly by a machine known as Guinevere as the first-ever National Lottery draw organised by The National Lottery's operator Camelot took place. The strapline 'It Could Be You' sent millions scurrying to newsagents with the dream of become millionaires. For the British film industry the same strapline seemed to apply as The Arts Councils of England, Scotland, Wales and Northern Ireland were assigned responsibilities for distributing Lottery money for film projects in 1995. The money mainly went on film production, although it should be remembered that some Lottery money was assigned for other film-related operations such as refurbishment work in cinemas or large grants such as the £15m assigned to the BFI London IMAX Cinema, which opened in 1999.

However, it was in the area of film production where a fierce debate raged about the validity of using public money to fund film production projects. Other media commentators also wondered whether the Arts Council, appointed by the Department of Heritage, was the appropriate body to administer such funds.

Lottery grants gave first-time directors a chance to try their luck, but many failed to ring the bell with either critics or box-office tills. Some, notably veteran film critic, the late Alexander Walker, railed against the principles behind public money being wasted on such speculative ventures when it might have been better used for good causes, such as keeping hospitals open. The poor performance at the box-office of the majority of the Lottery-funded films, some which turned out to be real stinkers, kept the debate neatly simmering.

At first it was generally assumed that money would be allocated to film-makers who needed extra finances to make their films. This involved them making a reasonable case on their application forms that their films stood a chance of being released. The bottom line seemed to be that money would be allocated if a film looked likely to repay the amount invested, a supposition that is generally not guaranteed in the world of film-making. It was widely assumed that Lottery funds wouldn't go to films intended to have a wide theatrical release. As such, post-1995, the top box-office UK films – *The Full Monty*, *Notting Hill*, *The World is Not Enough*, *Shakespeare in Love* (UK/USA, 1999), *Bean*, *Trainspotting*, *Sliding Doors* – succeeded without the help of Lottery funds, relying instead on commercial assistance afford them by the United States through sales and distribution deals.

Yet buoyed by the success of British films in the international market, in May 1997, with the government's blessing, the Arts Council announced three national Lottery-funded commercial franchises worth a cool £92.25m. The plan was to seize the moment and pool talent to create three mini-studios in an attempt to make commercially successful films. There were conditions attached. Initially, each franchise was given a period of six years to fulfill its individual projects and the Arts Council would nominally have to approve the funding of individual film proposals.

On paper the idea seemed like a bold move in the right direction since the film franchises consisted of film-makers with some track record of success. The awards also reflected the ambitions and targets set out by each franchise in their business plans. It all seemed very promising. It all went terribly wrong.

The Film Consortium

Lottery allocation: £30.25m

Number of films proposed: 39

Number of films released after six years: 16

The Film Consortium was made up of Greenpoint Films, a loose association of 10 film-makers: Simon Relph, Christopher Morahan, Ann Scott, Richard Eyre, Stephen Frears, Patrick Cassavetti, John Mackenzie, Mike Newell, David Hare and Christopher Hampton; Parallax Pictures, which featured directors Ken Loach and Les Blair and producers Sally Hibbin and Sarah Curtis; Scala Productions, which included Stephen Woolley, Nik Powell of Palace Pictures fame and Amanda Posey; and Skebra Films, which had been formed by Simon Relph in the 1980s.

By the mid-term review in early 2000 The Film Consortium had managed just over half a dozen film releases, the pick being *Hideous Kinky*, starring Kate Winslet. But other films like *Janice Beard 45 WPM* (UK, 1999), starring Rhys Ifans, Patsy Kensit and Eileen Walsh faired poorly. The Film Consortium could point to bad luck in losing Rank as its distributor when it was taken over by Carlton but generally its mid-term results were of the 'could do better' variety. By April 2000, the Film Consortium had been acquired by Civilian Content and eventually did do better over the next three years, scoring success with *24 Hour Party People* (UK, 2001).

Pathé Pictures

Lottery allocation: £33m

Number of films: 35

Number of films released after six years: 15

Pathé Pictures was a French-owned company operating in Britain. The franchise that won the Lottery bid consisted of Mike Leigh's production company Thin Man Films, Imagine Films, Allied Film-makers and Allied Films Ltd, which had made *The Lawnmower Man* (UK/ USA, 1991), NFH, Lynda Miles' Pandora Productions, Sarah Radclyffe Productions, Fragile Films, (which would produce *Spice World*) and MW Entertainment.

While eventually producing less than half of its original proposed total Pathé could boast a steady output of films such as *An Ideal Husband* (UK/USA, 1999), and the critically acclaimed *Ratcatcher*, which up to the end of the decade had done reasonably well. The franchise continued in a similar vein into the 2000s, producing diverse British films such as the dark horror *The Hole* (UK/France, 2001), featuring an early appearance from future Brit star Keira Knightley; the child-orientated comedy *Thunderpants* (UK/Germany, 2002); and the literary adaptation of *Girl With A Pearl Earring* (UK/Luxemburg/USA, 2003) starring Scarlett Johansson and Colin Firth.

DNA Films

Lottery allocation: £29m

Number of films: 16

Number of films released after six years: 5

This consortium consisted of Duncan Kenworthy, who had struck gold as a producer of *Four Weddings and a Funeral*, and Andrew MacDonald who had similarly mined success via *Trainspotting* and *Shallow Grave*.

Much to the chagrin of the film franchise sceptics, DNA Films was slow off the blocks andat the mid-term review it had still to release a film, although *Strictly Sinatra* (UK, 2000) and *Beautiful Creatures* (UK, 2000) had gone into production. Neither met with commercial or critical success. Rather than lose its franchise DNA was allowed to complete its six years and obliged by producing a genuine box-office hit in the zombie horror *28 Days Later* (UK, 2002).

The creation of the film franchises exposed a certain amount of naivety about how long films take to make and how money alone cannot guarantee success. The three franchises' original business plans now look wildly optimistic and understandably led to many column inches criticising the system and its administrator, The Arts Council.

The Arts Council of England had to wait a long time before witnessing real box-office success in *Billy Elliot* (UK, 2000). Only two other films, the romantic comedies *Shooting Fish* (UK, 1997) and *This Year's Love* (UK, 1999), succeeded in taking more at the UK box-office than they cost to make. However, the list of the top 20 Lottery-funded films shows an eclectic mix of British films featuring the established talents of Ken Loach (*My Name is Joe*), Mike Leigh (*Topsy-Turvy*) and Kenneth Branagh (*Love's Labour's Lost*); less mainstream films such as *Ratcatcher, Love is the Devil* and *Love and Death on Long Island* (UK/Canada, 1996); and familiar heritage films such as *An Ideal Husband* and *Mansfield Park* (UK/USA, 1999).

Top 20 all-time Lottery-funded list by UK box-office 1995–2000

	Title	Award (£m)	Budget (£m)	Box Office (£)
1	Billy Elliot	0.85	2.83	18,230,000
2	Shooting Fish	0.98	2.90	4,020,000
3	This Year's Love	0.75	2.75	3,600,636
4	An Ideal Husband*	1.00	6.50	2,893,170
5	Plunkett and MacLeane	0.95	9.30	2,779,315
6	Land Girls	1.50	5.50	1,573,783
7	Topsy-Turvy	2.00	13.50	1,163,994
8	Hilary and Jackie	0.95	4.90	1,040,788
9	My Name is Joe	0.50	2.50	949,228
10	Still Crazy	1.89	7.00	933,574
11	Hideous Kinky**	1.00	2.00	793,538
12	Mansfield Park	1.00	6.46	566,450
13	Love's Labour's Lost*	1.06	8.50	527,681
14	Divorcing Jack	1.00	2.70	469,961
15	Ratcatcher *	0.61	2.00	429,980
16	Love and Death on Long Island	0.75	2.50	394,372
17	There's Only One Jimmy Grimble*	1.60	3.31	352,173
18	Love is the Devil	0.36	1.00	277,366
19	Whatever Happened to Harold Smith?	0.50	5.64	253,530
20	The Winter Guest	0.50	4.50	250,689

* Pathé ** The Film Consortium

Box office figures as of 16 August 2001

Source: Nielsen EDI/Film Council/Screen Finance/BFI Film and Television Handbook 2002

It soon became clear that the entire film Lottery funding system needed a complete overhaul or Lottery monies would continue to be spent with no discernable benefit to the British film industry.

UK FILM COUNCIL

Responsibility for distributing Lottery funds in England was assigned to the new government-sponsored film body the Film Council (later rebranded the UK Film Council) headed up by its director John Woodward, and chairman Alan Parker, who had moved across from similar roles at the British Film Institute. Scottish Screen became the national agency responsible for the screen industries in Scotland, while the Arts Councils of Wales and Northern Ireland continued to distribute Lottery funds for their film projects.

The Film Council, which officially came into existence on 1 April 2000, had a wider remit to develop a sustainable UK film industry and develop a film culture in Britain via improved access to and education about the moving image.

Its first task was to introduce a structured system for Lottery funding. Weaknesses in the current system had been identified, particularly in the development of films, attention to scriptwriting and the lack of training opportunities for the next generation of film-makers. Starting with a package of £2m the Film Council set about creating three major funds and two smaller funds for training.

The Premiere Production Fund – £10m per year was to be set aside for the production and creation of popular mainstream films.

The New Cinema Fund – £5m per year was to be devoted to new film-makers working within new digital film technologies.

Film Development Fund – £5m per year was to be aimed at supporting the development of innovative and commercially attractive screenplays.

Film Training Fund – £1m per year was set aside for supporting training initiatives for scriptwriters and others working within the film industry.

First Movies – £1m per year was to be for children to help them make first short films using low-cost digital technology.

Essentially, the Film Council wanted to see an end to the production of films whose half-baked ideas, one-dimensional characters and awful scripts had somehow been rubber-stamped. The Film Council would allow the three film franchises to finish their allotted terms and again review their performances, while establishing the new film funds that would treat public money with better care.

Those who grumbled about Lottery distribution under the Arts Council now grumbled that the Film Council would become too powerful and influential in its distribution of funds. However, it is clear that the influx of Lottery cash, for better and for worse, boosted film production in the UK. Like it or not, the government had found a relatively efficient way of offering the industry a subsidy. Lottery funding for film production was here to stay.

In this section the fortunes of two Lottery films – *Billy Elliot* and *Ratcatcher* – are followed. *Billy Elliot* (made in 1999 although released in 2000) was the most successful of the Arts Council Lottery-funded films. *Ratcatcher* was an artistic and critical success but commercially uninspiring. Both films deserve their place in the cannon of the best of British. Without Lottery funding their production would have been much harder.

Billy Elliot (2000) (UK/France) UKCert 15

Director: Stephen Daldry

Screenplay: Lee Hall

Producers: Greg Brenman; Jon Finn

Production companies: Tiger Aspect; Working Title Films; BBC Films;, Arts Council of England; WT; National Lottery through the Arts Council of England

Production start date: 23/08/1999 **Budget:** £ 2.8m (estimated)

Distributor: UIP **UK Release date:** 29 September 2000

UK Box Office: £18,386,715 **USA Box Office:** $22m

Worldwide Box Office: $109.3m

Very late in the day, the much-maligned tenure of the Arts Council of England finally bore box-office success in the form of the comedy drama *Billy Elliot*, which became the most successful Lottery-funded film at the box-office just as the newly-formed Film Council was taking over the controls of the distribution of England's Lottery funds for film in 2000.

The film, made in 1999, struck a familiar chord with cinema audiences by serving up a rags to riches tale set against the backdrop of the miners' strike in the mid-1980s of a boy from the North East of England who chooses ballet dancing over boxing. This delightful premise throws up all sorts of issues about class, perceptions of male masculinity, sexuality, bereavement, family values and the north/south divide.

The film can be placed alongside *The Full Monty* and *Brassed Off* in not only capturing moments in Britain's social and political history, but also for portraying a sense of humour, which adds just enough sugar to take the bitterness away and make it accessible to wider audiences.

SYNOPSIS

Set in County Durham in 1984 at the height of the coal miners' strike, 11-year-old Billy Elliot lives with his father, Jackie, and his older brother, Tony, who are both on strike, and his grandmother who displays signs of senile dementia. Billy's mother died two years earlier. Billy's father pays 50 pence for Billy to go to boxing classes after school but Billy shows no aptitude to the sport. Instead, he is intrigued with a ballet class run by the chain-smoking Mrs Wilkinson. Tentatively, he joins in with the class and Mrs Wilkinson, noticing some natural ability, asks Billy if he wants to come back again.

When Billy's father finds out that Billy has been dancing instead of boxing he is horrified and forbids Billy to go to lessons again. Billy goes to Mrs Wilkinson's house in a middle-class suburb to explain the situation. Mrs Wilkinson tells him that she thinks he is good enough to audition for the Royal Ballet School in London. Billy agrees to take private tuition.

On the day that Billy is due to audition in Newcastle, Tony is arrested. Mrs Wilkinson comes to Billy's house and is met with hostility from Tony and Billy's father.

Billy's father finally relents at Christmas when Billy performs a dance of defiance in front of his father in the boxing hall. His father feels compelled to raise the money required for the audition, which involves crossing the picket-line and going back to work much to the horror of Tony, who stops him.

Billy's father accompanies Billy to London for his audition. Billy feels intimidated by his surroundings and takes out his frustrations by punching a boy. Feeling low, Billy is not able to answer any questions until a woman asks him to describe the sensations he has when he dances and Billy reveals the release and joy he gets from it.

After a tense wait, Billy gets accepted into the Royal Ballet School. Years later his father and Tony are seen attending a performance of Swan Lake at the Royal Opera House in Covent Garden where Billy is starring. Also in the audience is Billy's friend Michael.

HOW IT WAS MADE

Following the success of The Full Monty and Brassed Off it would be natural to assume that funding for Billy Elliot would have come easily. However, the number of production companies involved is testimony to the continued nervousness about British films, particularly ones with British themes and Northern accents. The film had a relatively low budget of £2.8m, an indication that the backers didn't anticipate another Full Monty in the making. Of that, £850,000 came from Lottery funding from the Arts Council of England.

The story of Billy Elliot came from Newcastle playwright Lee Hall, who had achieved some success with a BBC radio play in 1997, Spoonface Steinberg, about a nine-year-old autistic girl dying of cancer, which was adapted for television a year later. Hall pitched his 'art-house' idea for *Billy Elliot* to George Faber, head of BBC films in 1995, and was duly commissioned. Two years later, while Hall's other projects had seen fruition, Greg Brenman from Tiger Aspect called to check on *Billy Elliot*. The script underwent some pruning before being put aside for another two years before Hall's luck changed and with good timing he consulted his friend Stephen Daldry.

Working Title, flushed with success throughout the rest of the 1990s following *Four Weddings and a Funeral*, made some interesting choices. The film would be the first produced by its independent WT2 arm and be distributed by Universal Focus, a specialised film division of US major Universal. It also offered Daldry, who had come with a Royal Court Theatre pedigree and had directed hit plays such as *An Inspector Calls*, a chance to direct films. Daldry embraced the challenge, despite finding aspects of film-making completely different to theatre productions. His first foray into the medium came with the short film *Eight* (UK, 1998) about an eight-year-old Liverpool football supporter facing up to life after the death of his father. When Daldry received the script of *Billy Elliot* he was taken by the weighty intertwining threads of dance, identity, grief, creativity and conflict.

Hall's emotionally-charged script called for the lead role to be played by a boy who could not only act but dance as well and have the right regional accent. Jaime Bell, one of many hundreds of boys who auditioned for the part, had to go through more than half a dozen auditions before he was selected.

From the rest of the cast Julie Walters, who had made such an impression in the 1980's *Educating Rita* (UK, 1983), was the best known to audiences. In the 1990s she had appeared alongside Victoria Wood in TV comedy shows such as *Dinner Ladies* but had also starred in two dramatic films roles -- the low-budget *Girl's Night* (UK/USA, 1997) and *Titanic Town* (UK/Germany/France/Ireland, 1998). This time she could combine her comic and dramatic styles.

With a tight budget and a seven-week schedule, production began in August 1999 with much of the action shot in the village of Easington in County Durham and mining sequences taking place at Ellington and Lynemouth Mine in Northumberland.

The film, originally called *Dance*, screened at the Cannes Film Festival in May 2000 before its UK premiere in September 2000.

KEY ISSUES

As well as carrying the audience on Billy's slightly sentimental journey from impoverished mining community to fulfilling his dream in the best traditions of feel-good comedy films, *Billy Elliot* brings with it some serious issues in terms of grief, identity and self-expression. All this is fulfilled with the sinister brooding police presence that accompanies the backdrop of the miners' strike.

Billy's rocky road

Like *The Full Monty*, *Billy Elliot* examines and questions traditional notions of masculinity. Whereas *The Full Monty* focused on adult males, *Billy Elliot* looks to the future from the point of view of an 11-year-old-boy. Very early on in the film *Billy Elliot* is left under no illusions to his worth as a male when he is easily knocked out in the ring: 'You're a disgrace to them gloves, your father, and the traditions of this boxing hall.' Another kind of film might have led Billy into a *Rocky* type of regime. Instead, his journey to fulfilling his potential means that he has to join in with a girl's ballet class, challenge his father's authority, earn his brother's scorn and still strive to succeed as a dancer. The film is quick to cut to a clip of Fred Astaire dancing in *Top Hat* (USA, 1935), to prove a point that men can become successful dancers. Billy is naturally hesitant when joining in with the girls and when he tells the teacher Mrs Wilkinson that he feels like a sissy, she retorts: 'Well, don't act like one.'

During all this time the film cuts to scenes of male testosterone in action with the conflict between the striking miners on the picket-line and the policemen who have been drafted in to ensure that non-striking miners can get in to work. At one stage the gentile ballet class is intercut with shots of the strikers noisily confronting the massed ranks of police. These are poor role models for Billy. The hatred, aggression and frustration form a necessary influence, which on the one hand derives from a world that Billy does not want to belong to, and on the other gives him unchannelled energy from which he draws inspiration.

He chooses not to follow in his fathers' and brothers' footsteps by accepting his fate of becoming a miner and in so doing adhering to a form of gender stereotypes. His greatest influence is a woman, Mrs Wilkinson, who sees his true potential. She does not quite become Billy's surrogate mum but she does recognise the importance that Billy's mum played in his life when Billy recites his mother's letter almost word for word. Billy may feel that he has lost out on his childhood anyway and decides that he wants to become a ballet dancer.

The children in *Billy Elliot* are wise beyond their years. Debbie gives a frank and forthright assessment of her parent's relationship, analysing that her mother turned to dancing lessons as a compensation for a failed marriage. 'She's unfulfilled. That's why she dances,' she says matter of factly. Michael is equally sanguine and inquisitive about Billy's desire to become a dancer.

Luckily for Billy, Mrs Wilkinson comes from a middle-class background, which means that aspirations are easier to focus on than money. Billy also gets some mixed signals regarding his sexuality. Debbie fancies him and his best friend at school, Michael, whose father we learn dresses up in women's clothes, is seen experimenting with make-up and ends up giving Billy a kiss.

The blurring of sexual stereotypes also produces the statement from Billy: 'Just because I like ballet doesn't mean I'm a poof.' Ironically, taken outside of the confines of his harsh North East surroundings, Billy finally lashes out at the expense of a middle-class boy at his audition in London. On this occasion the violence that Billy has suppressed and expressed through dance is real and rather than earning his father's approval for acting like a man earns a stern rebuke from those conducting the interview.

Jackie Elliot's journey

To tease out gender roles, Billy's father is called Jackie. His journey in the film is harder since he feels he has to do what is best for everyone without the support of his wife. His outrage at finding that Billy has chosen ballet rather than boxing is followed by the assessment: 'All right for your Nana, for girls. No, not for lads, Billy. Lads do football... or boxing... or wrestling.' When Billy is barred from ballet he screams at his father: 'I hate you, you're a bastard.' Billy's father is quite clearly a hard man, but not impervious to this kind of jibe.

Billy's father is also challenged by his older son, Tony, also a miner. Yet he also steps out of line taunting his father: 'Since mum died you're nothing but a useless twat,' which leads to Billy's father punching him to the floor. Tony is eventually caught by the police and spends a night in the cells.

Jackie Elliot's breaking point comes at Christmas when everything seems hopeless and he breaks down. However, it is when Billy dances for his father, more as an act of defiance than an audition, that Jackie Elliot finally makes his boldest move and accepts Billy's desire to be given the chance to become a dancer.

In a peculiar role reversal he has to persuade Tony that Billy may have talent and should be given a chance. His ultimate sacrifice is when he crosses the picket-line to go back to work in order to fund the trip. In a symbolic scene, Tony begs his father not to compromise his principals but both come to accept that Billy has a right to shape his own destiny.

In the end Billy and his father are reconnected. This is charmingly shown in the film when Billy nervously asks his father: 'If I don't like it, can I still come back?' To which his father replies with a straight face: 'Are you kidding? We've let out your room.' The two then enjoy the joke.

Dancing in the streets

The choice of music is peculiar with Marc Bolan's glamrock band of the 1970s providing an unusual musical backdrop to the film. It is unlikely that in the mid-1980s Billy's brother would still be into T.Rex. We first see Billy bouncing on a bed throwing shapes to the tune of *Cosmic Dancer* from T.Rex's Electric Warrior album. This is an early indicator that Billy has a connection with music. Having just triumphed in Swan Lake the film closes to the ironic strains of *Ride a White Swan*. However, the T.Rex moments somehow add to the charm of the film and possibly speak to an audience who were in their early teens in the 1970s.

His breakthrough moment comes in the *I Love to Boogie* sequence where Billy dances with his teacher. The joy Billy experiences is shared by her and acts as a nicely timed exuberant fillip preceding the tear-jerking moment when Mrs Wilkinson shares Billy's mother's letter with him.

Two other tunes seem equally out of time in the film but are used to good effect. The first is The Clash's *London Calling*, which follows Tony as he is chased and caught and beaten by the police. This tension then leads to another of Billy's major dancing sequences, this time as he expresses his anger to the tune of The Jam's hit *Town Called Malice*. Both The Clash and The Jam hits come from a post-punk era of the late 1970s and early 1980s and are slightly out of context with the music scene of the mid-1980s even though they serve as symbols of rebellion.

The streets around where Billy lives, particularly with the hill showing the sea on the horizon, also lends itself to some effective photography as Billy is seen either skipping or jumping with the sea in the background. Bell excels in the role as a dancer by displaying his natural rhythm and thoroughly convincing us of his desire to succeed as a dancer.

Perhaps the key moment in the whole film is when one of the interviewers asks Billy what it feels like when he's dancing. Prior to this point we have shared Billy's joy and frustrations as a dancer by observing him. But when he finally articulates his feelings we know that dancing for him is cathartic: '…but once I get going… then I like, forget everything. And… sorta disappear. Sorta disappear. Like I feel a change in my whole body. And I've got this fire in my body. I'm just there. Flying like a bird. Like electricity. Yeah, like electricity.'

The culmination of those feelings are witnessed one last time when a mature Billy prepares to take the stage at the Opera House in London, to dance Swan Lake. His final flexing of muscles and preparations reveal themselves in his magnificent entrance.

Bereavement

Billy Elliot can be interpreted as a boy and his family overcoming bereavement. Death is seen as a box-office turn-off but the death of Billy's mother is handled sensitively. Billy is seen at her graveside, he answers questions from Debbie about how he feels, and at one point the loss manifests itself when he imagines her telling him to use a glass and not drink from the bottle of milk.

The piano, which belonged to Billy's mum, is used subtly as Billy is seen drawing comfort from its keys. Later on in the film, it is smashed up and the pieces used for firewood. 'Shut it, Billy, she's dead,' shouts his father when he is at his wit's end. The following scene shows Billy's father breaking down after wishing everyone a happy Christmas. The loss is shared as Billy's father comes to terms with what is left of his family.

The most moving scene is when Mrs Wilkinson reads a letter written to Billy from his mother, presumably when she knew she was going to die. We are touched when we realise that Billy knows the contents of the letter off by heart. And the letter itself exudes the total expression of love that a mother can have for her son. This very gentle moment is tapered off when Mrs Wilkinson says: 'She must've been a very special woman, your mother,' and Billy shrugs a reply: 'No, she was just me mam.'

The loss in the film can be read as a metaphor for the imminent loss of a community and an industry in the North East. Symbolically, it is not only Billy and his family who are in mourning.

The miners' strike

The miners' strike acts like background scenery to the main story. The brooding police presence, either passive or aggressive, is evident in most of the outdoor scenes. The conflict itself is seen in short, sharp cuts featuring miners on the picket-line or police banging their shields provocatively. Mrs Wilkinson's slovenly husband provides the only real discussion about the issues by repeating the government's policy on pit closures.

Daldry was keen to reference this period in Britain's industrial and social history, although he was wary that industrial disputes are not great box-office attractions. *Billy Elliot* contains enough humour and warmth to steer it away from the sharp end of social realist drama. Nevertheless, the scene in which Billy's father becomes a 'scab' by crossing the picket-line under police escort is utterly harrowing, particularly fuelled by the emotional intensity of preceding scenes.

By the end of the film Billy's scene overshadows the plight of the miners. They are seen going back to work as the strike is broken. Their future, unlike Billy's, is not assured.

SCENE ANALYSIS – PREPARE

Billy's early progress is captured in a sequence played out like one long rehearsal but really spreading the action over a period of time. In between rehearsal time we cut to a series of shots of Billy practicing at home, which provide some slapstick moments. Not only do we see Billy's dedication, growing self-belief and resolve, we also see Mrs Wilkinson as a hard taskmaster pushing him on.

The rehearsal sequence begins with the strains of *Get it On* by T.Rex linking the scene from the mobile library to the hall where ballet practice takes place. Our first shot is composed in a cinematic cliché with a camera above a spiral staircase looking down. At the bottom is Billy tentatively looking up the stairwell as the girls in their tutus rush up the stairs into the rehearsal space.

Having established Billy's return to rehearsals we cut to a shot of him in his darkened bathroom looking at the library book that he had recently taken from the mobile library. The sound of a tap running implies an alibi for his covert ballet activity. As he places the book on the shelf with pictures of two dancers in an arabesque position we hear Mrs Wilkinson's voice in the background start with 'OK, Billy Elliot, into the centre, I want you to watch carefully girls. First arabesque.' At this point Billy, in front of a large bathroom mirror, tries out the position. The sound of Mr Braithewaite's piano then switches the scene back into the ballet class where we see Mrs Wilkinson and Billy in front of a mirror (Mr Braithewaite caught in the reflection) with the girls either side of the mirror looking at Mrs Wilkinson holding Billy as he tries to find the correct position. Having found the right pose to Mrs Wilkinson's satisfaction in the hall we cut to Billy comically falling over in the bathroom, unable to execute the position on his own.

In the next shot Mrs Wilkinson is wearing her blue tracksuit and Billy is in his white top. As the shots return to the ballet class we see a subtle progression of time. When Mrs Wilkinson (in blue again) calls 'Spin it,' Billy is now wearing a blue top. As the class spin Billy looks out of place, appearing taller than all the girls in shot. In exasperation Mrs Wilkinson orders the class to: 'Look in the mirror.' As she does so we cut back to the bathroom. This time Billy is wearing his school uniform as he focuses on his face in the smaller mirror above the sink as the music from the class carries on in the background. His attempt at a spin merely knocks the library book off the shelf and Billy lets out a cry. The music stops and we cut back into the hall as Mrs Wilkinson berates the class. As she does, we cut back to Billy in the bathroom nursing his hand as we hear his father calling: 'What's going on?'

Billy is seen composing himself in the ballet class. This time the camera, which had previously surveyed the class in a long shot, now has Billy in the foreground. Billy's pirouette is captured in some quick cuts from the class and his bathroom. His next comedy moment is him landing in the bath at home and in Mrs Wilkinson's arms in class. Mrs Wilkinson's voice says: 'Up you get,' and Billy at home (drenched) and in the class rise. Back in the class Mrs Wilkinson apparently continues from where she just left off by saying: 'Find a place on that bloody wall, and focus on that spot.' Now Billy is wearing white in class and Mrs Wilkinson has a purple top on. Time has moved on even though the next cut back in Billy's bathroom shows him soaked as he follows her instructions by preparing again. In the bathroom Billy's agitation is clear as he fails to carry out a move. We cut back to a close-up of a similarly agitated Billy looking towards Mrs Wilkinson as she barks: 'Have you got the spot?'

At this point we get some obvious indications of time moving on when Mrs Wilkinson instructs: 'Prepare.' We then get a series of cuts of Billy at home in the centre of the picture absorbing her instruction – Billy in a yellow top in his bedroom, Billy wearing a jumper framed by some curtains, Billy lying in bed saying 'prepare', Billy wearing pyjamas in the bathroom. Then we hear Mrs Wilkinson shout: 'Go!' as we return to the class focusing on Billy in the foreground as he attempts the turn. The next sequence shows his progress as his unsuccessful turns are catalogued in another series of quick cuts ending in the bathroom where we see a full turn and a close-up of him smiling with satisfaction. Significantly, Mrs Wilkinson is now addressing him: 'Go Billy, go,' she cries. His smile is captured again when we cut back to a close-up of Billy in the class feeling that he has mastered his pirouette. He looks to Mrs Wilkinson for approval but she wipes his smile away by saying: 'What have I told you about that arm.' Billy's moody expression can now be seen as Mrs Wilkinson, the stern taskmaster, takes the class back to the bar and passes him but as she does she reveals her gentler side by giving him a sly wink of approval, which restores his smile and confidence. The scene, now featuring some uplifting, non-diegetic music, ends with an indication that Billy's resolve has been hardened when Mr Braithewaite challenges his masculinity by offering his own profound judgement on Billy's progress: 'You look like a right wanker to me, son.' However, now Billy is unfazed by these kind of jibes as the shots of him euphorically running and dancing home show.

REACTION

Billy Elliot confounded expectations and was greeted with general approval, even by the British press. The first indications that the film would succeed came at Cannes film festival where it drew a generous reception. In Britain it brought in more than £18m at the box-office – not a bad return for a budget of £2.4m. More importantly, it salvaged a tiny bit of credibility for Lottery-funding policies of the Art Council of England.

Most reviews tried to trace Daldry's theatrical influence on the staging of scenes in the film. However, much of the visual style came via veteran British cinematographer Brian Tufnano who had worked throughout the 1990s with Danny Boyle on both *Shallow Grave* and *Trainspotting*.

A couple of issues also inspired some interesting articles in the press. Madeleine Bunting writing in *The Guardian* in October 2000 dwelt on the issue of masculinity.

> 'We exiled men from home and children to work in factories and down mines, destroying the family units of the agrarian and pre-industrial cottage industry economy. Now heavy industry is finished, their masculinity is as redundant as their labour. *Billy Elliot*, like *The Full Monty*, is humourously playing with a history that lies heavily on the British heart: the decline of heavy manufacturing has destroyed not just communities, but souls.'

Akin Ojumu in *The Observer* in August 2000 assessed *Billy Elliot* in relation to aspirational social realist films of the late 1950s and early 1960s, such as *Saturday Night, Sunday Morning* (UK, 1960), and *Room at the Top* (UK, 1958), by balancing its 'gritty realism with joyous escapism.'

The film received three Oscar nominations for Stephen Daldry, Lee Hall and Julie Walters and picked up three BAFTA awards in 2001 for Best British Film, Best Actor in a Leading Role (Jamie Bell) and Actress in a Supporting Role (Julie Walters). The two actors also won in the Evening Standard British Film Awards with Walters picking up Best Actress and Bell gaining Most Promising Newcomer awards.

Ratcatcher (1999) (UK/France) UK Cert 15

Director: Lynne Ramsay

Screenplay: Lynne Ramsay

Producer: Gavin Emerson

Production companies: Pathé Fund Limited; Productions Lazennec; Holy Cow Films; BBC Films; Pathé Pictures; Arts Council of England; Studio Canal+; National Lottery through the Arts Council of England; BBC Scotland; Moonstone

Production start date: 03/08/1998 **Budget:** £2m (estimated)

Distributor: Pathé Distribution Limited **UK Release date:** 12 November 1999

UK Box Office: £437,694 **USA Box Office:** $0.2m

Worldwide Box Office: n/a

At first glance there seems to be few similarities between the working class boy does good feel-good film of *Billy Elliot* and the sometimes grim poetic beauty of *Ratcatcher*. One was made with plenty of appeal for a mainstream audience, while the other was more likely to appeal to an art house crowd. However, both benefited from Lottery funding, both featured an unprofessional boy actor in the lead role, both are set against the background of an industrial dispute, and both lead characters yearn to escape from their environments to a better life.

Ratcatcher was Lynne Ramsay's first feature film and not only showed touches of an assured visual artistry but drew critical acclaim. Many saw in Ramsay elements of the social realist tradition and comparisons were made between Ken Loach's *Kes* (UK, 1969) and the Bill Douglas trilogy *My Childhood* (UK, 1972); *My Ain Folk* (UK, 1973) *My Way Home* (UK, 1978). Ramsay herself preferred to cite French director Robert Bresson as an important influence.

Hers may not have been a film to fill multi-screens at the multiplexes but it revealed a genuine talent in stark contrast to many other first-time directors who had crashed and burned with their ill-conceived attempts at film-making.

SYNOPSIS

Set on a rundown council estate in Glasgow in the early 1970s during a refuse collectors' strike Ryan Quinn, a young boy, drowns in a canal after some harmless rough and tumble with James.

The canal haunts James. Despite being warned not to go back to it he goes there again and encounters a teenage girl, Margaret Anne, being bullied by a group of older boys. James sits next to her and they forge a fragile friendship.

James also befriends a young, simple boy from the flats called Kenny who loves animals. James encounters the old boys again who take him round to Margaret Anne's flat where she allows older boys to touch her sexually. James is encouraged to do the same but merely lies on top of her.

James steals some money from his father and takes a bus ride to a brand-new housing estate where he plays.

Later, as James and Margaret take an innocent bath together to cleanse themselves from lice, Kenny, who has been fishing for perch, falls in the canal but is rescued by James' dad.

The whole family attends a civic reception where the father is presented with a medal for bravery. He celebrates by going out with his mates while the rest of the family go home and dance to some old records. The cosy scene is shattered when James' dad returns home drunk and bloodied after being attacked by some boys. James' mother goes to him but he slaps her. James runs off to find solace with Margaret Anne as James' mother and father are seen making up by dancing intimately together.

As the army arrives to clear up the stacks of bin bags James is powerless when the older boys continue to torment Margaret Anne sexually. Kenny taunts James by saying that he saw him kill Ryan Quinn. James takes off and plunges into the canal.

The family, including James, is seen walking through the cornfield towards the new housing estate. We see James smile – the screen goes black – we see James underwater in the canal.

HOW IT WAS MADE

Good timing and fortune played its part in taking Ramsay from National Film and Television School graduate to directing her first feature. Her love of photography led her to enrol on the cinematography course at the film school but soon her restlessness and drive persuaded people on the course to allow her to make a film.

Ramsay's route to feature film involved her writing and directing some exceptional 'calling card' shorts. Her first was *Small Deaths* (1996) based on personal memories and experiences of childhood set in and around a Glasgow housing scheme. It was selected for the Cannes Film Festival in 1996, where it picked up the prestigious Critic's Prize. Her work gained the attention of producer Gavin Emmerson, who took on her next two shorts made in 1997 – *Gasman* and *Kill the Day*. The first of these, about two children reacting to their father's secret, was made by BBC Scotland, where head of drama Andrea Calderwood encouraged Ramsay to develop her ideas into a feature. *Gasman* was also screened at Cannes where this time it won the Jury Prize.

The BFI Production Board and Channel 4 Television backed *Kill the Day* about a drug addict trying to survive in and out of prison. Ramsay's good fortune came when Andrea Calderwood became head of production at Pathé, which had just entered bidding to become one of the three franchises to receive National Lottery funding. Finally, Ramsay received funding from French company Lazennec Productions, which had supported her short film work. The National Film and Television School alumni could begin work on *Ratcatcher* with the support of not only Pathé but also BBC Scotland. Other help came via BBC Films. It was clear that Ramsay had talent worth backing even in the uncertain world of feature film production.

She worked with regular collaborators from her film school days, cinematographer Alwin Küchler and editor Lucia Zucchetti, and from the outset had a clear idea of how the film should be made.

This included employing a mixture of professional and non-professional actors. The children in the film were personally selected after hundreds of auditions and although scenes were scripted she chose to work with the children, telling them what to say or allowing them to interpret the scenes using their own words. She also allowed a great deal of spontaneity to come through during the film.

KEY ISSUES

Ramsay's shorts had examined themes of families, childhood and a disenfranchisement brought about by poverty and class. These themes would be explored again in *Ratcatcher*. However, in an era where many of the successful British films seemed to have been made with television in mind, Ramsay's subtle, poetic visual style also caught the eye.

Childhood innocence lost, innocence regained

The piles of bin bags and the general disorder caused by the refuse strike act as the grim backdrop of the film but also serve as a metaphor for the unresolved chaos surrounding the lives of the children.

Having been involved in the accident that led to Ryan Quinn's death, James spends the rest of the film in a fragile state of mind. His innocence is first lost through playing, albeit roughly, with a friend. Actor William Eadie wonderfully evokes his haunted expression, anxiety and longing for a better life.

The deadly canal draws James to it like a moth to a flame. Here he encounters Margaret Anne who is set upon by a group of older boys and has her glasses thrown in the canal. This brutal teasing is taken a stage further when we learn that she serves as an object of adolescent sexual experimentation for the older boys. James, in contrast, shows no sexual desire towards Margaret Anne. Goaded by the older boys to 'have a pop' he awkwardly lies on top of her, unsure of what he is meant to gain by the experience. His relationship with her is tender. Margaret Anne, barely out of childhood herself, craves a physical contact with James that is to do with comfort rather than sexual desire.

This can be seen in the bathroom scene where both Margaret Anne and James take a bath together. They seem impervious to their nakedness as they splash around, playing with the soap and giggling like children half their age. The scene is closed with gentle humour as the two of them sit side by side eating sandwiches and wearing towels, rather like an old married couple.

James craves a simple type of intimacy. He cuddles up to Margaret Anne after he has witnessed his father striking his mother. Later, when he returns home having spent a night away he is joined on the sofa by his little sister Anne-Marie, who displays affection and concern as she shares an intimate embrace with her brother. Prior to this point Anne-Marie has merely bickered, told tales on James and generally given him two-finger salutes.

James achieves his release on his journey away from the slum of his home into the clean order of the new housing estate. We observe him playing around the housing estate as though it was a children's playground. Finally, his joy is released when he frolics by himself in the cornfield. It is here that he feels he can put his worries and the worries of his family behind him and maybe grow up securely.

If James' innocence has been lost then Kenny is a child who has somehow kept his naivety. His simple if hyperactive mind reflects a child who is embracing the world despite his awful surroundings. His enthusiasm and love for animals momentarily takes James away from his preoccupied feelings of guilt and remorse. When Margaret Anne asks James: 'Is he stupid or something?' James sticks up for his odd friend by saying: 'He's alright.' Sadly, Kenny's innocence, as he chooses to show James his birthday gift – a white mouse called Snowball – is brutalised by the cynical older boys who taunt him. Almost symbolically

Kenny releases his pet Snowball from further torment by sending it skywards on a balloon, unaware that in doing so he will kill it.

In the end James and Kenny fall out by dropping their childlike pretence and confronting each other with some harsh truths. James tells Kenny that he killed Snowball. Kenny replies that James killed Ryan. The breaking of these uncomfortable truths thrusts the boys back into the real world. Kenny also winds James up by repeating in an unlikely profoundly perceptive way: 'Poor cow, poor cow,' in relation to Margaret Anne's plight.

And yet throughout the film we see children acting like children on slides or in go-carts, full of affection and warmth. Ironically, they are also seen acting as pests, particularly when the army comes to clean up the rubble.

The older boys in the film seem to have no redeeming qualities about them at all. They appear brutal, instinctive, self-centred and self-satisfying, perhaps one step removed from the adult males they will shortly become. They end up attacking James's father, who despite being half-cut is doing a good deed by looking after a young girl's cat.

Somethin' stupid

When James' father brings home a big pot of paint, James' mother declares that it is grey, a point that he refutes good-naturedly by saying that it is pale blue. Ramsay paints an intriguing portrait of James' father by showing us his grey areas, which ultimately gives him some redeeming qualities.

On the one hand he is a weak man. He is frequently drunk and does not seem averse to flirting or going off with other women. He appears lazy and unmotivated and particularly harsh in relation to his son James, who hates him. Rather than stay with his family after he has won his award for bravery he chooses to have some drinks with his mates. In a drunken state, like a wounded animal, he lashes out and strikes his wife after some older boys in the street have attacked him.

On the other hand he is curiously gentle, particularly towards his younger daughter Anne-Marie who seems to adore him. She sits with him while he watches the Old Firm match on the telly. Another time he slips her a 50 pence piece, albeit from her mother's purse. In front of the family he slurs his love for the children's mother – and at that moment his drunken state convinces him, if not his wife, that his love is true. He also rescues Kenny from the canal in an instinctive act of bravery and tenderly speaks to the girl whose cat he takes charge of before he is attacked.

However, these good points do not cover his weakness. In the cold light of day he knows that the strongest person in the household is his wife – perhaps this is why he always seems to want to return home to her. Taken out of context the scene that shows James' parents dancing slowly to the tune of 'Somethin' Stupid' might reveal a loving couple but the truth of their relationship is different. While it is clear that James' mother loves his father – she talks to her children about how they used to jive together in the past – it is she who holds the family together. In fact her husband is like an additional child that she needs to clothe, feed and take care of despite the fact that he fulfils his traditional role as breadwinner by bringing in money for the household.

If the father is weak then the mother is strong and James quite clearly adores her. We see this more through looks and hugs than in words and an odd affectionate moment when James gently covers her toe, which shows through a hole in her tights. She also takes care of the children's welfare when she notices them itching. Her only moment of weakness comes when she hides and gets Anne-Marie to lie when the rent collector calls. However, she does this in the hope that the family can move to better surroundings.

The twisting, turning curtain unveiled

Opening with a slow-motion shot of a child enveloped in a curtain the film hints at a sense of foreboding, which seems to be realised when the child receives a smack from his mother. Ramsay is keen to keep her audience on its toes and offers us an unexpected twist at the beginning of the film. When Ryan Quinn rather than James dies we realise that he is not the main character and our attentions are reset as we follow the story about James and his family.

Midway through the film, which had been building itself into a series of bleak and oppressive events, the insertion of a fantasy sequence showing Snowball gliding through space to find the moon offers some unexpected light relief. This playful little scene comes as a release to the tension that had built up, culminating in Kenny's unwitting execution of his pet. She craftily returns us back to earth by showing us James asleep in front of the white noise of a television set.

We are also caught by surprise by other moments in the film such as James' bus ride, which turns out to be quite pleasant, and the awkward bathroom scene, which establishes an innocent relationship between Margaret Anne and James.

Finally, Ramsay leaves us with an enigmatic puzzle. Does the ending offer us a glimpse of hope or a glimpse of death? Does James become reborn at the end as his family walks happily through the cornfield to set up in the housing estate, or does James die by drowning in the canal? Do we want the last shot of the film to be James smiling at the camera in the cornfield, or submerged motionless in the murky depths of the canal? Ramsay ambivalently leaves us to make up our own minds.

The sound of silence

For audiences used to constant noise in their films from background music directing their emotions *Ratcatcher* comes as an oasis of calm. Its dreamlike quality often stems from many moments where there is no sound at all – Ryan lying dead on the banks of the canal, James and Margaret Anne sharing an awkward silence as he surveys the scab on her knee, Margaret Anne submerged underwater as James' father pulls Kenny out of the canal.

At other times the natural sounds of children playing outdoors and the splashes heard in water from the canal, the bathtub, or the bath punctuate the action. Elsewhere, the sound of TV programmes permeating living room spaces contrast with the dialogue.

Background music is used sparingly within the film but each time serves as a punctuation point. Indeed, the first snippet of non-diegetic music has a sequence which establishes certain situations within the film – James jumps off the wall as the hearse goes by, he returns to the brooding menace of the canal, he runs back to the flats past the ghostlike figure of Ryan's mother, before coming home and seeing his own mother asleep, followed by the drunken arrival of his father after a night out with another woman.

There is also a sequence when music is played from the record player in the flat, which give us several contrasting views in the story. James dances happily with his mother, but the happy atmosphere turns nasty when Da strikes Ma, leaving the two girls looking terrified (while the happy sounds of Lollipop play on in the background). As James seeks refuge in Margaret Anne's bed she asks him if he loves her to which he replies 'yes,'. The romantic notion is confirmed by the strains of Somethin' Stupid before the scene cuts to the shot of Ma and Da smooching away as though nothing had happened.

SCENE ANALYSIS – FRAMED

Away from the emotional pull of the narrative Ramsay offers the audience a strong visual palette to enrich the film. Her use of imagery throughout – sometimes working with contrasting shades of darkness and light, sometimes adding light – gives the film another dimension. Her visual style, photographed by Alwin Küchler, has scenes beautifully framed rather like pictures in a gallery to give the audience some additional symbolic information. Perhaps the most striking of these shots is taken during James' first visit to the new housing estate.

There is a subtle use of spatial expansion when James boards the bus and runs upstairs to the top deck where he occupies the front seats on the left hand side. At first he is framed in mid-shot and his reflection is clear in the window of the bus as he looks down and we get his point of view shot of the rubbish bags on the street. Margaret Anne passes and momentarily the action and sound slows, only then to return to a normal level as more bin bags are seen along the way. Out of the bin-strewn town we get a sharp cut taken from further down the bus with James standing as a tree comes into view and fields can be seen. As the bus approaches the tree, non-diegetic music is played, immediately lightening the mood as symbolically James' spirit rises as he leaves the town behind.

Our last view from the top deck of the bus features a wide long shot taken from the back of the upstairs deck as we get panoramic shots of the countryside.

The music halts when the bus stops. Now the sounds of birds can be heard as James gingerly walks down a road. He enters a building site and jumps into some sand near a cement mixer. There follows a series of shots showing him playing with materials on the site or climbing up on scaffolding.

As he reverently walks up a stairwell we are offered a high angle shot from above, which is broadly similar to shots used in the stairwells back home. In fact, his initial exploration of the new, empty rooms mirrors the earlier scene of him walking into the empty shell of Ryan's family's flat.

There follows a clever time and space shot; from the right hand side of the screen we see James leaning on a wall facing into the room. As the camera slowly pans across the bare wall it reaches a left hand partition where James now stands — this part fantasy shot captures his same reflective stance.

The camera then follows James into the bathroom as he lets out a sigh of joy as he sits down in the new bath (still wrapped in polythene) and turns on the unplumbed taps and finally urinates in the unconnected toilet, perhaps surprised at the consequences of his action.

As he walks down the stairs (again from the high angle above shot) and turns into the room we see a close-up of his face caught with light. The non-diegetic music again starts as we get a reverse shot to see the empty window frame.

From within the darkness of the room we see some blue sky and a wheat field. Almost magically, James climbs through the window and jumps into the field with the camera following his forward movement. A sequence of shots sees him frolicking joyfully in the field. The last shot shows James against a dusk-filled sky with cloud covering glimpses of blue. James is captured standing mid-shot to the left of the screen, perhaps facing the new houses. His brief moment of joy ends as he kicks a can along a road as he heads back home.

The framed window shots are repeated twice again in the film. On James' second visit when he cannot enter the house the framed shot of the cornfield doesn't carry the same kind of optimism and is represented by a bleaker, darker sky with raindrops visible on the newly-installed window, which now acts as a barrier. The framed shot of the cornfield is also used at the end of the film when the family is seen making its way towards a new life.

However, the film does not overplay the use of imagery and pulls off the trick of presenting a gritty, unsentimental social realist film softened with poetic imagery.

REACTION

At a time when British cinema releases seemed awash with gangster films *Ratcatcher* not only came as a relief but was met with universal critical approval. Ramsay was heralded as Britain's brightest new talent. The fact that she was a woman, one of only two per cent working in the industry, also seemed to be a reason to celebrate.

The film, which was shown in Cannes, received a positive response and drew two awards nominations there. *The Guardian*'s Jonathan Romney wrote: '*Ratcatcher* is a genuine art movie with just enough warmth creeping in to make its vision tolerable. Ramsay is not just a promising first-time director, but a fully-fledged visionary from the start.' These sentiments were echoed in other quarters of the film world. French critic Michel Ciment hailed *Ratcatcher* as the best debut by a British director in 15 years.

The accolades for Ramsay translated into awards as she won, among others, a BAFTA for Most Promising Newcomer, the New Director's Award at the Edinburgh Film Festival, Best Director at the London Critics Circle, a British Independent Film Award and the Sutherland Trophy at the London Film Festival.

Despite the critical approval and decent backing from distributor Pathé, the film performed modestly at the box-office. British audiences may have been flocking back to the cinema in their droves but they were much more likely to see *Star Wars 1*, *Notting Hill*, and *Austin Powers* than an art house film set in a decaying council estate in Glasgow. Additionally, the broad Glaswegian accents meant that the film had to be subtitled for a wider international audience.

CONCLUSION

Lottery funds for film production in 1995 meant that both Ramsey and Daldry were given a chance to cut their teeth as full feature film directors. However, there seemed a time in the late 1990s that the damage the turkeys made far outweighed the small gains achieved by the more successful films. Some felt that this was a period that did damage to the British film industry by over-producing films, many of which were either poorly devised or simply unable to find a distributor with a willing barge pole. The bottom line remained clear – without distribution a film cannot make money.

The debates about the profitability of Lottery-funded films rarely took into account the state of the distribution sector in Britain. *Billy Elliot*'s progress was clearly helped by being released on 335 screens by UIP. Meanwhile, films such as *The Winter Guest* (UK/USA 1996) did proportionally quite well having been released by FilmFour on 28 screens.

Despite vast improvements in film production during the 1990s, the overwhelming majority of British films still failed to set the box-office alight irrespective of their funding sources. As film production picked up, it became apparent that the area needing some attention was distribution.

FURTHER READING

Towards a Sustainable UK Film Industry
(Film Council, 2000)

The British Film Industry: a policy document incorporating the Government's response to the House of Commons National Heritage Select Committee. (London: HMSO, June 1995)

A Bigger Picture: the report of the Film Policy Review Group (Department for Culture, Media and Sport, 1998)

Icons in the Fire: The Decline and Fall of Almost Everybody in the British Film Industry 1984-2000 Walker, Alexander (Orion Publishing, 2005)

The Stats An overview of the film, television, video and DVD industries 1990-2003 (BFI National Library, BFI Information Services, 2006)

Contemporary British Cinema 16+ Source Guide Guides
Mettler, Erinna; Ormsby, Andrew; Reeve, David; Dupin, Christophe (BFI National Library, 2003) www.bfi.org.uk/filmtvinfo/publications/16+/

BFI Film and Television Handbook (BFI, editions from 1996–2005)

Selected reviews/articles/references

UK Film Council – www.ukfilmcouncil.org.uk

Scottish Screen – www.scottishscreen.com

Arts Council England – www.artscouncil.org.uk

Arts Council Northern Ireland - www.artscouncil-ni.org

Arts Council Wales – www.artswales.org.uk

National Lottery – www.lotteryfunding.org.uk

Medium Cool, by Nick James

Sight & Sound, Vol.8 No.8. (August 1998) P.12-15

Billy Elliot

Sight & Sound V.10 N.10 (1 Oct 2000) P.40 by Monk, Claire

Empire N.136 (1 Oct 2000) P.44 by Westbrook, Caroline

Cosmic Dancer by Lawrenson, Edward
Sight & Sound V.10 N.10 (1 Oct 2000) P.12-13

Masculinity in Question by Bunting, Madeleine
The Guardian, 2 October 2000, p 17

DVD – *Billy Elliot* (2 DVD Special Edition) – (Universal Pictures UK, 2005)

Ratcatcher

Sight & Sound V.9 N.11 (1 Nov 1999) P.50-51 by O'Sullivan, Charlotte

Empire N.126 (1 Dec 1999) P.50-51 by Lewis, Trevor

Ratcathcher
Kuhn, Anette (Palgrave Macmillan, 2008)

Cinema's Missing Children
Wilson, Emma (Wallflower Press, 2003)

What are you looking at? by Spencer, Liese
Sight & Sound V.9 N.11 (1 Oct 1999) P.16

Distributor Wanted by Kennedy, Harlan
Film Comment Vol.36, No.1. (Jan/Feb 2000) P. 6-9

DVD: *Ratcatcher* (Pathé Distribution, 2003)

7. GETTING DISTRIBUTED OR NOT

Breakdown of UK film distribution by releases and box-office 1990–1999

	1990	1991	1992	1993	1994	1995	1996	1997	1998	1999
20th Century Fox	4 £13.1m	21 £46.3m	15 £23.7m	9 £10.3m	13 £44.6m	17 £24.3m	16 £57.5m	25 £110.7m	17 £129m	22 £86.4m
Buena Vista	n/a	n/a	n/a	18 £44.2m	24 £66.3m	27 £74.1m	26 £89.9m	26 £89.6m	27 £98.0m	32 £118.5m
Columbia Tristar	7 £25.3m	17 £29.9m	19 £45.8m	13 £52.6m	22 £31.6m	20 £24.4m	13 £41.5m	19 £64.6m	15 £32.7m	26 £30.4m
UIP	17 £74.1m	31 £55.4m	23 £65.1m	28 £87.7m	25 £105.9m	25 £102.9m	29 £94.6m	20 £82.4m	36 £119.3m	39 £133.2m
Warner Bros.	19 £70.4m	35 £66.1m	33 £90.0m	23 £66.4m	27 £33.6m	34 £75.4m	20 £38.1m	21 £48.5m	25 £46.9m	19 £68.5m
Universal	n/a	n/a	n/a	n/a	n/a	n/a	n/a	n/a	n/a	14 £45.6m
Entertainment	n/a	8 £7.8m	12 £4.8m	14 £18.7m	19 £27.7m	23 £5.7m	20 £39.1m	29 £22.5m	22 £45.4m	24 £34.8m
Palace	5 £13.5m	25 £7.5m	n/a	n/a	n/a	n/a	n/a	n/a	n/a	n/a
Guild	4 £10.5m	11 £39.5m	12 £30.8	13 £17.0m	12 £4.3m	12 £19.9m	15 £13.3m	n/a	n/a	n/a
Rank Rank/PolyGram	6 £10.2m	22 £28.2m	18 £6.9m	15 £7.2m	22 £40.1m	14/7 £18.6m £5.8m	10/1 £6.0m £0.03m	n/a	n/a	n/a
PolyGram Rank/PolyGram	n/a	n/a	n/a	1 £0.02m	n/a	12/7 £14.4m £5.8m	21/1 £31.8m £0.03m	22 £55.7m	22 £25.4m	n/a
FilmFour	n/a	n/a	n/a	n/a	n/a	2 £0.03	14 £6.0m	13 £3.2m	12 £5.3m	19 £17.3m
Pathé	n/a	n/a	n/a	n/a	n/a	n/a		13 £13.9m	16 £3.1m	11 £21.0m
Others	n/a	97 £16.8m	107 £16.4m	108 £14.1m	113 £9.4m	91 £24.1m	80 £7.6m	96 £14.8m	137 £8.8m	187 £14.4m

Source: *Screen International/The Stats*

If film production in the UK during the 1990s was the horse, then film distribution was the horseman. The increase in the number of UK films did not go hand in hand with a proportional increase in the number of UK films released. The five major US distributors – 20th Century Fox, Buena Vista, Columbia TriStar, UIP and Warner Brothers – dominated throughout the decade-- and naturally enough focused on releases from America first, rarely taking a chance on the odd British film. As a result, the number of British films awaiting a theatrical release grew at a steady rate. Some went straight to video or television. Worse, many simply never saw the light of day.

With the exception of Entertainment, British distributors generally played second fiddle to the American behemoths and even then the decade witnessed some notable casualties such as Palace, Rank, Guild, PolyGram and FilmFour. Clearly the challenge was to crack the distribution nut if the British film industry was truly to thrive.

The majors

As multiplexes sprang up and British audiences rediscovered their appetite for films at the cinema it was inevitable that the five major distributors would benefit. The lion's share of the spoils was contested between UIP and Twentieth Century Fox. In terms of British releases UIP could rely on Bond films to boost its annual box-office returns, but it also benefited from films such as *Shakespeare in Love*, *Billy Elliot* and *Sliding Doors*. Twentieth Century Fox bagged the biggest British hit, *The Full Monty*, in 1997 and the following year *Titanic* cruised past it to become the most successful film at the UK box-office during the 1990s, ringing up a total of £69,025,646.

A sobering thought is that the biggest film of the 1990s featured an Anglo/American theme and co-starred British actress Kate Winslet. While the British film industry was finding its feet with budgets rarely going beyond £2.5m, *Titanic* was being shot in America, Canada and Mexico at an estimated budget of $200,000,000.

Other independent companies such as Guild, First Independent and Mayfair either fell or merged. Below the majors and the independents that challenged the, grew a plethora of companies that often released a single film. The exception was Entertainment and the emergence of Pathé, which finished the decade strongly.

Entertainment Film Distributors

The only British independent distribution outfit that not only survived the decade but sat at the table with the majors in terms of releases and box-office revenue was Entertainment. Founded in 1978 by producer Michael Green, the company is now run by brothers Nigel and Trevor Green.

It benefited from being the UK distributor of major American Studio New Line Cinema, which produced such hit films in the 1990s as *The Mask* (USA, 1994); *Se7en* (USA, 1995); *Boogie Nights* (USA, 1997); *Austin Powers International Man of Mystery* (USA, 1997); and *The Wedding Singer* (1998). Its success was also built on spotting potential hits such as Jane Campion's triple Oscar winner *The Piano* (Australia/France, 1993).

Entertainment's support of British films was less spectacular in terms of big box-office returns but the distribution arm scored some modest success with *Up 'n' Under* (UK, 1997), *This Year's Love* (UK, 1999) and *Lost in Space* (USA, 1998). Entertainment survived by careful choices, meticulous planning and not overreaching itself. In the 2000s it hit the jackpot by releasing *The Lord of the Rings Trilogy* (USA/New Zealand/Germany, 2001-2-3).

PolyGram

The table of distributors working in the UK charts the rise and fall of the independents with the end of Palace in the early 1990s and Rank in the mid-1990s. The rise and sudden fall of PolyGram (whose place at the end of the 1990s was taken on by Universal) came as a huge blow to the British film industry since its production and distribution operation came close to offering the UK a vertically aligned film outfit. When parent company Philips sold PolyGram to Seagram all that remained was a list of some of the top British films of the decade: *Four Weddings and a Funeral*; *Trainspotting*; *Bean*; *Lock Stock and Two Smoking Barrels*; and *Elizabeth*.

FilmFour

If the story stopped at the end of the 1990s FilmFour, which scored a big success with *East is East*, would be heralded as a British success. Unfortunately, it entered the new millennium searching in vain for its next big hit.

FilmFour also distributed non-British films such as *The Limey* (USA, 1999); *Dancer in the Dark* (Denmark/France/Sweden/Italy/Germany, 2000); and *The Warrior* (UK/France/Germany/India, 2001). However, British audiences were becoming more conservative in their non-Hollywood choices and dependent on a critical buzz to lead them to screens showing something different. In the end the buzz and the audience did not warm to films like *Charlotte Gray* and *Lucky Break*, both which on paper looked like they would do well. The problem in the British market has always been how to sustain future products if there are fallow years and Channel 4 brutally answered that question in 2002 by scaling down its production arm and pulled the plug on its distribution outlet.

Art house distributors

Below the majors and the wannabe majors came a host of mainly art house distributors such as Artificial Eye, Metro Tartan, ICA Projects. They generally issued a film per month to be screened on the small but dedicated art house circuit. However, it struggled against the tide of blockbusters and by the end of the decade foreign language films had dipped in audience appeal. Films such as Kieslowski's acclaimed *Three Colours: Red* (France/Switzerland/Poland, 1994) released by Artificial Eye took £511,253 at the UK box-office in 1994. By 1999 not even the high-brow publicity stimulated by Danish film-makers Lars Von Trier and Thomas Vinterberg in declaring their 'vow of chastity' in film-making under the banner of *Dogme 95* could generate more than £269,103 at the box-office when *Festen* (Denmark, 1998) was released by Blue Light. In the same year Columbia TriStar picked up

Tom Twyker's *Run Lola Run* for distribution but it only mustered £319,815 at the box-office. The most successful foreign language films needed to be bolstered by the foreign language Oscar win to gain a reasonable audience. Such was the case with *Life is Beautiful* (Italy, 1997) released by Buena Vista, which took just under £3m at the UK box-office.

Asian audiences

Perhaps the biggest surprise in the distribution market at the tail end of the decade was the steady rise in Bollywood films making their way onto screens in areas with large Asian communities. Distributors such as Eros and Yash Raj scored successes with their carefully targeted releases and the trademark spectacular musical sequences and coy romantic plotlines gave the somewhat dour looking low-budget British films a run for their money. The top Asian film *Hum Saath Saath Hain* (India, 1999) made £622,909 at the UK box-office, beating worthy British releases such as *Ratcatcher, Croupier* (UK/Ireland/Germany/France, 1997), and *Gods & Monsters* (UK/USA, 1998). The success of the Asian movies at finding a dedicated audience begged the question why couldn't British films achieve even better success in their own country?

Types of release for UK films 1984-2000

Proportion of films with a UK involvement that achieved;
a) Wide release. Opening or playing on 30 or more screens around the country within a year of production
b) Limited release, mainly in art house cinemas or a short West End run within a year of production
c) Unreleased a year after production

Year	(a)%	(b)%	(c)%
1990	29.40	47.10	23.50
1991	32.20	37.30	30.50
1992	38.30	29.80	31.90
1993	25.40	22.40	52.20
1994	31.00	22.60	46.40
1995	23.10	34.60	42.30
1996	19.00	14.00	67.00
1997	15.50	19.00	65.50
1998	22.70	21.60	55.70
1999	30.00	10.00	60.00
2000	22.50	12.20	65.30

Source: *Screen Finance/Nielsen EDI/BFI Film and Television Handbook 2001*

With such a competitive market and a UK audience weaned on Hollywood products, British films were always likely to struggle to make an impact against the giants. What was disappointing was how few films managed a wide release within a year of production and how many remained unreleased after a year of production.

Even in the bad old days of the 1980s the few British films that were made stood a better chance of being released than during the 1990s. In 1984, when UK attendances hit their lowest point, 50 per cent of British films managed a wide release and only six per cent stayed unreleased. By 1990, the picture had dramatically changed with nearly half the films on a limited release only. However, the most damning statistic was found from 1996 until the end of the decade when more than half the British films made still remained unreleased. This was the era of the multiplex boom but in many cases British films simply had to wait in line behind the bigger production and marketing budgets of their American counterparts, which not only boasted stars but had been largely responsible for rebuilding the UK's cinemas.

To succeed in this environment British film-makers had to convince distributors that their films would find a local and international audience. It is under such challenging circumstances that two of Britain's top auteur directors, Mike Leigh and Ken Loach, had to operate. Both had international reputations that were enhanced during the decade but reputations counted for little in the competitive climate of the 1990s. Ironically, both Leigh and Loach found a fair amount of commercial success but this tended to be in countries like France and Spain rather than among the popcorn munchers of Britain.

Secrets & Lies (1995) (UK/France) UK Cert 15

Director: Mike Leigh

Screenplay: Mike Leigh

Producer: Simon Channing-Williams

Production companies: CiBy 2000; Thin Man Films; Channel 4 Films

Production start: 30/05/1995 **Budget:** £2.5m (estimated)

Distributor: FilmFour Distributors **UK Release date:** 24 May 1996

UK Box Office: £1,969,910 **USA Box Office:** $13.4m

Worldwide Box Office: $52m

By the time Leigh came to make *Secrets & Lies* he had already secured a reputation as one of Britain's leading art house directors. In 1970 he made his debut feature film *Bleak Moments* but spent most of the next two decades working in theatre and for the BBC where his acclaimed quirky dramas *Nuts in May* (1976) and *Abigail's Party* (1977) established his reputation and cemented his unique style which involved months of improvisation with his actors. His second feature, *High Hopes* (UK, 1988) brought him back to the cinema's attention. In 1990 he made the quirky comedy *Life is Sweet* and followed it up with the darker and controversial *Naked*. *Secrets & Lies* would become a bittersweet film for Leigh. It enhanced his reputation on an international stage but the high level of critical acclaim was not matched with the same level of box-office success.

SYNOPSIS

After the funeral of her adoptive mother, Hortense, a black optometrist, is compelled to search for details about her birth mother. She goes to an adoption agency which dutifully hands over her adoption documentation. Hortense is shocked to discover that her mother was white. She decides to follow up enquiries on her own and trace her mother.

In the meantime white photographer Maurice is seen at work at weddings and in his studio taking a variety of portrait shots. Returning from work he encounters his wife Monica in a tense and irritable state and Maurice offers her sympathy and support. Maurice's highly-strung sister, Cynthia, a single mother, lives unharmoniously in a run-down council house with her 20-year-old daughter Roxanne, a street sweeper.

Hortense summons up the courage to meet Cynthia. Slowly in a café the truth is revealed and a distraught Cynthia realises that Hortense really is her daughter.

Hortense and Cynthia continue to meet each other and forge a relationship. When Maurice suggests that Cynthia and Roxanne come over to his house for a barbecue for Roxanne's 21st birthday, Cynthia invites Hortense along saying that she is a work friend.

The party starts very well, albeit with a certain amount of tension. Hortense's late arrival causes a minor stir but soon she sits uncomfortably with everyone else in the garden where she skirts around the issue of her relationship with Cynthia. However, things are brought to a head when Cynthia blurts out that she is Hortense's mother.

In the ensuing moments Roxanne, accompanied by Paul, storms out of the house while Maurice sets out to bring them back. More recriminations between Cynthia and Monica follow before the truth is revealed. Maurice states that Monica cannot have children and continues to get angry. This unexpected outburst prompts everyone to reveal their secrets to each other in an emotionally charged way that leaves Monica, Cynthia and Hortense hugging each other while Roxanne looks on bewildered but equally moved.

The final scene shows Hortense and Roxanne together at Cynthia's discussing their new-found status as half-sisters and the potential for getting to know each other much to the delight of a happier Cynthia, who is reconciled and reunited with both her daughters.

HOW IT WAS MADE

Leigh's reputation and his trademark improvisational directing style allowed him more licence than most when it came to funding the film. Prior to 1987, his credits read 'devised and directed'. However, he felt compelled to change this to 'written and directed' when people began challenging him on his style. His desire was always to achieve a realistic tone in his work, showing people as they really are.

To help him achieve this he selects his cast and they work together to create the characters and the situations, which eventually fulfill the premise of a story. Like his other work, the film of Secrets & Lies had no script but started as just an idea.

Many of Leigh's cast had worked with him before either in film, like Timothy Spall in Life is Sweet, or in the theatre, like Marianne Jeanne Baptiste who had starred in Leigh's play It's a Great Shame at the Theatre Royal Stratford East in 1993. Brenda Blethyn had recently won an award for Best Comedy Actress at the 1994 British Comedy Awards starring opposite Spall in Outside Edge. Phyllis Logan was probably best-known for her role in the long-running TV series Lovejoy but had made a handful of film appearances, including the comedy Soft Top, Hard Shoulder (UK, 1992).

With an assembled cast the characters grow organically as each actor starts the process of knowing all there is to know about their assigned role. Most of the performances are improvised over a period of months with Leigh guiding the actors and allowing them to create their own lines.

This method leaves funders, who desire a script, and some agents who cannot pitch a Leigh project to their clients, having to trust Leigh's judgement and reputation. Leigh's first ally was producer Simon Channing-Williams, who had worked with Leigh on his BBC projects and with whom he had formed Thin Man Films. Channel 4 agreed to release the film via its distribution arm FilmFour, while other funding came via French company CiBy 2000.

Leigh admits that it was not until the very end of *Secrets & Lies* that he and the cast knew how the issues would be resolved since the barbecue sequence evolved during the creation of the film. At a running time of 142 minutes, the film was also quite long for audiences brought up on 90-minute movies. Filming took place in and around London locations including Bethnal Green for Cynthia's house and Southgate for Maurice and Monica's house and photography studio.

KEY ISSUES

Hortense's journey to trace her birth mother would be quite a sufficient storyline in itself. However, her curiosity and determination leads her unintentionally into a family in crisis. Her search for her mother ultimately enables the family members to confront their secrets and express their pain.

Hortense – black and white

Hortense is a black woman who we first see at the funeral of her adopted mother. For the remainder of the film the music remains solemn, dominated by a mournful cello. For much of the film Hortense carries this motif with her and generally wears black, which subliminally acts as a reminder of her loss. Her emotions are fragile but she demonstrates a strength of purpose to find some sort of closure to her adoptive mother's death by taking the steps to find out and maybe contact her birth mother.

Her shock is to discover that her mother is white. In order to discover her identity Hortense's world has been turned on its head. Prior to this moment we have seen Hortense confide in her black friend, Dionne. Ironically, in light of future revelations, Dionne confesses to a sexual encounter with a total stranger. Hortense is slightly shocked but non-judgemental. She alludes to wanting to discover the truth about her mother without telling her friend that she is out to find her adoptive mother. Philosophically she states: 'We choose our parents,' and carries on to state that our parents inform us about the way we are. This is Hortense's secret. It is also noticeable that her tastefully decorated flat features white walls. There is also an ironic comic moment when Cynthia summons the courage to phone Hortense and the audience see Hortense wrapped in a towel about to take a bat, with a white face caked in make-up. The irony is that Hortense discovers that the answers she seeks are not straightforward black and white.

The film steers clear of any notions of colour prejudice. Monica's awkward moment when Hortense arrives for the barbecue and she goes to turn her away is possibly the only direct form of racism. Indeed, the colour of Hortense's skin is rarely seen as an issue.

The twist that the film provides is that she has been brought up in a secure loving middle-class black background, having attended university and gained a good career as an optometrist. She learns that her real mother comes from a working-class background, eking out an unfulfilled existence in a factory.

But in seeking the truth Hortense is prepared to face realities. She is non-judgemental and accepts Cynthia unconditionally. This acceptance leads to Hortense and Cynthia building a new relationship and Hortense bringing her period of mourning to a close.

It is only when she nervously accepts Cynthia's invitation to the barbecue that she feels compelled to lie to hide Cynthia's deep-rooted secret. However, by the end of the film Hortense is given a further fillip when Roxanne states that she would introduce Hortense as her half-sister.

Cynthia – woman on the verge of a nervous breakdown

If Hortense had a secure and loving upbringing then the opposite seems to apply to the needy, emotional Cynthia. Her antics, so despised by Monica, are excused by Maurice who explains: 'She can't help it; she never had enough love.'

Cynthia is, full of insecurities and unable to communicate with her daughter Roxanne without appearing to suffocate her. She is also jealous of Monica, who she perceives to be materialistic and a bad influence on her beloved brother Maurice. We learn that Cynthia had to sacrifice her life after her mother died in order to look after the family and as an impressionable young girl she became pregnant. It appears that Cynthia had many sexual partners but that ended with the birth of Roxanne.

She alludes to how attractive she still is by pointing out to a disinterested Roxanne how good her legs look and saying: 'I can still turn a few heads.' However, Cynthia is in crisis. Life has passed her by and she sacrificed most of her youth looking after her brother Maurice and then bringing up Roxanne. There is nothing much left for her and she perceives rejection from Roxanne, who is hostile and antagonistic to her and Maurice, who has moved away from the area and left the past behind.

Cynthia's clinging scene when Maurice comes to visit shows us the extent of her desperation. It is uncomfortable to witness. However, her moment of release comes when Hortense makes contact. Despite the shock and the pain of having a buried secret dug up and brought to the surface, Cynthia feels compelled to meet the daughter that she never knew.

The awkward first meeting between Hortense and Cynthia as they sit side by side in a café is contrasted with their next meeting when they sit as equals across the tables in a restaurant. Cynthia draws confidence from Hortense's desire to connect with her mother. In the café Cynthia rewinds the shame when as a 15-year-old girl she became pregnant and then the shame of the memory is exacerbated when she recalls that in fact she did have sex with a black man, a memory which she had all but erased. It is an irony that once she has overcome her shock Cynthia is even prepared to see a family resemblance. At one point she makes the remark to Hortense: 'You look more like me than my daughter does.'

Cynthia can see that giving Hortense up for adoption was ultimately the right thing to do since Hortense grew up in a loving and caring environment and gained a degree and a good job. This overwhelming sense of relief and the joy that her daughter not only has found her but wants to form a relationship with her brings about a change in Cynthia's confidence. Indeed, her relationship with Roxanne improves to the extent that she allows her daughter a tiny bit more space.

In the end, Cynthia's pride in Hortense betrays her secret when she reveals the truth at the party. This bolt out of the blue strikes Roxanne (since Maurice and Monica were aware of the secret). Ultimately, the shock therapy that brought comfort to Cynthia when she met Hortense is passed on to Roxanne, whose rage at her mother reaches boiling point. However, when the storm calms Cynthia has reconnected with both of her daughters and achieved peace of mind.

Monica – we're all in pain

Monica's pain is both physical and mental. The film shows her at her worst suffering from pre-menstrual tension and acting unreasonably to Maurice when he returns from work to find her frantically vacuuming the house. She also suffers from bad period pains, which serves as a cruel reminder to her that she is infertile. This shock revelation by Maurice comes after Cynthia taunts Monica about being selfish and not giving Maurice children. Prior to this moment Monica has come across as cold, unfeeling and rather selfish. However, the film does show Maurice and Monica in more normal circumstances, mainly in the scene when Stuart returns to the photography studio that he passed on to Maurice. During this scene their non-verbal exchanges suggest a couple that are actually quite in tune with each other's feelings and emotions.

To compensate for the absence of children, Monica throws her energies into using her artistic skills to create a beautiful home. However, the strain on her affects her relationship with her husband and brims out with deep resentment to Cynthia who has had no trouble bearing children that she didn't even want.

Our sympathy turns to Monica when she breaks down and cries uncontrollably. It is at this point that Cynthia's motherly instincts kick in and she feels Monica's pain and hugs her. Monica tenderly returns the favour and Cynthia breaks down and confronts the truth about Hortense's father. In finally revealing her secret Monica has not erased her pain but has eased the tensions between herself, Maurice and Cynthia. Monica has to deal with her husband's insecurity and declares that she loves Maurice: 'You don't know how much I love you.'

Maurice – There but for the grace of God

The key moment of the film arrives when Maurice finally explodes and forces everyone to show their hand: 'Secrets and lies! We're all in pain! Why can't we share our pain? I've spent my entire life trying to make people happy, and the three people I love the most in the world hate each other's guts, and I'm in the middle! I can't take it anymore!'

Maurice spends most of the film making people feel better about themselves. His outburst reveals his sensitive side as he tries to find a way of reconciling the antagonisms between Monica and Cynthia and Cynthia and Roxanne. He is, as his assistant Jane points out, 'lovely', and we see him trying to build bridges.

However, Maurice's love for those closest to him is also tested with the unexpected encounter with his former colleague and boss Stuart, who has fallen on hard times. During this encounter Maurice stands his ground when Stuart accuses him of ripping him off. But even then Maurice shows compassion to Stuart and helps him on his way. In the middle of the tense family conflic, Maurice and Monica see somebody who is worse off than themselves and for a moment this gives them a sense of perspective.

Defined by what we do

The film makes a point of showing us the work that people do somehow defines who we are. Hortense is an optometrist. This is generally perceived by everyone to be an unusual and interesting job. Symbolically, her job is to help people to see more clearly. Maurice's job also involves eyes, this time through the lens of a camera. Maurice owns and runs a successful photographic studio. Not only do the scenes of him at work offer some comic relief in the film but they also serve as portraits – tiny vignettes – of how appearances can be deceptive.

Cynthia works in a factory apparently making boxes, while her daughter Roxanne, who Maurice encourages to go to college, seems content working for the council sweeping roads. Her boyfriend Paul is a scaffolder and this fact impresses Cynthia when Maurice says that it pays well.

Out of all the protagonists Monica does not appear to work at all. The irony of this situation is revealed later in the film when we learn that she pushed for Maurice to take his cut of insurance money after his father died, a fact which riled Cynthia. Despite having the most in terms of material success, Monica's nest lays empty and unfulfilled.

SCENE ANALYSIS – TEA FOR TWO

In *Secrets & Lies* the scene between Hortense and Cynthia in the café is achieved in a single eight-minute take. Leigh had kept the actresses apart as much as possible to gain the spontaneity of the moment and make their performances seem natural. As a result he produces a compelling, honest scene. Over the course of four scenes we get to see Hortense and Cynthia gradually establish a relationship.

First we are taken to outside Holborn Underground station. The camera pans down from the Underground sign to street level where Hortense, arms folded, anxiously paces up and down lookings out for a woman she has never seen before – her mother. The camera stays on the opposite side of the road and so we get a candid camera type of feel as we observe the awkward meeting. The camera slowly follows Hortense as she walks to the entrance, our view momentarily obscured by a passing bus as Cynthia, looking anxious and lost, is revealed standing by the entrance.

There is a nice moment when Hortense passes Cynthia and the verité feel of the scene allows other strangers to walk into the frame, notably a white-haired woman carrying a suitcase. By a process of elimination Hortense approaches Cynthia. As she speaks the camera cuts to a closer shot. The first awkward exchange appears as if it will end soon as Cynthia understandably believes that a mistake has been made but her nervousness is betrayed by her saying: 'That's someone having a joke.' The strain begins to show on Hortense's face as Cynthia appears to crack up but she perseveres and suggests they have a cup of tea.

This scene is played out in one single long take apart from an initial establishing shot, which places the two of them inside the nearly empty café on a table sitting side by side. Cynthia says: 'They shouldn't go raising your hopes like that. 'Taint fair.' At this point we get a fixed camera shot, which frames Hortense and Cynthia together. Hortense wears black to Cynthia's white top, subtly underlining the film's 'black and white' motif. Behind them the café is empty although the world outside can be seen through the glass door at the entrance.

What follows is an intense scene played out without any background music, no distractions from other people, and no camera movement. What we see is what we get. It is a real exchange, filmed in real time.

The scene takes Cynthia back in time as she relives moments and learns consequences of her actions of putting her child up for adoption. Hortense is also absorbing the fact that the person sitting next to her is her birth mother. For both women this is a life-changing moment.

At one point we see a visible reaction on Cynthia's face when it dawns on her that she has been with a black man and so Hortense could be her daughter. Ashamed by this revelation she turns her back on Hortense and cries. Hortense holds her emotions under control and reacts impassively. She does not attempt to put her arm around Cynthia, nor does she offer words of comfort other than saying: 'You shouldn't feel ashamed'.

Cynthia's body language has her turn away and then turn to face Hortense. Of the two she makes more eye contact and appears more childlike than Hortense.

Cynthia faces Hortense when she explains that she had no knowledge that Hortense was black. She also cannot tell Hortense who her father was. When Cynthia notices that Hortense is disappointed not to learn more she pays Hortense a compliment: 'Look at you', she says with pride, but quickly reverts back to her lack of self-esteem by crying: 'I must be a disappointment to you.'

However, Cynthia's natural motherly instincts reveal themselves. In strange matter of fact interludes between tears Cynthia asks Hortense about her mother, father, boyfriends, jobs and siblings. At one point she even strikes the same nagging tone that she uses with her other daughter Roxanne – 'I bet you've got a boyfriend… nice girl like you.' Cynthia's natural good spirit also reveals itself when she emotionally states to Hortense: 'I bet your mum was proud of you. Wasn't she?' and then ironically adds: 'Of course she was, I'd have been proud.'

Yet Cynthia experiences terrible moments of pain when she confronts her past, particularly when reflecting that she has no husband and not even a boyfriend: 'I give them a wide berth, they got me into enough trouble as it is.' This last admission carries a double pang of pain – she had to give up her daughter for adoption and she lost out on having a proper relationship with a man.

Despite Cynthia's moments of distress Hortense feels compelled to ask uncomfortable questions. Understandably she tackles the issue of how Cynthia didn't even look at her when she was born. Perhaps the most pertinent moment comes when Cynthia cries: '"I was only a little girl meself - sixteen.'

Although some of Cynthia's answers affect Hortense she generally feels composed, betraying little emotion. However, right at the end when she recalls how her parents told her she was adopted on a flight back from Barbados, Hortense, gazes away from Cynthia as if recreating the moment of looking out the clouds from the plane.

Background music links the end of this scene to the more relaxed setting of the car journey home. Now Hortense and Cynthia are photographed in close-up in a reverse shot sequence. Cynthia is calm. Hortense admits that she needed to meet Cynthia. However, Cynthia goes back on the defensive and attempts to leave Hortense again by wishing her well but not wanting any more contact with her. This time the disappointment of a potential second rejection is etched onto Hortense's face.

For all we know this could be the last time the mother and daughter meet. Our next scene cuts to a close-up of Roxanne. Impervious to her mother's emotionally-charged secret, Roxanne picks up that Cynthia is no longer as hysterical as she has been before.

Cynthia merely says enigmatically: 'You've got to laugh sweetheart, else you cry.'

In the next scene Cynthia calls Hortense and we know that a relationship will be established. On the phone both women are calm and for the first time both are smiling and laughing. From an awkward initial meeting a new strong bond is developing between Hortense and her mum.

REACTION

Critically, many agreed that this was Leigh's most accomplished film to date. However, his art house credentials meant that commercially the film did not take off in the manner of a *Fully Monty* or a *Four Weddings and a Funeral*, netting a modest £1.9m in Britain.

Internationally, the film was feted and received a decent audience, particularly in France, which contributed to a far healthier worldwide box-office return of more than £12m. It also proved to be a stepping stone for Leigh. *Secrets & Lies* was given a high profile when it was nominated for five Oscars – Best Film, Best Director, Best Screenplay, Best Actress (Blethyn) and Best Actress in a Supporting Role (Jean-Baptiste). Although losing out at the Oscars, Blethyn picked up a Best Actress award at the Golden Globes and other awards flowed from European sources, namely the prestigious Palme d'Or at Cannes, where the film was premiered in May 1996. Blethyn also picked up a best actress award and the film won an ecumenical jury prize. Back in Britain it won three BAFTAs: Best Film, Best Screenplay and Best Actress (Blethyn).

Leigh's next project, again produced and distributed via Channel 4 and FilmFour, was *Career Girls* (UK, 1997) starring Katrin Cartlidge and Lynda Steadman. Many saw this film, made for a budget of £1.5m, as a disappointing follow-up to *Secret & Lies*. However, Leigh ended the 1990s with his most ambitious project to date, *Topsy-Turvy* (UK/USA, 1999), the story of the musical partnership between composers Arthur Sullivan and W.S.Gilbert in relation to the staging of their famous comic opera, *The Mikado*. This departure for Leigh meant he had a much bigger budget (£13.5m), including Lottery funding. He also parted company with Channel 4 in favour of the Lottery franchise to which he belonged, Pathé.

Land and Freedom (1995) (UK/Spain/Germany) UKCert 15

Director: Ken Loach

Screenplay: Jim Allen

Producer: Rebecca O'Brien

Production companies: Parallax Pictures; Messidor Films; Road Movies Filmproduktion GmbH; British Screen; European Co-Production Fund (UK); TVE Televisión Española; Canal+ España;, BBC Films; Degeto Film; ARD; Filmstiftung NRW; BIM Distribuzione;

Diaphana Films; Eurimages Conseil de l'Europe; Working Title Films

Production start date: 09/05/1994 **Budget:** £3m (estimated)

Distributor: Artificial Eye **UK Release date:** 6 October 1995

UK Box Office: £889,640 **USA Box Office:** $0.2m

Worldwide Box Office: n/a

The art house cinema scene took a bit of a battering during the decade but auteurs such as Mike Leigh, Peter Greenaway and Sally Potter enriched an already eclectic mix of films. Perhaps the busiest of the British art house directors during this period was Ken Loach.

The 1990s saw him returning to prominence as a feature film director after a period of absence in the 1980s. His 1990s work shows a broad range of politically motivated social realism dramas like *Riff Raff*, *Raining Stones* and *Ladybird, Ladybird* (UK, 1994), which focus on the lives and struggles of ordinary working class people. In 1995 Loach, who took advantage of European funding opportunities, produced a British film about the Spanish Civil War of 1936-39 called *Land and Freedom*. This move marked a departure from the grimy British kitchen sink dramas associated with Loach and was to continue with *Carla's Song* set in Nicaragua before he returned to home soil for *My Name is Joe*. Like the other British art house directors, Loach knew that his core audience lay in Europe rather than in America.

SYNOPSIS

In present day Liverpool after the death of her grandfather David, Kim sorts out his possessions and goes through a suitcase, which contains cuttings, photos and letters from a time when he fought as a volunteer in the Spanish Civil War. She learns that David, an unemployed worker and British Communist party member, volunteered to join the fight against the fascists in Spain. Kim learns about David's history through letters he wrote to his fiancé Kitty.

On a train David stumbles upon some friendly militiamen who sign him up to a detachment loyal to the Marxist revolutionary POUM organisation. The reality of his task becomes apparent when David receives basic training with antiquated equipment. David notices a Spanish woman in his multinational unit called Blanca who he awkwardly finds out is in a relationship with the bold Irishman Coogan.

The drudgery of the unit's entrenched skirmishes is brought to an end when it liberates a village from the small occupying fascists army. In the process Coogan is killed by a sniper while arguing with David over a round of ammunition. Blanca grieves for Coogan while David feels a mixture of shock and guilt.

Free from their fascist oppressors the villagers agree that collectivism is the best way to serve the revolutionary cause. After a heated debate the POUM unit decides to stay as a militia rather than join the New Popular Army.

During a training drill for new recruits David is injured when his rifle backfires and he is sent to Barcelona for treatment. There he unexpectedly meets Blanca and the two share a night of passion. However, their relationship is thrown apart when Blanca discovers that David has signed up with the Stalinist International Brigade, despite her protestations about Stalin's treachery.

David then finds himself at the centre of a working class uprising in Barcelona against the popular front regime. During a skirmish he encounters an Englishman from Manchester who is fighting against David despite both of them signing up to fight against the fascists. Disillusioned with fellow socialists fighting each other David tears up his Communist party card and returns to his militia unit where he is reconciled with Blanca.

To their disbelief the POUM militia are ordered to disband by the Republican Army and the leaders of the unit are arrested for allegedly colluding with the fascists. In the confusion that follows Blanca is shot dead.

Back in the present David's coffin is lowered into the ground and his granddaughter reads out a poem by William Morris. She scatters Spanish soil that David had brought back with him to England in his red neckerchief, which she then clasps aloft in a salute of solidarity.

HOW IT WAS MADE

From the outset Loach and Jim Allen, who had worked with Loach in the 1970s on the TV political drama series *Days of Hope* and his recent films *Hidden Agenda* (UK, 1990) and *Raining Stones* set out to make a film about the Spanish Civil War which would expose the role of Stalinism in betraying the Spanish workers' fight against General Franco's fascist regime. Creatively they needed to find a framework that would explain the complexities of the Civil War and still act as a compelling human drama.

Their idea was a double-barrelled device, which was to show everything through David's eyes in the form of flashbacks conveyed via letters written to his fiancé and have David's granddaughter (and thereby the audience) absorb this subjective information. David's personal knowledge and grasp of events is passed on to us as our own knowledge unravels the story.

With their agenda set Loach and Allen used George Orwell's *Homage to Catalonia*, where the author served as a soldier on the Aragon front, as an influence to construct their story. The film-makers also cited other reference works including Victor Alba's history of the POUM and *The Spanish Civil War* by historian Hugh Thomas.

Their research also involved seeking out survivors from the Civil War who were part of the POUM, the Marxist revolutionary group, and drawing on their actual experiences and incorporating them into the plot.

Funding proved a problem and the budget of £3m was exceptionally small for a project with such grand ambitions. *Saving Private Ryan*, by comparison, had a budget of £50m. Nevertheless, Loach was able to take advantage of the European Co-Production Fund, British Screen, BBC Films and Working Title on the British side with further funding from Spain and Germany and support from Eurimages. His own company, Parallax Pictures, also had support from Sally Hibbin and Rebecca O'Brien, who produced the film.

Loach's casting reflected his working style, which features elements of unscripted dialogue and a naturalistic approach. In *Land and Freedom*, which was filmed in the region of Aargon in Spain, he took a mix of professional actors, notably Ian Hart who had just won an Evening Standard British Film Award for Most Promising Newcomer for *Backbeat* (UK/ Germany 1994), as the working class idealist, David. Other members of the militia were trade union activists and the scene where collectivism is debated featured people from a village and professional actors such as American Tom Gilroy. Loach also had the actors speak in Spanish and Catalan where necessary to gain authenticity, even if this meant that the film would carry subtitles.

Beyond that the film was shot in chronological order with the actors learning the plot as the action took place, enabling them not only to achieve a level of camaraderie as a group of actors but also to engage emotionally at dramatically critical moments such as when Coogan and Blanca are killed.

Several distributors had picked up Loach and Parallax for their previous films – Enterprise for *Hidden Agenda*, Mayfair for *Riff Raff*, First Independent for *Raining Stones*, and Artificial Eye for *Ladybird, Ladybird*. Perhaps reflecting the European nature of the film, specialist European art house distributor Artificial Eye was again onboard to distribute the film in the UK. *Land and Freedom* received its world premiere in Spain on 7 April 1995 before transferring to the Cannes Film Festival and an eventual release in Britain in October.

KEY ISSUES

Loach and screenwriter Allen succeed in presenting a film where no prior historical knowledge is necessary in order to understand the motivation of its main character David, who acts as our historical guide through the turmoil and chaos of the Spanish Civil War. We share in many of the intimate political debates and gain an understanding of the complex issues surrounding the Civil War and Loach and Allen's interpretation of events.

Betrayal of ideals

The core theme of *Land and Freedom* is Loach and Allen's assertion that the Spanish Civil War could have been won had it not been for Stalinism. However, its main character David remains a supporter of the working class struggle throughout the film. His first betrayal comes from the fact that in England he is unemployed. With no prospects of work and a rallying cause to stimulate him, he chooses to leave his fiancé behind and help his fellow workers in Spain fight the fascists.

During the raid on the village David feels guilt that he contributed to Coogan's death by arguing about a round of ammunition when the Irishman is shot by a sniper. It is little consolation to David that the sniper, who turns out to be a priest, is caught. The villagers show no remorse as the priest is executed and tell how he betrayed them by tipping off the fascists with information he gleaned from the confessional. These events profoundly effect David who declares in one of his letters that: 'I'm not the man I was,' and dismisses his 'daft romantic ideas.'

The next betrayal shows Blanca disgusted that David has betrayed the revolutionary cause presented by the POUM in favour of joining the Communist International Brigade. 'Stalinists are betraying the revolution,' she cries. 'You don't see – you don't want to see.'

Stung by her fierce rejection David finally experiences his political awakening among the chaos and confusion in the siege of Communist headquarters when across the barricade he encounters a volunteer from Manchester who is fighting with the anarchists: 'Why aren't you over here with us?' he calls. Neither man seems to know. Disillusioned David tears up his Communist party card.

When David rejoins the POUM militia he declares profoundly: 'I saw a lot of things with my own eyes – things I didn't want to see.' However, the final betrayal is played out when the Communist-backed army declares the POUM illegal and accuses them of supporting the fascists. The scene comes after a bitter struggle to hold a position fighting the fascists and the injustice and disgust is given an extra emphasis. However, Loach is careful not to leave the notion that the fighting has all been in vain. Despite the outcome to David's personal crusade he still regrets nothing.

Collectivism

One of the key scenes in the film is when people from the village engage in a debate about whether or not to collectivise the land. During the sequence we see David being updated by translations of what is being said. However, Loach manages to set his audience in the intimate scene with a fly on the wall style.

The debate first starts on a local level with some villagers seeing the necessity of combining forces to provide food for those fighting in the war. This issue is muddied by the man with a small holding who agrees that effort should be made to feed those fighting but not at the expense of his own plot of land which he wants to continue to farm as his own. He argues that his hard work should be rewarded and not penalised by a collective approach. Within moments the issue has taken on wider proportions when the villagers are asked to consider the bigger picture of the struggle. Gene Lawrence, an American who is with the POUM militia, says that the revolutionary talk is scaring potential allies and urges a concerted effort to win the war against the fascists. His voice represents the Communist standpoint that winning the war must come before revolutionary reforms.

His argument is counterbalanced by a German view, which points to how postponing revolutionary action in his native land led to the rise to power of Hitler. By now the debate has moved from the localised issues of a small village to the global issues of democracy and world politics. Those debating political and ideological issues are foreigners who are standing up when they speak as opposed to the villagers, dealing in life and death matters of hunger, who remain seated.

In the end the villagers vote in favour of collectivism. As an audience we follow the debate in much the same way that David has followed the development of the Civil War. As a footnote to this important political debate, today's audiences, spoon-fed on endless TV reality shows, may subconsciously relish the 'it's your time to vote' moment.

Following on from this comes another chance to absorb the information when the POUM militia vote on whether to stay as a revolutionary militia or join the communist backed New Popular Army, thereby securing better equipment to fight the fascists. Gene, staying true to his principles, chooses to leave the militia, while David stays despite agreeing with the logic behind joining a more organised army. Again, by giving us both sides of the argument, Loach engages with the audience.

Story or history?

Loach was careful to call his film *A Story From the Spanish Revolution*. This was not a documentary about the Spanish Civil War, although it contained some actual newsreel footage. Rather it was a considered drama about the conflict told unapologetically from the point of view of a young working class idealist.

Irrespective of historical accuracy *Land and Freedom* succeeds in conveying David's personal journey from idealism to disillusionment. Loach skilfully takes us with David through training camps, language difficulties, battles and mixed emotions to a growing political awareness. In this way Loach creates a personal drama that engages us emotionally as he attaches elements representing complicated political ideologies to his characters.

Loach needed to frame the fiction within the realms of actual historical events. As a matter of convenience he created an English speaking POUM militia but in doing so brought together an assortment of nationalities that bonded for the same cause. The camaraderie is well observed and Loach's naturalistic style makes it feel authentic.

The debates on collectivism and whether or not the POUM militia should integrate into the Popular Army were used as illustrations of issues rather than historical signposts. However, other incidents such as the execution of the priest and the trading of insults rather than bullets over the barricades are all based on eyewitness accounts.

Those objecting to the historical inaccuracies in the film point to the fact that Loach concentrated on a small area in Aargon which led to the impression that this is where the heart of the war was fought and it is heavily biased in favour of the POUM to the detriment of the International Brigade. They were also unhappy with implications that arms were held back from the militias by the Communists.

However, Loach remained adamant with his stance that Stalin sabotaged the Spanish workers struggle in order to forge an alliance with Britain, France and the US.

Drawing a Blanca

This story about the Spanish revolution uses Blanca as the heroic and beautiful symbol of that struggle. She serves several purposes in the dramatic and politic aspects of *Land and Freedom*. The first impression we get of her is false when David is teased into believing that Blanca is a prostitute. To his embarrassment he discovers that she is in a relationship with Coogan. This is significant on a couple of levels. First, it establishes the sexual politics within the group, but second and less obvious Blanca is an anarchist (represented by her red and black scarf) who has joined up with the Marxist revolutionary POUM. This point establishes the initial confusion of people of different political views fighting together against the fascists. David also accidentally joins the POUM when he is unable to locate a Communist brigade.

Blanca also represents, in a sketchy form, the role women played in the war. She is shown in battle but later on we learn that women are not allowed to bear arms and Blanca is seen behind the front line administering First Aid. The other woman in the unit, Maite, is seen as the cook of the unit.

Loach also uses the character of Blanca as an emotional catalyst and allows for a romance of sorts between her and David to develop as a simmering theme. David is attracted to her but backs off when he learns that Coogan is her man. Ironically, his part in Coogan's death unites David and Blanca in grief and he embraces her. Unexpectedly Blanca joins David in Barcelona where for one evening they leave their political ideals and struggles behind and make love not war.

Their tender liaison is shattered when Blanca learns that David has joined the International Brigade, which was his intention in the first place. At this point her role in the film is to act as the moral conscious and she exclaims: 'Stalinists are betraying the revolution.' Their lovers' tiff is based on what Blanca perceives is David's political naiveté and in this respect she represents the views of Loach and Allen.

The emotional pay-off comes not in a heroic Hollywood-style embrace but in Blanca's status as a martyr when she is clumsily shot by the Popular Army who are asking the POUM to lay down their arms. Blanca is buried in collectivised land (soon to be taken again) and achieves her freedom. Symbolically the revolution is seen to end with Blanca's death and we learn no more about the outcome of the Civil War, or indeed what happened to David and his comrades from the POUM unit. Instead, we hear David reflect Loach's view of the struggle: 'Had we succeeded here – and we could have done – we would have changed the world.'

We can be heroes

The opening and closing shots of the film provide a suitable contrast in assessing David's life. In the first instance we witness the death of an unremarkable old man seemingly living on his own, in a not very pleasant block of flats ironically daubed with anarchist and National Front graffiti. By the end of the film we have shared his remarkable story of idealism, naiveté and courage and our opinion of the old man has changed considerably.

The funeral scene is neatly linked to the funeral of Blanca with a shot of David's coffin being lowered into the ground in the present following on from her burial in the past. Somehow the emotional intensity of the two funerals is held as Kim scatters the Spanish soil onto David's coffin and offers an emotional and defiant farewell to her grandfather that she apparently never really knew.

SCENE ANALYSIS – WHY AREN'T YOU OVER HERE WITH US?

David's encounter with a volunteer from Manchester who is fighting against him is the point where he abandons the ideologies espoused by political parties and makes his own mind up. He is prompted to find out for himself beforehand when Blanca, enraged that he has joined the Stalinist-backed International Brigade, storms out on him in Barcelona.

Loach enters a stage in the film where he must demonstrate how factions formally fighting together against the fascists now turned against each other in a complex turn of events in the Spanish Civil War.

His first devise is to take the audience back to the room in present time where David's granddaughter absorbs cuttings and letters. As she picks up a cutting we hear a voiceover from David explaining the situation in quite simple terms. 'It's dead complicated Kit, and difficult to explain. The trouble is the struggle seems to be falling apart in front of our eyes. No one trusts anyone anymore. Anarchists and POUM are pulling one way, Communists another. It's mad.' At this point David's granddaughter can be seen looking at a *Daily Worker* paper with the headlines: 'Spanish Trotskyists Plot With Franco' followed by a sub-heading which reads 'Documents Reveal Secret Link-up With Fascist H.Q', and written in pen by the side of this statement underlined in capitals is the word LIES! This emphasises the point David has just made in his letter but he goes on to state that he will continue to place his trust in the Communist party.

We cut to David in Barcelona as his voiceover continues by introducing the next scene. He concludes: 'There's shootings. Comrades against comrades – the fascists must be laughing their heads off. Anyway, I've just got orders to join a squad of Government supporters. It seems that we're being sent to defend Communist HQ. No choice. I'm not looking forward to it.'

We see David and a group of armed men wearing red neckerchiefs being led to the headquarters by a policeman but they encounter fire from a group of anarchists distinguished by their red and black neckerchiefs. A shot taken from the Communist position onto the square below shows a CNT (anarchist) truck drive through the streets as if to further explain the two sets of anti-fascists about to take part in the stand off.

David can then be seen with his men at their vantage point at the Communist headquarters, which is taken from the right side of the screen as they look down on the street below. An old woman hurries across the road carrying two bags. Meanwhile our attentions are returned (from the point of view of David's unit) to the opposing side of the street where a black and red banner declaring 'Comite Regional de Cataluna' (AIT) is evident as volunteers are seen preparing barricades. As the camera surveys David and his unit from their side a loudspeaker announcement (given to the audience via subtitles) establishes that the attack carried out on the Telephone Exchange (which was maintained by the anarchists) was an attack on working people. At this point the film has provided as much factual information as possible before the shooting starts.

Another woman is seen from the point of view of David's unit walking hurriedly across the square with a basket of food as shots are fired. Bravely she places her bag down and implores to both sides: 'You should be killing fascists – not one another'. The absurdity of the situation is shown as David's unit urges her to go home. The anarchists are also seen urging her to get out of the way. She flees from the firing when her basket is hit. David (speaking in Spanish) apologises to her.

Both sides now trade fire and the screen fades to black before establishing a night time shot of the stand-off. The darkness in the scene where only outlines of figures are visible adds to the confusion as two sides previously both fighting the fascists now turn on each other. Across the divide the men are heard to trade insults and snippets of propaganda: 'You don't even know who's your enemy. You idiots.'

Suddenly a British voice is heard. David calls out: 'Are you English? Where are you from?' We see David rise from his position and look across to his fellow Brit whose dark outline can just be distinguished as he is framed in long shot in the middle of the screen resting his gun on sandbags.

The highly-charged bickering between the opposing Spanish factions is now replaced with an absurd exchange between the man from Manchester and David. He calls: 'What are you doing here?' David replies: 'Don't know' but counters immediately with: 'Why aren't you over here with us.' There follows an almost exact reply, as if it is David's voice in echo: 'Why aren't you over here with us.' Neither men can explain the situation.

The apparent good-natured banter between the Spanish factions ends when a grenade is lobbed over from the Communist side to the anarchist position. Both sides return fire and the battle continues. However, David's disillusionment starts to kick in as he falls back near a wall and in Spanish states: 'No more. Never. We are not enemies.'

REACTION

Land and Freedom won the FIPRESCI International Critics Prize and the Ecumenical Jury Prize at Cannes. Despite the political theme it drew widespread acclaim from film critics: 'Loach's movie is a visceral, emotional and intellectual experience, and among the finest films of the decade,' declared Philip French in *The Observer*.

It also set up vigorous debate among academics and political parties from the Left. The film's historical inaccuracies and its bias were revealed in several articles, one by Santiago Carillo, former head of the Spanish Communist party, attacking the film. Other reactions came from veterans of the Spanish Civil War who served in the International Brigades. Some were antagonistic to Loach's stance, others more sympathetic to what he had attempted to do.

The overall impression was that Loach had made a bold film about a subject, particularly in Spain, that had appeared dormant. Indeed, many young Spaniards were drawn to see the film and it performed well at the Spanish box-office.

In Britain it achieved good art house returns of more than £800,000 but Loach and his producers were unhappy with distibutor Artificial Eye for not placing the film in multiplex cinemas. In an article in *Premiere* he said: 'To catch people who wouldn't normally go to see a certain film, you have to mount a rather bigger campaign than the one [Artificial

Eye] mounted.' Artificial Eye responded by pointing to the poor box-office performance at multiplexes of *Ladybird, Ladybird*, but this merely frustrated the producers who saw *Land and Freedom* as Loach's most commercial, accessible film as proved by the returns from Spain and also from France.

Sadly, *Land and Freedom* would be Allen's last collaboration with Ken Loach for the writer died in the summer of 1999. Loach's next film, *Carla's Song*, was set among the political upheavals in Nicaragua and this time featured an idealistic Glaswegian bus driver who meets and falls in love with Carla, a Nicaraguan refugee. The screenplay was written by Paul Laverty, who appears in *Land and Freedom* as the Scot in the POUM militia unity. Laverty had first-hand experience of the struggle between the US-backed guerilla contras and their attempts to overthrow Nicaraguans democratically elected by the Sandinista government. The former lawyer would become Loach's regular screenwriter through the remainder of the decade and into the 2000s.

CONCLUSION

It is noticeable that Britain's two most celebrated art house directors should find more commercial success in France and Spain than back home. Both men are respected in the British press but without the backing of an American major their work has failed to be widely distributed.

While much of the effort in the 1990s was to bolster the British production sector, a similar effort was not evident when it came to distribution. While an art house audience remained loyal to independent films there seemed little opportunity in Britain to cross over and find a larger audience. Equally, younger audiences were being successfully weaned off anything that might appear foreign and seemed to embrace the American cultural hegemony — at their local cinemas at least. Art house directors, even popular ones like Leigh and Loach, not only had to battle to get funding for their projects, they then had to battle to get their films shown to wider audiences even on the back of festival accolades and awards.

But if it was tough for independent film-makers then PolyGram's sudden and shocking demise in 1999 showed how fragile the British film industry was. The absence of a distribution-led industry would always make film-makers vulnerable.

With the notable exception of Working Title, which secured a US major for its distribution outlets, many British film-makers operated on a one-stop shop basis. Any success a film garnered at the box-office rarely saw its way back in funding another film. By the end of the decade it seemed that any notions of a sustainable film industry in Britain needed to address the issues of distribution, not just locally but globally where the market offered potentially greater rewards for the type of films that Leigh and Loach were interested in making.

As it stood, the British distribution sector at the end of the 1990s was either sprinkled like confetti with dozens of companies releasing a handful of films, or spread thinly into niche markets where operators released a film a month and then crossed their fingers and hoped that their release would succeed.

By 2002 the UK Film Council, whose two foundations stones were to 'develop a sustainable UK film industry' and ' develop film culture in the UK by improving access to, and education about, the moving image,' was on the case investigating a specialised distribution and exhibition strategy for the UK, which would encompass all forms of cinema.

FURTHER READING

British Cinema of the 90s
Murphy, Robert (ed.) (BFI, 2001) Chapter 8 – Hollywood UK by Watson, Neil

A Better Picture: A consultation paper on three financial measures
(UK Film Council, January 2002)

A Better Picture: A digest of consultation responses
(UK Film Council, April 2002)

Never A Sure Thing, by Dobson, Patricia
Sight & Sound Vol.7 No.9. (September 1997), P.22-24

The Great British Movie Mountain, by Westbrook, Caroline
Empire No.100. (October 1997), P.150-154

The Stats An overview of the film, television, video and DVD industries 1990-2003
(BFI National Library, BFI Information Services, 2006)

BFI Film and Television Handbook (BFI, editions from 1990–2005)

Selected reviews/articles/references

Film Distributors' Association – www.launchingfilms.com

Secrets and Lies

Sight & Sound V.6 N.6 (1 June 1996) P.51-52 by MacNab, Geoffrey

Empire N.84 (1 June 1996) P.32 by Cavanagh, David

The Cinema of Mike Leigh: a Sense of the Real
Watson, Garry (Wallflower Press, 2004)

Mike Leigh: interviews
Movshovitz, Howie (University Press of Mississippi, 2000)

Contemporary British Cinema 16+ Source Guide Guides
Mettler, Erinna; Ormsby, Andrew; Reeve, David; Dupin, Christophe (BFI National Library,
2003) www.bfi.org.uk/filmtvinfo/publications/16+/

Land and Freedom

Sight & Sound V.5 N.10 (1 Oct 1996) P.51 by Kemp, Philip

Empire N.77 (1 Nov 1995) P.48 by Nathan, Ian

Film For a Spanish Republic by Christie, Ian
Sight & Sound V.5. N10 (1 Oct 1995) P.36-37

Loach on Loach,
Fuller, Graham (ed.) (Faber and Faber, 1998)

The Cinema of Ken Loach: Art in the Service of the People
Leigh, Jacob (Wallflower Press, 2002)

The Revolution Betrayed: An Interview with Ken Loach by Potton, Richard
Cineaste v.22, n.1 (Winter, 1996) P.30

Freedom Fighter by Brealey, Louise
Premiere (UK) V.3 N.12 (April 1996) P.20

8. CULTURALLY DIVERSE

Glancing at the top British films in the 1990s one would be hard pressed to match the vision portrayed on the screen with the multi-cultural make-up of the audience flocking back into cinemas, particularly in the large cities. According to census data the most significant change to the British population from 1991 and 2001 was the increase in the number of people from different ethnic backgrounds and countries. Although 92 per cent of the population is still white, during the 1990s the population grew by 4 per cent of which 73 per cent was made up of minority ethnic groups with black Africans doubling during the decade followed by increases in Bangladeshi, Pakistani and Chinese groups.

The analysis of what constitutes a typically British film spilled over to black British and Asian British film-makers. If it was hard for white first-time film-makers to get their films made then it was doubly difficult for black and Asian film-makers to secure funding and the 1990s are something of a desert, with the occasional oasis, when it comes to finding films made by, or about, the black or Asian experience in Britain.

Some might argue that this is an example of deep-rooted prejudice, while others say that black and Asian themes do not have sufficient crossover appeal to woo a large audience. Another view about the problems facing black and Asian film-makers in Britain was not to do with race but aesthetic considerations, which seemed to inflict many would-be British film-makers in the 1990s irrespective of skin colour.

As a rule of thumb many of the new British film-makers in the 1990s focused on getting their films made first and worried about the target audience and the possibility of making money later.

At the beginning of the 1990s Channel 4, BBC and the British Film Institute's influential production board were on hand to seek out new work and cater to minority audiences. Midway through the decade the National Lottery kicked in to give many first-time film-makers the chance to get their films made, but success was no longer to be measured on artistic integrity as the multiplexes sprang up. The art house circuit was engulfed and minority or niche films generally struggled to be screened to large audiences. Distributors and exhibitors could justifiably point to the rising numbers returning to the cinema, mainly to see Hollywood films. If this is what the public wanted then why mess with a winning formula?

It is within this context that black and Asian film-makers had to work in the 1990s. It appeared that the risks in investing in black and Asian films were too great, particularly when there were many films made by white first-time directors, writers and unfamiliar actors falling down like ten-pins in a bowling alley. However, black and Asian film-makers were thrown a lifeline via America through the hip hop music scene and the relative success of African American films such as *Do the Right Thing* (USA, 1989); *Boys N the*

Hood (USA, 1991); and *Waiting to Exhale* (USA, 1995). There were also obvious crossover international hits such as *Malcolm X* (USA, 1992) and *What's Love Got to Do With It* (USA, 1993), which showed that a commercial audience existed for cinema with black cultural themes.

Black music seemed to be the hook to enable British black Afro-Caribbean films to be made. This was partly due to the calculation that there was a sufficient young white audience interested in black music and style to make such films viable. It is fair to say that Asian film-makers had to find another route into the British cinema and they did this by joining the quirky social comedy route, which proved successful for the likes of *The Full Monty*, *Brassed Off* and *Little Voice*.

BRITISH BLACK AND ASIAN BRITISH FILMS IN THE 1990S

There had been signs of an opening up of cross-cultural perceptions in the 1980s with films like Stephen Frears' successful *My Beautiful Launderette*, Julien Temple's unsuccessful *Absolute Beginners*; and John Akomfrah's documentary on race relations in *Handsworth Songs* (UK, 1986).

My Beautiful Launderette's writer Hanif Kureishi again joined forces with Frears for *Sammie and Rosie Got Laid* (UK, 1987) and was backed by Working Title and PolyGram for his directorial debut *London Kills Me* but found more success via his BBC TV drama *The Buddha of Suburbia* (1993). Kureishi also wrote the screenplay based on his short story for the film *My Son the Fanatic* (UK, 1997), which was produced by the BBC.

Following Kureishi's successes the 1990s began with the promise of a more diverse cinema when Issac Julien, a key figure in the 1980's black British film movement and co-founder of Sankofa, a film collective dedicated at finding a voice for black film culture, made his directorial feature film debut with the BFI-funded feature *Young Soul Rebels*. The film, set in the late 1970s around a pirate radio station run by Chaz and Chris, dealt with issues of sexuality, gender and national identity while also featuring black soul music, punk rock, a gay romance and a murder thriller to boot. The film, which picked up the critics SACD Award (Society of Dramatic Authors and Composers Award) at Cannes, earned praise from some critics, not sadly for the quality of the film but because it was a black film made by a black film-maker.

A year later *The Crying Game*, a film that dealt with themes of sexuality, gender and identity also showed a distinctly diverse side of British life and successfully wrapped it up within the genre of a political thriller. The casting of American actor Forest Whitaker as the black soldier, primarily to boost international sales, disappointed many who would have championed the cause of black British actors.

British Black and Asian Films in the 1990s

Title	No of screens	Box Office (£)
Ama (UK, 1991)	1	8,230
London Kills Me (UK, 1991)	3	30,749
Young Soul Rebels (UK, 1991)	4	33,246
Bhaji On the Beach (UK, 1993)	5	309,715
Wild West (UK, 1992)	4	30,349
Brothers in Trouble (UK, 1995)	2	6,422
Welcome II the Terrordome (UK, 1995)	2	4,085
Franz Fanon Black Skin White Mask (UK/France, 1996) (Documentary)	1	1,684
Babymother (UK, 1997)	5	62,928
Dancehall Queen (USA/Jamaica, 1997)	2	98,808
My Son the Fanatic (UK, 1997)	16	130,616
Sixth Happiness (UK, 1997)	1	2.480
The Girl With Brains in Her Feet (UK, 1997)	13	21,115
Guru in Seven (UK, 1997)	14	19,792
East is East (UK, 1999)	80	10,374,926
A Room For Romeo Brass (UK, 1999)	13	91,389

Source: Nielsen EDI, BFI The Stats: An overview of the film, television, video and DVD industries 1990-2003

In 1992, Channel 4 funded Bhaji on the Beach, a gentle comedy about a group of Asian women from the Midlands who set off on a day trip to Blackpool. Dir Gurinder Chadha won the Evening Standard Award for Newcomer to British Cinema for the film and again the critics were doubly pleased to see an Asian British film directed by an Asian woman. However, the film did not light the blue touch paper and the rest of the decade was a frustrating time for Chadha, who ironically went to America to make the gentle multi-racial comedy What's Cooking? (UK/USA, 2000) before waiting nearly 10 years to pick up where Bhaji on the Beach had left off with Bend it Like Beckham (UK/Germany, 2001) and Bride & Prejudice (UK/Germany, 2004).

Considering Britain is a multi-cultural society it seems remarkable that a decade can throw up under 20 black British or Asian British films. Of these only half a dozen deal directly or indirectly with Afro-Caribbean culture in Britain and even then *Dancehall Queen* was based in Jamaica. The majority of the funding for the films came via Channel 4, BBC Films and the BFI, but the yield given on these films was low, with most struggling to be shown on more than a few screens. The startling exception to this was the surprise hit *East is East*.

GOODNESS GRACIOUS ME

It is noticeable that more Asian British films were made with unusual themes. *Wild West* focused on an Asian band obsessed with country and Western music; while *The Sixth Happiness* was a fictional biography of the life of disabled author Firdaus Kanga growing up in Bombay's Parsee community. The late 1990s saw Asian British culture become more prominent in the media with the sketch comedy show *Goodness Gracious Me* successfully transferring from BBC Radio 4 to BBC2 and making stars of the British Asian actors and writers Sanjeev Bhaskar, Kulvinder Ghir, Meera Syal and Nina Wadia. The show poked fun at mainly Indian stereotypes – often portraying them in exaggerated form or inverting situations such as the sketch where a group of Indians go for 'an English' instead of a curry. Bollywood films were screened in multiplexes and cinemas in areas with a high Asian community and soon they would take more at the box-office than the few top foreign language films that reached British screens. It is possible that all these factors helped *East is East*, which looked at a mixed raced Muslim family in 1971 Salford, become such a big hit.

BLACK AND WHITE

Black actors, unlike their American counterparts, generally had to play second fiddle to white British or American actors. Marianne Jean-Baptiste became the first Black British person to be nominated for an Oscar in her performance of Hortense in Mike Leigh's *Secret's & Lies* but instead of leading to more roles in Britain the actress went to America where she landed a part as FBI agent Vivian Johnson on the American TV series *Without A Trace*. There was another first when Ngozi Onwurah became the first black female director with *Welcome II the Terrordrome*. Julien Henrique's *Babymother* was also interesting in that it featured no white British characters.

Meanwhile, hit film *Notting Hill*, was taken to task by the critics for its lack of black or Asian faces within its supposed cosmopolitan London setting (although there are some very minor black and Asian characters in the film).

The Girl With Brains in Her Feet explored the adolescent world of a girl from a mixed race background, but like most of the films featuring black actors race was rarely raised as an issue. In the other top British films *The Full Monty* boasted a black character in the shape of Paul Barber as Horse (although originally the film was thought to have more black strippers) and Vas Blackwood as Rory Beaker in *Lock, Stock and Two Smoking Barrels*.

Looking at black themed films in the 1990s is rather like peeling a layer off an onion of the British film industry. It is easier to champion the performance of *East is East* than analyse the failings of *Welcome II the Terrordrome*. The good news is that public-funded organisations like Channel 4, BBC and the BFI were prepared to give British black and Asian film-makers a chance to make films. The bad news is that by the end of the decade this artistic benevolence was becoming rare. Black actors and film-makers would have to try harder to get their projects off the ground because the risks were still seen to be great. Problems with development and training common to the whole British film industry caused more blockages than opportunities and many black film-makers were caught in Catch 22 scenarios where the opportunities to show off their talents were hampered by a lack of opportunities to make films in the first place. There were exceptions, of course. Remi Adefarisin, a black director of photography, was busy during the 1990s working on films like *Sliding Doors*; *Elizabeth* and *Onegin* (UK/USA, 1998). However, he started his apprenticeship in television in the late 1970s and in a highly competitive world, time, opportunities and experience are rare commodities.

And yet the British Asian film experience proved a point that there exist audiences ready to take on niche programmes. The two films examined in this section – *East is East* and *Babymother* – show films with contrasting fortunes. *East is East* shows that audiences can be found for films with multicultural themes, while *Babymother* stuck to its guns of staying within a relatively small niche market.

East is East (1999) (UK) UK Cert 15

Director: Damien O'Donnell

Screenplay: Ayub Din-Khan (Based on the play by Ayub Din-Khan)

Producer: Leslee Udwin

Production companies: Film Four Limited; Assassin Films; BBC; MEDIA Programme of the European Union;, FilmFour

Production start date: 05/10/1998 **Budget:** £2.40m (estimated)

Distributor: FilmFour **UK Release date:** 5 November 1999

UK Box Office: £10,374,926 **USA Box Office:** $4,177,818

Worldwide Box Office: n/a

The unusual creative mix *East is East* sounds like the type of racist joke comedians like Bernard Manning used to perform on *The Comedians*, Granada TV's stand-up show of the 1970s; the film was written by a British Pakistani (Ayub Din-Khan), directed by an Irishman (Damien O'Donnell) and produced by a woman, Leslee Udwin, who was born in Israel and brought up in South Africa. But this cocktail of cultural influences was no joke, but rather a blend that came together to create an unexpected British hit comedy. Kipling's poem on which the title of the film is based suggests that: 'East is East and West is West, and never the twain shall meet'. Essentially, the film debunks this notion by showing us a mixed race British family growing up in 1970s Salford where the twain have definitely met and produced seven children.

East is East may be yet another quirky comedy to come out of Britain in the 1990s but it also deals with weighty topics such as cultural identity, domestic abuse and racial integration. The fact that it is partially autobiographical serves as a mirror on Britain's growing multi-cultural society in the 1970s.

SYNOPSIS

Set in Salford in 1971 Pakistani chip shop owner George Khan is married to Ella, an English woman, and they have seven children – six boys – Nazir, Abdul, Tariq, Maneer, Saleem, Sajid – and one girl, Meenah. The family gather for the arranged marriage of the oldest son, Nazir, but at the last moment Nazir flees the ceremony. George ostracises Nazir from the family. Life eventually gets back to normal with George and Ella running the fish and chip shop with Auntie Annie.

Taking council from the Mullah at the local mosque George, who is worried that his children are not growing up in the Muslim tradition, decides to meet Mr Shah and arrange a marriage for Tariq and Abdul. He keeps the arrangement a secret as the family take a pleasant trip to Bradford.

Back in Salford Abdul joins Tariq for a night out at the disco where Stella and her best friend Peggy join them. As Tariq and Abdul return home worst for wear, Sajid, who needs to go to the toilet, overhears George's plans to marry off Tariq and Abdul. Tariq is furious when he discovers and smashes a watch bought for the ceremony. He tries to leave home and goes to stay with Nazir but is followed by Meenah, Saleem, Stella and Peggy. Nazir and his partner come back to Salford in a Rolls Royce with a notion to confront George but Ella dissuades them and they leave before George arrives back home.

In the end the Shahs with their ugly daughters arrive in Salford and under orders the families gather and engage in awkward small talk. However, tensions rise between Ella and Mrs Shah. The whole thing falls apart when Saleem returns with his 'sculpture' of a cast of female genitalia, which accidently lands in Mrs Shah's lap. The Shahs leave the house in disgust. George goes to attack Ella but this time he is stopped by the rest of the family. Ella and George, both affected in their own ways by the experience, are then seen gingerly reconciled in the chip shop.

HOW IT WAS MADE

Based on his own experiences of growing up in a mixed race family in Salford and owning a fish and chip shop, Din-Khan is represented in the play and the film by Sajid, the youngest of the family. Former actress, Leslee Udwin, who had appeared in the ill-fated BBC soap *Eldorado* (1993), was looking for her first producing project, loved the play, which had been a sell-out hit at the Royal Court Theatre in London, and approached Din-Khan to develop it into a feature film. She then sought funding, which came principally from FilmFour and BBC Films.

Her next task was to pick a director and she turned to Irishman Damien O'Donnell who had championed the outsider in his first short film *Thirty Five Aside* (Ireland, 1995) about a young boy who is an outcast at his new school because he didn't like football. More time was spent on development with help from the MEDIA programme and securing funds.

Of the cast only Linda Bassett as Ella had appeared in the stage play. Her husband partner was Om Puri who starred in two earlier Asian British films *My Son the Fanatic* and *Brothers in Trouble* (1995). Lesley Nicol had played in Granada's hospital drama *Staying Alive* (1997) and regular TV actor John Bardon had appeared in the BBC sitcom *Get Back* (1992). The rest of the cast, made up of the Khan children, were mostly newcomers to film work though some had TV experience with the exception of young Jordan Routledge, who was set to make his screen debut.

KEY ISSUES

With its semi-autobiographical outlook *East is East* is rather like looking at an old family photo album. The children are raised in Britain and increasingly feel the pull of integration rather than adhering to their father's rather mixed messages of following rules on dress, behaviour and food. But it would be wrong to view this film, coming as it does in a pre-9/11 world, as an attack on Islam but rather as a rough personal portrait of an aspect of Pakistani culture caught against the backdrop of the India-Pakistan war and the controversy sparked by Enoch Powell speeches. However, the film uses humour to convey its messages and to defuse any offence or tensions. In less skilled hands *East is East* could have backfired, but the film succeeds principally as comedy first and then, behind the laughs, as a social commentary.

Played for laughs

The comic credentials of *East is East* are established from the opening shots when most of the Khan siblings are seen in the midst of a Catholic procession carrying a crucifix and a statue of the Virgin Mary through the grey streets of Salford. Alarm bells sound when they hear that their father has returned home early. As he joins Ella to observe the procession his children, still holding their religious icons, do a quick back double to bypass their father before rejoining the procession. This more or less sets the comic tone of the film, which contains a delightful array of visual jokes: after his circumcision Sajid is carefully carried home by his father until he reaches the house and bumps Sajid's head on the doorway; a new-fangled space hopper is burst when the van parks in Bradford; Sajid's toggle gets caught in the door when he is caught taking a pee in his parents bedroom; Meenah deliberately boots a football through Mr Moritmer's window which hosts a picture of Enoch Powell and Powell's face is replaced by that of Mr Mortimer; Nazir's partner's Afghan hound is seen regally looking out of the Rolls Royce as it leaves the Khan's terraced street; and the randy mongrel dog leaps on Mrs Shah as a final humiliation during her awful visit to the Khans.

There are many other subtle and unsubtle jokes which serve to keep the tone light and the audience not far from the next laugh. The film is unkind in its humour by making the hapless Peggy, Stella's fat friend, a figure of fun. It also serves up two pantomime ugly sisters as Tariq and Abdul's prospective wives, but leads to Auntie Annie cutting through the hypocrisy of the moment and turning to the stunned Tariq and Abdul with the droll observation: 'You're lucky you pair aren't you? Landing a couple of belters like these!'

Generally, the film skates a fine line in trying not to offend, despite often using language that would sound offensive out of context. However, the good-natured tone and vibrant performances give the film its energy. There is a lovely short non-verbal sequence when Sajid is being pursued through the house by Tariq, Meenah and Abdul and seeks support of his brothers Manner and Saleem. One absolves himself through prayer while the other first nods him to the place of safety only to repeat the same nod to the pursuing group. If it wasn't for the culturally significant secret Sajid was keeping this scene could have been repeated in any affectionate look at a squabbling family. However, East is East is a film where cultural clashes and questions of identity are the main cause of tension.

Curry and chips

The cultural pick and mix of the film is evident throughout as two cultures seemingly converge. The Khan children are unable to immerse themselves fully into the British way of life under the harsh regime instigated by their father despite their mother often turning a blind eye and understanding their desires to break out.

Abdul is curious to find out what British culture is about and he joins Tariq at a disco. Later, much to the surprise of his workmates, he is seen having a drink on his own on his stag do as he prepares to marry a woman he has never met, a stark contrast to the ribald antics his work colleagues inflict earlier on a British colleague about to be hitched.

Abdul is inquisitive but unsure of his position in British society.

Maneer is more obedient and seems most likely to follow Islam, unlike Tariq who is quite adamantly against his Pakistani roots. He denies his identity at the disco by calling himself Tony and is accepted by the bouncers. Abdul meekly assumes an assumed identity of Arthur, while the oldest brother Nazir changes his name to Nigel.

Meenah rebels in her tomboy antics and her reluctance to wear a sari. In one playful moment she performs a parody Bollywood-style dance to a classic tune *Inhi Logonne* from the film *Pakeezah* (India, 1972) Dir Kamal Armohi, dressed as she is in white overalls and holding a broom at the back of the chippy. It is a peculiar cross-cultural performance not good enough to be authentic Bollywood but not bad enough to be mocking that culture.

George is a strict disciplinarian but the film shows him quite literally fighting a losing battle. On many occasions the Khan children and sometimes Ella are put on red alert with the news that: 'My dad's coming.' There are a long list of crimes that they try to conceal such as eating sausages and bacon, Meenah wearing a skirt in the house, Saleem studying art and not engineering, Tariq snogging a white girl and slipping out to discos at night, and Nazir running off from his wedding to shack up with his male business partner. In a culture where patriarchs dominate and generally gain respect, George is thwarted at each step of the way. Ironically, his only truly obedient son Maneer gets a beating when he covers up for Tariq's rage.

A key scene between Tariq and his father allows both sides of the cultural clash argument come to the fore. George begins by demanding respect. 'Pakistani son always shows respect,' he says, to which Tariq replies: 'Dad, I'm not Pakistani. I was born here. I speak English, not Urdu.' Rather than react violently George tries to reason with his son and delivers some home truths of his own. 'I am trying to show you a good way to live. You no English. English people never accepting you. In Islam everyone equal. See. No black man, no white man. All Muslim. Special community.'

Tariq responds by wishing to be able to make up his own mind. George then rather destroys his own argument by warning Tariq off English women, who he claims are 'no good.' Tariq responds by saying: 'Well, if English women are so bad, why did you marry my mum?' George is riled by this and grabs Tariq by the throat and demands respect, to which Tariq seemingly backs down. He finishes the discussion by saying that he will marry a Pakistani and then concludes by saying that he will then marry an Englishwoman: 'Just like my dad.'

If George's relationship with his children is stormy then his marriage to Ella is far more complex. The two genuinely seem to have affection for each other and Ella seems to understand the contradictions in George's life. She does berate him for his hypocrisy saying that he is a Muslim when it suits him and even forces him to accept that Nazir, their eldest son, still exists: 'He's not dead, he's living in Eccles,' she says matter of fact.

Despite voicing her disapproval of matters, such as the way George handles the arranged marriage to Tariq and Abdul, Ella supports him. Her breaking point is reached when George beats Maneer in front of her. She responds by saying: 'I will tell you this for nothing, I am not going to stand by and watch you crush them one by one because of your pig bloody ignorance.' Her unfortunate use of the term 'pig' leads to George lashing out in a rage in what is the film's most uncomfortable moment.

Remarkably, Ella's loyalty to George returns in the next scene. As they watch an uncannily ironic moment from the children's programme The Clangers she puts her foot down with her children when they start voicing defiance about the visit of the Shahs: 'As long as you're living under his bastard roof, you'll do as you're told. Do you hear me!' In the end Ella obeys her husband's wishes – up to a point.

While George does not emerge with much credit during the film, it is quite a remarkable feat that this wife-beating, bigoted, ignorant man still can elicit a modicum of sympathy. Deep down his motives seem sincere and they are to do with protecting his family within a British cultural setting, which he has both embraced and yet rejected, as symbolised by his request for half a cup of tea.

'Mum, mum the Pakis are here!'

For today's audiences brought up on a diet of political correctness the racist language in *East is East* comes as a bit of a shock, even if it does accurately reflect the language of the day. The Khan children freely use the word 'Paki' as a derogatory term for other Pakistanis.

The racism is never seen as the main issue. Mr Moorhouse is the token white racist, seen supporting Enoch Powell and giving us his prejudiced credentials when a van arrives outside the Khan's house. 'See. You let one of 'em in, and the whole fucking tribe turns up.' The great irony is that two of his family members, the spotty grandson Ernest who fancies Meenah and greets George Khan with 'Salaamu Alaikum' and his granddaughter Stella, who is besotted with Tariq, do not subscribe to his views.

At one point Stella declares: 'I'll never let the colour of your dad to come between us.' Elsewhere, the film shows how racist remarks were once misconstrued as good-natured when Abdul is referred to as Gunga Din by a work colleague. Outside the disco two Asian boys are turned away but Tariq, alias Tony, is allowed in. Ignorance is also at the heart of George Khan's racism. In the hospital he mutters 'bastard Indian' under his breath when he encounters an Indian doctor. However, despite the footage of Enoch Powell, the film does not show too much in the shape of hostile racism towards the Khan family. If anything, it potrays an almost idyllic notion of an integrated Asian family whose main struggles comes from within the confines of their home.

The family way

One of the endearing aspects about *East is East* is how the Khan family minus the father, who refers to his children as 'bastard', are tightly knit. The most moving scene reflecting this solidarity is when they all congregate around a phone box on a rainy night to talk to Nazir, who George has disowned. Sajid refers to him as 'our kid' while Tariq merely wants to know what the 'talent like in Eccles'. Ella is rather like a hen with her chicks around her. She concludes her conversation with Nazir by asking: 'You are happy now, aren't you son?' The happiness of his children is a sentiment that never seems to be apparent in George's mind.

At one stage Ella reveals her insecurities when she asks Aunt Annie whether she is a good mother to which she receives the ironic reply: 'No, I think you're an awful friggin' mother.' Ella's compassion and empathy is later shown when she comforts her white friend, also married to a Pakistani, who breaks down after telling Ella about her daughter's marriage.

Ella ends the film defending her family's honour during the failed linking up with the Shah's grotesque family. She cannot tolerate the snobbishness of the Shahs, who appear to be more middle-class than the Khans. Ella's loyalty is tested to the limit when the Shahs suggest that the boys moved to Bradford. Her understanding is that the daughters-in-law always move in with the husband's family. The accidental skirmish with Saleem's 'sculpture' which unfortunately lands in Mrs Shah's lap leads to a face off: 'I will never allow my daughters to marry into this jungly family of half-breeds,' declares Mrs Shah. Ella finally stamps her authority, which not even George can contest when she retorts to Mrs Shah's insult. 'Who the frig do you think you are coming here and saying my house isn't good enough for my daughters? Well, your daughters aren't good enough for my sons, or my house. If I hear another word against my family I will stick that fanny over your bastard head.'

The comic confrontation, which sees the removal of the Shahs from the household is followed up with a far serious matter where Ella retains and wins the moral high ground by putting her family first. In a scuffle the Khan family declare an end to George's ways despite his fierce protestations. Even Maneer cannot bring himself to support his father. Ironically, with Sajid's hood accidentally ripped off by Abdul as he tries to restrain his father, the family are brought to an uneasy, tearful truce, which implies a change in the future.

SCENE ANALYSIS — STAGING THE SHAHS' VISIT ON FILM

East is East was adapted by Ayub Din-Khan from his own stage play. The scene featuring the Shahs' visit is perhaps the most stagey moment in the film in the way it is shot, but it also contains cinematic devices to move the comic drama to its final conclusion. The scene also encapsulates the core themes of the film, starting from comedy and ending near enough in 'kitchen sink' melodrama.

As George helps Mr Shah into the dentist chair we are given a wide-angled shot of the 'parlour', which fits everyone into the shot. This particular shot gives the impression of a theatre set, the camera situated in the 'fourth wall' of the room, perched just above Mr Shah's shoulder. But this is not to be filmed as a static scene. While the script alone can tell us that the meeting is an absolute disaster the facial reactions of the cast members provide accurate non-verbal communication to the events as they unfold.

Early on Abdul's close-up face is caught in a zoom shot as he sees his less than beautiful betrothed for the first time giving him a toothy smile. He barely conceals his horror as he forces out a smile. The camera cuts to Tariq smirking at his brother while daughter number two enters the frame. Again, the camera zooms into his face as he looks with disbelief at the ugly sister he is supposed to marry. She in turn looks bemused. Tariq's angry gaze turns to his father George, who is then set into the frame, and a cut to Ella looking unimpressed by her husband's choices.

The strained conversation results in a series of pregnant pauses, gaffes, entries and exits, which are caught in close-up reaction shots. Naturally, the cinema can direct the audience's attentions to these moments and add more detail than in the live environment of the stage play.

Mrs Shah: The thing is all these little houses look the same.

(Mr Shah looks across disapprovingly at his wife.)

Ella: Meenah would you fetch the tea, love?

Meenah: (with parody of posh voice): Righty-ho.

(Leaves the room with a big smile in the direction of her mum).

Ella (referring to Sajid): Sorry about him, Mr Shah. He's just been circumcised.

(George glares at Ella. Ella responds by lowering her eyes as if to acknowledge the faux pas. Mrs Shah looks unimpressed.)

Mrs Shah: Where did you get this sari?

(George pauses with his tea as he waits for Mrs Shah's comment. Ella looks across hoping for some support only to hear the choice of sari, which Meenah didn't want to wear, being attacked as untraditional.)

Aunt Annie: (arriving) Didn't know you had visitors.

(Ella smiles knowing full well that she did.)

George: They're good boys. Bring no trouble.

(Tariq looks up with hatred towards his father. George, feeling slightly uncomfortable, receives the look.)

Ella: (In response to sound outside) Maneer cock, see what those too are up to.

(He leaves the room holding the door just for a few seconds as he smirks across at his luckless brothers Abdul and Tariq.)

Auntie Annie (leaving): Congratulations again. Tarra, George.

(George lowers his eyes as if things could not get worse. Ella smiles unconvincingly as if to offer him support.)

Mr Shah: Wouldn't it be more convenient if your sons were to come to live with us?

(Camera pans across as Adbul looks across to Tariq who in turn looks up towards Ella.)

Mrs Shah: I would have thought that you would have been grateful with the extra space. I know I would.

(A series of quick reaction shots has Ella looks towards George, Mr Shah smile, a stern George look back towards Ella, Ella look concerned, and Mrs Shah look as though she has achieved a *fait accompli*.)

The scene is cut up with Saleem's arrival, which is filmed in the dining room. This allows for his sculpture to be revealed in all its glory to the audience before it makes its unwanted journey into Mrs Shah's lap. The visual comedy so apparent throughout the film is again timed to perfection, but while the scene could equally be played out with comic timing on stage, the small details that the camera captures squeezes extra humour out of the incident.

With Saleem's artwork in situ in Mrs Shah's lap there is a pause. Saleem, in close-up lying on the floor looks up and quickly notices the two ugly Shah daughters. Ella and the rest of the children near her are framed at the doorway gazing in the direction of Mrs Shah's lap. We cut to a close-up of Mrs Shah looking down. From her point of view she sees Saleem lying prone ahead of her with his object of art in her lap. We cut to her scream. Saleem responds with a scream of his own (presumably provoked by the sighting of his potential sisters-in-law) and all hell is let loose.

When Ella finally hits back at Mrs Shah she is caught in the centre of a frame surrounded by her six children with Sajid hanging on to her sleeve. Although this scene could be represented effectively on stage it is given greater impact as the camera zooms closely into her face as she tells Mrs Shah to leave. We are also afforded a shot from outside the Khan's house as Ella quite literally shows Mrs Shah the door.

Our last view of the Shahs is also unique to the screen as we witness a long shot from across the road as the great dane bounds over and leaps on Mrs Shah (in cartoon comedy fashion) while Mr Shah looks on apparently unfazed.

REACTION

East is East received good reviews in Britain dealing as it did with the relatively unexplored theme of growing up in multi-cultural Britain. *Evening Standard* film critic Alexander Walker recognised this when he declared the film to be: 'Fresh, frank, impudent and self-mocking, it marks a giant leap over the threshold of multicultural casting and ethnic British cinema.' Meanwhile, Christopher Tookey writing enthusiastically in *The Daily Mail*, stated: 'The masterly screenplay and lively direction are by exciting new talents. Its warmth and generosity of spirit deserve to make it a smash hit around the world.' Reaction from Asian British communities was more mixed with some objecting to what they perceived to be negative stereotyping of Asians and Muslims.

It also scored well on the festival scene and garnered a neat haul of awards including the Alexander Korda Award for Best British Film at the BAFTAs, Best Film at the Evening Standard British Film Awards, and the London Critics Circle and a Special Award for Outstanding Achievement in International Cinema at the Awards of the International Indian Film Academy.

The creative team of film debutants O'Donnell, Din-Khan and Udwi, all received warm acclaim and the £2.4m budget was handsomely reaped back at the box-office with returns in Britain passing £10m. Of the cast members Om Puri was singled out for capturing pathos in his performance as George and Linda Bassett was applauded for her feisty yet-down-to-earth portrayal of Ella.

In the US, the marketing of the film was unusual in that its poster played down the role of Asian characters. Though not the runaway hit of *The Full Monty* it performed reasonably well State-side.

Babymother (1998) (UK) UKCert 15

Director: Julian Henriques

Screenplay: Julian Henriques; Vivienne Howard

Producer: Parminder Vir

Production companies: Channel 4 Films; Formation Films; Arts Council of England; National Lottery through the Arts Council of England

Production start date: 21/09/1997 **Budget:** £2m (estimated)

Distributor: FilmFour Distributors **UK Release date:** 11 September 1998

UK Box Office: £62,928 **USA Box Office:** $5,115

Worldwide Box Office: n/a

Written and directed by Julian Henriques, *Babymother* was one of the few films made in the 1990s by a black film-maker about the Afro-Caribbean community. It features an all-black cast and is set within the confines of Harlesden in London. As films go *Babymother* was not among the top films of the 1990s in Britain, neither was it designed as a sociological critique on single mothers living in housing estates, rather it was to be a vibrant musical. If it was down to its bold ambitions and the fact that it managed to be made at all, then *Babymother* should be classed a success. However, as with many British films of the 1990s, it seemed to lack the extra stages of development that might have helped it realise its full potential and help it cross over to a mainstream audience.

SYNOPSIS

Set within the black Afro-Caribbean community in Harlesden, Anita is known to her friends as 'Nita' and is the babymother (or young mother) of two children called Anton and Saffron.

When Byron, the 'babyfather' of the two children and a reggae recording artist, cuts Anita out of a performance, she suggests to her best friends Sharon and Yvette that they form a group themselves.

Returning late again to pick up her children Anita sees an ambulance, which has arrived too late to save her mother Edith. Her sister Rose tries to console Anita but she remains frosty. Eventually, Rose explains to Anita that she and not Edith is her real mother, a conclusion that Anita has guessed.

Without Edith's support and having ostracised her real mother Rose, Anita is forced to spend more time looking after her children. Gradually, her responsibilities overwhelm her and she breaks down. Her response is to compose a tune called Babymother. She returns to Sharon and Yvette (with her children in tow) and they agree to raise £350 for a recording session.

Their fundraising efforts prove fruitless but then record producer Ceasar offers Anita a free recording session if he will go out with her. Reluctantly Anita goes off with him but he reneges on the deal. Byron returns from a tour and after a doorstep reconciliation Anita lets him back into his flat and her life. She takes his money (leaving him an IOU note) and arranges the recording session.

Byron is unhappy to learn that Anita has plans of a music career of her own, especially since Anita has made contact with promoter Bee. Sharon fights Anita when she learns about her and Caesar but with their record getting local airplay the group makes up.

Byron is stunned when Anita beats him in the Artist Clash competition. Anita seals victory by dedicating her song to Edith and, crucially, her mother Rose (who is there with Anita and Byron's children).

HOW IT WAS MADE

It took around five years for the team of director Julian Henriques and producer Parminder Vir to get *Babymother* made. In 1987 the two had founded Formation Films and were noted for their TV documentary work. Henriques' interest in London's reggae dancehall scene prompted him to make the drama musical short *We the Raggamuffin* (UK, 1992) for Channel 4.

Henriques wanted to expand the theme into a feature. He didn't set out to make an all-black movie in London but once he had established the setting in Harlesden it seemed to him that there wasn't the need for a mixed cast. This bold choice meant that pitching the film gave the film-makers a unique selling point, or at least something unique, because the assumed wisdom was that black films don't sell. In an interview with the *Black Film Bulletin* Henriques reveals the layers of risks involved in making the film: 'Basically, when you say black movie you just about double the stakes in the eyes of the backers. Making any movie with a first-time director, writer and a first-time producer in this case and unproven cast – that is a big risk. Then you add to that, that it is a musical and it is going to be shot on a tough estate and it is an all-black cast and you have stacked up, without realising it, the risk factor to a very considerable extent.'

Another calculated risk was to have original songs throughout the film, the bulk of which were written by established reggae artist Carroll Thompson (known as the Queen of Lovers Rock) and sung by Trilla Jenna (known as the Queen of UK Dancehall music).

Casting an all-black cast where the principle character was a woman under the age of 25 who could act and sing proved another challenge. The casting of Anita caused the biggest problem and actress Anjela Lauren Smith was called back for dozens of auditions before finally landing the role. Having set their action around a specific area of London, it seemed unlikely that any black American actor could be persuaded to step into that environment convincingly and with the constraints of a small budget Henriques chose to look for British black actors.

Don Warrington was possibly the best-known black actor with a host of TV credits beyond his most popular role from the late 1970s as Philip in ITV's sitcom *Rising Damp*. Similarly, Vas Blackwood also had a string of TV credits but an association with the character of Lennox in BBC's long-running sitcom *Only Fools and Horses*. Corinne Skinner-Carter was an established actress who had appeared in *Empire Road* (1978), BBC's groundbreaking attempt at a drama based around a multi-racial society in Birmingham. Wil Johnson and Suzette Llewellyn had some TV experience behind them but the rest of the cast were made up of relative newcomers.

Channel 4 and the Arts Council of England also recognised that Henriques had come up with a unique project in an area that had not been touched before and he was trusted to see the project through with minimal interference. Naïvely they worried more about the artistic, social and multicultural significance of such a film rather than the best ways of making box-office returns.

Henriques and Parminder Vir looked at targeting a young mainstream mainly black audience – while not discounting young whites who were into black culture. *Babymother* was targeted at cinemas areas with large concentrations of black people – Lee Valley in Edmonton, the Premier in Peckham and the Ritzy in Brixton. But risks have their price and marketing funds for the project amounted to just £60,000, a tiny drop in the ocean compared with the £750,000 spent on *Trainspotting*. The film-makers, like many first-timers in the 1990s, hoped for word of mouth to sell their film. In the end *Babymother* was released in September 1998. Its hopes rested on a small release on just five screens.

KEY ISSUES

For all its verve and musical energy *Babymother* doesn't quite reach the show-stopping climax of *The Full Monty*, nor does Anita's relationship with Rose convey the emotional intensity displayed between Hortense and Cynthia in *Secrets & Lies*. What the film does give us is a feisty, fiercely ambitious young woman, who is prepared to take on her lover and the father of her children in order to achieve her goal.

Be a mother to your child

For much of the opening period of the film you would be forgiven if you forgot that Anita, who is still very young herself, is the mother of two young children. Most of the time she is seen leaving them with her 'mother' Edith, or else turning up late to pick them up. Anita depends on an extended family and a support system, primarily so that she can go out and have fun with her mates. The film does not attempt to hide the youthfulness and early on there is a scene showing her two well-behaved children looking on as Anita, Sharon and Yvette exuberantly dance and sing, acting more childlike, than the children themselves.

However, the film manages to convey a shift in Anita's perception and a reluctant acceptance of her responsibilities after Edith dies. From this point, simply palming the children on to others is no longer an option. Fortunately, this enforced maturity also acts as a creative impulse for Anita, who finds music the best way to articulate her feelings.

The film generally shows Anita with a loving attitude to her children. The only time she seems cross with them is when Anton puts on a tune by his father Byron.

Byron plays the role of an absent 'babyfather', happy to roam unfettered with his responsibilities as suggested by his liaison with Dionne. In his opinion the role of bringing up the children falls squarely on the shoulders of the mother. Perhaps this is why he believes that there is: 'only room for one musician' in the family – or perhaps that is just his ego talking. However, when Byron is around he is affectionate towards his children, who always seem to call for him in his absence. Indeed, there are indications that Byron may be true to his word and home to stay when he drops the children off to school.

The best role model for a parent in the film is the oldest character Edith, who it transpires brought up Anita as her own with no qualms or fuss and apparently no male present. Indeed, Rose also talks of the absence of her father and how it broke her heart at the time she was giving up Anita. Rose in the end may be a success but as a *babymother* herself she actually abandoned her child. By the end with Rose and Anita reconciled the *Babymother* song carries with it a double-edged reference. By the end of the film the *babymothers*' union certainly seems in a stronger position than that of the babyfathers.

Token white actors

The action takes place in and around the streets of Harlesden and all its actors are black. There are no token white actors at all. A year later critics observed that *Notting Hill* gave a false impression of London by hardly showing any multi-ethnic faces in the neighbourhood. Ironically, the flamboyant costumes and elaborate hairstyles worn by Anita and her 'posse' make the women look like they have just stepped out of carnival in Notting Hill. Indeed, the opening shot of the girls dancing in the streets of Harlesden are quite stunning (and the costumes remain so throughout the film) and it is only the sight of red London buses that remind the audience that the action is taking place in London and there are white people, though not too many, in the background. However, it would seem very hard to know where or how to fit a white actor into this environment without it seeming contrived.

For once, the focus isn't about black and white issues but it concentrates on a local scene. This is an interesting and bold move for the film-makers to take. The film provides a contrast between the bleak housing estate where Anita lives and the vivid colours worn by her energetic friends as they exercise their version of 'girl power' through their girl group Nita, Sweeta and Nasty. Ultimately, the film seems easier to be defined as a musical for a black dancehall crowd than a social commentary about black single mothers.

Fairytale of Harlesden

Despite its original songs and the modern dancehall settings *Babymother* at times feels like an updated old style musical. When we first see Anita and Byron in the rehearsal studio Byron is singing and in true musical tradition Anita joins in. Later the two lovers engage in their tiff by singing across a grim, grey council estate as though it was a set from West Side Story. Indeed, the film carries elements of the musical genre throughout whether through live performances or in a rather self-conscious MTV-inspired video sequence. The film doesn't quite get to the 'let's do the show here' moment, but it comes close when Anita and her 'crew' storm the stage in the film's finale.

Anita's story is set around a series of conflicts with Byron, but most importantly with her 'mother' Edith and her 'sister' Rose. After Edith dies we learn that Rose is in fact Anita's real mother. Anita's burning ambition is to become a singer and have hit records. Success she believes will help her provide for her children and gain respect from Byron and independence from those around her.

For the first half hour of the film Anita is full of energy. She is seen dancing with her mates, working out at the gym, or playing pool. During this time she loses her man Byron to Dionne, loses her 'mother' Edith, and learns the truth about her real mother. Something has to give and finally the upbeat and defiant Anita has a breakdown, which is represented neatly in a framed shot showing her almost in silhouette crying outside her dark and dingy flat. Her grief and despondency do not last long and as she takes her responsibilities onboard she launches into action with her lifeplan.

The film has a fairytale ending of sorts with Anita going head-to-head with a disgruntled Byron during the artist clash at the dancehall. Triumphantly, Anita dedicates her last song to her grandmother Edith, her mother Rose and her children.

Grey areas

The vibrant opening titles of the film establish the characters that will take part in the action, except it becomes clear as the film develops that the part of Dionne has been sacrificed to help to progress the story. While there are some areas in the film that tend to work as the 'live' performance numbers, other moments possibly required further thought.

A major criticism of many British films in the 1990 was that they suffered from lack of script development. This was an issue picked up by the Film Council in its formative statement *Towards a Sustainable UK Film Industry* (2000) where it noted:

'All sectors of the industry agree that the lack of support for script development results in finished films which are too often sub-standard and subsequently wholly or partially rejected by the distribution sector.'

Unfortunately, there are moments in *Babymother* that reflect this concern. The fact that Anita has lost her 'mother' and then learns that Rose is her real mother is never discussed between her and Byron, nor does Rose in her new status of mother seem to enquire about Byron and his relationship with Anita.

Similarly, there are some moments when the dialogue might have been tightened up. At the reception after Edith's funeral Yvette and Sharon discuss Byron's absence but somehow don't strike the right kind of gravitas with the glib: 'Not showing up is pure rubbish.' Equally unconvincing is how easily Sharon accepts Anita's apology after Anita's unwise encounter with Cesar. 'Really, sorry,' more or less does the trick – although Sharon has worked out that Anita's actions were designed to get free studio time.

Despite Sharon's assertion that: 'The music business is nasty, Byron taught you that lesson for sure', Anita and her friends' musical path is relatively simple – recording, radio and then blow established artist off stage. It feels harsh to pick faults but parts of *Babymother* sometimes feel like a work in progress rather than the finished article.

SCENE ANALYSIS – MAKING A MODERN MUSICAL

One of the intriguing aspects of *Babymother* is the way the film is prepared to take on the musical genre and insert it within the confines of the dancehall culture of Harlesden. Singing obviously takes pride of place in the way music is used throughout the film with performances evident in dancehall scenes, studio recordings and home rehearsals. All these elements make sense within the context of the storyline. Elsewhere, music is used throughout the film in diegetic, performance and non-diegetic forms.

However, in the scene where Byron tries to apologise to Anita after cutting her out of his act we see the film moving into the traditional singing mode associated with old musicals where actors burst into song. In this modern musical version the scene is controlled enough to appear plausible but nevertheless it reflects on the ambitions of the film-makers that they were prepared to take risks.

In the preceding scene, set in Anita's flat, Anita, Sharon and Yvette are seen bouncing around on sofas. Anita, pencil in mouth, is coaxing Sharon to join in. On the floor Anita's children Anton and Saffron are seen on the floor looking up at their *babymother* and friends. Anita has a lyric sheet in her hand and looks over to her two friends as they gain confidence in their singing and dancing. They sing to a backing track but it is not clear whether this is actual or overdubbed.

We first see Byron outside Anita's door hearing her group rehearse. The concrete-clad balcony walkway gives us a grim reminder of the grey, unglamorous world Anita and her friends actually inhabit. The group's rehearsal in the lounge is interrupted by the sound of a car horn. A sharp edit takes us to a close-up shot of Anita at the top of the balcony looking down, the grey colours of her surroundings for once matching the colours of her top.

We hear Byron call: 'Nita.' As she shakes her head in disbelief we are given a reverse shot from her point of view showing Byron sitting on top of his car with one door open to allow the speakers to play his backing track. Byron's colourful red attire and smart car mark a sharp contrast with his surroundings as he attempts to woo Anita back against a background of soulless paved concrete, waste bins and rubbish. As the latter day Romeo attempts to woo his Juliet (balcony and all) in not quite a lavish Hollywood-style ballad, the scene errs on the side of veracity.

The camera takes us down to street level as we hear and see Byron sing his song, opening with: 'Forgive me, don't come easy.' By the time he sings 'sorry' we cut to a long shot from his point of view where he surveys Anita flanked on either side by Sharon and Yvette, who appear within open window frames looking down and mocking Byron.

He continues unperturbed by pouring his heart out. Behind Byron we see some people occasionally walk by without paying much heed to the scene, almost as if a bloke sitting on a bonnet singing was a natural occurrence on their estate. One set of women attempt to make a gesture in his direction but otherwise move on. In this respect the scene shares the musical's slight sense of the surreal when all other actions are either suspended or accommodate the show tune to be performed.

As Byron sings: 'forgive me for I'm easy' we return to the close-up of Anita who smiles, and asks Sharon: 'What do you think?' Another shot of the three women shows Yvette barking towards Byron – undermining his romantic notion. As Byron continues to sing an incredulous looking Sharon joins Anita in her close-up frame with both friends now shaking their heads while suppressing smiles.

At street level the camera has moved from the side to capture Byron from the front as the next few close-up shots intensify the affect Byron and his sugary, sweet melody are having on Anita. Rather than swoon, Byron's ploy is scuppered when Anita bursts into her harsh retort singing: 'I don't care.' Now the modern musical aspect of the film kicks in. Whereas Byron's backing track came from his car, Anita's backing track comes from nowhere, just like in the old musicals when a full orchestra might strike up as the artists sang.

We now cut to Byron in close-up as he stops singing and implores Anita to stop. From this point he is no longer the centre of attention in the scene. As we get a reaction shot of Byron still trying to talk to Anita the full group in their long shot are witnessed in full flow – the shambolic presentation of the lounge replaced with a feisty, tight performance.

Byron gets the message, jumps into his car and leaves. We see his departure from Anita's point of view. Yet the musical number is brought to an end, not on a high note, but with a bump back to earth as a shot from the balcony looking along the walkway shows Anita's timid children standing forlornly after hearing their father and their mother bickering through the medium of song. Now background music is introduced as Anita turns to go to her children and says to her friends. 'I've gone too far.'

This scene also acts as a foretaste of the climax of the film when Anita and her crew bound onto the stage to take Byron on again as they reprise their 'I don't care' assault, which ultimately gives Anita her game, set and match moment. It should also be noted that while Wil Johnson overdubs his own vocals and lip-synchs to himself, Anita's main vocal performances are lip-synched to singer Trilla Jenna.

REACTION

In the film world timing and luck often play a big part in how a film will be received. *Babymother* was released in the same week as *Saving Private Ryan*, which meant column inches were devoted to Spielberg's epic. In Britain the predominantly white middle-class, middle-aged male reviewers gave the film poor reviews. While acknowledging its cultural significance they also pointed to its failings. But not all reviews were bad. In *Sight & Sound* Stuart Hall wrote: 'Anita, Sharon and Yvette make the Spice Girls look like convent fifth formers at a Sunday afternoon tea party.'

Derek Elley in *Variety* also praises the film from a technical point of view: 'On a technical level, pic is extremely impressive with smooth cutting; rich, saturated colors that bring out the best in Annie Curtis Jones' costumes; fine widescreen lensing and a moody, coloristic score by John Lunn to fill the gaps between the nine songs.' However, his review is less impressed with the story's lack of tension.

Commercially *Babymother* took more than £60,000 at the British box-office, which most would agree would be a poor return for the £2m budget. But for a film targeting a niche market it didn't do too badly; its screen average was a respectable £3,840, which stands up well compared with other British releases which had bigger totals and wider releases such as *Ratcatcher*, (15 screens, average £3,492), *Land Girls* (30 screens, £2,516), *Plunkett and Macleane* (345 screens, average £2,204). Nevertheless, the notion that black films do not have commercial clout persisted.

CONCLUSION

Babymother, with its theme of strong women pitting their talents against a male-dominated music scene, unintentionally narrowed its audience appeal. The uncomprising style of the film with only black actors, unknown lead actors and unfamiliar new tunes makes it a fascinating film purely on the levels of marketing and distribution. The fact that it was the first black British musical and featured an all-black cast should have been a major selling point but the ambitions of the film-makers perhaps became greater than the final product itself. Despite concentrating on the reggae dancehall scene in London the film carried with it something of the exuberance and energy of a Bollywood movie.

East is East on the other hand looked less like a Bollywood movie but more than a modern British comedy. Of the two cultures, Afro-Caribbean and British Asian, it seemed that topics featuring Asian diaspora had more box-office clout. This seemed to be true with the success of *Bend it Like Beckham* and to a lesser extent *Anita and Me* (UK, 2002), which were no doubt helped by the success of *East is East*.

Babymother certainly helped to show the sparsity of black-themed films. Paradoxically, the strength and weakness of British films in the 1990s is that they took chances with themes that had not been previously explored. Where the majority of films fell short of their expectations was taking care with their scripts and how the films could be sold to buyers, not just in Britain and abroad. The success of East in East finally showed that not only could multi-cultural issues be the subject matter and that audiences could learn a bit about different communities, but also that there were audiences for the films. Yet as one door appeared to open the terror attacks in America in September 2001 and the accompanying fears led to another being shut.

FURTHER READING

Black in the British Frame: The Black Experience In British Film And Television
Bourne, Stephen (Continuum International Publishing Group Ltd.; 2nd revised edition, 2001)

Tears of Laughter: Comedy-drama in 1990s British Cinema
Mather, Nigel (Manchester University, 20006)

A Fuller Picture: The commercial impact of six British films with black themes in the 1990s
Wambu, Onyekachi and Arnold, Kevin (Black Film Bulletin and the British Film Institute, 1999)

British Cinema of the 90s
Murphy, Robert (ed.) (BFI, 2001) Chapter Eleven – Black British Cinema in the 90s: Going Going Gone by Alexander, Karen

The Stats An overview of the film, television, video and DVD industries 1990-2003
(BFI National Library, BFI Information Services, 2006)

BFI Film and Television Handbook (BFI, editions from 1990–2005)

Selected reviews/articles/references

Black British Film and Television: 16 plus source guide
Clarke, Nicola; King, Andrea, Ker, Matt (BFI National Library, 2000)

Another kind of British and Exploration of British Asian films by Sawhney, Cary
Cineaste N 26, V.4 (Autumn 2001) P. 58-61

East is East

Sight & Sound V.9 N.11 (1 Nov 1999) P.36-37 by Spencer, Liese

Empire N.126 (1 Dec 1999) P.105-107 by Nobil, Ali

Eastern Premise, by Applebaum, Steve
Film Review (December 1999), P. 29, 70-71

Home cooking and strong curry sauce by Walker, Alexander
Evening Standard, (4th November 1999)

East is East
Harris, Crispin (Film Education study guide, 2003)

Babymother

Sight & Sound V.8 N.9 (1 Sept 1998) by McGrath, Melanie

Empire N.112 (1 October 1998) P.44 by Griffiths, Nick

Variety (28 September 1998) P.38 by Elley, Derek

A Rage in Harlsden by Hall, Stuart
Sight & Sound V.8 N.9 (1 Sept 1998)

Baby Mother Shows Poor Grosses But Healthy Earnings by Prescod, Marsha
Black Film-maker V.2 N.6 (1 Jul 1999) P.10

9. TYPICALLY BRITISH

If ever a can of worms was worth opening then defining what constitutes a British film would be worth the effort, if only to witness the wriggling spectacle of definitions. For the average cinema-goer a British film is a usually a matter of perception and would consist of one or more of the following elements:

British cast (predominantly)

British director and script (and other British production team or crew)

British locations

British cultural content

There is, of course, the official government definition, which roughly follows the above elements but allows crucial exceptions.

WHAT QUALIFIES AS A BRITISH FILM?

The value of getting the stamp of approval from the Secretary of State for Culture, Media and Sport for qualifying as British lays in the advantageous tax treatment, which improved during the 1990s and which the producers of the film gain. In order to qualify a film has to either satisfy the criteria placed under Schedule 1 of the Films Act 1995, or comply with terms established in an international co-production agreement which includes the UK. In the former case roughly four criteria have to be met.

1. The film needs to have been made by a company registered and controlled in the UK or within the European Union, or in a country with which the European Community has signed an Association Agreement.

2. Seventy per cent of the production cost must be spent on film-making activity in the UK.

3. Seventy per cent of the cost of labour should go to 'citizens or ordinary residents of the Commonweath, EU/EEA or a country with which the European Community has signed an agreement.'
    However, there is an allowance for this cost to have one non-Commonwealth/EU/EEA/Association person (such as the case of Julia Roberts in *Notting Hill*) to be deducted from that 70 per cent. Also, if the film-makers wish to use two non-Commonwealth/EU/EEA/Association people then 75 per cent of the labour costs are taken into account (providing one of them is an actor).

4. No more than 10 per cent of the playing time of the film should be made up of previously certified film material or film by another film-maker.

The qualifying criteria for co-production treaties rely on the appropriate share of production costs being met. They are:

No less than 40 per cent for bilateral agreements.

No less than 20 per cent for convention agreements.

No less than 10 per cent for multilateral agreements.

CULTURALLY BRITISH

However, the 1990s saw the global environment change. Boundaries and borders became blurred and somehow the qualifying criteria managed to miss some films such as the multi-Oscar-winning *Sense and Sensibility*, that seemed typically British and encourage other films which didn't seem British at all, such as *Judge Dredd* (USA, 1995), to benefit from tax incentives.

Emma Thompson received all the plaudits when she won an Oscar for her screenplay adaptation of Jane Austen's novel of *Sense and Sensibility*. Surely, this was a typically British film? It was the type of period costume drama that became labelled as a heritage film and consisted of lush English locations and a literary heritage that had 'Made in England' stamped all over it. Furthermore, the cast featuring the likes of Alan Rickman, Colin Firth, Hugh Grant and Kate Winslet oozed those peculiar British authoritative and yet charming acting qualities for period pieces that international audiences and particularly Americans seem to lap up. And yet Ang Lee was the Taiwanese director of the film, money for it came from Columbia Studios and most of the post-production work was carried out abroad. Nevertheless, the press and public generally recognised it as a triumph for British cinema - and paradoxically it was.

Indeed, the 1990s saw a spate of 19th century literary adaptations: Emily Brontë's *Wuthering Heights* (UK/USA, 1992); *Mary Shelley's Frankenstein*; Charlotte Brontë's *Jane Eyre* (UK/USA/France/Italy, 1996); Thomas Hardy's *Jude* and *The Woodlanders* (UK, 1997); and two more Jane Austen works – *Emma* (UK/USA, 1997) and *Mansfield Park* (UK, 1999). A couple of Henry James adaptations also had some British involvement – *Portrait of a Lady* (1996) and *Wings of the Dove* (UK/USA, 1997).

These films mined a rich vein of British talent and were a boon for costume designers and locations managers who scoured stately homes of England for just the right period pomp and precision. It could be argued that the films were aimed away from the traditional youth audience, even though literary adaptations are always handy for school course work.

NATIONAL HERITAGE FILMS

The 1990s saw evidence of British films playing to their strengths by offering audiences a rich serving of historical costume dramas. Kenneth Branagh sparked off an interest in Shakespeare with his interpretations of *Much Ado About Nothing*, *Hamlet*, and *Love's Labour's Lost* and his performance in Oliver Parker's *Othello*. *Richard III* (UK/USA, 1995), starring Ian McKellen in a fictitious 1930s Britain, also attempted to update Shakespeare.

The move to mix heritage and comedy produced the multi-award winning romantic fictional comedy *Shakespeare in Love*, starring American actress Gwyneth Paltrow. It combined classic elements of heritage found in the historical drama *Elizabeth*, (which incidentally also featured actors Geoffery Rush and Joseph Fiennes) and the romantic comedy of Hugh Grant vehicles of the 1990s and indeed Paltrow's own *Sliding Doors*.

Along with *Elizabeth*, the British monarchy was the subject of two other successful films – *The Madness of King George* (UK/USA, 1993) and *Mrs Brown* – both proving that films about the British royal family are still a unique selling feature.

Merchant Ivory Productions was noted for specialising in period pieces depicting stories from the early half of the 20th century. Its major success in the 1990s came early on with *Howards End* and *The Remains of the Day*. Other attempts at evoking this era included *Wilde* and George Orwell's *Keep the Aspidistra Flying* (UK, 1997).

Leading British art house directors also tapped into the heritage resource, or at least costume dramas or period pieces, albeit providing audiences with a collection of slightly more challenging works than the picturesque spectacles provided by other British popular literary adaptations during this period: Derek Jarman – *Wittegenstein* (UK/Japan, 1993); Peter Greenaway – *Prospero's Books* (UK/Netherlands/France/Italy/Japan, 1991); *The Baby of Mâcon* (UK/Russia/France/Germany, 1992); Sally Potter – *Orlando* (UK/Russia/Italy/France/Netherlands, 1992); Mike Leigh – *Topsy-Turvy* (UK/USA, 1999); Ken Loach – *Land and Freedom* (UK/Spain/Germany, 1995).

Britain's strong celluloid association with the Second World War was not in such evidence during this time – instead Hollywood chose to re-explore the war film genre in films such as *Saving Private Ryan* and *The Thin Red Line* (USA, 1998). However, Anthony Minghella's *The English Patient* (USA, 1996) and *The Land Girls* (UK/France, 1997), gave two fresh approaches to films about the Second World War. Meanwhile, the First World War came under greater scrutiny with films such as Gillies MacKinnon's *Regeneration* (UK/Canada, 1997), Richard Attenborough's *In Love and War* (USA, 1996) and *The Trench* (UK/France, 1999).

But heritage films were not just confined to English stories. Two Scottish folk heroes, William Wallace and Rob Roy, were depicted in films released in the same year: *Braveheart* and *Rob Roy* (USA, 1995).

To a lesser degree the Welsh also tapped into the heritage market with two Welsh-language films, which both received Oscar nominations in the Foreign Language Film section. *Hedd Wynn* (UK, 1992) was set around the First World War and *Solomon and Geanor* (UK, 1998) (which was also filmed in English) was set in 1911. Technically these were two British films but could hardly be classified as typically British. Easier to pigeon-hole were the top Welsh-themed films of the decade *The Englishmen Who Went Up a Hill But Came Down a Mountain*; *Twin Town* (UK, 1997); and *House of America* (UK/Netherlands, 1997).

NOT ALL THAT BRITISH

Set in Northern Ireland during the Troubles in the 1970s *Titanic Town* can be added to the Scottish and Welsh films as a way of muddying the waters of what we assume to be typically British. However, there is further confusion when trying to class films where the investment and creative talent come from abroad but the films are partly shot in Britain. *Star Wars Episode 1 – The Phantom Menace*, immediately springs to mind since some of it was filmed at Leavesden Studios, Hertfordshire.

Equally perplexing are films such as the multi-Oscar-winning *The English Patient*, which feels like it should have been classed as a British film on the basis of its cast, its director and a certain cultural content, but it was in fact filmed in Italy and Tunisia and funded by American money.

Some argue that the best litmus test for determining the national origins of any film is to trace its money trail. This means seeing who stumped up the money to make the film in the first place and, crucially, who benefits financially once the film is released. If we were to follow this route then we would soon learn that the majority of British films make money for Hollywood studios. Despite the hype and excitement of box-office hits and Oscar celebrations the British film industry is, in truth, a cottage industry that survives largely due to its creative talents and technical expertise rather than its financial clout. But the money trail argument is complicated because money, whether it comes from Hollywood or Europe, does get reinvested in creating British films. The surprising success of *Four Weddings and a Funeral* meant that Working Title, courtesy of Universal, could follow up that success with *Notting Hill*.

In an interview at the NFT during the 1980s the great British director Michael Powell talked about his classic film *the Life and Death of Colonel Blimp* (UK, 1943) and pointed out the folly of analysing the country of origin too deeply: 'This is a 100 per cent British film but it's photographed by a Frenchman, it's written by a Hungarian, its musical score is by a German Jew, the director was English, the man who did the costumes was Czech – in other words it was the kind of film that I have always worked on with a mixed crew of every nationality, no frontiers of any kind.'

THE OSCARS ARE COMING

Another annual event in the film calendar, which still acts like a barometer to gauge how well British films are doing, are the Academy Awards and guarantees the British media with two stories per year – the Brits that are up for nomination and then the Brits that have won.

Below is a list of the British Oscar winners of the 1990s. On the one hand the list confirms the depth of British talent with many award winners working on Hollywood films, on the other it reveals that the majority of top British films of the decade – *Four Weddings and a Funeral*, *Trainspotting*, *The Full Monty* – didn't get a look in according to the members of the Academy of Motion Pictures Arts and Sciences. The outstanding exception was *Shakespeare in Love*, which picked up an impressive haul of seven gongs (six going to British participants).

During the 1990s the Best Director award went to two Brits – Anthony Minghella and Sam Mendes – and the top acting awards went to Jeremy Irons, Anthony Hopkins, Emma Thompson, Judi Dench and Michael Caine, which is hardly representative of the performers – the likes of Hugh Grant, Kate Winslet, Robert Carlyle and Ray Winstone – who dominated British screens.

Elsewhere, Britain dominated the Animated Short categories with Aardman Animation enjoying a cracking good time picking up two Oscars for its Wallace and Gromit films.

British Oscar winners 1990–1999

1990 held in 1991

Jeremy Irons – Best Actor: *Reversal Of Fortune*

John Barry – Best Original Score: *Dances With Wolves*

Nick Park – Best Animated Short: *Creature Comforts*

1991 held in 1992

Anthony Hopkins – Best Actor: *The Silence Of The Lambs*

Daniel Greaves – Best Animated Short: *Manipulation*

1992 held in 1993

Emma Thompson – Best Actress: *Howards End*

Ian Whittaker – Best Art Direction: *Howards End*

Simon Kaye – Best Sound: *The Last Of The Mohicans*

Tim Rice – Best Original Song: (A Whole New World) *Aladdin*

1993 held in 1994

Richard Hymns – Best Sound Effects Editing: *Jurassic Park*

Nick Park – Best Animated Short: *The Wrong Trousers*

Deborah Kerr – Career Achievement Honorary Award

1994 held in 1995

Ken Adam & Carolyn Scott – Best Art Direction: *The Madness of King George*

Elton John & Tim Rice – Best Song: (*Can You Feel The Love Tonight*) *The Lion King*

Peter Capaldi and Ruth Kenley–Letts – Best Live Action Short: Franz Kafka's *It's A Wonderful Life*

Alison Snowden and David Fine – Best Animated Short: *Bob's Birthday*

1995 held in 1996

Emma Thompson – Best Adapted Screenplay: *Sense and Sensibility*

James Acheson – Best Costume Design: *Restoration*

Lois Burwell and Peter Frampton – Special Achievement In Make Up: *Braveheart*

Jon Blair – Best Documentary Feature: *Anne Frank Remembered*

Nick Park – Best Animated Short: *A Close Shave*

1996 held in 1997

Anthony Minghella – Best Director: *The English Patient*

Stuart Craig and Stephanie McMillan – Best Art Direction: *The English Patient*

Rachel Portman – Best Original Score Musical or Comedy: *Emma*

Tim Rice and Andrew Lloyd Webber – Best Original Song: (*You Must Love Me*) *Evita*

1997 held in 1998

Peter Lamont and Michael Ford – Best Achievement In Art Direction: *Titanic*

Anne Dudley – Best Original Score Musical or Comedy: *The Full Monty*

Jan Pinkava – Best Animated Short: *Geri's Game*

1998 held in 1999

Best Film: *Shakespeare in Love*

Judi Dench – Best Actress in a Supporting Role: *Shakespeare in Love*

Tom Stoppard – Best Original Screenplay: *Shakespeare in Love*

Martin Childs and Jill Quertier – Best Art Direction: *Shakespeare in Love*

Sandy Powell – Best Costume Design: *Shakespeare in Love*

Stephen Warbeck – Best Original Score Musical or Comedy: *Shakespeare in Love*

Jenny Shircore – Best Make–up: *Elizabeth*

Andy Nelson – Best Sound: *Saving Private Ryan*

1999 held in 2000

Sam Mendes – Best Director: *American Beauty*

Michael Caine – Actor in a Supporting Role: *Cider House Rules*

Peter Young – Art Direction: *Sleepy Hollow*

Lindy Hemming – Costume Design: *Topsy-Turvy*

Christine Blundell, Trefor Proud – Make up: *Topsy-Turvy*

Kevin MacDonald, John Battsek, – Documentary Feature: *One Day in September*

Phil Collins – Original Song: *(You'll Be In My Heart) Tarzan*

TYPICALLY BRITISH IN THE 1990S

It is clear that the 1990s saw the usual crop of heritage films to bolster the British film industry. However, what emerged during the decade were more local British films with quirky, contemporary themes – brass bands in *Brassed Off*, pigeon fanciers in *Little Voice*, local rugby clubs in *Up 'n' Under*, football fans in *Fever Pitch*, and East End gangsters in, well, several films, including *Face*, *Lock Stock and Two Smoking Barrels*, and *Essex Boys*. Equally prevalent were British politics and conflict with trade unions as witnessed in *The Full Monty*, *Brassed Off* and *Billy Elliot*. Youth culture came kicking and screaming onto the screens led by *Trainspotting* and followed by *Boston Kickout* (UK, 1995), *Twin Town*, and *The Acid House* (UK, 1998).

And finally there was Hugh Grant and the rom com team of Working Title and Richard Curtis who not only presented a typically stereotyped view of Britain to an international audience but allowed a series of more down-to-earth comedies to be made, such as *This Year's Love, Martha Meet Daniel, Frank and Laurence* (UK, 1998) and *Bedrooms and Hallways* (UK, 1998).

This section looks at two typically British films – *Shakespeare in Love* and *Sense and Sensibility* – that were both funded by American companies and were both perceived by international audiences to be British.

Shakespeare in Love (1999) (UK/USA) UK Cert 15

Director: John Madden

Screenplay: Marc Norman; Tom Stoppard

Producers: David Parfitt; Donna Gigliotti; Harvey Weinstein; Edward Zwick; Marc Norman

Production companies: Miramax Films; Universal Pictures; Bedford Falls Company

Production start date: 02/03/1998 **Budget:** £15m (estimated)

Distributor: UIP **UK Release date:** 29 January 1999

UK Box Office: £20,814,996 **USA Box Office:** $100.2m

Worldwide Box Office: $289.1m

British costume drama was about the safest gamble any producer could make. The 1990s showed that the success of this peculiarly British genre had no reason to abate – witness the successes of *The Madness of King George*, *Sense and Sensibility* and *Mrs. Brown*. However, not even the wildest optimist either side of the Atlantic could have predicted that *Shakespeare in Love* would ring up such a bountiful jackpot. The film won seven Oscars, making it the most successful Oscar-winning British film of the 1990s and was heralded as another triumph for the British film industry.

But was that the case? The film was produced and distributed by American companies, co-written by an American, starred and co-starred an American, and many of the 314 screens in Britain, which hosted its release in 1999, had been built by Americans.

Shakespeare in Love, the fictional account of how William Shakespeare fell in love and wrote *Romeo and Juliet*, is the epitome of a typically British film in the 1990s in that it is full of contradictions. Not only was it a sumptuous costume drama, it was also a crowd-pleasing and a romantic comedy. It craftily weaves elements from *Romeo and Juliet* into the plot but keeps its tone not far from Blackadder II territory. Its cultural content is routed in the heritage of Elizabethan England but its commercial sensibilities play to the needs of a 20th century audience. The makers of *Shakespeare in Love* also allow part of the plot to act as a parody of the entertainment industry by showing funding problems and the odd compromises that need to be made to get a piece of work shown.

SYNOPSIS

Set in London in 1593, Philip Henslowe, owner of the Rose Theatre, is heavily in debt to moneylender Hugh Fennyman, who tortures Henslowe. Henslowe not only promises Fennyman a new play by up and coming playwright Will Shakespeare but also makes Fennyman a partner in the forthcoming production. Unfortunately Shakespeare is suffering from writer's block.

Disguised as Tom Kent, rich merchant's daughter Viola is the last to take part in an audition for actors and she catches Shakespeare's attention by declaiming his lines rather than those of his great rival Christopher Marlowe. The rivals meet in a tavern where Marlowe helps Shakespeare out with some plot ideas for the new play.

Soon Shakespeare discovers that Viola and Tom are the same person and rapturously Viola and Shakespeare engage in a romance, protected by Viola's nurse. The affair stimulates Shakespeare's creative juices and the pages of the new play flow, much to the relief of Henslowe and the growing delight of Fennyman.

In the meantime Viola is betrothed to Lord Wessex and they go to Greenwich where the Queen decides whether to approve her match with Wessex. The Queen is sceptical that love can be portrayed accurately in a play and a wager of £50 is made that no such play can be written.

Back in London a skirmish occurs between Burbage, owner of the Curtain theatre, and Shakespeare. The scuffle leaves Shakespeare's company victorious, although celebrations are doubly cut short. First Viola as Tom Kent learns that Shakespeare is married and secondly the news arrives that Marlowe has been murdered.

Viola and Shakespeare are reconciled but this leads Viola's identity to be revealed by the young John Webster. Tilney, Master of the Queens Revels, exposes Viola as a woman and promptly closes down the Rose.

A magnanimous reprieve comes from Burbage who allows the play to be performed at his theatre. Posters are made up and fall into the hands of Viola as she is married to Wessex. Sam, the boy playing Juliet, finds that his voice has broken. Much to Shakespeare's joy Viola steps in as Juliet.

Tilney interrupts the play once more by trying to arrest the whole company. This time Queen Elizabeth, who has been in the audience, prevents him. Diplomatically she lets the company off the hook, insists that Wessex pays Shakespeare the wager and suggests a new play for Shakespeare. Viola and Shakespeare bid each other a tearful farewell as she sets off to Virginia.

HOW IT WAS MADE

Despite being acquired by The Walt Disney Company, Miramax held onto its position as the USA's leading independent production and distribution company in the 1990s. It had supported less obvious British films in America such as *The Crying Game*, *Priest*, and *Brassed Off* but had also gone down the British costume drama route with films like *Restoration* (1995), *Emma*, which also starred Gwyneth Paltrow, and *Mrs. Brown*, which starred Judi Dench. As early as 1992, *Shakespeare in Love* was mooted as a project with the likes of Julia Roberts, Daniel Day-Lewis and Kenneth Branagh touted as possible cast members.

The fact that there are five credited producers indicates the long drawn out process of getting the project off the ground. The British contingent consisted of David Parfitt, who had enjoyed success with Branagh as part of Renaissance Films and had gone down the costume drama route with *The Madness of King George* and *Wings of the Dove*.

The British line continued when John Madden was picked to direct the film largely on the strength of his own costume drama about Queen Victoria, *Mrs. Brown*. Although the main idea of the story came from American writer and co-producer Marc Norman, respected British writer Tom Stoppard, who had also dabbled in showing Shakespeare from another point of view with his stage play of Rosencrantz and Guildenstern are Dead, was drafted in to help tighten up the story.

Casting for the film featured an almost chocolate box-style selection of British actors: Simon Callow from *Four Weddings and a Funeral*, Tom Wilkinson from *The Full Monty*, Jim Carter from *Brassed Off*, Imelda Staunton from *Sense and Sensibility* (and *Much Ado About Nothing*), Rupert Everett from *The Madness of King George*, and of course Judi Dench from *Mrs Brown*. Added to this was Colin Firth, fresh from his 'steamy' performance in the role of Mr Darcy in BBC's production of *Pride and Prejudice* (1995).

Casting Will Shakespeare required someone to pull off the role of well-known genius playwright, accomplished actor and star-crossed lover. Joseph Fiennes, who had recently been seen in *Stealing Beauty* (UK/Italy/France, 1996), fitted the description.

The American stars for the film were Gwyneth Paltrow, who not only had starred in two recent British films – *Emma* and *Sliding Doors* – but had a convincing posh English accent to boot, and Ben Affleck who was to pick up an Academy Award for his screenplay in *Good Will Hunting* (USA, 1998). The two would become 'romantically' linked for a while. Finally, and perhaps unusually, another recent Academy Award winner, Australian actor Geoffrey Rush, who had starred in *Shine* (Australia/UK, 1996), was chosen to play the often luckless proprietor of the Rose, Henslowe.

The film required an entire Elizabethan set to be constructed featuring both the Rose and the Curtain theatre and Shepperton Studios witnessed the transformation from a boggy field into a convincing Elizabethan London set. This was after all a big budget production bankrolled by Universal and Miramax and shows not only how persuasively money talks in the film business but also what it can achieve in terms of sets and designs.

The backbone of the design team and indeed much of the crew, including production designer and costume designer, were British. Beyond Shepperton, locations included the Thames at Barnes for the taxi ride sequences and the beach at Holkham, Norfolk.

With only a few weeks to go before its release in November 1998 an extra scene was added between Viola and Shakespeare as a results of feedback from test screenings

With the scene duly inserted for greater clarity *Shakespeare in Love* was unravelled to an unsuspecting world.

KEY ISSUES

Shakespeare in Love pushed a lot of buttons and then some. It had the broad popular appeal of a straightforward rom com with enough action, sex and laughs to even occupy a multiplex-targeted teenager's attention span. It was also a visual treat – for those more interested in costumes than drama there was plenty to admire. The film also appealed to a more sophisticated audience who would get the many Shakespearian references and either guffaw at them or tut-tut at historical inaccuracies or, worse, some downright liberties taken by writers Norman and Stoppard. In total it was part comedy, part tragedy, part romance, part pantomime and even part Shakespeare.

Bringing Shakespeare to life

The paradox of William Shakespeare is that beyond his genius and his unique cannon of work very little is actually known about him as a person. This afforded Norman and Stoppard to take a sketchy picture of what was known about the bard and deliver him onto the screen using broad brush strokes.

First they tackled Shakespeare as a writer with the amusing premise that he was suffering from writer's block. We see Shakespeare sitting at his desk willing the words to come but instead screwing up pieces of paper and depositing them around his room. His confidence is regained by his visit to a distinctly 'Freudian' doctor/apocathery who gives Shakespeare a charm to release his muse.

In truth, the insecure Shakespeare differs only slightly from the writer whose quill is sharp. Even on his way to see his doctor and warding Henslowe off there is a mischievous playfulness about this Will Shakespeare, which spills into arrogance – 'God, I'm good' – when he is on fire.

The historical debate about Shakespeare's sources and the conspiracies surrounding Christopher Marlowe – that he may have had a hand in some of Shakespeare's work – are neatly presented as Shakespeare devours the scraps of advice given to him by Marlowe in structuring what will become *Romeo and Juliet*. Shakespeare may be cocky but he is astute enough to know when to take good advice. The film projects Marlowe as the top writer of the day, much to Shakespeare's childish jealousy. But that itself proves a nice running joke when Shakespeare passes himself off as Marlowe when confronted by Lord Wessex. This comedy even spills out to tragedy when we learn about Marlowe's mysterious death (as indeed in real life it was a mystery) and Shakespeare believes that he has been responsible.

Shakespeare also gets help from Viola as she gives him the outline of the plot for *Twelfth Night*. Of course, this is Shakespeare we are dealing with and we are left in no doubt that once he gets going there is a genius at work. Norman and Stoppard give Shakespeare just the right level on intensity to suggest that there is stuff 'locked up there'.

Perhaps Shakespeare is less convincing as a lover and as a swashbuckling fighter. History tells us that he married Anne Hathaway and then went to London (these facts are played for laughs in Shakespeare's 'psychoanalysis session'). Also scholars tell us that Shakespeare's sonnets were written for a man rather than a woman. However, the film runs a parallel construction between events in Shakespeare's life as he falls for Viola and the plot of Romeo and Juliet. But whereas Romeo is a bit of a dreamer, the film shows Shakespeare to be more of a man's man, comfortable in a tavern of ill-repute, handy with a sword and dictated by his desires. His feminine side appears to come out in his poetry and his display of emotions. He is every inch a modern action hero with shades of Erroll Flynn.

Shakespeare in *Shakespeare in Love*

As well as effectively running a parallel story of Romeo and Juliet within the film – the Capulets are represented by the Curtain Theatre, the Montagues by the Rose – Shakespeare/Romeo first believes his muse/love is Rosaline and the famous balcony scene is parodied, including the line: 'What light from yonder window breaks?' and plundered as much from Zefferelli's famous film version as Shakespeare's play itself. In this scene Viola's nurse acts as the crossover foil as she calls Violet in – just as the nurse calls Juliet in.

There are moments of delight when the film and the play cross over and merge as one. The balcony scene is cut between Sam the actor opposite Viola as Tom Kent going through the lines, to Will and Viola enacting the same lines until it reaches the two lovers' moment of parting and a complicated role reversal takes place. Shakespeare says – from the play: 'Good night, good night. As sweet repose and repose and rest Come to thy heart as that within my breast. O wilt thou leave me so unsatisfied?' Viola corrects: 'That's my line' and Shakespeare entwines the two by admitting that it is his line as well.

Elsewhere, bang on cue Burbage and his men storm into rehearsal just as Henslowe's players are about to stage the fight scene between the Capulets and the Montangues, which gives another visual joke as Henslowe checks his script.

However, *Shakespeare in Love* doesn't just confine itself to lines from Romeo and Juliet. There are references to Hamlet early on when Shakespeare talks to Henslowe about the progress of his forthcoming play: 'Doubt thou the stars are fire, doubt that the earth doth move.' Viola first comes to Shakespeare's attention when she prefers to recite lines from *Two Gentleman of Verona* than from Marlowe's *Dr Faustus*. Other lines come from *Sonnet 18* – 'Shall I compare thee to a summer's day?' and, of course, the film cleverly resolves its ending by giving Shakespeare, by royal command, the outline of the plot for *Twelfth Night*. *Shakespeare in Love* contains cross-dressing, mistaken identities, ghosts and the play within the play motifs.

Back to the future

Although much effort was made to create Elizabethan England with a story set in the 16th century, *Shakespeare in Love* delights in nudging its audience with 20th century sensibilities. Early on, as Shakespeare is seen brooding in his room, one of his discarded papers lands in a 'tourist' mug from Stratford on Avon.

Much humour is derived from the deadpan boatmen who are basically modern day cabbies. Twentieth century screwball comedy lines are placed in a 16th century context as Will Shakespeare chasing after Tom Kent issues the time-honoured instruction: 'Follow that boat.' The boatmen conform to their cabbie stereotype by saying: 'I had Christopher Marlowe in my boat once,' or 'Strangely enough, I'm a bit of a writer myself.'

Shakespeare is clearly meant to be on a psychiatrist's couch (which hadn't been thought of in the 16th century) when he goes for help with his writer's block. This is Woody Allen territory as is the increasing participation of Fennyman in the play, a homage to Allen's *Bullets Over Broadway* (USA, 1994) perhaps. Norman and Stoppard also contrive to deliver the corniest line from the whole film when Henslowe states: 'The show must…' and Shakespeare urges 'Go on.'

By permission of Mr Burbage

Another interesting strand that manages to keep a foot firmly placed in the 20th century is *Shakespeare in Love*'s sly satire on the entertainment business, which deals with theatre but can just as easily be transported to film. Intentionally or otherwise, the film serves as a neat microcosm of the relationships between the British film industry and its rich American benefactors.

Early on Fennyman tots up how much money he will make for two performances of Henslowe's promised new play and calculates a figure of £20. Henslowe protests that he still has to pay the actors and the authors to which Fennyman, without skipping a beat, suggests a share of the profits. Henslowe replies that there's never any and Fennyman retorts: 'Of course not.' In a nutshell the two men have explained the system of deferred payments, which helped to fund some British films during the 1990s and left many actors and authors out of pocket.

A sideswipe is also made at the benefactor. Fennyman is a bit of a thug and Shakespeare craftily gets him onside by offering him the part of the apothecary in *Romeo and Juliet*, which Fennyman's ego greatly accepts. The stuttering Wabash also gets a minor part purely because he is Henslowe's tailor. However, a bigger ego in the shape of top actor Ned Alleyn shows contempt for Fennyman when he declares that he is 'The money.' Ned puts him in his place by saying: 'Then you may remain so long as you remain silent.' How many film-makers wish that was true of the people who put up the money for their productions and then proceed to interfere.

Ned Alleyn = is a small parody of the star system. Shakespeare is seen constantly fanning his ego and persuading him to play the part of Mercutio (which Shakespeare claims is the title of the play), even though the main roles are Romeo and Juliet. In this respect American Academy Award writer and actor, Ben Affleck, also plays second fiddle to up-and-coming English actor Joseph Fiennes.

There is also time for a joke at young male audiences when Shakespeare speaks to a young John Webster, who was to become a famous Jacobean playwright noted for two dark pieces, *The White Devil and the Duchess of Malfi,* and the boy states: 'Plenty of blood. That is the only writing,' a point he reiterates later when Queen Elizabeth asks whether he liked the play and he answers: 'I liked it when she stabbed herself, your Majesty.'

There is also the not so subtle joke on the poster which parodies the long pre-title credits associated with most films today, including names of sponsors and producers. The poster reads:

> By permission of Mr Burbage
>
> A Hugh Fennyman Production
>
> Of Mr. Henslowe's Presentation
>
> Of The Admiral's Men in Performance
>
> Of The Excellent and Lamentable Tragedy
>
> Of Romeo and Juliet
>
> with Mr Fennyman as the Apothecary

SCENE ANALYSIS – BETTER THAN A PLAY

One thing that is common throughout the staging of *Romeo and Juliet* is the sense of pace and movement. It is typified by the speed in which it takes us through the events on and off stage. On stage the camera often makes circular movements around the actors and more often than not we are afforded a perspective from the actual stage, so we often get to see the audience in the theatre from the actor's perspective. The film is generous to those with a short attention span in the way it flits from one position to the next. Each shot is so well composed that there is a natural rhythm to the scenes performed on stage, which are occasionally broken up by characters in the film making their way to the theatre.

As Wabash walks onto the stage towards the audience attempting not to stutter we literally sees what he sees – the whole circular theatre as the camera settles down centre of stage looking out at the whole audience. Wabash prepares to speak and we are shown a shot of a section of the audience in the pit looking up towards him. A close-up of Wabash shows him gaze in their direction before stuttering to other parts of the theatre. This small sequence is intercut with a shot of Shakespeare backstage in despair. But as Wabash finds his courage he begins the prologue. As he does the camera zooms away from him in an upward movement and we cut back to Shakespeare looking up with a mixture of surprise and relief. Our next shot shows Wabash from behind addressing the stage and the camera slowly drifts upwards and away. As he speaks the lush background music enters, signalling a moment of emotional relief.

With the prologue still being proclaimed we see Viola (fresh from her wedding) and her nurse rushing through crowded streets in the direction of the theatre. The volume of the background music overtakes the volume of the prologue. The music is faded down at the point that Wabash comes off stage and encounters Shakespeare who congratulates him. Shakespeare then looks from the wings towards the stage and we get his point of view shot of the play beginning.

In keeping with the speed of the scene our attentions are now drawn to Will as Juliet whose voice has broken. No sooner have we learned this than Shakespeare and Henslowe are locked in discussion deciding what to do (and cracking 'the show must go on' joke). The solution appears as we see Viola and her nurse take their seats. They pass Burbage and seconds later Henslowe is debating with Burbage about the lack of a Juliet. The camera movement again is evident as it swings from Henslowe and Burbage across to Viola in the next aisle. When Henslowe asks Viola 'Do you know it?' the background music strikes up again and soothes us with the knowledge that Viola will step in and save the play.

Once again the story within a story is interrupted with an outdoor shot. This time Wessex is seen riding towards the theatre. Again we see him enter the theatre with the sound of the play in progress and the background music easing us along to the next key moment - Juliet's entrance. We see a shot of Shakespeare leaving the stage to applause but slumping down backstage. We return to a shot of the stage cut with a reaction shot from the pit of the audience clearly enjoying themselves and the background music fades out again.

As the cue for Juliet to come on stage is spoken by Ralph Bashford playing the Nurse: 'What ladybird' we get fast cuts adding layer upon layer of plot – Will Kempe as Juliet trying out his lines; Wessex up in the stalls looking for Viola; Shakespeare on the floor backstage clutching his head in despair; and finally Henslowe pulling Will Kempe as he attempts his entrance. Viola's entrance is met with sighs from the audience and a set of reaction shots – the two actors on stage; Shakespeare looking up; a close-up of a disgruntled Wessex in the stalls; Viola's nurse crossing herself and finally Burbage telling Henslowe backstage: 'We'll all be put in the clink'.

With Viola on stage as Juliet the background music fades in gently for our next emotional nudge. The sumptuous costumes and elegant settings allow for many of the shots to have exquisite framing. One shows Shakespeare in the wings looking lovingly on stage towards Viola. At first he is seen in a mid-shot caught between curtains and scenery. The camera moves slowly towards him as we then get a reverse shot of the object of his affection, Viola. This small sequence itself could be entitled *Shakespeare in Love*, since that is what Shakespeare's gaze manages to convey as the two lovers are caught in close-up and Viola looks across at a smiling Shakespeare and returns a smile to him. The intimate moment is broken when Viola speaks her first line and we cut to a fight scene.

Backstage Shakespeare finally meets Viola and speaks to her and the blurring between the film and the play is perfectly illustrated as the two move forward to embrace. A crafty cut shows a close-up of that embrace and the camera pulls away from the couple as they release each other only to reveal that we are on stage with them and they are reciting words from the play. Music again informs us of the double-edged emotion of the scene the two lovers are enacting.

As the fatal potion is presented in close-up we see the friar and get a sweeping movement, which then reveals Viola as Juliet on stage. The constant camera movement gives the play its own sense of continuation. The apothecary's nervous entrance on the stage allows more in-jokes as he cuts Shakespeare's lines short but maintains the urgency of the scene.

Romeo and Juliet's death scene is included in some detail to add a sense of drama and closure to the play. Again camera movement is key when Viola as Juliet awakes to find her Romeo dead beside her. Her waking sigh is matched with a sigh from the audience. Viola's nurse blurts out that Romeo is dead leaving the camera to pull away from the shot of Viola looking up to the audience and seeing Romeo beside her. It moves back towards her as she takes Romeo's dagger and we get a cut to the audience reaction at stage level before Juliet takes the dagger to herself. We see her from above before cutting back to a reaction shot of Viola's nurse and finally Juliet/Viola rests with Romeo/Shakespeare on stage, the two now completely intermeshed with their on and off stage personas.

Wabash ends the play with his epilogue. Again the camera pans upwards away from his close-up to reveal the stage. The background music accompanies him lightly. A final set of cuts reveal the tension backstage as the audience is stunned into silence. Finally, applause and reaction shots ring out around the theatre and as Viola and Shakespeare stir from their positions the background music strikes up in earnest and the cast take their curtain call and Viola and Shakespeare embrace in true Hollywood style. The final high shot taken from 'the Gods' down onto the stage could have marked the end of the film. However, it merely allows for the climax to be curtailed and the remaining breathless elements of the film to be resolved with the arrival of Tilney's men, the unexpected appearance of Queen Elizabeth and the conclusion of the wager.

REACTION

To paraphrase from the film: 'Strangely, it all turns out well.' That the film landed seven Oscars is perhaps 'a mystery' (see page 232). Not far behind was a clutch of BAFTAs for Best Film, Best Performance by an Actress in a Supporting Role – Judi Dench, Best Performance by an Actor in a Supporting Role – Geoffrey Rush, and Best Editing – David Gamble. The success was reflected in its performance at the box-office, bringing in more than £20m in the UK. In the USA the film topped the $100m mark, placing it in the top 20 films of 1998. Impressive worldwide box-office figures rang to the tune of $289.1m.

Back in the UK the press gave the film good reviews with the exception of *The Guardian*'s Jonathan Romney, who observed: 'Sniping at what's already been celebrated as a major national triumph always looks not-quite-cricket, but Madden's film is transparently one of those things that the British Do So Well, and the Americans fund so handsomely. It sets out to provide more than your money's worth, but *Shakespeare In Love* falls some way short of infinite jest.'

Meanwhile, Janet Maslin made the following point: 'Far richer and more deft than the other Elizabethan film in town (*Elizabeth*), this boasts a splendid, hearty cast of supporting players. (The actors in both films, like Fiennes, do notably better work here.)'

It is interesting that *Elizabeth* should be regarded as the poor relation since it was a fully-fledged, big budget British film. Romney's point is valid for costume dramas are things that 'the British Do So Well'. Turning to a typically British genre to secure revenue for future productions did not seem a bad idea – even if in the case of *Shakespeare in Love* the funding came from America.

Under the guiding hand of Harvey and Bob Weinstein Miramax continued to support British films, including costume dramas like *Mansfield Park*), *An Ideal Husband*, and *Love's Labour's Lost*; and a ream of British films ranging from the edgy *Velvet Goldmine* (1998) to the box-office hit of *Bridget Jones's Diary* (2001).

For a brief moment in the late 1990s Paltrow became an adopted Brit, largely due to her convincing accent. Her successes in British films continued with *Sliding Doors* and teaming up with British director Anthony Minghella for another Miramax film, *The Talented Mr Ripley* (1999). In December 2003 she married Chris Martin from the band Coldplay, thereby cementing the assumed connection that she had with Britain.

Sense and Sensibility (1995) (USA) UK Cert U

Director: Ang Lee

Screenplay: Emma Thompson (based on the novel by Jane Austen)

Producer: Lindsay Doran

Production companies: Columbia Pictures Corporation; Mirage Enterprises; Good Machine

Production start date: 04/1995 **Budget:** £ 9.4 m (estimated)

Distributor: Sony Pictures International **UK Release date:** 23 February 1996

UK Box Office: £13,632,700 **USA Box Office:** $43m

Worldwide Box Office: $135.1m

Two hundred years after its first draft (the novel was published in 1811) *Sense and Sensibility* was committed to film in a sumptuous production which featured a top-notch British cast, a top-drawer Taiwanese director in Ang Lee and a top screenplay from one of the film's star's Emma Thompson, who went on to win an Academy Award for her adaptation of Austen's early work.

If costume dramas have been the staple diet of hit British films then the industry was given healthy servings of Jane Austen in the 1990s. Along with *Sense and Sensibility* two other Austen novels were turned into films: *Emma*, and *Mansfield Park*. On top of this was the acclaimed BBC serial *Pride and Prejudice* and a version of *Persuasion*, which was released theatrically in America. Of Austen's major works only *Northanger Abbey* remained untouched by film or television.

On the surface Austen's world of the English country gentry, manners, morals, wit and romance seem rather dated to modern audiences. However, the themes interwoven in the novels appear, albeit in diluted form, in *Four Weddings and a Funeral*. Furthermore, Austen's plotlines would find other outlets in contemporary films such as *Clueless*

(USA, 1994), loosely based on *Emma* and later on in the successful adaptation of Helen Fielding's 1996 best-selling book *Bridget Jones's Diary*, which had loose connections with Austen's *Pride and Prejudice*.

SYNOPSIS

On the death of their father (Tom Wilkinson) the Dashwood women comprising Mrs Dashwood (Gemma Jones), Elinor (Emma Thompson), Marianne (Kate Winslet) and Margaret (Emilie François) learn that they are left with little money. The spoils of their estate are assigned to the sympathetic John Dashwood (James Fleet) and his domineering wife Fanny (Harriet Walter) who knocks down her husband's suggestions of a share of the money to his sister and her children.

The Dashwood women spend an uncomfortable time with John and Fanny. The tension is relieved with the arrival of Fanny's brother, the coy but charming Edward Ferrars (Hugh Grant), who strikes up an amiable relationship with Elinor, much to the delight of Marianne and Margaret but not so Fanny. Just as Elinor and Edward seem to be getting close he is called away to London, which prompts Mrs Dashwood to take up the offer from her rich relation Sir John Middleton (Robert Hardy) to live in a cottage on his Devonshire estate.

They meet his mother-in-law, the robust, redoubtable gossip Mrs Jennings (Elizabeth Spriggs) and the serious, gentlemanly Colonel Brandon (Alan Rickman) who takes a shine to Marianne, although it is not reciprocated. Instead, Marianne falls for the dashing John Willoughby (Greg Wise), who arrives on his horse to her rescue when she stumbles and twists her ankle while walking in the rain.

The two sisters receive blows to their relationships. At the point when Willoughby seems to be proposing to Marianne he declares that he is called away to London, leaving her perplexed and heartbroken. Elinor's hopes are crushed when she meets Lucy Steele (Imogen Stubbs) who reveals, in strictest confidence, that she is secretly engaged to Edward.

The sisters' misery is lifted when Mrs Jennings invites them up to London. However, Marianne's despair grows daily as none of her notes to Willoughby receive a reply. Elinor keeps her heartbreak to herself as she has to endure Lucy Steele's nagging friendship. At a ball Marianne is devastated when she meets Willoughby who acts as though they barely know each other. His behaviour is finally explained when it transpires that he has become engaged to a rich heiress.

Lucy confides in Fanny that she intends to marry Edward whereupon she is banished from the household and Edward's inheritance is cut off. Colonel Brandon learns about this and, considering Edward to have acted honourably, offers him a parish on his estate, but he gets Elinor to convey that news to Edward. Brandon also relays the story of how Willoughby had fathered a child by the daughter of the woman that he had once loved. This scandal meant that Willoughby was cut off from his inheritance leaving him potentially penniless, which explains his sudden departure to London and his match to an heiress.

A despondent Elinor and Marianne return home via Somerset where they stay with Mrs Jennings well-meaning daughter Charlotte (Imelda Staunton) and her grumpy husband (Hugh Laurie). Their estate is within walking distance of where Willoughby lives and Marianne cannot resist walking towards his grounds in the rain. She falls gravely ill and her recovery coincides with an appreciation of Colonel Brandon and the two end up betrothed.

Hearing the news that Lucy Steele has become Mrs Ferrars the Dashwoods are surprised by the arrival of Edward to their cottage. Their confusion is cleared up when they learn that Lucy Steele had married Edward's brother Robert (Richard Lumsden). With the door now open Edward and Elinor are free to marry.

In the end Marianne marries Colonel Brandon while Elinor marries Edward, leaving the forlorn Willoughby who married for money and not for love to overlook the happy ending.

HOW IT WAS MADE

It would be wrong to think that successful costume drama in the 1990s was the sole preserve of the British film industry. Columbia Pictures had released the Oscar nominated *Little Women* (USA, 1995), as well as supporting British productions such as *The Remains of the Day*, which starred Thompson. Her star was on the rise as she was nominated for Best Actress Oscar in the film. Despite the split with husband Kenneth Branagh she was highly regarded, particularly in America.

In many ways *Sense and Sensibility* was her film as she took on the acting role but provided the adapted material, which perfectly balanced the integrity of Austen's work without pandering too much to 20th century sensibilities, even if this meant many rewrites in order to get the balance right.

The other major influence in making this quintessential English film was Taiwanese director Ang Lee, who had recently scored an international success with the gently observed drama *Eat, drink, man, woman* (Taiwan, 1994). With the typical back-up associated with British costume dramas – locations, top actors and fine costumes – Lee was to provide another element to the mix.

Lee was keen to have Thompson play the part of Elinor (even though in the book Elinor was 19). Thompson obliged and added slightly more emotional depth to her apparent rejection by Edward and a greater sense of maturity and worldliness than the flighty romantic character of her younger sister Marianne.

The cast was full of familiar British actors and some soon to become familiar faces. Hugh Grant's star was rising as a result of *Four Weddings and a Funeral* and his role of Edward is played with Charles' slight stammer from that film. James Fleet also plays to type as the hen-pecked John Dashwood. Even with the benefit of hindsight it is hard to chart Kate Winslet's career pre-*Titanic* and yet the actress had made an impressive impact in Peter Jackson's dark study of overbearing friendship in *Heavenly Creatures* (New Zealand/ Germany, 1994). Elsewhere, we have the brooding presence of Alan Rickman contrasting with Greg Wise's dashing flamboyant charm and a marvellous supporting cast consisting of some hardy perennenials – Robert Hardy, Imelda Staunton, Imogen Stubbs, Harriet Walter, and Elizabeth Spriggs – and a scene-stealing cameo from Hugh Laurie as a world-weary, irritated cynic trapped among the nineteenth century chattering classes.

Some of the filming took place at Shepperton Studios and around Greenwich and Somerset House in London, but the remainder of the film was shot in the South West of England in Devon, Somerset and Wiltshire. The task of finding suitable locations fell to the South West Film Commission. Obviously heritage films stood the most to gain from the plethora of stately homes and lush green rolling landscapes accompanied by sheep and the stunning backdrops added to the appeal of the film. Efford House in Plymouth became the Dashwood's humble cottage, while Montacute House in Somerset passed for Cleveland and the church at Berry Pomeroy, Devon was chosen for the closing scene.

For all its Britishness the two main production companies were Columbia Pictures and Sydney Pollack's Mirage Enterprises (which English director Anthony Minghella joined forces with in 2000 thereby giving it an Anglo/American association.) Shooting took place in April 1995 and received its premiere in America first in December 1995 before waiting two months for its English release.

KEY ISSUES

Jane Austen's *Sense and Sensibility* is constructed around twists and revelations where characters that seem too good to be true end up being disappointing and those perceived as dull but worthy come good in the end. The film offers its audience a gateway to the book. It not only captures the essence of the novel but also throws up issues of love, money and integrity.

Adapting Austen

The beauty of adaptations is that those who are familiar with the material will go into the film with their expectations already set. Those unfamiliar with the text are given a helping hand to understand why a particular novel was worth adapting in the first place and, if the film succeeds, to whet their appetites to read the original. In *Sense and Sensibility*, Thompson pulls off the feat of remaining true to the spirit of Austen's novel while at the same time ensuring that cinematically the film does not drag.

As a necessity Thompson does away with some characters that would slow the story down and so Lady Middleton in the novel is absent in the film and is largely replaced physically by Mrs Jennings, who is seen to accompany Sir John Middleton to the Dashwood's cottage when they move in. Another omission is that of Mrs Ferrars, Edward and Robert's mother. The ghastly Fanny more or less fulfils the same role of blocking Edward's romance with Lucy Steele. Lucy's sister Anne also goes awol in the film, but she is rather a peripheral character in the book.

Thompson does take a few liberties in establishing relationships. More time is devoted to comparing Edward to Willoughby. The scene with Edward coaxing Margaret from under the table in the library by talking to Elinor about the source of the Nile belongs to Thompson, as do the scenes where Marianne and Willoughby recite poetry to one another, even though the book clearly states that their interest in books and poetry were entwined.

In the book Willoughby first appears on foot carrying a gun with two pointers playing round him. In the film he is established as a dashing figure riding to the distressed Marianne on his horse and in this way the audience gets a good idea of what the man is all about. Equally revealing (and absent from the novel) is Brandon visiting Marianne with freshly picked flowers, while Willoughby arrives with handpicked wildflowers, which Marianne says that she prefers.

The book also takes us through the story at a more leisurely pace (eventually we get to read the full contents of Marianne's frantic notes to Willoughby). Certain scenes are either missed out (Edward visiting Barton where it is observed that he carries a lock of hair in a ring) or combined in the same event (Lucy Steele meeting Robert Ferrars at the same ball where the Dashwoods see Willoughby behaving in a cool way to Marrianne). Thompson also delights in creating a comic turn in the gruff Mr Palmer by neatly giving Hugh Laurie some terse retorts.

Perhaps the biggest omission from the film is the scene where Willoughby arrives dramatically at Cleveland to confess to Elinor just as Marianne (whose severe illness is condensed in the film) has survived her illness. In the film Thompson cleverly transposes this lengthy scene into a short passage where she gives Willoughby the benefit of the doubt when talking to Marianne. The decision not to use the Willoughby scene was more to do with the pacing of an already complex story. We later see Willoughby on the brow of a hill looking down at the wedding of Marianne to Colonel Brandon, which more or less tells us of his remorse and regret and ties in with Elinor's brief re-appraisal of Willoughby's nature.

The importance of being prudent

Elinor and Marianne represent *Sense and Sensibility*. With an economy of detail Austen perfectly describes their character traits starting with an assessment of Elinor.

'She had an excellent heart;—her disposition was affectionate, and her feelings were strong; but she knew how to govern them: it was a knowledge which her mother had yet to learn; and which one of her sisters had resolved never to be taught.'

'Marianne's abilities were, in many respects, quite equal to Elinor's. She was sensible and clever; but eager in everything: her sorrows, her joys, could have no moderation. She was generous, amiable, interesting: she was everything but prudent.'

Thompson's performance as Elinor requires her to show control of her emotions. Her romance with Edward is ridiculed when she allows herself to tell Marianne that she 'esteems him.' Any passion that she feels is buried deep.

Her character carries a vast degree of self-integrity, highlighted in the scenes where she meets Lucy and becomes her confidante even though her heart has been broken. This control of emotions is put to the test when Brandon gets her to tell Edward the good news that he will have a parish on Brandon's estate, thereby securing the marriage to Lucy. Despite her emotions Elinor looks at the bigger picture and always does the honourable thing. For her, feelings should be private. It comes as a relief therefore to witness her outpouring when Edward turns up and the Dashwood family realise that Lucy married his brother Robert, leaving the coast clear for Edward to propose to Elinor.

Born romantic

If Elinor's sense belongs in the 19th century then Marianne seems bursting to join the 20th century and do away with the conventions of the old society. She recognises that 'there is something wanting' in Edward but is swept off her feet by Willoughby. he is flash and vain (in modern days he would turn up in an expensive motor car – as it is he drives his carriage with its bright yellow wheels at full tilt).

Marianne declares: 'To love is to burn; to be on fire like Juliet or Guinevere or Elenore.' Marianne is burnt indeed, but not in the way she had imagined. Her heart dictates her actions and her feelings are worn on her sleeve. For a while she and Willoughby seem like the perfect match. It seems harsh that Marianne – a hopeless romantic able to recite Shakespeare's *Sonnet 116* off by heart – discovers that there is more to life than love. While her passion is fierce the reality of her relationship is that in the end Willoughby puts his financial security ahead of love.

In the novel we learn that Marianne was 'born to discover the falsehood of her opinions.' Colonel Brandon seems a poor substitute for Willoughby and there is a sense in both the film and the novel that Marianne ends up with the sensible option. However, given the choice her heart would dictate that she should have been with Willoughby instead of ending up with an honourable man twice her age in Colonel Brandon.

Four weddings and a near death experience

Austen's rural, class-driven society is neatly encapsulated in the weddings that take place. Although this is a tale of 19th century life there are strange parallels with the modern day in arranged marriages and people marrying for money rather than love (known today as gold diggers). However, in Austen's age the helpless role of women is rather well-illustrated even though her two main characters show a good deal of spirit, wit and intelligence. Class mattered and money, greed and possessions were foremost in people's minds.

The four marriages in the film show something about social standing: Willoughby marries Miss Grey for money rather than love; Robert marries the flighty Lucy knowing that his financial position is secure; Brandon (who is 35) marries Marianne (who is 19) for love, proving he is not just a colonel but a gentleman to boot; and finally Edward marries Elinor for love but would have married Lucy and lived in poverty. In all these cases the men call the shots and the women suffer and wait in silence or gossip endlessly.

The men in Sense in Sensibility all carry secrets to do with women – Edward is engaged to Lucy, Brandon has a ward, Willoughby has made Eliza pregnant (out of wedlock too), and Robert has his eye on Lucy (although this secret is not so apparent in the film).

In the end the women are left to fret or to gush with relief. Marianne's near death experience basically extinguishes her feisty spirit so enflamed by the dashing charms of Willoughby and she finally becomes submissive to Colonel Brandon's worthy nature – not to mention his sizeable large estate.

Ang Lee's angle

The choice of Ang Lee as director raised a few eyebrows but his vision definitely adds to the aesthetic appeal of the film. The film is often composed like an oil painting and late night shots are bathed in soft glowing lighting. His touches are often subtle but not to the extent that they interfere with the basic flow of the story.

Early on in the film Elinor, having accepted Edward's hankerchief, offers to show him the tree house. As the couple leave Mrs Dashwood enters the shot and a smile appears on her face. As she walks out of shot the camera looks up to the top of the stairs where we see Fanny looking down with disapproval.

In another scene Elinor is left in distress by Edward's absence and Mrs Dashwood enters the room to comfort her. The camera gently pulls away from the shot to leave them in their private moment. Later on another shot from above the stairs shows three rooms where each Dashwood woman retreats in a moment of high drama. Elsewhere the subtle looks between people are captured. The novel is largely written through Elinor's perspective and this is shown when she sees how intensely Colonel Brandon looks at Marianne at their first meeting.

SCENE ANALYSIS — ON THE BALL

The ballroom scene gives ample opportunities for the film to show off its wares and we see a whole array of posh frocks, the interior of a stately home, some choreographed dancing and the pulling of taut emotional heartstrings where no one except Marianne actually seems to say what they mean.

As with many of the evening scenes, the lighting is subtle and a warm golden glow from candle lights creates an atmospheric effect. The camera tends to track the movement of the characters, particularly when Mrs Jennings first enters the room. The scene is mapped nicely so that Mrs Jennings takes us in to see Fanny. She in turn points her fan and leads us to meet her brother in what turns out to be a tease. Seen from the back Lucy and Elinor, framed together, prepare to meet him only for his brother Robert to turn round.

Throughout the film non-verbal communication is conveyed by looks between characters. Marianne is captured giving Robert a look of hefty disapproval when he states that Edward Ferrars has 'no special acquaintance here to make his attendance worthwhile.' Fanny, on the other hand, is captured with a look of satisfaction that Edward and Elinor are not to meet up again. Equally, Robert cannot hide his look of disappointment when Mrs Jennings urges him to dance with Elinor and Elinor herself can only muster a false smile as Robert declares that: 'It would be my honour.' Robert in fact would much rather dance with Lucy and boldly asks her for a dance later.

As Robert leads Elinor into the main ballroom the camera follows them and then sweeps upwards to give us an overhead view of most of the room with couples dancing. By now the background music, which accompanies the dancers, is more noticeable than before. As the dancers line up we are taken back to ground level and the intricate formation dance unfolds with the camera keeping tightly on Robert and Elinor as they weave between dancers and exchange banal pleasantries. Just as the scene looks as though it is going nowhere Elinor exchanges one partner and links up with Willoughby, thereby taking us into a further part of the plotline.

Elinor's exchange with Willoughby demonstrates the tight cauldron of emotions. Rather than burst out with 'Where have you been Willoughby?' she merely greets him. Willoughby himself responds with the formal: 'How do you do Miss Dashwood' rather than 'look, I can explain everything.' Our next mapping point inevitably has a close-up shot of Willougby looking over his shoulder and catching sight of Marianne. His face betrays no emotion as he continues to dance. Marianne, on the other hand, causes as a bit of a scene as if on cue the music stops, the dancers divide and she runs across the crowded room to greet him with: 'Good God Willoughby, will you not shake hands with me.'

At this point Marianne, in close-up, is framed looking up at him with a smile on her face. When we get the reverse shot Willoughby is looking down upon her with a look of resignation. Marianne's expression quickly changes and she addresses his peculiar behaviour by saying: 'Willoughby what is the matter, why have you not come to see me?' As the music strikes up for the next dance Willoughby politely declines to engage with his soul mate and leaves. This time the camera takes us to a close-up of Elinor's reaction of sympathy towards her sister before returning to capture Marianne's stunned expression.

Marianne follows Willoughby as the scenes mapping exercise takes us into yet another room as we observe Willoughby returning to his party from Marianne's point of view. As he does we only see the backs of the small group that he has joined. As Elinor joins Marianne at the door we then see Miss Grey turn her head around, sheepishly followed by Willoughby. With Miss Grey and Willoughby framed together we make the connection that they are a couple. Their gaze is captured as the camera takes us to a close-up shot of Marianne's reaction. We hear Willoughby mutter who the Dashwood women are and also get to hear a sly putdown by a member in his group say something about their 'country fashions'. Miss Grey takes Willoughby's arm and they turn back to their group and completely cut off Marianne.

Elinor leads Marianne away from the room and as she starts to faint. Mrs Jennings blunders in again as the camera follows the three women through the room. Mrs Jennings beckons Lucy who is seen holding Robert's hand as they cut away from their dance. As Robert and Lucy rejoin the dance we are left with our final non-verbal piece of communication as Fanny, dancing with her husband, quickly throws a guilty look in the direction of the departing Dashwoods.

This scene has moved the story on by revealing Colonel Brandon's earlier doubts about Willoughby to be true and taken Lucy away from her enchantment with Edward into her brother's care, and also heralding a point where both Marianne and Elinor share a broken heart.

REACTION

Sense and Sensibility was nominated for six Oscars and Thompson won the award for Best Writing – Screenplay Based on Material from Another Medium. Her adaptation also won a Golden Globe, London Critics Circle Film Award and an Evening Standard British Film Award 1997 (an honour that she shared with John Hodge for *Trainspotting*). Thompson also picked up a BAFTA for Best Performance by an Actress in a Leading Role.

Winslet's performance as Marianne won her a BAFTA for Best Supporting Role and a Best Actress Award (which included her role in *Jude*) at the Evening Standard British Film Awards.

Reviews were equal in praise for Thompson's adaptation and Lee's sympathetic treatment, which many felt added a refreshing dimension to the standard British costume drama. In his *Variety* review Todd McCarthy wrote: 'The choice of Lee to direct this so specifically British and period film, and his great success in doing so, will no doubt be the source of much wonderment.' Lee picked up a Golden Berlin Bear award at the Berlin International Festival.

The film was a big domestic and international box-office success, ringing up more than £13.5m in the UK, which seemed a good return on the £9.5m that Columbia Pictures had invested.

Hot on its heels came the Miramax version of *Emma*, starring Gwyneth Paltrow and featuring a post-*Trainspotting* Ewan McGregor. The film was a success if not to the same degree as *Sense and Sensibility* although Rachel Portman did win an Academy Award for Best Original Score. In 1999 Miramax and the BBC teamed up with the aid of Arts Council Lottery funding to create *Mansfield Park* starring Frances O'Connor and Jonny Lee Miller (also from *Trainspotting*). However, this version proved less successful at the box-office, perhaps as a result of too many Jane Austens in a short period of time.

CONCLUSION

Not for the first time in the 1990s it is possible to see in both *Sense and Sensibility* and *Shakespeare in Love* how Americans put their finance and faith in the expertise of British actors, technicians and creative talents. *Shakespeare in Love* may have been a typically British film and one that celebrated all the British film industry strengths both in front and behind the camera but nobody in Britain could really get away with too much tub thumping because the film simply would not have been made or released on such a successful scale without considerable American backing.

However, the fact that the film gave us such a romanticised view of England and all things to do with Shakespeare was also a British strength. These were unique features and ones that had international appeal.

Fans welcomed the spate of Jane Austen adaptations in the 1990s. *Sense and Sensibility* rather raised the stakes in the classy way it was presented. Much of its success was down to Lee's slightly different visually aesthetic angle and Thompson's slick adaptation was perfect for a 20th century audience prone to fidget if the action slackened.

FURTHER READING

English Heritage, English Cinema
Higson, Andrew. (Oxford University Press, 2003)

The British Film Industry, Second Report, Session 1994-95, Volume I.
(London, HMSO, 8 March 1995).

British Cinema of the 90s
Murphy, Robert (ed.) (BFI, 2001) Chapter 12 – Fewer Weddings and More Funerals:
Changes in Heritage Film by Church Gibson, Pamela

The Stats An overview of the film, television, video and DVD industries 1990-2003
(BFI National Library, BFI Information Services, 2006)

BFI Film and Television Handbook (BFI, editions from 1990–2005)

Selected reviews/articles/references

Film Education – www.filmeducation.org/filmlibrary.html

Adaptations, Heritage Film and Costume Drama 16+ Source Guide Guides

Forbes, Tess; Goodson, Susanna; Khan, Ayesha; Sharp, David; Thomas, Wendy; Kerameos, Anastasia; Williamson, Tracey; Currant, Sarah; Crabbe, Victoria; Evers, Bronia (BFI National Library, 2006)

DVD: *Sense and Sensibility* – Collector's Edition (Sony Pictures Home Entertainment, 2006)

Shakespeare in Love

Sight & Sound V9. N.2 (1 Feb 1999) P53 by Kemp, Philip

Empire N.116 (1 Feb 1999) P20. by Nathan, Ian

Comedy, love, and a bit with a dog by Romney, Jonathan
The Guardian, Friday January 29, 1999

Film Education Shakespeare in Love – www.filmeducation.org/secondary/shakespeareinlove

DVD: *Shakespeare in Love* (Universal Pictures UK, 2004)

Sense and Sensibility

Sight & Sound V.6 N.3 (1 March 1996) P.50-51 by Monk, Claire

Empire N.81 (1 March 1996) P.33 by Brown, Deborah

Jane Austen on screen
Macdonald, Gina and Macdonald, Andrew F. (Cambridge University Press, 2003)

Sense and Sensibility: study guide
Dixon, Rod (Film Education, 1996)

Passionate Precision by Lyons, Donald
Film Comment V.32 N.1 (1 Jan 1996) P.36-41

Cautionary Tale by Fuller, Graham
Sight & Sound V.6 N.3 (1 March 1996) P.20-22

10. END OF THE DECADE — BOOM OR BUST?

Top 20 films at UK box-office 1990-2000

Title		Distributor	Box Office (£)
1	Titanic (1998)	Twentieth Century Fox	68,971,532
2	The Full Monty (1997)	Twentieth Century Fox	52,232,058
3	Star Wars Episode 1 (1999)	Twentieth Century Fox	50,928,328
4	Jurassic Park (1993)	UIP	46,564,080
5	Toy Story 2 (2000)	Buena Vista	43,491,021
6	Men In Black (1997)	Columbia Tristar	35,800,000
7	Independence Day (1996)	Twentieth Century Fox	37,010,000
8	Notting Hill (1999)	Universal	31,006,109
9	Gladiator (2000)	UIP	30,907,687
10	Chicken Run (2000)	Pathe	29,514,237
11	A Bug's Life (1999)	Buena Vista	29,310,536
12	The World Is Not Enough (1999)	UIP	28,576,504
13	Four Weddings and a Funeral (1994)	Rank	27,762,648
14	The Lost World (1997)	UIP	25,800,000
15	Austin Powers 2 (1999)	Entertainment	25,772,822
16	The Sixth Sense (1999)	UIP	25,407,279
17	Toy Story (1996)	Buena Vista	22,486,389
18	The Lion King (1994)	Buena Vista	21,923,399
19	Mrs Doubtfire (1994)	Twentieth Century Fox	21,227,668
20	Shakespeare In Love (1999)	UIP	20,814,499

Source: Nielsen EDI, BFI The Stats: An overview of the film, television, video and DVD industries 1990-2003

By the mid- to late 1990s British cinema seemed to be not only on the road to recovery but showing signs of good health. The efforts at the beginning of the decade to inject life into the film production sector had paid off and 1996 witnessed the production of 128 British films aided by a combination of tax incentives, lottery funding and co-productions with America and to a lesser extent Europe. By anyone's standards this was a phenomenal leap from the 30 produced in 1989.

Hand in hand with the rise of the multiplex cinemas admissions rose throughout the decade, ending strongly with 139.7 million in 1999 compared with 97.3 million in 1990. Although British audiences were lured by American blockbusters, a crop of British films barged their way to box-office success – *The Full Monty*, *Notting Hill*, *Four Weddings and A Funeral*, and three James Bond films – proving that homespun success had a global as well as a domestic audience. Furthermore, if the strength of an industry is defined by the amount of Oscars it picks up then *Shakespeare in Love*'s haul of seven Academy Awards implied that it was robust.

Had the decade ended a year earlier in 1998 there would have been genuine reasons to be bullish about the prospects of the British film industry in the new millennium. A combination of PolyGram, Working Title, FilmFour and BBC Films were now well-established and making commercially viable films. There was also the promise of the three Lottery film franchises DNA Films, The Film Consortium and Pathé making an impact and the newly-formed Film Council would soon be outlining plans to distribute Lottery money via The Premiere Fund, the New Cinema Fund and the Film Development Fund. The distribution nut was harder to crack but Entertainment, PolyGram, FilmFour and Pathé occasionally took on the might of the majors.

However, the balloon was burst in 1998 when Philips, the Dutch company that owned PolyGram, decided to sell it on to Seagram. PolyGram's film division had functioned as a production and distribution company led by Michael Kuhn and overseen in Britain by Stewart Till, and not only financed British films but nurtured and supported British talent. The table of the top 30 UK films of the decade clearly shows PolyGram's influence and ability to steer films to popular success. Arguably, without PolyGram we would not have spent so much time looking at the talents of Danny Boyle, Duncan Kenworthy, Richard Curtis and Hugh Grant to name but a few, or the partnership it established with Working Title run by Tim Bevan and Eric Fellner. The dream of a European-based studio system to take on the might of the Hollywood Studio system was effectively over.

PolyGram's demise was much worse than the falls of Goldcrest, Palace Pictures and HandMade Films a decade or so earlier because the film division was still producing hits. Indeed, *Notting Hill*, released in 1999, was to be PolyGram's final hurrah.

But it would be wrong to assess the decade of British cinema merely in commercial terms. By looking at a selection of films featuring British actor Ray Winstone and actress Helena Bonham Carter (who have not featured in other films in this book), it is possible to encapsulate the trends and shifts that defined British cinema in the 1990s. Alongside their successes the celebrated actors starred in films that suffered from either a lack of a wider distribution or no distribution at all.

Top 30 UK films at UK box-office 1990-2000

	Title	Distributor	Box Office (£)
1	The Full Monty (1997)	Twentieth Century Fox	52,232,058
2	Notting Hill (1999)	Universal	31,006,109
3	Chicken Run (2000)	Pathe	29,514,237
4	The World Is Not Enough (1999)	UIP	28,576,504
5	Four Weddings and a Funeral (1994)	Rank	27,762,648
6	Shakespeare In Love (1999)	UIP	20,814,499
7	Tomorrow Never Dies (1997)	UIP	19,584,504
8	Billy Elliot (2000)	UIP	18,386,715
9	GoldenEye (1995)	UIP	18,245,572
10	Bean (1997)	PolyGram	17,972,562
11	Sense and Sensibility (1996)	Columbia TriStar	13,632,700
12	The Beach (2000)	Twentieth Century Fox	13,332,236
13	Sliding Doors (1997)	UIP	12,434,715
14	Trainspotting (1996)	PolyGram	12,433,450
15	Snatch (2000)	Columbia TriStar	12,326,923
16	Lock, Stock and Two Smoking Barrels (1998)	PolyGram	11,784,141
17	Spiceworld (1997)	PolyGram	11,401,855
18	East is East (1999)	FilmFour	10,374,926
19	Kevin & Perry Go Large (2000)	Icon	10,247,636
20	Little Voice (1998)	Buena Vista	8,502,367
21	The Commitments (1991)	Twentieth Century Fox	8,285,701
22	The Borrowers (1997)	PolyGram	8,003,575
23	Angela's Ashes (1999)	UIP	7,753,488
24	Waking Ned (1998)	Twentieth Century Fox	7,055,261
25	Mary Shelley's Frankenstein (1994)	Columbia TriStar	6,034,999
26	Elizabeth (1998)	PolyGram	5,536,790
27	Much Ado About Nothing (1992)	Entertainment	5,505,603
28	Emma (1996)	Buena Vista	5,283,225
29	Eyes Wide Shut (1999)	Warner Brothers	5,259,066
30	Mickey Blue Eyes (1999)	Universal	5,192,599

Source: Nielsen EDI, BFI The Stats: An overview of the film, television, video and DVD industries 1990-2003

RAY WINSTONE

Ray Winstone's reputation as an actor was enhanced during his appearances in British films during the 1990s despite any obvious box-office success. His hard man image was utilised in films such as *Ladybird, Ladybird*; *Nil By Mouth* (UK, 1997); and *Face*. He also turned in a harrowing performance in *The War Zone* (UK/Italy, 1998), a story about incest. Of these films *Face*, produced by BBC Films and distributed by Twentieth Century Fox yielded the biggest return at the box-office (£1,197,547). However, the other films drew critical acclaim. Interestingly they featured two British actors who had found fame in Hollywood in the role of director.

Gary Oldman's *Nil By Mouth*, is a disturbing autobiographical account of the lives of a South East London working class family dealing with domestic violence, drug abuse, petty crime and drunkenness. As an actor Oldman had moved to Hollywood to play villains. Returning to South East London he earned much praise for the stark honesty of his work, drawing comparisons with Loach's own social realist tradition, which continued to be realised in *Ladybird, Ladybird*.

Equally disturbing was Tim Roth's directorial debut in *The War Zone*, providing Winstone with yet another challenging role as a father who commits incest. UIP and FilmFour backed *Ladybird, Ladybird* and *The War Zone* respectively with limited art house screenings (seven and eight screens), which yielded small-box office returns of under £200,000. *Nil By Mouth* was backed by Twentieth Century Fox on more screens (61) and did considerably better by bringing in £789,171.

However, Winstone also appeared in two films that showed the fragile nature of the British film cinema during the 1990s – *Fanny & Elvis* (UK/France, 1999) and *Five Seconds to Spare* (UK, 1999). *Fanny & Elvis* was a comedy, which on paper looked like it would turn out as another quirky British hit featuring Kerry Fox, David Morrissey, Jennifer Saunders and Ben Daniels alongside Winstone. Sadly, this film with a £3.2m budget drawn from Arts Council of England Lottery funds and the Film Consortium, Granada, France 2, Cinéma, Canal+, Scala Productions and supported by the MEDIA Programme drew in a meagre return of £161,656. UIP distributed it on 135 screens but it averaged just £529 per screen. Likewise, *Five Seconds to Spare*, a thriller based on the novel *The Dwarfs of Death* by Jonathan Coe, looked on paper like it would do well, but it never managed a theatrical release and eventually found its way onto DVD in 2003. BBC1 finally screened it on 13th November 2005.

In 2000 Winstone donned some speedos and put in another top-notch performance as a retired gangster in *Sexy Beast* and seemed at home alongside British acting stalwarts Michael Caine, Bob Hoskins, Tom Courtnay, David Hemmings and Helen Mirren in *Last Orders* (UK/Germany, 2001).

HELENA BONHAM CARTER

At the beginning of the decade Helena Bonham Carter was associated with costume dramas and roles in Merchant Ivory Productions such as *Room With a View* and *Maurice* and indeed the 1990s began with a role in *Howards End*. The film brought *Merchant Ivory* three Oscars and further success followed by *The Remains of the Day* which was nominated for eight Academy Awards. Merchant Ivory didn't enjoy such a degree of success for the rest of the decade but unlike many others the company continued to make films in the 2000s with the likes of *The Mystic Masseur* (UK/India, 2001) and *The White Countess* (UK/Germany/USA/China, 2005), which was to be Merchant's last film before his death in May 2005.

Bonham Carter was to join forces (professionally and for a while personally) with Kenneth Branagh in *Mary's Shelley's Frankenstein*. The film cost £19m and was one of those peculiar 'is it a British film'. It featured a strong British cast and was filmed at Shepperton Studios but funded mainly came from the US and Japan. Similarly, *Margaret's Museum* (UK/Canada, 1995), which afforded her a grittier role, was set within an isolated mining community in Nova Scotia and so didn't seem like a British film at all, even though it was a Canadian UK co-production that received funding from Skyline Film and Television and support from British Screen. Distributed by Metrodome on just four screens the film didn't pick up a big audience.

The same was not true of *The Wings of the Dove*, based on the Henry James novel, which gave Bonham Carter a best actress Oscar nomination. The film was financed by Miramax and distributed by Buena Vista and drew in a reasonable audience for a costume drama.

However, Bonham Carter also appeared in a couple of films that on paper seemed like they should do well. The first was the Lottery-funded Keep the *Aspidistra Flying*, based on George Orwell's novel and co-starring Richard E Grant. It was the Opening Gala film of the London Film Festival in 1998. It received a small release by First Independent, a distributor that would not survive to the end of the decade. Bonham Carter also starred with Sam Neill in *The Revengers' Comedies* (UK/France, 1998) a BBC Film which had a US release as *Sweet Revenge* but not a UK one and it ended up being screened on BBC2 on 30 December 1999.

During the decade, Hollywood called for Bonham Carter and gave her some roles to took her away from her costume drama image. They included *Mighty Aphrodite* (USA, 1995), *Fight Club* (USA/Germany, 1999) and Tim Burton's remake of *Planet of the Apes* (USA, 2001).

In 2003 she played Anne Boleyn to Winstone's Henry VIII in Granada TV's drama. Both Winstone and Bonham Carter cemented their reputations in British films during the 1990s but their appearances in less successful or downright unsuccessful films tells its own story about the fragile nature of the industry in Britain. Were the films that didn't get wider releases really so unworthy? Or were too many Hollywood films playing on British screens?

HOLLYWOOD RULES UK

During the 1990s the British film industry had seen intense scrutiny from various governments on ways to improve the industry - by the National Heritage Committee in March 1995, by the Advisory Committee on Film Finance in July 1996, and by the Film Policy Review Group in 1998.

In 1996 the Advisory Committee said: 'The British film industry is at present poorly organised to take a substantial share of the world film market. It is largely comprised of small independent producers. Multinational media companies dominate the distribution and exhibition sectors. This contrasts with the situation is the US, where film is one of the country's largest industries and where the Hollywood studios integrate production and distribution (and, overseas, exhibition), giving them almost total control over the value chain.'

Quite simply, the British film industry could not compete on a global stage without joining forces with the dominant forces in Hollywood and to a lesser extent those in Europe. If support from America stopped then it would be reduced to a cottage industry. It is also worth reflecting that in the 1980s the British film industry saw its life flashing before its eyes and only substantial American investment into production, distribution and exhibition revived it.

Britain offered America creative and technical talents, not to mention excellent studio facilities, while the Americans offered finance and back-up promotional support. Without it British films would struggle to be made, struggle to be sold and struggle to be released.

BUILDING A SUSTAINABLE UK FILM INDUSTRY

The creation of the Film Council in 1999 to bolster the British film industry led to a reality check delivered to the film industry in November 2002 in a keynote address by Sir Alan Parker, chairman of the Film Council. At the beginning of the 1990s efforts were concentrated on improving film production by encouraging investment from abroad. Now the emphasis had switched to calling for a distribution-led industry.

During his speech Parker urged for mindsets to be altered. Tellingly he implored:

'We need to abandon forever the 'little England' vision of a UK industry comprised of small British film companies delivering parochial British films. That, I suspect, is what many people think of when they talk of a 'sustainable' British film industry. Well, it's time for a reality check. That 'British' film industry never existed, and in the brutal age of global capitalism, it never will.'

The theme of inward looking was picked up elsewhere when he stated: 'We have to stop defining success by how well British films perform in Milton Keynes. This is a big world – really successful British films like *Notting Hill* can make up to 85 per cent of their revenues outside the UK.'

Sir Alan Parker concluded with the observation: 'We have to stop worrying about the nationality of money. We want to encourage investment into our film industry from anywhere in the world – without tearing up the roots of cultural film production.' Indeed, his biggest film of the 1990s, *Evita* (USA, 1996), was a case in point. It received its funding from America and was shot at Shepperton, in Hungary and in Argentina with a cast featuring Madonna, Antonio Banderas and Jonathan Pryce and an international crew.

If American money combined with British talent produced hit films like *Notting Hill*, which in turn would lead to investment in other films, then this meant that British studios, actors and technicians would be employed. Furthermore, American money meant that the beloved British company Aardman Animation could expand its already popular slate of short films by going into full film production on a much bigger scale, which it did with its first feature *Chicken Run*.

In the end the public were surely not too bothered by the nationality of the films they watched. Their definitions were simply whether or not they were any good.

Notting Hill (1999) (UK/USA) UK Cert 15

Director: Roger Michell

Screenplay: Richard Curtis

Producer: Duncan Kenworthy

Production companies: Notting Hill Pictures; PolyGram Filmed Entertainment; Working Title Films

Production start date: 20/04/1998 **Budget:** £15m (estimated)

Distributor: Universal Pictures **UK Release date:** 21 May 1999

UK Box Office: £31,006,109 **USA Box Office:** $116.1m

Worldwide Box Office: $363.1m

From the creators of *Four Weddings and a Funeral* – or so the publicity read – came an attempt to prove that its formula for a successful British movie could work again. Richard Curtis scripted another rom com, produced by Duncan Kenworthy and featuring the charms of Hugh Grant. All that was required was an American actress co-star (to sell the film) and a good supporting middle-class British cast. Billing it as the follow-up to *Four Weddings and a Funeral* could also do the film's prospects no harm.

In some ways *Notting Hill* represents an end of term account of how far the British film industry had progressed from its bleak outlook in 1989. However, it would be wrong to dismiss it as a Brit rom com by numbers because the craft of the film and its knowing way to push the right buttons turned it into not only one of the most successful films of the year but one of the top releases of the decade.

It also signalled the last moments of PolyGram's brave attempt to compete with the Americans in engaging in a studio system from production, distribution and onto exhibition. PolyGram's sudden demise foresaw a period of boom and bust in the British film industry where fortunes relied heavily on American support.

SYNOPSIS

Divorced travel bookshop owner William Thacker lives and works in his favourite part of London – Notting Hill. He shares his house with a blue door with his eccentric, unkempt, Welsh flatmate, Spike, and he works with his cheery but gormless colleague Martin. His world is turned upside down when a world famous actress casually walks into his life.

Popping out to buy orange juice William walks straight into Anna Scott, soaking both of them with the juice. With his house yards away he persuades the star to go and clean up. She leaves him with a kiss and an unlikely romance develops. Posing uncomfortably as a journalist from *Horse and Hound* at a press launch for her new film, William asks Anna out that evening. Anna is unfazed by the evening spent with his friends and she dates William again. However, he beats a retreat when he learns that Anna's boyfriend is in town.

When Scott is splashed over the tabloids due to some nude photos surfacing she unexpectedly chooses to seek sanctuary with William at his home in Notting Hill. Eventually, she persuades William to go to bed with her. However, their morning bliss is short-lived when a posse of press photographers install themselves on William's doorstep to snap photos of him, Anna and even Spike. Anna is furious and after calling for a chauffeur leaves.

Through the next six months William becomes morose but gradually believes that he has moved on after his strange affair with Anna. However, on a tip by his friend Max he learns that Anna is back filming in London. He overhears her dismiss him to a fellow actor and fears that his moment of hope is gone.

Anna unexpectedly calls at William's bookstore and asks him to see her more often and give her a chance in love. William at first declines but comes to his senses and with the backing of all his friends they track Anna down to a press conference at the Savoy where the two are reconciled.

HOW IT WAS MADE

The starting point of the film came from Curtis conjuring up the consequences if a very normal bloke somehow ended up dating a very famous person. He then chose Notting Hill as an area since he lived on its doorstep and thought it would be the cool type of place that an American actress would want to explore.

The team that brought the world *Four Weddings and a Funeral* more or less came back together with Duncan Kenworthy again producing. Although he was at pains to state that *Notting Hill* was not a sequel to *Four Weddings*, it was clear that people would note the similarities and have certain expectations about another rom com starring Grant. Early on it was even suggested that Mike Newell might direct, but he had already plumped for the American comedy drama *Pushing Tin* (1999). Instead, Roger Michell, who was noted for his theatre and TV work with BBC adaptations of Jane Austen's *Persuasion* and *The Buddha of Suburbia*, took to the helm as director.

Having secured Grant to once again play Curtis' alter ego on screen, attentions turned to the role of Scott, who had to be convincing as a world famous Hollywood actress. Casting proved simpler than the producers had imagined since Julia Roberts, the first choice, was enthusiastic for taking the lead.

The all-important back-up British cast featured the crop of familiar TV faces from BBC sit coms such as Emma Chambers, known to many as Alice, from the Curtis BBC sit com the *Vicar of Dibley*, Tim McInnerny who had played Captain Darling in Curtis/Ben Elton scripted *Blackadder Goes Forth* and James Dreyfus who played DC Goody in Elton's BBC sit com the *Thin Blue Line*. Welsh actor Rhys Ifans who had starred in *Twin Town*, and Gina McKee who had appeared in BBC2's hit drama *Our Friends in the North* came through as emerging talents. Added to this was Richard Macabe who had appeared in Michell's *Persuasion*, stalwart actor Hugh Bonneville and a cameo from Perrier award-winning comedian Dylan Moran.

Despite having two high-profile actors in Roberts and Grant, the team decided to film as much on location in Notting Hill as possible and Portobello Road, Westbourne Park Road and even the Coronet Cinema become the essential backdrop to the romantic story. Filming eventually took place in April 1998.

Ironically, the production and location team's biggest headache came when wishing to shoot the red carpet clips around the Empire Leicester Square since the film would receive its world premiere at the same cinema in May 1999.

KEY ISSUES

Where *Four Weddings and a Funeral* had been a surprise and welcome hit, *Notting Hill* was a different beast, albeit honed from the *Four Weddings* mould, but this time with a great deal more confidence. The makers of *Notting Hill* knew that they had the potential for lightning to strike again and this faith in the overall marketability, skill and execution of the film was rewarded.

However, as many a producer and film-maker will testify, success in the film business is never guaranteed. On one level *Notting Hill* is just an amiable, neatly assembled, crowd-pleasing rom com; on the other it is a film that used a blueprint from another to construct its success.

In your dreams, mate

'This is the sort of thing that happens in dreams – not in real life,' stammers William as he sits in front of Scott, the world's most famous actress. *Notting Hill* is constructed as a male fantasy, dream come true. It has a fairy tale opening when Anna walks into William's bookshop, a fairy tale middle when Anna seeks refuge in William's house after a tabloid scandal rocks her world, and a fairy tale ending when Anna and William live happily ever after.

In suspending our disbelief we identify with William's assertion that meeting Anna was 'surreal'. Indeed, for anyone who has brushed shoulders with a star in an everyday life situation there is a complex moment of believing you know the person from their work, but at the same time not knowing that person at all. Anna sums this up when she quotes from actress Rita Hayworth: 'They go to bed with Gilda; they wake up with me.' Anna clarifies the point by stating: 'Men went to bed with the dream.'

William strikes it lucky pretty much throughout the film and seems unaware of his good fortune by coyly declaring: 'Well, I suppose in the dream scenario I just – ahem – change my personality because you can do that in dreams and walk across and kiss the girl.' His rude awakening comes later when he discovers that the world's most famous actress' boyfriend is back in town to which he declares: 'This is a fairly strange reality to be faced with.'

The fairly strange reality is also faced to comic effect with the reaction from William's friends at the dinner party, which Anna attends. This ranges from the gushing star-struck awe dished out by Honey to the impervious happy oblivion maintained by Bernie.

Yet the theme of separating the real from the image is illustrated by the scene of the lads in the restaurant talking about Anna based on her persona as portrayed in the papers, with one of them tastefully remarking that: 'she's absolutely gagging for it.' William's gallant attempt to intervene leads him to declare: 'The person you're talking about is a real person and I think she probably deserves a little bit more consideration.'

In the end the dreamlike fantasy world which unites Anna and William is conveniently unravelled when she states: 'The fame thing isn't really real you know,' and then proceeds to say the film's most infamous line: 'Don't forget, I'm also just a girl, standing in front of a boy, asking him to love her.' William, naturally ruins the moment by not falling into Anna's arms and adopts a pragmatic approach – but after coaxing from his friends and an unlikely denouement in front of the world's press – his dreams do come true and the rich American actress gets her poor British bookshop owner.

Calling the shots

One minor element running through the film is the relationship between the hopeless, failing Brits and the successful, rich Americans. William runs a failing travel bookshop, Tony's restaurant venture closes after several months, and Bernie is made redundant from his highly-paid job in the City. Max and Bella are happily married but their misfortune is experienced as a result of Bella's accident that leaves her wheelchair-bound and unable to have children. For all their cheerful optimism Spike, Honey and Martin are never going to set the world on fire. This point is illustrated in Max's preamble to the last brownie contest when he declares: 'Having you here, Anna, firmly establishes what I've long suspected, that we really are the most desperate lot of under-achievers.'

In stark contrast Anna is a success story earning $15m on her last movie, picking up an Oscar and treating William to a gift of an original Chagall painting to replace his poster copy.

Anna's dominance manifests itself in her relationship with William. In most cases she calls the shots. She gives William an intense passionate kiss after she returns to his flat for a bag. She then summons him to meet her at a press interview. Admittedly, William does ask her out to Honey's birthday meal but Anna is soon back to her bossy best by scaling a fence to get into the private communal gardens and again kissing William. She then blows hot and cold by first inviting him up to her room at the Ritz only to reveal that she has a boyfriend. However, she comes back into William's life using his house as a bolthole and initiates sex (after he has acted like a gent and slept on the sofa). She then breaks his heart when the press photographers are encamped outside William's house, snapping cruelly: 'Newspapers last forever. I'll regret this forever.'

Despite his attempts to see her on the set of her film it is Anna again who comes back into the bookshop and declares a desire to stay with William. He declines the offer but then makes his bold move to agree to see her at a crowded press conference – where else?

Spike

When Anna Scott and William Thacker aren't conforming to the rom com model – meet unexpectedly, fall in love, argue, make up, live happily ever after – they are given some good lines. Hers tend to be smart retorts, while his are self-deprecating or slightly surreal observations – it is the role of Spike as the unkempt fool that enhances the comic aspect of the film.

He comes close to stealing the film from the star-studded lovers. Ifans gives the character a physical presence, which complements his daft, sometimes corny lines. We see him modelling three tasteless t-shirts in an attempt to get off with a woman, mistaking mayonnaise for yoghurt, donning William's wet suit and appearing in his underpants to the waiting press. The latter scene is nicely played when Spike returns to the house and checks himself out in the mirror: 'Not bad, not bad at all. Well-chosen briefs, I'd say. Chicks love grey. Mmm. Nice firm buttocks.'

Although he is meant to represent the flatmate from hell – never cleaning, never taking messages and never out when you want him to be – Spike manages the trick of being quite likeable. However, whether anyone whose romantic life was as complicated as William's would ever open up to 'Spikey' is another matter.

Anna Scott – film star

Another strand running through the film is a not too detailed look at the film industry as experienced by Scott. In the opening sequence we see her star status as photos of her appear on the cover of *Empire*, *Newsweek* and *Marie Claire* magazines. Her image is also plastered on the side of London buses and she is observed in videos.

The endless round of press interviews focus on William's inept performance as a journalist of Horse and Hounds interviewing the stars of Scott's sci-fi romp, Helix. We also see William helping Anna rehearse her awful lines for her next blockbuster. When William alludes to Jane Austen and Henry James, Anna declares: 'You never get anyone in *Wings of a Dove* saying: 'Inform the Pentagon, we need black star cover'.' But as if to keep its finger on the pulse of the times we also see Anna shooting a costume drama at Kenwood House, Hampstead – an American-funded film with a British crew. She also attends a press conference and later on we catch glimpses of her and William at the premiere of her latest film.

Strangely, despite all these scenes Anna's status is largely seen from William's point of view. No one at Honey's birthday meal probes her about her career. For comic effect we learn about stunt bottoms, but Anna's craft as a leading actress seems largely based on looks rather than acting ability, as witnessed from the few clips we see of her in other films.

Four Weddings and a *Notting Hill*

It is inevitable that *Notting Hill* should be compared with *Four Weddings and a Funeral*.

Both succeed in their rom com intentions but the bigger budget afforded to *Notting Hill* shows – it was made for £13m more than *Four Weddings*. There is nothing in *Four Weddings* as showy as the *Ain't No Sunshine When She's Gone* sequence when William walks continuously through the market streets of Notting Hill passing through the seasons of the year and experiencing sun, wind, rain, snow and spring again.

Four Weddings featured a strong ensemble cast. While *Notting Hill* also gives William a group of friends, these characters merely provide back-up support for his story. There are other love interests – Max and Bella, Honey and Spike – but they are minor.

For those seeking connections Grant more or less reprises his character from Charles to William written for him by Curtis. Ironically, Grant played the Curtis characters so successfully that he declared that people assumed that he was that character in real life. Once again Grant's character falls for an American woman and the film finishes almost with a knowing wink to the audience with a wedding scene.

Generally though *Notting Hill* and *Four Weddings and a Funeral* can stand alone on their own merits and their similarities are really down to the personnel involved in making them. Nevertheless, *Notting Hill*'s associations with its former film did no harm whatsoever in promoting it when it was released.

SCENE ANALYSIS – I'M ALSO JUST A GIRL STANDING IN FRONT OF A BOY

Both *Four Weddings and a Funeral* and *Notting Hill* have a parallel scene when the female love interest turns up unexpectedly and utters memorable lines. In the case of *Four Weddings* a drenched Carrie finally melts to Charles' charms when she says wistfully: 'Is it raining. I hadn't noticed.' *Notting Hill* obliges by putting Scott and William back in similar territory with Scott finally falling for William.

The scene is interesting for the awkwardness of the moment, the physical distance that Anna and William keep from each other, and their static nature. It is also played out with the absence of background music, which would otherwise break the tension or might lead the audience to the wrong emotional conclusion.

The first point to note is how the world's most famous actress has dressed down to greet William. Unlike the first time she entered William's shop, she now wears a blue cardigan with matching blue skirt and top and flip flops – no shades, no beret, no cool jacket.

William moves forward to greet her but keeps his distance. As the two speak we get midshots taken from behind their shoulders in a leisurely shot reverse shot sequence. For a couple who are in love their nervous gestures, forced smiles, awkward silences, and coy glances allow for the scene to maintain a level of tension, that is broken by a series of interruptions.

First, Anna breaks the strained small talk by pointing to the wrapped gift she has brought for William. She seems embarrassed to be handing over a present to someone she has treated quite badly. William walks forward and thanks Anna whose smile is replaced by a nervous look. Both Anna and William look down to the gift as if not wishing to achieve too much eye contact with each other.

For once, William seems more relaxed than usual, feeling the game is up and the need to chase Anna has finished. As Anna attempts to not only apologise to William but also to suggest that they meet again, we get a close-up shot of her face, met by a close-up reaction of William. However, the camera then cuts away to a longshot as Anna appears to summon up her courage repeating: 'The thing is, the thing is…'

Her train of thought is interrupted when from behind her shoulder we see the bookshop's resident eccentric walk through the door and break her flow. William assertively dismisses the man and he prompts Anna to continue. She states in a nervous voice whether William would want to see her 'a little or a lot maybe.' Once more we get a close-up of Anna's face as she asks William if he could like her again. In assertive mode William points out that he had overheard her conversation with the actor at Hampstead when she dismissed him out of hand.

This tense moment is interrupted when Martin appears and tells William that his mother is on the phone. William turns to look at Martin but then returns to face Anna while still addressing his colleague. There follows a slight comic interlude where Martin is left alone with Anna and true to form mistakes her work with that of Demi Moore.

When William returns we are somewhat surprised when he politely declines Anna's request to restart their relationship. Again Anna's reaction is caught in close-up and after a pause her forced smile returns and she says: 'Yes' in response to William's 'No.' As Anna nervously attempts to say farewell we cut to a close-up of William who explains his reasons for not seeing Anna, citing that his heart would not recover from another rebuff. As he speaks his face breaks into occasional smiles and his eyelids blink nervously as he explains his decision contrasting Beverly Hills and Notting Hill.

With their relationship on a knife-edge Anna says: 'Fine. Good decision. Good decision,' but her smile carries no conviction. Starting off with a more serious demeanour Anna plays her last card with a slight hint of tearful tremor in her voice: 'Don't forget, I'm just a girl, standing in front of a boy asking him to love her.' Again Anna's face is contorted by a forced smile, which manages to convey more pain than pleasure.

Had all gone well for Anna we would have caught her embracing William in a close-up. Instead, William is observed with a rather non-plussed look on his face. There follows yet another awkward silence and the camera cuts away to a long shot. Anna walks forward and gives William a tender, if fraternal, kiss on his cheek before backing away awkwardly with a final gesture in the direction of the wrapped gift. As she leaves the shop, and presumably William's life forever, he is observed motionless from behind, his hands rigidly placed behind his back.

Notting Hill calls the audience's bluff by building up a scene that by its association with *Four Weddings and a Funeral*, would end with a resolved conclusion. Instead, it merely allows for the film to steer its way to the press conference finale. In order to do this William, (in front of all his friends) recalls the scene that we have just seen enacted and carefully repeats Anna's 'just a girl in front of a boy' line as the penny finally drops and the madcap dash to achieve the happily ever after ending that the film demands takes place.

REACTION

Notting Hill was perceived as another crowd-pleaser. It triumphed at the box-office with receipts of more than £31m in the UK, making it more successful than *Four Weddings and a Funeral*. Of course, the impact the film had was lesser due to the steady rise in British films since the early 1990s.

It picked up modest recognition, winning the Audience Award at the BAFTAs and the Peter Sellers Award For Comedy, Evening Standard British Film Awards 2000 but the real triumph of the film was that a winning formula had been tried again with favourable results.

On both sides of the Atlantic the press seemed to enjoy the film with some comparisons being made with the press conference scene in *Roman Holiday* (USA, 1953), while others tried to give Grant the status of a modern Cary Grant. Reviewers felt that Roberts brought more to the table than Curtis's previous female love interest Andie MacDowell and Rhys Ifans was singled out for his comic performance. Critics were divided by the on-screen chemistry between Grant and Roberts, some finding it hard to fathom why a film star would fall for such a patent loser.

Curtis received praise from Peter Bradshaw in *The Guardian*, who wrote 'Mr Curtis is unashamedly a writer with a strong, personal style and, by virtue of diligent crafting under the editorial eye of his wife, Emma Freud, produces witty, literate scripts with proper gags.' But there were also snipes about the film, particularly the lack of a cosmopolitan depiction of *Notting Hill* and even references to the way that it pandered to a commercial audience, Peter Preston, also writing in *The Guardian*, remarked: '*Notting Hill* will be a success because it has been constructed not to fail.'

Chicken Run (2000) (UK/USA) UK Cert U

Directors: Peter Lord; Nick Park

Screenplay: Karey Kirkpatrick; [Jack Rosenthal]

Producers: Peter Lord; David Sproxton; Nick Park

Production companies: DreamWorks LLC; Aardman Chicken Run Limited; Pathé Image; Aardman Animations; [Allied Film-makers]

Production start date: 15/09/1997 **Budget:** £27.40m (estimated)

Distributor: Pathé **UK Release date:** 30 June 2000

UK Box Office: £29,514,237 **USA Box Office:** $106.8m

Worldwide Box Office: $225m

With the year-on-year increase in video sales, family entertainment was big business not just in the cinema but in the home too. A whole generation of children spent a good proportion of the 1990s endlessly watching their favourite Disney films. Disney was canny in its releases and spread its classic films out while making something of a comeback in the cinema with *The Lion King* (1994), which addressed a new audience. However, its traditional drawing methods were being replaced by computer-generated illustrations. In turn, the release of *Toy Story* in 1995, credited as being the first CGI feature, created a whole new animated ball game. The race was on to create more CGI films, complete with top-drawer actors to voice over its characters, and to wow and entertain audiences of all ages. The future seemed bright – the future seemed digital.

Top video retail films 1991–2000

1991 – *Fantasia*	1996 – *Toy Story*
1992 – *Cinderella*	1997 – *Independence Day*
1993 – *The Jungle Book*	1998 – *Titanic*
1994 – *Snow White and the Seven Dwarfs*	1999 – *A Bug's Life*
1995 – *The Lion King*	

Source: BVA, BFI The Stats: An overview of the film, television, video and DVD industries 1990-200

In Britain the lucrative family film was a genre that British film-makers by and large had overlooked with some exceptions such as *The Wind in the Willows* (UK, 1995) and *The Borrowers*. While animated entertainment did pretty well on children's television with programmes like *Thomas the Tank Engine*, it seemed that the prerogative for family feature film entertainment would remain in the hands of Disney Studios.

Arguably one of the most successful British film production studios of the 1990s was the Oscar award-winning Aardman Animations, based in Bristol. Formed by Peter Lord and David Sproxton in the 1970s, Aardman first came to attention via the creation of a stop-motion plasticine character called Morph who used to appear in the BBC programme *Take Hart*. In 1985 Nick Park joined Aardman and in 1989 *Creature Comforts*, his vox pop film featuring animated animals mouthing real vox pop interviews, won an Oscar for Best Animated Short. Park would become synonymous with his creations of Wallace and Gromit, who had three cracking short films released in the 1990s by the BBC – *A Grand Day Out* (1991), *The Wrong Trousers* (1993) and *A Close Shave* (1995) – with the latter two winning Oscars.

Buoyed by its Oscar successes, Aardman took its first steps into feature film work by signing a five-picture deal with Hollywood studio, DreamWorks. Aardman had conquered a TV audience and an international audience with its quirky British shorts – now it remained to be seen if it could pull off the trick with a full-length feature and whether its unique take on colloquial British life circa 1950s would avoid interference from its American partners. In 1995 *Chicken Run*, a prison escape caper, was hatched.

SYNOPSIS

Set in a chicken farm somewhere in Yorkshire, England, farmer Mr Tweedy is convinced that his chickens are plotting an escape, much to the annoyance of his overbearing wife, Mrs Tweedy. Meanwhile, feisty chicken Ginger is determined to escape with the rest of her chickens for a better life of freedom.

Matters come to a head when during a roll call Mrs Tweedy pulls out the luckless Edwina who has not been laying any eggs and takes her into a shed to kill her for a roast dinner. Mrs Tweedy, dissatisfied with the yield the eggs are providing for her business, invests in a

273

chicken pie-making machine.

Ginger's hopes are changed when she sees Rocky, the lone free-range rooster from America, crash into the chicken farm hurting his wing in the process. Ginger urges Rocky to help to teach the chickens to fly, which he reluctantly agrees to do after Ginger discovers that he has escaped from a circus and threatens to turn him in.

Having put on a party to cheer up the chickens the mood is changed again when the pie-making machine is installed and Mr Tweedy takes Ginger for the first pie. Rocky bravely assists in the rescue when he and Ginger land inside the machine facing perilous close shaves before putting a spanner in the works which forces the contraption to fail, much to Mrs Tweedy's displeasure.

Back in the chicken coop Rocky and Ginger share a tender moment on top of the roof but in the morning Ginger finds that he has gone. Ginger turns to Fowler and gets him to explain the RAF. Inspired by his answer she rallies the chickens to build a flying machine to escape over the fence.

Rocky reappears, wracked with guilt after seeing a poster for Mrs Tweedy's pies. He helps Ginger with the ramp and they manage to scramble onto the flying machine, chased by Mrs Tweedy. The chickens escape to an idyllic new life and many little chicks are seen hearing the stories of bravery from Fowler.

HOW IT WAS MADE

While the world was being enthralled by computer-generated animation Aardman Animations resolutely stayed with its unique but very time-consuming stop-motion plasticine animation. This was to be its first excursion into the world of full-length feature films and Park felt reluctant to debut with a Wallace and Gromit adventure. Instead, in quite a bold move, the Aardman team took to chickens as the lead characters. It determined to maintain the quirky Britishness of its work and by and large DreamWorks was happy to let it have its way.

In 1995, Lord and Park started the two and a half year process of designing the characters and creating a detailed storyboard before any filming took place. Providing development support, Pathé joined them midway through. By 1997, DreamWorks had come on board and injected the necessary funding to get such a big project off the ground. Essentially Lord and Park's starting point was to create a version of the classic film The Great Escape (USA, 1963) — with chickens!

American Karey Kirkpatrick, who had recently adapted Roald Dahl's James and the Giant Peach (UK/USA, 1996), for the animated film came on board as screenwriter and worked closely with Lord and Park on the film.

Lord and Park had met Mel Gibson while they were attending the Oscars and discovered that he was a fan of Wallace and Gromit. They tested their lines for Rocky using lines from the Mel Gibson film *Maverick* (USA, 1994), upon which the character of Rocky was loosely based.

BBC's hit sit com *Absolutely Fabulous* provided a couple of voice members. Rocky's romantic lead Julia Sawalha, known to many as the sensible daughter Saffron, voiced Ginger and Jane Horrocks, who played Bubble, voiced Babs. Elsewhere, the double act of rodents came courtesy of Timothy Spall and Phil Daniels, while Miranda Richardson was heard as the dastardly Mrs Tweedy. With the exception of Mel Gibson, the cast made no effort to alter their regional accents, as witnessed by comedian Lynn Ferguson's role as the Scottish 'Mac'.

With a script sorted out the voice actors were brought in to interpret the characters models which had yet to be finalised. Some sound tweaking occurred later on but the voiced characters informed the animators on how the physical characters might look in the film.

By the time it came to making the film a huge crew of more than 180 representing 30 sets, and 18 animators assembled to undertake the painstaking stop-motion project, which took 18 months. The meticulous process meant that each individual movement in each frame of each shot was done by hand. With film running at 24 frames per second, which yields approximately one minute of film action per week, this really was intensive labour but also a labour of love.

The heads and the hands of the main figures were made from plasticine and the chickens were technically awkward to get right in terms of replicating real movements and so the team adapted their figures for flexibility. Their main bodies were adapted from plasticine casts and the joins between torso and head neatly covered with an array of scarves. However, some CGI work was necessary in post-production and also to achieve effects such as the gushing gravy.

With sound effects and music added to the action shots nearly five years after its original conception *Chicken Run* was ready to be released.

KEY ISSUES

For Aardman Animations the question was whether it could translate the success of its short films into an 80-minute feature film? On top of that came the added pressure of working with a major Hollywood studio and pleasing its paymaster while still holding on to Aardman's unique artistic integrity. Most of all, its decision not to go with Wallace and Gromit and instead hatch an entirely new film with new characters was a gamble.

The great escape

For the older audience the joy of watching *Chicken Run* was the anticipation that the film would pay homage to John Sturges' Christmas favourite *The Great Escape*. In fact, *Chicken Run* goes further with various other references ranging from other films – *Indiana Jones* (in Rocky and Ginger's escape from the pie machine) and *Stalag 17* (the coup where the chicken's do their planning is 17) to TV's *Star Trek* when Mac mimics Scotty's oft-quoted line: 'The engines can't take it.' Mrs Tweedy is also referred to as a 'cling-on' as she hangs by the string of lights as the plane is airborne.

The subtle and not so subtle references come thick and fast; the chicken who lays no eggs and is taken away to be eaten is called Edwina as a dig at former Health Minister Edwina Currie who once claimed that most of Britain's egg production was infected with the salmonella bacteria.

However, the blueprint from the film is clearly *The Great Escape*. Ginger doubles up on the roles played by Steve McQueen 'the cooler king' Hilts (she is taken to the coal bunker as punishment and replicates his baseball using a vegetable) and Richard Attenborough 'Big X' Barlett (as the driving force behind the escape attempts). Rocky also gets to parody Steve McQueen's role in the film when Captain Hilts asks Bartlett how many men he is planning to take out. Bartlett says: '250' to which Hilts replies: 'You're crazy. You oughta be locked up.' In *Chicken Run* the scene is replayed with Rocky saying: 'Let me get this straight. You want to get every chicken out of here at the same time?' To which Ginger responds: 'Of course,' leading Rocky to say: 'You're certifiable!'

Elsewhere, Gordon Jackson's role as 'Mac' 'Intelligence' is transferred straight across to the chicken called Mac; Fowler pays homage to David McCallum's dispersal role by releasing nuts and bolts concealed in his trouser legs; Ginger also gets to play Charles Bronson's Danny The Tunnel King, including authentic tapping with spade on rail as she is pulled forward. Finally, albeit not so directly, Fetcher and Nick are scroungers, as portrayed in the original film by James Garner as Hedley.

Despite many references to the Second World War, *Chicken Run* is not a direct parody of the film beyond the main premise. As much as it plays homage to other British war movies of the 1950s, the presence of Rocky as an American and the romantic interest in the film creates an interesting tension between Anglo American relations.

Who do you think you are kidding?

From the start the Aardman team insisted that *Chicken Run* was to be an Aardman movie featuring old-fashioned caricatures with regional accents and typically British expressions. In this respect *Chicken Run* stays very firmly in the post-war British tradition. Mrs Tweedy is seen running through her accounts using pounds shillings and pence as her currency and throughout the film characters use words and phrases such as 'Poppycock!',

'Codswallop', 'Well chuffed, I was', 'Face the facts, ducks,' 'You great lummox!', 'You stupid Norbert,' and 'heading for a fearful prang'. These expressions help to maintain a strong cultural identity without any need for translation.

The same is not true for the Scottish character Mac, whose accent Rocky fails to understand every time. This sly reference may be intended as a gentle ribbing of the Americans who couldn't understand films like *Trainspotting* (where some dialogue was reshot and the actors spoke slower). In any case Ginger, with Julia Sawalha's clear annunciation, is able to translate.

Elsewhere, Fowler gets to run through stiff upper lip officer class clichés including: 'When the senior officer called for a scramble, you'd hop in the old crate and tally-ho! Chocks away!' or 'Good grief! The turnips bought it.'

Fowler's character is antagonistic towards Rocky – 'Pushy Americans. Always showing up late for every war. Overpaid, oversexed and over here!' – and so also gets to follow the thread of American G.Is coming to Britain. The film gently exploits this strand by playing upon the cliché. The chickens are thrilled by Rocky's presence and are in awe of all things American. He obliges by flattering them with his charm. When asked why he came to England he replies: 'Why, all the beautiful English chicks, of course.'

Rocky, the all-action American hero, turns out to be not all that he's cracked up to be and ends up merely in a romantic role, rescuing and winning over Ginger. He also gets some good smooth lines of his own: 'Hey, easy Miss Hard Boiled. I think you're turning soft'. In the end it is the daft old plucky Brit Fowler who saves the day by flying 'the crate' out of the chicken farm. Ginger too is an all-action heroine who casts Mrs Tweedy adrift to a gravy splashdown on the dangling line and it is her passion and determination that wins the day.

At the end of the film when the credits have finished there appears to be a gentle swipe wafted towards the way of Hollywood when Fetcher and Nick pour scorn on Rocky's 'big shot' status: They conclude that: 'Showbiz folk are all the same.' Fetcher claims: 'The rats are the stars,' to which Nick complains ironically: 'We do all the hard work. He gets all the credit.'

A children's film for adults

There's more corn in *Chicken Run* to fill Mr. Tweedy's chicken feeder several times over, which makes it perfect for children and adults alike. Lord and Park were asked whether the film was aimed at children or adults, to which they cleverly replied that it was aimed at the child within themselves. Getting children into the cinema was not a problem since they could see the film purely on its own merit as a colourful, cracking yarn about chickens escaping from a chicken farm run by an evil woman and her gormless husband. It was also unusual that female characters were given such prominent roles – after all there are no female roles in *The Great Escape* – and so girls may have welcomed the slight change in gender roles from the usual stereotypes.

In keeping with the spirit of Wallace and Gromit, the humour is gentle and even Rocky's brash intervention is often dampened down. Apart from the scene where Edwina gets the chop the film is free from the dark side, which often seems a prerequisite to children's entertainment. Instead, *Chicken Run* always looks on the bright side of life and is accompanied by a supply of verbal and visual jokes – 'It's raining hen,' 'You call this pay? It's chicken feed,' 'The Lone Free Ranger', 'Poultry in motion!' 'Chocks away!' – some which might go over the heads of young children but get picked up by adults.

SCENE ANALYSIS – MRS TWEEDY'S CHICKEN PIES

Rocky's attempts to rescue Ginger from the chicken pie machine would be complex enough if it involved live-action characters, but even with plasticine heroes the thrills and spills come as thick and fast as the gravy meant for the pies.

The scenes of peril demonstrate the ingenuity and inventiveness of the action sequence. Along the way the camera work, tight editing and the lighting are also worth noting as we are led breathlessly from one moment to the next.

1. Ginger dangling upside down is released down a long shoot as Rocky, slipping and sliding on a conveyor belt, fails to catch her.

As Ginger is released into the shoot we get a shot from Ginger's perspective and the camera carries out a slight spiralling downward motion as we see Rocky leaning over the entrance with the woodened beams of the shed behind him. Then the metallic walls of the shoot become apparent before we cut back to a shot from Rocky's level of him looking down into the shaft.

2. Rocky tumbles down the long shaft when he accidentally releases the vegetables by standing on a lever.

As Rocky flies out of the shaft he is filmed from below and just as he falls out of shot we get his point of view angle as he heads towards rotating blades. Again the camera gives a slight tilt before cutting back to Rocky who heads straight towards the camera once more. This time as he goes out of frame we cut to a close-up of a bar and Rocky just grasping onto it.

3. Rocky catches up with Ginger as both find their feet trapped in pastry dough. A giant rolling pin device comes into view and just as Ginger looks like getting squashed Rocky bounces over, grabs hold of a rotating pulley and lifts them away from the rolling pin. Their fall is broken as they land into the centre of some flattened dough.

The lively music accompanying the action stops as Rocky and Ginger avoid the giant rolling pin, providing a false respite as Ginger calls out: 'look out'.

4. A rounded pastry cutter swings down and entraps Rocky and Ginger in the centre of a tin foil container. They are lifted up in a tin foil carton encased with pastry, which is sent off on a conveyor where chopped vegetables fill the trays and are to be topped off with gravy, which is fired from a gun.

We see an extreme close-up of the gun pointing straight at Rocky and Ginger, complete with a tiny dribble of gravy coming out. We cut to Rocky juggling a carrot, which is then stuffed into the barrel of the gun.

5. Rocky and Ginger are squashed by a device, which adds the upper crust of pastry to their tin carton.

Along with the music and Rocky and Ginger's yells we have the sounds of the machine in action. When Rocky and Ginger 'high five' after avoiding the gravy their celebration is interrupted with a circular, almost space age flashing device which stamps them and then emits a little radio signal sound.

6. They pop out of the top layer of pastry only to find that they are in the centre of an oven.

Encased within their pastry we see a close-up, set against a black background, of the tin foil and pastry and the shapes of Rocky and Ginger struggling to burst out - which they do.

As the flames of the oven fire up the camera moves quickly around Rocky and Ginger, who are still in their tray until all the flames are lit. As the camera completes its circular movement we get to see their escape route out of the oven door. The lighting in the oven subtly changes so that when Ginger and Rocky run towards the door they are lit up with a glowing orange light.

When Ginger returns for Rocky we are afforded a high overhead shot. There we witness the comic shapes that Rocky has made in all the pies as Ginger weaves her way between the pies to rescue him.

Again the music reaches a false crescendo when we see another extreme close-up of the oven door closing and Ginger just grabbing her hat in time as it shuts.

7. Rocky wipes himself clean while the whole system seems about to blow up with a spanner seen wedged between the cogs and the gravy pressure monitor reaching a critical pitch.

As the machine prepares to explode under the pressure we see several quick cuts to close-up shots of machinery parts – the spanner in the works, a slight tilted angle on a display saying System Blockage with a red light flashing, Mrs Tweedy turns, another slightly tilted angle of the Gravy Pressure gauge going into its red zone, Mr Tweedy in the foreground being lit by flashing lights pulls levers while Mrs Tweedy shouts at him in the background, the bolts fly out as gravy seeps through the seams and finally cogs are released before we get back to Rocky and Ginger running.

8. Rocky and Ginger race away from the cogs, which have become loose and roll after them. Their final escape from the machine comes as they reach the packaging exit where boxes line up. Lying on a box Rocky is stamped with a Mrs Tweedy's Chicken Pies label. Finally, they are free and escape just as Mrs Tweedy pulls the plug on the machine.

The sequence also gives us a romantic shot when Rocky and Ginger land on one of the boxes and we see a close-up of Ginger momentarily nestling beside Rocky before getting up to avoid the label.

The scene ends with a great final comic moment as the hapless Mr Tweedy thinks he has fixed the problem. Mrs Tweedy is seen with a pie carton mixture in her hand. Mr Tweedy turns to her and we get an extreme close-up of Mrs Tweedy delivering the pie to his face. As we hear the splurge we cut to the pie label as Ginger slaps it onto a wall in the chicken coup.

One of the greatest testaments to Aardman Animations' craft is the seemingly effortless way characters engage in such action sequences. It is hard to believe that these scenes are undertaken with a painstaking stop-action process. Yet the joy of watching these films is the attention to detail. The studio lovingly creates sets worthy of any Hollywood blockbuster and inserts its characters to act and react accordingly.

REACTION

Critics generally gave *Chicken Run* the thumbs up. Its success was reflected in box office receipts of more than £29m in the UK, making it the third most successful British box-office film of all time (behind *The Full Monty* and *Notting Hill*) and the third most successful film of 2000 (behind *Gladiator* and *Toy Story 2*). It also did excellent business in America, making more than $106m and rewarding DreamWorks' faith in the Bristol studio. DreamWorks' investment showed in its promotion of the film, which used such tags as 'This ain't no chick flick!' It also ran a trailer which parodied the trailer for *Mission Impossible 2* (known as *M:I-2* referring to *Chicken Run* as *C:R-1*). This may have worked as a clever marketing device, but leant more towards American culture than the pastiche of *The Great Escape* and was perhaps not entirely in keeping with the essence of the movie.

There would be no Oscar glory for the Aardman team, despite efforts to have *Chicken Run* nominated in the Best Film category. As a result of the interest coupled with the success of the CGI *Toy Story 2* (1999), a Best Animated Feature category was included for the 2002 Academy Awards. The film did pick up its share of nominations and settled for the Peter Sellers Award for Comedy – Evening Standard British Film Awards 2001.

The issue of Britishness and DreamWorks involvement would follow Park and Lord where they observed a subtle difference in attitudes in relation to the inclusion of Mel Gibson as Rocky. They stated that this was met with approval from Americans they spoke to but a slight sense of suspicion from some Brits. At a time where the future of the British film industry was under the spotlight the increasingly familiar article appeared. This time Andrew Pulver, writing in *The Guardian*, bemoaned the fact that the American audience got to see the film first: 'the decision to prioritise *Chicken Run*'s US box-office run is determined by one simple factor: it is not really British at all. Like the large majority of the films by which mainstream British cinema defines itself *Chicken Run* is bought and paid for by a foreign company. In *Chicken Run*'s case, it is DreamWorks SKG'.

However, to say that *Chicken Run* was not a British film does not take into account the amount of British artistic and creative talent that went into its making. To quote from a discussion between Nick and Fetcher it really boiled down to which came first - chicken or egg. In the case of *Chicken Run*, Aardman was given the money to make the film (as part of a five-film deal with DreamWorks). Without that funding it is unlikely that the scale and investment could have matched Aardman's ambitions to go into feature film production. Aardman would have been lucky to receive a fraction of the £27m spent on the feature had it stuck to British funding. Surely in the end the thing that mattered was that the film was a success and a British one at that.

Chicken Run's success carried on through the inevitable video release, nestling in at number four in the British video chart for 2000 (behind *Star Wars Episode 1*, *Toy Story 2*, and *Gladiator*). By the end of the decade DVD, with its bonus features, director's commentaries and deleted scenes, was slowly overtaking VHS as the format of choice. Initially, the retail market for DVDs suggested a slightly more adult audience before DVD machines hit consumer stores with a vengeance in the early 2000s. Nevertheless *Chicken Run* still made it into the top 10 DVDs for 2000.

CONCLUSION

Sure as eggs are eggs Aardman Animations could pride itself that its name was guaranteed to bring in a family audience who knew that they would be entertained with something that was typically British. Even with the financial assistance and full back-up from DreamWorks, it pulled off the coup of producing a film with its stamp on it. *Chicken Run* signalled a trend that would continue into the next decade of British family-orientated films. Up to that point they had been few and far between.

In 1997 author J.K. Rowling published her first novel, *Harry Potter and the Philosopher's Stone*. By 1999, following the phenomenal success of the Harry Potter books, Rowling sold the film rights to Warner Bros. with the proviso that the principal cast be kept strictly British, thereby echoing Aardman's request to maintain its British cultural status. In the next decade Harry Potter would dominate the family market, which in turn led to more family-orientated films being made. Aardman, in the meantime, had already cemented its reputation as a beloved British institution.

For the makers of *Notting Hill* the fact that lightning could strike twice was utilised in the 2000s. The British hit formula was to continue, albeit in a slightly refined way, particularly in the case of Hugh Grant's persona, which developed a more cynical aspect in the next decade with two Bridget Jones films and *About a Boy* before returning in the Curtis rom com fest *Love Actually*.

Whereas *Chicken Run* teases Americans about their special relationship with Britain, *Notting Hill* more or less admits Britain's reliance on America through the uneasy relationship between Anna Scott and William Thacker. She may find Thacker attractive but she still calls the shots and generally makes him feel insecure. This sums up the power base behind the emergence of British films in the 1990s.

If British cinema can be defined in such a way then the 1980s will be remembered for Collin Welland's passionate assertion that 'the British are coming'. This proved to be a false dawn. By the 1990s the statement that seemed to sum up British cinema in the 1990s came from another Oscar winner, Emma Thompson, who in October 2001 gave her frank opinion in a university newspaper about the myth surrounding the British film industry: 'The very phrase 'British film industry' depresses me. I don't think we've got a film industry and never have had.'

However, it is important to separate the distinctions. Instead of thinking of the British film industry, it is easier to think in terms of films made in Britain. Thankfully, the 1990s will be remembered for its wide range of British films – *The Full Monty*, *Trainspotting*, *Four Weddings and a Funeral*, *East is East*, *Secrets and Lies*, *Shakespeare in Love*, *The World is Not Enough*, *Ratcatcher*, *Notting Hill*, *Sense and Sensibility*, *The Crying Game* – rather than the money that financed them.

The next decade would be less extravagant by comparison with fewer risks being taken and, as a result, fewer edgier films such as *Trainspotting*. The 1990s gave many first-time directors their first chance with contrasting results. Nevertheless, in the 2000s trusted and tried formulas from the 1990s were to reap benefits with the Bridget Jones films representing the rom coms, *Bend it like Beckham* building on films like *Bhaji on the Beach* and *East is East*, and Bond films again reviewing the formula with *Casino Royale* (UK/USA/Germany/Czech Republic, 2006). Films made in Britain still made an impact on the international stage but there would no longer be calls for a sustainable film industry in Britain – that dream belonged firmly routed among the optimism of British cinema in the 1990s.

FURTHER READING

British Cinema of the 90s
Murphy, Robert (ed.) (BFI, 2001)

The British film business
Baillieu, Bill and Goodchild, John (John Wiley & Sons, 2002)

Report to the Secretary of State for National Heritage
(Department of National Heritage, July 1996)

A bigger picture: the report of the Film Policy Review Group.
(Department for Culture, Media and Sport, 1998)

The Stats An overview of the film, television, video and DVD industries 1990-2003
(BFI National Library, BFI Information Services, 2006)

BFI Film and Television Handbook (BFI, editions from 1990–2005)

Selected reviews/articles/references

UK films to smash British market share by Scott, Mary
Screen International N. 1237 (3 Dec 1999)

Notting Hill

Sight & Sound V.9 N.6 (1 Jun 1999) P.49-50 by O'Sullivan, Charlotte

Empire N.120 (1 June 1999) P.18-19 by Caroline Westbrook

Notting Hill Great by Jones, Alan
Film Review (1 June 1999) P.66-69

Interview with Roger Michell by Blair, Iain
Film + Video V.16 N.6 P.89-92

Chicken Run

Sight & Sound V.10 N.8 (1 Aug 2000) P.41-42 by Newman, Kim

Empire N.134 (1 Aug 2000) P.60 by Errigo, Angie

How Aardman Got a Free Range Run by Katzenberg, Jeffrey
Screen International N.1266 (7 July 2000) P.24

Rushes: The Bigger Picture
Sight & Sound V.10 N.1 (1 Jan 2000) P.4-5

DVD: *Chicken Run* (Pathé Distribution, 2000)

INDEX OF TABLES

Number of Films Produced in the UK 1980-90 8

Breakdown of Percentage of Films Released in the UK by Country 64

The UK Video/DVD Market 1990–2000 66

UK Cinema Admissions 1990–2000 93

Multiplex Sites and Screens 94

UK Sites and Screens 1990–2000 94–5

Top Films at the UK Box-Office 1990–2000 95

Number and Value of UK Films 1989–1999 121

Top Production Budget of Films made in the UK 1990–9 122

Top 20 All-Time Lottery-Funded List by UK Box-Office 154

Breakdown of UK Film Distribution by Releases and Box-Office 1990–1999 177

Types of Release for UK Films 1984–2000 180

British Black and Asian Films in the 1990s 205

Top 20 Films at the UK Box-Office 1990–2000 257

Top 30 Films at the UK Box-Office 1990–2000 259

Top Video Retail Films 1991–2000 272

INDEX

1985 Film Act   8–9, 39, 42

Aardman Animations 5, 231, 263, 272–6, 280–1

Aardman Chicken Run Limited   272

Abbott, Steve   109

ABC   97

Abraham, Jake   54

Academy Awards/Oscars   6–8, 16, 19, 26, 29, 32, 39, 45, 63, 108, 118, 123, 140, 165, 178, 180, 190, 206, 228–34, 236, 240, 243–4, 246, 252–3, 258, 261, 267, 273–4, 280, 282

Affleck, Ben   236, 240

Aird, Holly   82

Allen, Jim   190, 192–4, 197, 200

Apted, Michael   137, 140

ARD   190

Artificial Eye   179, 191, 193, 199–200

Arts Council of England   5, 41, 43, 124–5, 151–3, 155–7, 165, 216–19, 253, 260

Assassin Films   207

Atkinson, Rowan   134, 137

Attenborough, Richard   5, 7, 35, 40, 229, 276

Austen, Jane   132, 228, 244–53, 265, 268

Babymother   205–7, 216–25

Backbeat   123, 125, 193

BAFTAs   18, 60, 108, 118, 137, 165, 173, 190, 216, 243, 252, 271

Baptiste, Marianne Jean   183, 190, 206

Barber, Paul   102, 206

Bardon, John   209

Bassett, Linda   209, 216

BBC Films   27, 29, 67, 123–4, 128, 156, 158, 165, 167, 190, 193, 205, 209, 258, 260–1

BBC Scotland   124, 165, 167

Beaufoy, Simon   99, 101, 109

Bedford Falls Company   234

Bell, Jaime   158, 161, 165

Bevan, Tim   70, 126, 258

Bhaji on the Beach   123, 205, 282

Billy Elliot   126, 53–65, 73, 78, 233, 259

Billy MacKinnon Media   124

BIM Distribuzione   190

Black, Jack   73, 80

Blackwood, Vas   206, 219

Blethyn, Brenda   183, 190

Bond, Samantha   141, 144

Bonneville, Hugh   265

Bower, David   131

Boyle, Danny   44–5, 52–3, 164, 258

Branagh, Kenneth   15, 27–36, 128, 153, 228, 236, 246, 261

Brassed Off   5, 99, 109–19, 127, 156–7, 204, 233, 236

Brenman, Greg   156, 158

Briers, Richard   28, 32

British Film Commission   43–4

British Film Fund Agency   8

British Film Institute (BFI)   9, 14, 69, 124, 151, 155, 204–5, 225

BFI Production Board   14, 43, 203

British Screen Finance Limited   9, 39, 43

Broadbent, Jim   16

Broccoli, Barbara   137, 139

Brosnan, Pierce   138, 143, 145, 147–8

Brown, Ralph   20

Buena Vista International   70, 95, 177, 180, 257, 259, 261

Callow, Simon   11, 236

Carlton Film Distributors   125, 129, 152

Carlyle, Robert   46, 52, 75, 102, 109, 122–3, 141–2, 147, 231

Carter, Helena Bonham   11, 33, 35, 258, 261

Carter, Jim   236

Cattaneo, Peter   99, 101, 109

Chadha, Gurinder   123, 205

CiBy 2000   121, 181, 184

Cinema Exhibitors' Association   10

Cine-UK   97

Chambers, Emma   265

Channel Four/Channel 4   9–12, 14–18, 44–6, 67, 71, 73, 80, 82, 99, 101–2, 109, 111, 118, 122–4, 127–9, 131, 167, 179, 181, 183, 190, 203, 205–6, 216, 218–19

Channing-Williams, Simon   181, 183

Chariots of Fire   7–8, 13

Chicken Run   257, 259, 263, 272–83

Children's Film Foundation, The   8

Cinematograph Film Council   9

Cleese, John   141, 143

Columbia Pictures Corporation /Columbia Tristar   177, 179, 228, 244, 246–7, 253, 257, 259

'Cool Britannia'   5, 44, 71, 80, 139

Coltrane, Robbie   141, 144

costume drama   44, 140, 228–9, 234, 236–7, 243–4, 246, 253, 261, 268

Crying Game, The   14–26, 35–6, 43, 204, 236, 282

Curtis, Richard   126, 129, 131, 133, 137, 233, 258, 263–5, 269, 271, 281

Cusack, John   70–6, 79–80

Daldry, Stephen   156, 158, 162, 164–5, 173

Daniels, Phil   274

Danjaq LLC   137

Davidson, Jaye   18, 26

Degeto Film   190

Dench, Judi   11, 141, 231–2, 236, 243

Department for Culture and Sport (DCMS)   41, 227

De Vincentis, D.V.   70, 72, 76

Diaphana Films   191

Din-Khan, Abu   207–9, 213, 216

Disney   68, 70–2, 235, 272–3

DNA Films   44, 153, 258

Dogstar Films   70, 73

Doran, Lindsay   244

DreamWorks SKG   272–4, 280–1

Dreyfus, James   265

DVD   6, 8, 66, 68, 70, 90, 92, 148, 260, 281

Eady Levy   8–9, 39

East is East   5, 127, 179, 205–16, 225, 259, 282

Elton, Ben   32, 265

Emerson, Gavin   165

Entertainment (distributor)   27, 178–9, 257–9

Eon Productions   137–9

Eurimages   42, 191, 193

European Co-Production Fund (ECF)   42, 190, 193

Eurotrustees   15, 18

Evans, David   80, 83, 87

Evans, Stephen   27

Everett, Rupert   236

Feirstein, Bruce   137

Fellner, Eric   126, 258

Ferguson, Lynn   274

Fever Pitch   67, 70–1, 80–91, 233

Fiennes, Joseph   229, 236, 240, 243

Figment Films   44–6, 53

Film Consortium   44, 152, 258, 260

Film Council/UK Film Council   5, 15, 43–4, 154–6, 201, 221, 258, 262

Film Four   10–11, 118, 127, 173, 177–9, 181, 184, 190, 207, 209, 258–60

Filmstiftung NRW   190

Finn, Jon   156

First City Features 27

Firth, Colin 75, 82, 89, 153, 228, 236

Fitzgerald, Tara 111

Fleet, James 133, 245, 247

Flemyng, Jason 54

Fletcher, Dexter 54

Ford, Alan 54

Formation Films 216, 218

Forthcoming Productions 123

Four Weddings and a Funeral 5, 10, 72–3, 95, 119, 122, 126–37, 148, 153, 158, 179, 190, 230–1, 236, 240, 247, 257–9, 264–6, 268–9, 271, 282

Full Monty, The 5, 69–70, 95, 99–110, 112–13, 115, 118–19, 122–3, 141, 151, 156–7, 159, 164, 178, 204, 206, 216, 219, 231–3, 236, 257–9, 280, 282

Francois, Emilie 245

Frears, Stephen 10, 70, 73–4, 77, 52, 204

Gallivant 124

Gemmell, Ruth 82

Gibson, Mel 274, 280

Gigliotti, Donna 234

Gilroy, Tom 193

Gandhi 7–8, 13

Glasgow Film Fund 45, 124

Goldcrest 11, 13–14, 125, 258

Good Machine 244

Grant, Hugh 80, 111, 126, 129, 131–3, 137, 228–9, 231, 233, 245, 247, 258, 264–5, 269, 271, 281

Greenaway, Peter 6, 14, 42, 191, 229

Hall, Lee 156–8, 65

Handmade Films 11–14, 53, 125, 258

Hardy, Robert 245, 247

Hart, Ian 123, 193

Henriques, Julian 216–19

Herman, Mark 109, 111–12

Hibbin, Sally 152, 193

High Fidelity 66–7, 70–80, 83, 90–1, 126

Hjejle, Iben 73

Hodge, John 44–7, 252

Hollywood 6, 14, 17, 28–9, 32, 39–40, 52, 61, 64, 68, 75, 81, 95, 98, 106, 121, 125, 137, 140, 179, 181, 197, 203, 223, 229–31, 243, 258, 260–2, 265, 273, 275, 277, 280

Holy Cow Films 165

Hornby, Nick 67, 70–4, 76, 80–3, 86, 89–90

Horrocks, Jane 274

Hoskins, Bob 12, 124, 260

Howard, Vivienne 216

Ifans, Rhys 152, 265, 268, 271

Impact Pictures 125

Issacs, Jeremy 10

Johnson, Wil 219, 224

Jones, Gemma 245

Jones, Vinnie 54–5, 60

Jordan, Neil 14–21, 24, 26, 36, 121

Keaton, Michael 29, 32

Kenworthy, Duncan 129, 153, 258, 263–5

Kirkpatrick, Karey 271, 274

Kismet Film Company 124

Kötting, Andrew 124

Kureishi, Hanif 10, 131, 204

Land and Freedom 42–3, 123, 190–202, 229

Laurie, Hugh 35, 246, 248

Lee, Ang 228, 244, 246, 250–1, 253

Leigh, Mike 5–6, 152–3, 181–4, 190–1, 200, 206, 229

Leonard, Robert Sean 32

Lionheart TV International 123

Llewellyn, Suzette 219

Llewelyn, Desmond 141, 148

Loach, Ken 5–6, 42, 101, 122–3, 152–3,

166, 181, 190–200, 229, 260

Lock, Stock and Two Smoking Barrels 5, 44, 53–62, 127, 206, 259

Logan, Phyllis 183

Lord, Peter 271, 273–4, 280

London Film Commission 43

Luiso, Todd 73

Lumsden, Richard 246

Macabe, Richard 265

MacDonald, Andrew 44–5, 153

Macdonald, Kelly 45–6

MacDowell, Andie 129, 131, 271

MacKinnon, Gilles 124, 229

Madden, John 233, 236, 243

Marceau, Sophie 141–2, 145, 147

Mayfair (distributor) 15, 26, 178, 193

McCourt, Emer 122

McGregor, Ewan 45–6, 52–3, 75, 111, 253

McGuire, Victor 54

McInnerny, Tim 265

McKee, Gina 265

McKidd, Kevin 52

McLean, Lenny 54, 56, 60

Meadows, Shane 5, 124

MEDIA Programme (European Commission) 42, 207, 209, 260

Merchant Ivory 11–13, 29, 127, 131, 229, 261

Messidor Films 190

Michell, Roger 263, 265

Miller, Jonny Lee 46, 253

Minghella, Anthony 123, 128, 229, 231–2, 243, 247

Mirage Enterprises 244, 247

Miramax 17, 26, 53, 109, 111, 118, 234–6, 243, 253, 261

Moonstone 165

Moran, Dylan 265

Moran, Nick 54

Moriarty, P.H. 54

Much Ado About Nothing 15, 27–37, 128, 229, 236, 259

multiplex 5, 7, 15, 39, 63, 70, 93–9, 166, 178, 181, 199–200, 203, 206, 237, 258

My Beautiful Launderette 10, 73, 204

National Film Finance Corporation 9

National Lottery 5, 41, 43, 121, 151–7, 164–5, 167, 173, 190. 203, 216, 253, 257–8, 260–1

New Cinema Fund 15, 155, 258

New Crime Productions 70, 72

Newell, Mike 72–3, 128–9, 131, 137, 152, 265

New Labour 5, 40–1, 44, 61, 139–40, 142

Nicol, Lesley 209

Nippon Film Development and Financing 15, 18

Noel Gay Motion Picture Company 44

Norman, Marc 233, 236–9

Notting Hill 42, 71, 73 80, 126, 151, 173, 206, 220, 227, 230, 257–9, 262–71, 280–2

Notting Hill Pictures 263

O'Brien, Rebecca 190, 193

Odeon 96–8

O'Donnell, Damien 207–9, 216

Palace Pictures 11, 13–18, 26–7, 36, 82, 125, 152, 177–9, 258

Paltrow, Gwyneth 60, 148, 229, 236, 243, 253

Parallax Pictures 122, 152, 190, 193

Paragon Entertainment Corporation 13, 53

Parfitt, David 27, 234, 236

Parker, Alan 90, 154, 262–3

Pasolini, Uberto 99, 101–2

Pathé 44, 125, 152–3, 165, 167, 190, 258–9, 272, 274

Pathé Distribution Ltd. 165, 173, 177–8, 257–8, 272

Pearson, Neil 82

Pink, Steve 70, 72, 76

PolyGram Filmed Entertainment 6, 52–3, 55, 90, 123–4, 126–7, 129, 131, 177–9, 200, 204, 258–9, 263–4

Posey, Amanda 80, 90, 152

Postlethwaite, Pete 111, 114

Powell, Nik 13–14, 16–19, 26, 36, 82, 123, 152

Priest 102, 123, 236

Productions Lazennec 165, 167

Prominent Features 109, 111

Puri, Om 209, 216

Purvis, Neal 137, 140

Puttnam, David 5, 40, 125

Radclyffe, Sarah 126

Ramsay, Lynne 5, 165–7, 169–71, 173

Rank 93, 95–6, 125, 129, 152, 177–9, 257, 259

Ratcatcher 128, 153–5, 165–75, 180, 224, 282

Rea, Stephen 19, 86

Redwave Films 99, 101

Reeves, Keanu 29, 31, 121

Renaissance Films 27, 29, 236

Revolution Films 124

Richards, Denise 141–2

Richardson, Miranda 18, 26, 274

Rickman, Alan 228, 245, 247

Riff Raff 102, 122, 191, 193

Ritchie, Guy 53–8, 60

Roache, Linus 123

Road Movies Filmproduktion GmbH 190

Robbins, Tim 75

Roberts, Julia 42, 227, 236, 265, 271

Rosenberg, Scott 70, 72, 76

Rosenthal, Jack 271

Routledge, Jordan 209

Rush, Geoffrey 229, 236, 243

Samuel Goldwyn Company 27, 29

Sarah Radclyffe Productions 125, 152

satellite television 9, 39, 63, 66–7, 70

Sawalha, Julia 274, 276

Scala Productions 26, 123–4, 152, 260

Scott Thomas, Kristin 131, 137

Scott-Thomas, Serena 144

Seagram 6, 126–7, 179, 258

Secrets and Lies 127, 181–90, 219, 282, 234, 236, 244–55, 259, 282

Sense and Sensibility 33, 228, 232–3

Shakespeare in Love 151, 178, 229, 231–43, 253, 257–9, 282

Shakespeare, William 15, 27–33, 35, 229, 233–43, 249, 257

Sharp, Lesley 102

Showcase 97–8

Simmons, Rudd 70

SKA Films 53, 55

Skinner-Carter, Corinne 219

Skyline Film and Television Productions 124, 261

Slattery, Tony 20

Small Faces 124

Smith, Anjela Lauren 218

social realism 5, 100, 118, 122, 162, 164, 166, 172, 191, 260

Softley, Iain 123

Sony Pictures International 244, 254

Spall, Timothy 187, 274

Spriggs, Elizabeth 245, 247

Springsteen, Bruce 75

Sproxton, David 271, 273

Statham, Jason 54, 60

Staunton, Imelda 28, 236, 246–7

Steve Tisch Group, The 53, 55

Sting 54–5

Stoppard, Tom 232–3, 236–9

Stubbs, Imogen 245, 247

Studio Canal + 125, 165, 260

Strong, Mark 82

Styler, Trudie 55

Summit Entertainment 53, 55

Tall Stories 124

Tarantino, Quentin 45, 53, 60

television 5, 7–9, 15, 27, 43, 48–9, 51, 54, 63, 65, 67–8, 83, 87–8, 111, 127, 148, 151, 157, 167, 170, 177, 190, 207, 244, 273

Thatcherism 48–9, 100, 102–3, 110

There's Only One Jimmy Grimble 125, 154

Thin Man Films 152, 181, 183

Thompson, Emma 6, 27–9, 32–3, 228, 231–2, 244–5, 248–9, 252–3, 282

Tiger Aspect 156, 158

Top Five Productions 70

Tomlinson, Ricky 122

Touchstone Pictures 70–2

Trainspotting 5, 10, 44–54, 60–1, 102, 118, 122, 127, 141, 151, 153, 164, 179, 219, 231, 233, 252–3, 259, 276, 282

Truly, Madly, Deeply 123, 128, 131

TVE Televisión Espanola 190

Twentieth Century Fox Film Corporation 95, 99, 102, 177–8, 257, 259–60

Twentyfourseven 26, 124

UCI 93, 98

Udwin, Leslee 207, 209, 216

UGC 97

UIP 95, 138, 156, 173, 177–8, 234, 257, 259–60

Umbi Films 123

United Artists Corporation 137–8

Universal Pictures 44, 124, 126, 234, 263

Vaughn, Matthew 53, 55

video 6, 8, 14–15, 39, 54, 65–6, 68, 70, 87, 103, 148, 177, 227, 281

Vir, Parminder 216, 218–19

Virgin Cinemas 97–8

Wade, Robert 137, 140

Walter, Harriet 245, 247

Walters, Julie 158, 165

Warner Village 94, 98

Warrington, Don 219

Washington, Denzel 29, 31

Weinstein, Harvey 234, 243

Welland, Colin 7, 282

Welsh, Irving 44–6

Whitaker, Forest 18, 204

Wildgaze Films 80

Wilkinson, Tom 102, 109, 123, 236, 245

Wilson, Michael G. 137, 139

Winslet, Kate 95, 124, 152, 178, 228, 231, 245, 247, 252

Winstone, Ray 231, 258, 260–1

Winterbottom, Michael 5, 124

Wise, Greg 33, 245, 247

Wonderland 124–5

Woolley, Stephen 13–19, 26, 36, 82, 121, 123, 152

Working Title 10–11, 70, 73, 80, 126–7, 129, 131, 156, 158, 191, 193, 200, 204, 230, 233, 258, 263

World Wide Web 64–5

World is Not Enough 68, 128, 137–51, 257, 259, 282

Zeta-Jones, Catherine 80

Zwick, Edward 234

STILLS INFORMATION

The publisher has attempted to correctly identify the copyright holders of the images reproduced herein and believes the following copyright information to be correct at the time of going to print. We apologise for any omissions or errors and will be delighted to rectify any errors brought to our attention in future editions.

The Crying Game © Palace / Channel Four / Aquarius Collection; *Much Ado About Nothing* © Samuel Goldwyn Company / Aquarius Collection; *Trainspotting* © Figment Films / Channel Four / Aquarius Collection; *Lock, Stock and Two Smoking Barrels* © SKA Films / Aquarius Collection; *High Fidelity* © Touchstone / Working Title / Aquarius Collection; *Fever Pitch* © Channel Four / Aquarius Collection; *The Full Monty* © Twentieth Century Fox / Aquarius Collection; *Brassed Off* © Channel Four / Miramax / Aquarius Collection; *Four Weddings and a Funeral* © Working Title / Polygram / Channel Four / Aquarius Collection; *The World is Not Enough* © United Artists / Eon / Aquarius Collection; *Billy Elliot* © BBC Films / Aquarius Collection; *Ratcatcher* © Pathé Pictures / BBC Films / Aquarius Collection; *Secrets and Lies* © CiBy 2000 / Channel Four / Aquarius Collection; *Land and Freedom* © Parallax Pictures / Aquarius Collection; *East is East* © FilmFour Ltd / Aquarius Collection; *Babymother* © Channel Four / Arts Council of England / BFI Stills, Posters and Designs; *Shakespeare in Love* © Miramax / Universal Pictures / Aquarius Collection; *Sense and Sensibility* © Columbia Pictures / Good Machine / Aquarius Collection; *Notting Hill* © Working Title / Polygram / Aquarius Collection; *Chicken Run* © DreamWorks / Aquarius Collection.

Also available

Studying British Cinema: The 1960s

Danny Powell

Also available

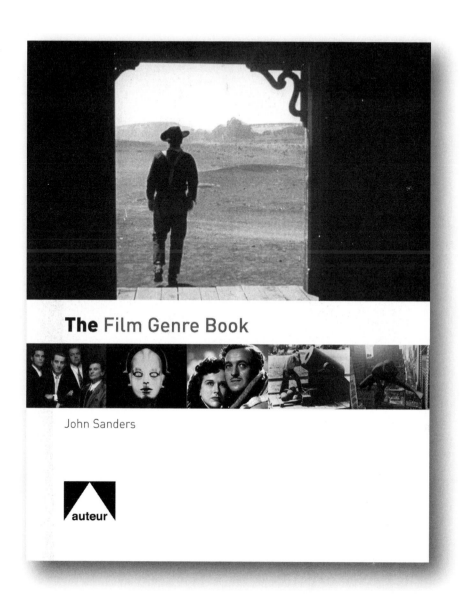